Confronting Genocide

Confronting Genocide

Judaism, Christianity, Islam

Edited by
Steven Leonard Jacobs
Marc I. Sherman, Bibliographic Editor,
Institute on the Holocaust and Genocide,
Jerusalem, Israel

LEXINGTON BOOKS

A division of
ROWMAN & LITTLEFIELD PUBLISHERS, INC.
Lanham • Boulder • New York • Toronto • Plymouth, UK

LEXINGTON BOOKS

A division of Rowman & Littlefield Publishers, Inc.
A wholly owned subsidiary of The Rowman & Littlefield Publishing Group, Inc.
4501 Forbes Boulevard, Suite 200
Lanham, MD 20706

Estover Road
Plymouth PL6 7PY
United Kingdom

Copyright © 2009 by Lexington Books

British Library Cataloguing in Publication Information Available

Library of Congress Cataloging-in-Publication Data

Confronting genocide : Judaism, Christianity, Islam / [edited by] Steven Leonard
Jacobs.
    p. cm.
  Includes bibliographical references and index.
    ISBN 978-0-7391-3588-4 (cloth : alk. paper) — ISBN 978-0-7391-3589-1 (pbk. :
alk. paper) — ISBN 978-0-7391-3590-7 (electronic)
  1.   Genocide—Religious aspects—History. 2. Rape—Religious aspects—History.
I. Jacobs, Steven L., 1947–
  HV6322.7.C654 2009
  201'.76—dc22   2009005541

Printed in the United States of America

Contents

Introduction: Genocide in the Name of God: Thoughts on Religion and Genocide

In his academically autobiographical essay, Israel W. Charny, one of the true doyens of the field of genocide studies, related the following:

> A second section [of the 1994 work *The Widening Circle of Genocide*] was devoted to religion and genocide by Leonard Glick. There is quite a story to be told about how many years it took before we succeeded in getting this important open treatment of the subject of religion as both setting the expressed moral direction of Thou Shalt Not Kill [*sic*], while in itself being responsible for so many genocidal killings over the centuries. Before Leonard Glick's fine contribution, there had been several well-known scholars in the field of religion who had agreed to do the project and then dropped it at a very late stage, almost without explanation. To me, it seemed that what happened was that they were unable to tell the truth about the religious establishments with which they were variously connected.

If truth be told, the reason for such difficulty is far more significant than that of personal "religious discomfort." Those whose field is religious studies come late to the study of genocide, and, thus, that which is commonly identified in the popular mind as "religion" is all too often overlooked as an important factor in contributing to either the implementation and perpetuation of genocide, or as a foundational underpinning and rationalization for such collective acts. To be sure, even where the evidence is incontrovertible (e.g., the Armenian, Rwandan, Darfur [Sudanese] genocides), it is approached from the perspectives of historians, political scientists, sociologists, and the like, with no attempt to address the theological frame out of which religions operate or their institutional structures—buildings, liturgies, curricula, etc.—which proceed from those orientations. An example of this tendency is the otherwise excellent text edited by Bartov and Mack (2001), *In God's Name: Genocide and Religion in the Twentieth Century*, papers delivered at a 1997 conference held at the United States Holocaust Memorial Museum, Washington, D.C. This volume focuses primarily on the Holocaust, the most documented of genocides, and less on Armenia, Rwanda, and Bosnia, through the five significant questions with which the editors were concerned. A focus on theology or institutions would have necessitated a very different set of papers in the main, with more work needing to be done, not only on Christian "preparations" for genocide, but with regard to both the Jewish and Islamic concepts of exclusivity ("chosenness") and their relationship to genocide (Jacobs, 2003/2004).

Then, too, many of those who study religion, like many of their colleagues in the academy, are themselves distanced from parochial religious commitments or heretofore have not chosen to address this intersection of religion and genocide. For those whose own religious commitments exercise a primary influence, Charny is, quite possibly, somewhat correct: to chastise or denounce their own communities for active presence in a given genocide or failure to speak out against it, and meanwhile remain faithful adherents of that religious tradition, becomes painfully problematic if not downright onerous, burdensome—or worse. Slowly, however, addressing this topic of religion and genocide is beginning to change as scholars, both inside and outside the field of religious studies, realize the all-too-prominent role of religion in this horror. Indeed, Professor Henry R. Huttenbach, City College of New York, recently wrote:

> Thus, religion—meaning the faithful, the doctrine, the clergy and their institutions—can *easily* be prompted to buttress genocidal thought and action in a wide array of capacities. The religion-genocide nexus needs to be carefully studied in general, and, in particular, must be carefully monitored in times of social crisis. The worst-case scenario would be to continue underestimating, or even denying, that the nexus exists. *It is the task of scholars to expose and explore it, and for policy-makers to dismantle the religion-genocide connection.* (Huttenbach, 2004: 23; emphasis added)

With the exception of Kuper's seminal essay (1990) and Glick's essay, noted above (1994), all of the contributors herein wrote specifically for this book, thus answering, at least initially, Huttenbach's challenge. (None, however, are policy-makers.) All the essays are discomforting in their own right and this initial volume opens the door to yet more research, field work, writing, etc., by scholars, policy-makers, and concerned citizens of all countries—and not only those who define themselves as "religious" or scholars of religion.

Part I, "Textual Warrants for Genocide," on the study of texts held sacred and used/abused by religious communities, provides the framework and logical beginning point for any discussion and subsequent discourse on this nexus between religion and genocide:

For Leo Kuper, lawyer and sociologist, himself a "pioneer of genocide studies," the initial point of entry must be an examination of the sacred texts of the three dominant monotheistic traditions—Judaism, Christianity, Islam—realizing in the process the religious differences between genocidal perpetrators and victim-recipients and noting, too, how fundamentalist understandings enhance the texts' central significance for those committed to them. Kuper died before the September 11, 2001 attacks on the United States, and how the perpetrators of 9/11 "read," and thus understood, Qur'anic passages as validating their behaviors has yet to be fully critically examined by religious studies scholars. Carefully, however, Kuper does note that ultimately such work is "indeterminate," and that further exploration must address the larger cultural context in which religion functions, the very nexus—to use Huttenbach's term—that religious studies addresses.

My own contribution to this discussion is to focus specifically on the sacred texts of these three monotheistic traditions—Torah, New Testament, Qur'an—by citing what I continue to regard as representative examples of those texts, which read out the other and pave the way for pregenocidal behaviors, texts exclusivising the in-group (Jews, Christians, Muslims) by claiming both inherent superiority and privileged access to God. I also suggest that, given the reality of continuing genocides, the "midrashic" way of reading such texts, historically linked to the Jewish religious tradition, may very well be the only way to move such conversations about sacred text forward.

Chris Mato Nunpa's essay addresses a genocide little examined in the United States outside of those recipient communities whose historical legacies are the events themselves. He does so, however, by addressing what he regards as the "divine sanction" that both the Hebrew Bible and the New Testament to allot to genocide, most particularly in the two textual affirmations of "chosen people"—ness and "promised land"—ness, neither of which was applied to the Native Americans themselves, but which seemingly validated the behaviors of white, largely Christian persons and groups who attacked them, displaced them, and murdered them. Growing up on the Reservation (or "Rez" as he has referred to it in personal communications with the editor), he personally experienced the too-frequent use of biblical texts in the churches there, accompanied by continuous denigration of his own religious and cultural ways of life. Much more research and writing are thus needed by scholars of religion addressing specifically the Native American experience in this country and the religious commitments and rationalizations of the perpetrators themselves.

Lutheran theologian and Holocaust scholar James Frazer Moore in his essay suggests a new direction for religious studies research in relation to genocide. Noting that the Rwandan genocide took place in the aftermath of Good Friday and Easter Sunday, to what extent, he asks, was the liturgical theology of Roman Catholicism manipulated by those committed to the practice of genocide in the most Catholic of African countries? He further raises the larger question—yet to be explored not only with regard to Rwanda, but in other cases of genocide as well—about the use of religious myth, religious practice, and the actual texts of Christian worship in legitimating genocidal violence. (It should also be noted, therefore, that issues of myth, texts, and worship, of course, are among the central concerns of those who study religions.)

Gary Phillips, addressing the Balkan genocide, sees a decided linkage between unholy violence and Holy Bible, and quests for explanation. Significantly, he regards the nineteenth century Serbian national epic *The Mountain Wreath* as paralleling the Gospel of Matthew's condemnation of the Jews as the anti-Christ—except that in the case of the Bosnian genocide, it is the Muslims who fit the analogy so as to deserve genocidal extermination and annihilation. Thus, for Phillips, such thinking becomes translated into a nationalist-racist ideology undergirded by religious thought. The horrific tragedy that frames his essay again reminds the reader that in this "nexus" our overarching primary concern must be the human beings involved, those who survive the genocide as well as those who do not, and what he calls the "real world impact" of the use of such texts as they manifest themselves in different cultural settings.

Part II, "Religion and Mass Violence: Empirical Data and Case Studies," begins with anthropologist Leonard Glick's (previously published) essay which draws distinctions between localized religion (a term brought to prominence by a fellow anthropologist, the late Clifford Geertz), specifically Judaism, and the universalist religions of Christianity and Islam. No religion, however, escapes its genocidal potential because of its orientation. The ongoing crises between Israel and her Arab neighbors, and more pointedly between Israel and the Palestinians—in which both sides condemn the other as having "genocidal intent"—is more often than not inflamed by paralleling rhetoric, which has yet to be explored as such by religious studies scholars. The missionizing thrusts of both Christianity and Islam, over the course of their own histories, have sustained a genocidal degradation, annihilation, and extermination of both peoples and groups that continues in the present moment, ofttimes with Islam and Christianity at loggerheads with each other. Though the United Nations Special Commission of Inquiry on the genocide in Darfur, Sudan, genocide has rejected the term genocide as applicable as recently as 2005, the perpetrators have, in the largest numbers, been Muslims and the victims Christians. The newness of these events has not, however, yet allowed religious studies—and other—scholars to fully examine the data.

Richard L. Rubenstein, profound Holocaust thinker and scholar, minces no words in acknowledging the "significant part" played by religion in the perpetration of genocide, as well as the "genocidal potentiality" of Islam, and chooses to reexamine an early "genocide of the twentieth century," that of the Armenians by the Turks. Even while affirming the essentially secular orientation of the Young Turks and their newly formed state, the Armenians' "choiceless choice" between conversion to Islam or death was a religious one. For Rubenstein, defining a targeted group as radically evil, and thus as "enemies of God," provides a powerful legitimation of genocide. Unremitting mass murder on the part of those who commit it can then become a seeming defense of truth, goodness, and even civilization itself.

Mohammad Omar Farooq writes about a lesser-known genocide in 1971 in Bangladesh (formerly East Pakistan), which he regards as a clear case of the abuse of Islam—both religion and text—for the purpose of genocide by the ruling elite. The implications of his essay in the present post-9/11 moment, and the credibility given by those in positions of religious, governmental, and political power to Harvard professor Samuel Huntington's thesis of the "clash of civilization" (Huntington, 1996) are particularly timely. What does it say about religions, their institutions, their texts, their manner of practice if they can be too easily recruited into the practice of genocide? What countermeasures, if any, are to be taken by various religious communities themselves, as well as by others, to correct, prevent, and inhibit such abusive manipulations?

Paul Mojzes's lengthy essay provides a thorough historical overview of complex occurrences of what took place in the Balkans, both at the beginning and at the end of the twentieth century, and draws upon a large variety of documentary evidence not readily available to those unfamiliar with or unread in the native languages. He also makes an important distinction between genocide and "ethnic cleansing," and turns his attention as well as to the question of justice for the perpetrators and the role of religion in this tragedy. Drawing the critically important distinctions between "genocide," "ethnic cleansing," "mass murder," "democide," and "politicide" is important for scholarly work examining both instances of large-scale megadeath as well as contemporary manifestations of such. These distinctions have widespread, international legal implications translating into nation-states' abilities to punish the guilty, maintain the viability of judicial systems and overall governmental function, and so on. From the "on the ground" perspective of the victims themselves, however, both the living and the dead, the distinctions are irrelevant to their experiences.

Presbyterian scholar and thinker Stephen R. Haynes sees parallel situations. Addressing both the Holocaust and the case of Rwanda, and, like

Donald Dietrich, realizes that both confront issues of Christian complicity and Christian credibility. He also raises four questions worthy of further exploration: (1) Why is Rwanda an exceedingly unattractive venue for Christian self-examination? (2) Why is it important for Christians to ask *theological* questions in the aftermath of Rwanda? (3) What are the lessons for Christians who want to remember Rwanda? (He posits four.) (4) Why does the genocide in Rwanda present us with compelling evidence of the "ineptitude" of Christian leaders and institutions in resisting genocide?

Part III, "Alternative Readings of Troubling Texts: Religion as a Force against Violence," opens with David Patterson's strongly theological essay, faulting not only intellectuals and scholars but all serious persons steeped in what he calls the "ontological mode of thought," freed from any sense whatsoever of the absoluteness of the God of Abraham, Judaically understood, and the demands such a God makes on humanity. He thus forcefully argues that there is more of a relationship between such thinking and genocide than there is between "religion" and genocide, and that this mode is framed by categories of thinking that lead to genocide, and then makes a case for *religious* teaching as the only antidote to genocidal ideologies. As a counter argument to "normative" academic-intellectual thinking, Patterson's comments are worthy of serious reflection—and response.

Historian Paul R. Bartrop's essay on the relationship between a denial of the Ten Commandments—long understood as a genuinely Judaic contribution to the civilizing of humanity, and one taken over by both Christianity and Islam and incorporated into their own religio-theological and moral-ethical structures—and the acts of genocide as we understand them by the Nazis in the Holocaust, the Rwandans, the Bosnian Serbs, Croats, and Muslims raises even further complicating questions of the role of religion as foundational to pregenocidal and genocidal activity. For Bartrop, too, then, religion has become a "root cause" of genocide and the very antithesis of what it is supposed to be.

Christian scholar Henry F. Knight turns to the same biblical texts as does Judaic scholar Zev Garber, but Knight's treatment of the issue of fundamentalism in all three monotheistic traditions that directly involves textual readings and understandings, and does take some issue with Garber, seeing the destruction of Amalek as divinely sanctioned. For him, however, the central issue is that of "mythologizing the other," which in turn becomes a justification for genocide. Long understood to be a central category of examination by religious studies scholars, the role, place, and function of myth in religious—and other—communities may yet prove a valuable contribution toward improving our understanding of the relationship between religion and genocide. Knight also addresses the conceptions of reconciliation, hospitality, and vulnerability in the post-Holocaust world of today's genocides, and, by implication, suggests how communities, perhaps by drawing upon other aspects of religion, can engage in the process of post-genocidal rebuilding.

Part IV, "Theologies and Practices of Reconciliation," starts with a chapter by John K. Roth—philosopher, Holocaust scholar, committed Christian—in which the repeated term "uselessness" is central: the uselessness of violence and suffering inflicted upon the victims—of the experience of those who have been so brutalized—and the negative uselessness of knowledge learned about a genocide but not used in further or future prevention. Additionally, using as his point of departure a different understanding of restitution to Jews by Christians after the Holocaust, he thus opens a new avenue of thinking about Knight's concept of reconciliation: that is, how after the genocide, perpetrator groups and victim groups, who now find themselves living together can begin any sort of "dialogue of healing." The cases of Rwanda (e.g., the contemporary work of psychologists Erwin Staub and Yael Danieli) and Bosnia come immediately to mind, though the precedent was set in the case of the Holocaust with the children and grandchildren of victimizers and victims coming together in dialogue—Jews and Germans and others—and may prove useful in other settings.

Catholic theologian Donald Dietrich sees "a surprising moral inconsistency" between the position of the Roman Catholic Church and the publication of the document "We Remember" with regard to the Holocaust, and the lack of a comparable document in the case of Rwanda, which he regards as "astounding." For him, evidently, this failure is the result of the Church—his Church—refusing to recognize its own historic role as complicitous in both scenarios. He also addresses the complex topic of ecclesial repentance and its demands in the context of genocide and dialogue with others.

Like Dietrich, fellow Roman Catholic scholar and professor of social ethics John T. Pawlikowski too realizes the logical disjunct between the document "We Remember" as a response to the events of the Holocaust and the document and the lack of any official document in the case of Rwanda. For him, his Church "has remained largely silent" and thus by doing so provides its followers with little or no moral guidance in how to address this or any future genocide.

Judaic scholar Zev Garber calls for a far closer reexamination of biblical texts, following Kuper, specifically the Hebrew Bible together with rabbinical commentaries, as they relate to the genocidal destruction of the seven nations understood to be ancient Israel's enemies (Deuteronomy 7:2 and 20:17), and argues that there is no divine sanction for genocide whatsoever suggesting that such is more an "evolving cultural imperative" and less a religious warrant. His work thus suggests a direction for *all* religious studies and other scholars of texts, particularly in this area of genocide: a far more careful reading of not only sacred religious texts, but political texts and public speeches and media presentations (radio, television, film) as they are understood by religious communities, nation-states, and others, and used to foment and carry out genocide.

Concluding this collection is Carol Rittner's essay about the unholy trinity of rape, religion, and genocide. Institutional religions, primarily the providence of males, are criticized for failing to address and condemn the use of rape as a tool of genocide, blindly perpetuating their own gender biases, and evincing little if any compassion to the female victims. Her essay is disturbing, to say the least, and as do many others opens doors to further study and investigation.

The essays that comprise this volume are not intended to be the final word on the questions of religion and genocide and the interconnection between the two. They are, at best, a preliminary exploration of a too-little addressed topic in a relatively new field—genocide studies—whose own origins are only of post–World War II vintage. Since 1990, however, numerous volumes, many by reputable scholars or extremely competent journalists, have addressed the topic of "religion and violence." Of more than thirty volumes examined, only four—in addition to Bartov and Mack's (2000) *Genocide in God's Name: Genocide and Religion in the Twentieth Century*—even include the word "genocide" in their titles: two, Anzulovic (1999) and Sells (1996) are concerned with Bosnia; one deals with the genocide of Native Americans (Tinker, 1993) and one, most recently, with Rwanda (Rittner et al., 2004). Clearly, much more research is needed, more publications are warranted, and more conversations must take place. Ideally, this volume is a contribution to present and future work.

A project such as this one is truly a collaborative effort. The editor gratefully and appreciatively acknowledges with profound thanks all the contributors who so graciously and immediately responded to the initial invitation to write for *Confronting Genocide* and for their patience from initial submission to final product. Their willingness to participate, it is hoped, is reflected in the finished volume. (Any errors, of course, remain with me.) To my colleagues as well in the Department of Religious Studies at the University of Alabama—Tim Murphy, Maha Marouan, Steven Ramey, Ted Trost, and Chair Russ McCutcheon—for providing an interactive and intellectually stimulating environment conducive to research, writing, and thinking about issues large and small, thank you. Very, very special thinks are also extended to Ms. Toby Whitman, typist extraordinaire, and Mr. Bernard Pucker of the Pucker Gallery, Boston, Mass., for permission to use Samuel Bak's painting *Crossed Out II* for the front cover. Acknowledgement with grateful appreciation must also be extended to Taylor and Francis to republish Leo Kuyper's essay "Theological Warrants for Genocide" (Autumn 1990) form *Terrorism and Political Violence*, 2(3): 351–379; and Transaction Publishers, New Brunswick, N.J. (and series editor Israel W. Charny) to republish Leonard Glick's essay "Religion and Genocide" (1994) from *The Widening Circle of Genocide [Genocide: A Critical Bibliographic Review,* Volume 3], 43–74. And to my spouse, Dr. Louanne Clayton Jacobs, whose love and support enable me to examine, yet again, the worst of which we human beings are capable, but who always brings me back into the light: this book is dedicated to you.

Steven Leonard Jacobs
Tuscaloosa, Alabama
August 25, 2008

I

TEXTUAL WARRANTS
FOR GENOCIDE

1

Theological Warrants for Genocide: Judaism, Islam, and Christianity

Leo Kuper

ABSTRACT

Religious differences between victimizers and their victims are a common characteristic of genocides and genocidal massacres. Often the significance of these religious differences is very clear, as in the religious persecutions of the Middle Ages, the Armenian genocide, the Holocaust, the root and branch annihilation of settlements during the partition of India, the massacres of Hindus in East Pakistan (Bangladesh), the threatened genocide against the Baha'is in Iran, and the seemingly interminable conflicts in southern Sudan. At other times, the influence of religious difference is more indirect, compounded with many other elements, for example in Uganda under Amin, or the massacres of Ibos in northern Nigeria.

This article concentrates on one aspect of religious differentiations, the theological warrants for genocide in the sacred texts in the interrelated religions of Judaism, Islam, and Christianity. The influence of these texts is analyzed in historical perspective, with emphasis on the broad social context, and the power to engage in genocidal action. The contemporary spread of religious fundamentalism enhances the significance of these texts, as notably in Israel and its occupied territories, where the clash of religious fundamentalisms introduces a particularly threatening extremist element in the ongoing conflict.

INTRODUCTION

The intimate relationship of religious difference to genocide was very clear
in the Middle Ages with its religious wars, the persecution of heretics, the
annihilation of the Albigensians and other dissident sects, the Crusades,
and the pogroms. And it is a continuing element in genocide to the present day. When the United Nations adopted the Genocide Convention in
1948, defining the crime in essence as the deliberate destruction of a group
in whole or in part by killing its members, or deliberately inflicting on the
group conditions of life calculated to bring about its physical destruction, it
described the victims as racial, ethnic, religious, or national groups.

However this understates the significance of religious difference, since a
common characteristic of genocide is the presence of religious difference between perpetrators and victims, whether racial or ethnic or national groups.
The religious difference is often superimposed on other elements of differentiation—of race or ethnicity, cultural heritage, inequality in economic and
political participation and in human rights, and a measure of segregation
or territorial concentration. The religious affiliation then becomes part of a
distinctive social status, and often contributes at a deep formative level to
alienation from other groups in the plural structure of the society.

The general theme of this article deals with one aspect of the religious element in genocide, namely the legitimation of genocide in the sacred texts and
its consequences, with special reference to the interrelated religions of Judaism, Islam, and Christianity. The new movements of religious fundamentalism in the three religions enhance the significance of these genocidal texts.

The emphasis in this discussion on theological warrants for genocide
introduces a one-sided perspective on the sacred writings. These writings
also offer many precepts of the highest ethical order, which would encourage conciliation and the peaceful resolution of conflict. The teaching of the
Sermon on the Mount, for example might have prevailed in the relations
of the Catholic Church to dissident Christian sects and to Jews: It has been
influential in many other contexts. So too, Judaism and Islam are religions
of the highest ethical principles, aspiring to a utopian or messianic realm
of universal peace. But the presence of religious difference in so many annihilatory conflicts and massacres is strong argument for the need to analyze
the potential significance of the religious element in genocide.

THEOLOGICAL AND SECULAR
LEGITIMATIONS FOR GENOCIDE

Systems of belief have a quite variable and often indeterminate influence on
action. They may serve as rationalizations, or as justifications, for courses of

action already decided upon, in which case it is as if the courses of action had sought out their own legitimizing ideologies. Thus Ruether and Ruether in their recent study *The Wrath of Jonah—Crisis of Religious Nationalism in the Israeli-Palestinian Conflict* choose as their theological paradigm the Book of Jonah so as to convey the message that God is not the God of one people only, but created and loves all nations, wishing them "to live together in the peace that springs from repentance and obedience to the one God who created them all, rather than in violence and desire for the annihilation of the other."[1] The sacred text serves them as a justification or sanctification for their advocacy of ethnic conciliation. Similarly the Puritan identification of native Americans as Canaanites and Amalekites was clearly an ideology of colonization, motivated by conflicts with the indigenous inhabitants of the land and rationalized or justified by the sacred texts.[2]

In other cases, beliefs have an intimate and motivating relationship to action. But they do not act in isolation. They are part of a general societal context. Thus in medieval Europe, it was in areas of rapid economic and social change, and of serious overpopulation, that age-old religious millenarian prophecies concerning the last days took on "a new, revolutionary meaning and a new explosive force."[3] So too, Nazi ideologies gained their genocidal force in the period of threatening change and disorientation which followed the First World War. There were the traumatic aftereffects of the brutal destruction of human life, the dislocations of modernization, the radical challenge to traditional values and political ideologies, the disastrous economic slump with the downward mobility of the lower middle class, and the influx of large numbers of displaced European Jews. Indeed one has only to reflect that while an ancient sacred text might provide a continuous warrant for the annihilation of vilified or demonized groups, the mass killings carried out under its authority are intermittent. Only under a particular combination of social forces is the sacred legitimation activated.

The religious facilitation of genocide is only one of the many available legitimizing warrants. The bioracial ideology developed by Nazi doctors, who played a key role in the killing centers, drew on the "scientific" metaphor of healing. It portrayed the Germanic race as an organic unit in need of curative care by purification and revitalization. And since it was exposed to the debilitating influences of the mentally and physically impaired, and since its survival was threatened by contaminating contacts with Jews, the eradication of these elements was perceived as a curative device-healing by killing.[5]

Traditional Communist theory provides no explicit mandate for genocide or mass killing. But it does offer a Manichean perspective on the relations between the bourgeoisie and the workers, an apocalyptic vision of the liquidation of the bourgeoisie, and a historical process leading inexorably to the triumph of the workers' utopia. In these circumstances, there would be no particular obligation to keep members of the bourgeoisie needlessly alive, and historical necessity might indeed offer encouragement to assist in their liquidation.

Capitalism, too, might yield a warrant for genocide, as Rubenstein argues plausibly in his analysis of the British government's policy toward the Irish during the Great Famine of 1846–1848.[6] But it would operate more by indirection in allowing the free market to take its "natural" course, than by active involvement in the annihilation of populations. Indeed, many ideologies have yielded warrants for genocide with varying degrees of plausibility. There are the ideologies of colonization, with their associated racial and evolutionary theories; the animal analogies, used with devastating effect on many hunting and gathering groups; the supporting ideologies of racial and ethnic domination; the imperatives of imperialist expansion.

Within this plethora of legitimizing ideologies is there anything distinctive in the theological warrants to justify their treatment as a separate category? It cannot be found in self-righteousness, which is encouraged by many ideologies. Nor can it be found in the indifference to the suffering of the victims, nor in the joyous abandon with which the perpetrators sometimes engage in the atrocities of mass murder. Nor are the apocalyptic and utopian visions restricted to religious revelations.

It is probably in the rewards, the punishments and the dichotomies that the religious, other-worldly realm outstrips the secular dispensations of this world. The rewards might range from the remission of sins to an eternity of heavenly bliss (as for those who fall while serving in the holy war of the Islamic Jihad against the unbeliever). The punishments that human beings inflict on each other are horrendous, but hardly comparable to the torments of the Christian hell, though they were anticipated in the Auto-da-fe of the Holy Inquisition, and approximated in the Nazi death camps. In the rewards, punishments, and dichotomies of the religious realm, the imagination is emancipated from the limitations of realistic and technological restraints, and may give itself over, utterly, to unspeakable atrocity or ineffable bliss. However, it should be noted in the case of Judaism that the genocide theme precedes the largely first century creation of the theological concepts of Heaven, Hell, immortality, and martyrdom.

One anticipates that different systems of belief, with their varied structures of rewards, punishments, and dichotomies, would have different affinities for religious persecution and genocidal conflict. In ancestor cults there would seem to be no basis for religious intolerance. Polytheistic religions can readily accommodate other deities, though they may nevertheless be exclusive. Religions in which the devotees seek to attain mystic union with the divine and a state of cosmic benevolence should be remote from intolerance.

Of all the systems of belief, it seems that the most threatening to other groups may be the monotheistic religions, dedicated to the worship of the one and only true God and in possession of the ultimate revelation. It is with three such interrelated religions that this paper deals.[7]

Christianity and Judaism are genetically linked in the sense that Christianity arose out of Judaism, and accepts the revelations of the "Old" Testament. Originating in the same geographic milieu, Christianity was in competitive relations with Judaism, seeking converts among Jews and among idol worshippers of the environing society. As for Islam, it was strongly influenced by the Judeo-Christian tradition, though its primary background is Arab, and it grew out of the problems existing in an Arab Meccan society.[8]

JUDAISM

In commenting on the significance of the sacred texts for genocidal action in the three religions, it is important to bear in mind that in Judaism, in contrast to Christianity and Islam, it was only for a brief period prior to the Diaspora that the sacred texts could yield effective theological warrants for destructive violence against other groups. In the Diaspora there was not the necessary conjunction of religious faith and secular power. This does not imply that Jewish communities in exile were powerless to act against apostasy and heresy or that they were always without centralized organization and authority. Excommunication in its different forms could be a formidable weapon. But the available sanctions were by no means adequate for the suppression of dissident-sects. Thus Hasidism gave rise to a major schism in Judaism, which the rabbinical centers were powerless to prevent. This is not to suggest that if there had been the necessary conjunction of spiritual authority and secular power, the response might have been the annihilation of the sect. Its purpose in referring to Hasidism is to draw attention to the difference between Judaism, Christianity, and Islam in the potentiality for destructive violence. It must be noted, too, that during the Diaspora rabbis developed a special concept of nonviolent resistance which produced heroic instances of martyrdom, a concept which shaped Jewish consciousness and conduct.

Prior to the Diaspora, there was a period in which Judaism did command the necessary power for destructive violence. This was during the conquest of Canaan and the establishment of the kingdom of Israel. The legitimation for destructive violence was provided by the doctrine of *herem.* This concept contains within it the ambiguity inherent in many taboos, between the sacred and the profane, the beneficent and the malevolent. It is defined as "the status of that which is separated from common use or contact either because it is proscribed as an abomination to God or because it is

consecrated to Him."⁹ On the one hand, it served to promote the militant
dedication to monotheism. And from another aspect it may be viewed as
an ideology for the conquest of Canaan.

The biblical injunctions against idol worship and other abominations
unto the Lord were particularly severe.¹⁰ They specifically proscribed idol
worshippers and other nonbelievers, as being under the sanction of *herem.*
The Torah applied the destructive form of *herem* to Israelites who wor-
shipped gods, whether individual Israelites or an entire community. This
was the most destructive form of *herem* extending also to the proscription of
the possessions of the victims. Human beings were to be put to the sword
and their possessions burnt. There are no biblical accounts of the destruction of dissident sects with Judaism itself.

The condemnation by *herem* was also applied to the seven nations inhabiting the land promised to Israel. Not a soul of these was to be left alive
"lest they lead you into doing all the abhorrent things that they have done
for their gods and you stand guilty before the Lord your God."¹¹ However,
the spoil of these nations was not *herem.* But the commandment to destroy
Amalek and his people extended also to their possessions, the Amalekites
having attacked the Israelites with great cruelty during their wanderings in
the desert.

There was a further form of *herem,* which did not derive from divine
injunction, but originated by voluntary act. An enemy might be proscribed
as a votive offering to God, designed to secure His favorable participation
in the coming battle. It seems plausible, as suggested in the *Encyclopedia
Judaica,* that this was the original form of the enemy *herem,* and that it was
later transformed into a blanket proscription of the seven nations inhabiting the land promised to Israel, and rationalized as a protection of the
purity of Israel's religion.¹² Colonizing zeal would have intermingled with
religious faith. But whatever the relationship between these motivations,
there were a number of genocides in the early period of the wars of settlement, as notably in Jericho. However practice, as exemplified in biblical
accounts, was by no means consistent with the sacred commands. Professor
David Lieber comments that most historians do not accept the biblical accounts as representing historical reality, and to the extent that populations
were massacred, it was part of the "holy war" concept which Israel shared
with all of its pagan neighbors.

Now, after millennia of dispersion, Israel again commands effective military power. But there is no clear conjunction of religious faith with military
power as in many of the neighboring Islamic societies. Indeed, it is difficult
to define the relations between Judaism and the state of Israel, they are so
charged with contradiction, ambiguity, and compromise.

While the State of Israel is formally secular and democratic, it is a Jewish
state, which renders problematic the meaning of secular, and indeed, Ela-

zar and Aviad view the national and religious elements as inextricably tied together.[13] They argue that even the "nonreligious Zionists" were never able to govern without religious groups. Hence "God and the Covenant have always been, somehow, a part of the government as they are somehow a part of the state, making the religious condition of Israel extremely complicated and one which even challenges comprehension."[14]

In terms of a status quo agreement with religious groups prior to independence, Sabbath is an official day of rest, Jewish dietary laws are observed in public institutions, religious school systems are maintained and funded by the state, and matters of personal status, primarily marriage and divorce, are governed by religious law.[15] This is some indication of the significance of the Orthodox religious groups, now greatly enhanced by their role as third parties in the electoral struggles of the major contestants for political power, and by the massive influx of traditionally oriented refugees from the Arab world.

At a different level, and more profoundly, traditional religion in contemporary Israel is a source of the sacred symbols, beliefs, and practices needed to legitimate the social order, mobilize the population, and integrate the society, while transmitting its dominant values and worldview.[16] The return to Israel is a return to the traditional homeland, and for the religiously oriented, a return to the land God promised to the children of Israel. Many of the sacred holidays in the Jewish calendar commemorate historic events in biblical times. Liebman and Don-Yehiya comment that "these holidays are increasingly interpreted according their religious origin . . . but they are also invested with national meaning in a manner consistent with a reinterpretation strategy. . . . Traditional religious symbols penetrate, and are incorporated into, the civil religion," though this does not imply "a generalized return to traditional religion."[17]

While religion contributes to the integration of Israeli society, it is also divisive. The very nature of Israeli society as a Jewish state excludes Arabs, and this combined with the need for internal security, relegates Arabs to a diminished civil status as a dominated minority, notwithstanding the declared policy of political democracy.[18] The divisiveness extends also to the Jewish population in the form of conflict between an extreme Orthodoxy aggressively seeking to impose its certitudes and religious practices on the nonreligious or mildly conforming majority, while the specially favored institutional status of Orthodox Judaism and the concomitant exclusion of Reform and Conservative Judaism are a further source of division.[19]

Probably the major integrating factor which restrains the conflicts within the Jewish population is the hostility of much of the outside world, and the perpetual state of war maintained by neighboring Arab states against Israel, with the denial of Israel's right to exist, and the threat of genocide. This hostility exemplifies a traditional view of Jewish-Gentile relations, expressed

in the phrase "Esau hates Jacob," and as actualized in the annihilation of
European Jews in the Holocaust.[20] It is the Holocaust which "plays a critical
role in Israeli civil religion," its memorial Yad Vashem, assuming a "sanctity
not only because it symbolizes six million Jews who died but because it
symbolizes the Jewish people and culture of the Diaspora whose suffering
and death legitimize the Jewish right to Israel."[21] It is a secular legitimation
infused with sacred sentiment.

The contradictions between the ethnic exclusiveness of Jewish religious
nationalism and the universalist ideals of a secular democratic state profoundly affect the status of Palestinians both within Israel and in the occupied territories, as Ruether and Ruether demonstrate in *The Wrath of Jonah*.
They argue that within Israel, Palestinians have been rendered politically invisible and economically exploited by a policy of "fragmentation, isolation
from contact with Israelis and from one another, proletarianization (that is,
loss of land and reduction to a paid labor force in the lowest sectors of the
Israeli economy), economic and educational underdevelopment, political
neutralization and co-optation."[22]

So too, in the occupied territories, policy is directed to making the Palestinians "invisible" by appropriation of land and water, integration of basic
services, and of labor and markets in the economy of Israel, establishment
of Jewish settlements which "serve literally as armed camps, not only in
defense of their settlements, but in aggressive retaliation against incidents
such as stone throwing," and military control "for all matters essential to
daily life under a constant regime of restrictions and harassments."[23]

This severe uncompromising indictment is consistent in general outline
with the oppressive policies pursued in the history of colonization and in
the military pacification of occupied territories, with the denial of the right
to self-determination by the conquered peoples. These conflicts tend to
be intractable, and this is particularly the case where there is the seeming
authority of sacred texts. At this level, the Jewish right to Israel is a return
to the Holy Land, to the biblical world with its covenant and promises, its
prohibitions and sanctions, its moral precepts and paradigms. It is a return
to the world of the prophets and of messianic expectations.

Many circumstances encourage these expectations. It was surely incon-
ceivable that after millennia of exile and persecution and the overwhelming catastrophe of the Holocaust, Israel should be reestablished in its
traditional homeland. And was not the victory of the Six-Day War against
the massed armies of the Arab states, and the liberation of Jerusalem and the
holy places "some special revelation of God's intentions, evidence of the
fulfillment of messianic promises?"[24] And how should one interpret the victory in the Yom Kippur war which caught the Israeli army by surprise and
which many Israelis feared would end in defeat and annihilation? Following Rabbi Yehuda Amital, should it not be comprehended in its messianic

dimension and, indeed, viewed as a struggle against Western civilization and its impurity?[25]

However, comprehension as a messianic dimension permits many interpretations with different concepts of messianic redemption, as in the confrontation between Christianity and Judaism, between the Christian concept of redemption as an event in the spiritual realm, reflected in the private world of each individual, and the Judaic concept of redemption as a public event taking place in the visible world and within the community.[26] So, too, in Israel, there are varied interpretations of the messianic dimension and its contemporary significance.

If the messianic era is to include Isaiah's vision of a world in which "the wolf shall lie down with the lamb and the leopard shall lie down with the kid," then the fratricidal nature of group relation is the Middle East and of the Arab-Israeli confrontation would represent the absolute antithesis to this idyllic cosmic transformation. It would certainly seem to exclude the belief that Israel was now in an era which represents the beginnings of redemption. But this is a difficulty that can be transcended theologically, as the late Uriel Tal documented in his analysis of the "Foundations of a Political Messianic Trend in Israel."[27]

One solution is to detach the Utopian cosmic transformation from the messianic era as referring to the world to come. According to this view, "the messianic era finds its empirical expression in the concrete political change Israel has wrought, the essence of which is the abolition of political subjugation or exile." A second solution finds evidence of cosmic transformation in "the return to the soil, life within nature, the agricultural achievements, the secular creativity, . . . the Zionist activity, the military victories upon the holy soil, the blood spilt on this soil and for its sake." This view substitutes the attainment of a prophetic messianic age for the political messianic age of the first solution.[28]

Some expressions of the messianic trends in Israeli society, with their fundamentalist immersion in the biblical world, have serious implications for Israeli-Arab relations. The messianic movement, Gush Emunim, is dedicated to the settlement of the land in its biblical entirety as its contribution to the redemptive process and in fulfillment of God's commandment to the children of Israel.[29] Conflicts over land are a particularly explosive issue. Then too, at the level of human rights, the introduction of the biblically defined status for strangers (*gerim*) would derogate from the constitutional rights of the Arab residents. And Tal, in his analysis of these issues, quotes from an article by Rabbi Hess on "The Commandment of Genocide in the Torah," in which he proclaims that "the day will come when we will all be called to fulfill the commandment of this religiously commanded war, of annihilating Amalek"—the commandment of genocide.[30]

The position of Rabbi Hess has had virtually no support, even in extreme Orthodox circles. The fundamentalist messianic movement Kach, on the other hand, has a significant following. It is organized as a right wing political party under the leadership of Rabbi Meir Kahane [1932–1990].[31] In contrast to Gush Emunim, which does not conceive of an Arab evacuation as an inevitable consequence of its settlement activities, Kach is committed to the "total eviction of the Arabs."[32] The title of Rabbi Kahane's (1980) book, *They Must Go*, declares this unequivocally.[33]

Kahane's argument rests partly on secular grounds: the ultimately insoluble contradiction between a Jewish state of Israel and a democratic state in which Arabs and Jews have equal rights; the illusion that two large nations can occupy the same land in peaceful coexistence, when they differ in every possible respect; and the imbalance between an Israeli-Arab birthrate, which is the fourth highest in the entire world, and a modest Jewish birthrate.[34]

His movement, however, derives its emotional and compelling force from fundamentalist interpretations of biblical texts and messianic expectations. The Jewish people is the Chosen of God, unique and holy. Its right to the Holy Land of Israel derives not from favor or historical residence, but from "title granted by the Builder and Owner . . . to serve the Jewish people, so that they have a distinct, separate place in which to fulfill their obligation" under the Covenant. "There can be no others who freely live there, let alone share sovereignty and ownership." A religious creation, the State of Israel is the beginning of redemption, with final messianic redemption dependent on faith.[35]

In his analysis of Kach, Sprinzak draws attention to "Quasi-Fascist" manifestations in its antialien sentiment and racist symbology, in its propaganda and personality cult, and in its legitmation of violence and the engagement of some of its followers in anti-Arab atrocities.[36] It should be emphasized, however, that neither fundamentalism nor messianism necessarily carry any threat to other groups. But when they are associated with theologically grounded legitimation of violence, they may set in motion an extreme process of polarization and escalating conflict. These potentialities are somewhat restrained by the constitutional structure of Israeli society, the integrity of its judicial process, and the democratic orientation of many of its citizens. However, there remains the danger of a catastrophic confrontation between Judaic and Islamic fundamentalism.

ISLAM

Current movements of Islamic fundamentalism or of Islamic radicalism, seeking a return to an Islamic social order and a traditional way of life, enhance the relevance and significance of the sacred texts and teachings. These texts offer models and precepts for action with great versatility and applicability to the most varied demands and interpretations of contemporary situations.

In contrast to the animosity of Christianity for Judaism, Islamic doctrine was relatively tolerant. Islam was not initially in competition with Judaism for converts. In medina, where Muhammad first established himself, an early conflict with Jewish tribes was resolved by their defeat. There was no basis for antagonism in different interpretations of the Old Testament, since Islam did not retain the Old Testament. "The Qur'an was not offered as a fulfillment of Judaism, but as a new revelation superseding both the Jewish and Christian scriptures, which had been neglected and distorted by their unworthy custodians." And the rejection of Muhammad's claim to be the Messenger of God was "less significant, less wounding, less of a reproach than the Jewish rejection of Christian claims."[37]

In the relationship of Islam to other religions, Judaism and Christianity were specially favored. There is a general acceptance in Qur'anic teaching of the prophetic revelations as of "universal import," and Jesus is recognized as a Messenger of God, as one prophet in a series of prophets. This line of prophecy, however, is conceived as culminating in the mission of Muhammad, "the seal of the prophets." His revelation is the final, the perfect revelation.[38] Within the series of prophets and prophecies, the privileged position of Jews and Christians rests on their status as "Peoples of the Book."

Lewis comments that there are many passages in the Qur'an, in which hard words are used about the Jews, but that these passages are concerned for the most part with the Prophet's own conflict with them, and are to some extent balanced by other passages, speaking more respectfully, and prescribing a measure of tolerance.[39] Rahman, in a commentary on Islam, observes that the Qur'an "deplores the diversity of religions and religious communities, which it insists is based on willful neglect of the truth, and denounces both Jews and Christians as "partisans, sectarians," with "each sect rejoicing in what itself has." He comments further that the Qur'an in fact envisages some sort of cooperation between Judaism, Christianity, and Islam, and invites Jews and Christians to join Muslims in such a goal.[40]

The world, in early Islamic juristic doctrine, consisted of two zones, the Abode of Islam (*dar al-Islam*), where Muslims ruled, and the Abode of War (*dar al-harb*), the rest of the world. This is, of course, a sharp and threatening dichotomy. A less threatening conception includes a third zone, the Abode of Peace, those countries or powers with whom Muslims have peace pacts. But peace with non-Muslim states was viewed as provisional, and ideally of limited duration.[41]

The divisions into religious zones, defined in relationship to Islamic imperium, reflected the Muslim mission to expand the territory and rule of Islam throughout the world. The duty was to continue until the universal domination of Islam had been attained. The means for this expansion were persuasion, conversion, submission, and the *jihad*, usually equated in Western writing with the notion of "holy war."[42] It was one of the gates to paradise, with rich heavenly rewards assured to those who devoted themselves to it, and the revered status of martyrs for the fallen.[43]

The Peoples of the Book, the scriptural peoples (Jews, Christians, Zoroastrians, and by special interpretation other groups), could live in the Islamic state without conversion, conditional, however, on submission to Muslim rule and payment of a special tax. Their status of *dhimmis* (tolerated peoples) secured them protection and the right to follow their own religions, but under conditions of discrimination, and acceptance of inferiority and humiliation.

This discrimination varied on the whole from tolerance and acceptance in times of Islamic strength and creativity to oppressive restraint and persecution when Islamic power was under threat or disintegrating. It has varied too in different countries, being highly repressive in Morocco and in Iran. "Expulsion, forced conversion, and massacre—all three of rare occurrence in Sunni lands—were features of life in Iran up to the nineteenth century."[44] Discrimination also varied under different regimes. The messianic movement of the Almohads was highly intolerant of deviations from its version of Islam. Lewis writes that it was probably in the period of Almohad rule (twelfth century) "that Christianity was finally extirpated from North Africa. Jews, too, suffered badly in North Africa and Spain and—exceptionally in Muslim history west of Iran—were given the choice between conversion, exile and death."[45]

There was, thus, no theological warrant for genocide against "scriptural peoples" who submitted to Islamic rule. But in the extension of Islamic rule and in the refusal to submit these peoples were exposed to the threat of mass killings. They were also vulnerable as protected groups, as *dhimmis*, if some members failed to conform to the required standards of submissive behavior. Thus, the populace might engage in the massacre of religious groups, should their members overstep the conventional bounds of respect and humility or attain too high an office, as in the massacre of Jews in Granada in the eleventh century.[46] However, this may be a more general characteristic of systems of domination, though rarely expressing itself in the extreme form of the annihilation of a people. One recalls the biblical story of Esther, Mordecai, and Haman in the reign of Ahasuerus, or the extra-legal sanctions for submissive behavior in racist and caste societies.

The Turkish genocide of Armenians in 1915–1916 was not a reaction to transgression against the standards appropriate for former Christian *dhimmis*. There is wide agreement that the Young Turk government was motivated by an extreme chauvinistic nationalism, and not by religious fanaticism. But it unleashed religious fanaticism in the most varied strata of Turkish society, which participated extensively in the genocide. The declaration of a *jihad* by the Sultan on the outbreak of the First World War must surely have inflamed religious passions within the Ottoman Empire, though it was primarily directed to Muslims outside the Empire where it had little effect.

There was the same pattern of religious atrocities in the genocide as in the massacres of 1895–1896 under the Sultan Abdul Hamid II, the forced conversions under the threat of death, the seizures of children to be brought up as Muslims, the atrocities against priests—humiliated, tortured, murdered—and the desecration and destruction of holy places.[47] Lepsius documents these atrocities, but he balances his account by reference to the protests of many responsible government officials and Turkish citizens against the deportations and extermination, attributing responsibility to the government, ruling under the Committee of Union and Progress, and acting through the provincial representatives of the Committee, the militias they recruited from Kurdish tribes, bands of brigands and criminals, and the army and police.[48]

The theological dispensation of conditional tolerance for religious difference extended to the "scriptural peoples," was not available for idolaters or pagans. The alternatives for them were conversion or destruction. They were always under threat of the *jihad*, though this might be deferred until circumstances were favorable, or on payment in goods.[49]

The juristic interpretations of *jihad* were derived primarily from the Prophet's teaching and conduct as they evolved during his lifetime, in response to changing circumstances. There was thus room for variation in emphasis and conception, and for conflicting interpretations by the jurists, and also the possibility of selecting different models for action. The resulting flexibility in the doctrine of *jihad* lent itself readily to adaptation in changing historical contexts of action.

The *jihad*, as the means for the extension of Islam and for its defense, was appropriately invoked against the Crusaders. However, the Islamic *contra-jihad* only attained its full expression after appreciable delay.[50] This is surprising, given the fact that the Crusades were after all religious wars directed against the Muslim infidel, and that the first Crusade, launched by Pope Urban II, with promises of spiritual rewards, was already accompanied by genocidal massacres in the conquest of Jerusalem, and by indiscriminate massacres and terrorism perpetrated by the crusading Tafurs.[51]

The *jihad* was also appropriately invoked against the colonizing powers, for example by Abd al-Qadir against the French in Algeria. His campaign was conducted with great courage and persistence, and with careful observance of the prescriptions of Islamic law, but it was overwhelmed by the French Army's war of extermination.[52]

The doctrine also lent itself to adaptability in response to the decline in Arab power, and the assaults of modernization and Westernization with their negative perceptions of the *jihad* as "Holy War." Khaddurie's *War and Peace in the Law of Islam* is an example of a modern response to contemporary pressures on the Islamic world.

Khaddurie defines the *jihad* in its juridical theological meaning as "exertion of one's power in Allah's path, that is, the spread of the belief in Allah, and in making His word supreme over the world." This *jihad* obligation might be fulfilled, according to the jurists, by heart (combating the evil persuasions of the devil), by tongue and hands (supporting the right and correcting the wrong), and by war (in fighting against unbelievers and the enemies of faith). *Jihad* as war is equated by Khaddurie with *bellum justum* as in ancient Rome, to which Khaddurie adds "*pium*, that is in accordance with the sanction of religion and the implied command of gods."[53] Of particular significance is the fact that the greater part of his book is devoted to the Law of Peace, regulating the relations between Muslims and non-Muslims, and Islamic Law of Nations.

Peters explores the same theme in his analysis of the Islamic response to colonialism. In a section on new interpretations of the *jihad-doctrine*, he comments that some modernist authors interpret *jihad* as "Islamic international law" by reason of its adaptability to modern conditions and its humane rules; and they emphasize its venerable antiquity, having been formulated and applied "when, in the rest of the world, international relations were still dominated by barbaric anarchy and the savage law of the jungle." But it would appear from the analysis that these new interpretations have more theoretical or ideological significance in the defense against Western attacks, than practical application.[54]

These ancient injunctions seem irrelevant to the contemporary scene, in which Islamic states are confronted by the entrenched power of the West, with its massive nuclear armaments, and by the worldwide representative organizations of the Christian churches, and at a time too, when Third World nations wield appreciable influence in international affairs. Nevertheless, these ancient doctrines continue to exert an influence in certain contexts, notably in the struggle against Israel, and in the assertion of an Islamic identity in reaction to the disintegrating pressures of Western industrialization and its secular ideologies. Bernard Lewis traces many of these continuities in his writings. Fatah, the main Palestinian guerrilla organization, is a technical term for an Islamic conquest gained in a holy war, while Fatah's regiments are named after three battles won in holy wars for Islam against non-Muslims.[55] In Egypt, in the manual of orientation issued by the supreme command in 1965, the wars in Yemen and against Israel were presented in terms of a *jihad*, the enemies being opponents of social justice and human betterment, namely imperialism, Zionism, and Arab reactionaries. The manual issued to the Egyptian troops in June 1973 described the enemy quite simply as the Jews.[56]

The fundamentalist reaction to the disorientation of Western colonization, imperialism, and materialism revitalizes the Islamic continuities. It seeks the return to an all-embracing Islamic way of life, traditionally conceived, and dedicates itself to the service of the Islamic community. In the contemporary theocratic regime of Iran the commemoration of the martyrdom of Husayn in 680 is the major ceremonial event in the Shi'ite holy calendar. It reaffirms the ineffable prestige of martyrdom in the service of Islam, introducing a theological weapon of great and deadly versatility.[57] And the attempt to eradicate the Baha'i religion, denied recognition under the Iranian constitution, is presumably an expression of a fundamentalist rejection by the theocratic regime of religious dissidence that arose with Islam itself.

Continuities with Christian anti-Semitism[58] begin to enter the Islamic world in the high Middle Ages, and with the incorporation of Greek Orthodox Christians into the Ottoman Empire. But "the real penetration of modern-style anti-Semitism, however, dates from the nineteenth century." It was introduced by Christian Arab minorities, and actively encouraged by consular and commercial representatives and by priests and missionaries.[59] Now, in reaction to the establishment of Israel, and the humiliating defeat of the Arab armies, the themes of Christian anti-Semitism have become a major ideological weapon in the war against Jews.

The chapter headings in Bernard Lewis's analysis of Semites and anti-Semites summarize the progression from a problem of internal conflict within Palestine, through its extension to Zionism as the enemy, and its final expression in the war against Jews. In the process, there is an internalization of Christian anti-Semitism, encouraging some reinterpretation of traditional Islamic teaching.

A large anti-Semitic literature in Arabic, of Christian and European or American origin, draws on an iconography with the familiar grotesque caricatures of the anti-Semitic press in the Christian world.[60] This literature includes nine different Arabic translations and innumerable editions of the notorious forgery, the inflammatory *Protocols of the Elders of Zion*, which purveys the myth of a world Jewish conspiracy;[61] and Lewis comments that the volume of anti-Semitic publications, the eminence and authority of those who write, publish, and sponsor them, their place in school and college curricula, their role in the mass media, would all seem to suggest that classical anti-Semitism is an essential part of Arab intellectual life at the present time—almost as much as in Nazi Germany.[62]

It is by no means only Islamic communities that are the recipients of this anti-Semitic propaganda. On the contrary, some of the Arab countries and Iran are now the main centers for the dissemination of international anti-Semitism throughout the world.[63] And the Arab states, in association with the Soviet bloc and many Third World countries, use their oil-rich prestige to influence the proceedings and resolutions of the United Nations, where the demonization of Israel (and of Jews) attains its ultimate manifestation in routine rituals of outcasting and degradation.

As a result of the Israeli War of Independence and the ideological polarization of group relations, and under the stimulus of widespread persecution, mounting harassment, and occasional massacre, there has been a general flight of Jews from the Arab countries to Israel. The ancient Jewish communities are now virtually extinct, with sizable remnants remaining only in Morocco and Tunisia.[64]

CHRISTIANITY

Some of the variables of general relevance to technological warrants for genocide may be derived from an analysis of the especially intimate relationship of Christianity to Judaism. Others are more specific to this relationship. This is true of the variables related to the genetic linking of Judaism and Christianity, with Christianity developing out of Judaism. These include Jewish reactions to the Christian revelation, and the Christian view of the Judaic revelation. Do Christians regard it as superseded? And how do they react to the refusal of Jews to accept Jesus as the Messiah or the Son of God? What is their response to the Jewish rejection of the claim that with Jesus the final messianic age had arrived? Is there any basis in Christianity for the transformation of religious controversy into social anti-Semitism? Was the refutation of Judaism implicit in Christian theology in any way connected with the anti-Semitism prevalent in Western history and its culmination in the annihilatory anti-Semitism of the Nazis?[65]

Rosemary Ruether's major contribution to the analysis of these issues conveys in the title of her book, *Faith and Fratricide*, her perception of Christian theology as laying the foundations for fratricidal persecution. She traces the development of an anti-Judaic tradition in the New Testament, arguing that this was the Church's response to the negation of its messianic interpretation of the Scriptures by official Judaism.[66] Christians became the people of God, Jews the apostate people, unbelieving toward the Gospel, and murderous toward its messengers and the prophets who preceded them.[67] The relationship is one of thesis and antithesis, without hope of resolution, save in the last days when the righteous and repentant remnant of Israel will be gathered into the community of redemption. It is only recently that the Catholic Church has moved toward a more tolerant attitude in the search for mutual understanding between Christians and Jews, and in the recognition that God's saving truth is also operative in the other world religions.[68]

The antagonism of Christianity for Judaism remains, however, deeply embedded in the sacred writings, in the very foundations of Christianity, and this leads Ruether to enquire whether it can be rooted out entirely without destroying the theological structure of Christianity.[69]

Rubenstein argues to somewhat similar effect from a different perspective, that of the dissonance between Judaism and Christianity, each tradition being in the position of "disconfirming other" to its rival. He views the bitter anti-Jewish animus of some of "Christianity's most saintly personalities" as serving to reduce this dissonance. "The same genius, energy, and imagination which led them to initiate a universal religious civilization also impelled them to attack and discredit those whom they perceived to be challenging even by their silent unbelief, the very foundation on which Christian civilization was constructed, faith in Christ as the Savior of mankind."[70]

The reprobation of the Jews is based on the assertion that they rejected Jesus as the Christ. But this final act of apostasy is projected backward, yielding a view of Jewish history as a trail of crimes.[71] These negative aspects were much expanded by the Church Fathers, giving rise to an extensive thesaurus of derogatory epithets and antagonistic dichotomies. Christian inwardness and authenticity are contrasted with Jewish legalism, Christian universalism with Jewish particularism. Christianity is the fulfillment of that which Judaism "foreshadowed" in the "fleshly way."[72]

Baum, in his introductory exposition of Ruether's argument, refers to "the radical distinction between the believing church and the blind synagogue, between the Israel of the spirit and the Israel of the flesh, between the heavenly and the earthly Jerusalem. Eventually all the dichotomies of salvation between spirit and flesh, light and darkness, truth and self-righteousness, were projected on the opposition between church and synagogue until the Jewish people became the embodiment of all that is unredeemed, perverse, stubborn, evil, and demonic in this world."[73]

The social consequences for the vilified group of this theological anti-Judaism were dependent on the power to act in the secular realm. It is only when power is joined to religious belief that the sacred texts can become effective warrants for destructive action against other groups. And Ruether analyzes the transformation of religious belief into discriminatory social practice.

The potential for this transformation was already realized in the Roman Empire in the fourth century, when Christianity was transformed from a persecuted faith into the established religion of the empire, with the emperors acting as exponents of the theological view of the Jews and as priest kings of the Christian theocratic empire.[74] Imperial and canonical law had prohibited intermarriage and sexual relations between Jews and Christians; commensality was also forbidden (the Council of Elvira, *circa* 315). The Emperor Theodosius (378–395) made it a crime of adultery, punishable by death, for any Christian man or woman to marry a Jew or Jewess. There were restraints on social relations between Jews and Christians, exclusion of Jews from public office (Synod of Clermont, 535), prohibition of Jewish employment of Christian servants (Synod of Orleans, 538), burning of the Talmud and other books (Twelfth Synod of Toledo, 681), Christians not permitted to patronize Jewish doctors (Trulanic Synod, 692), Christians not permitted to live in Jewish homes (Synod of Narbonne, 1050), and the imposition of special burdensome taxation on Jews (Synod of Gerona, 1078). Later anti-Judaic laws decreed the marking of Jewish clothes with a badge, forbade the building of new synagogues or the repair of old ones, imposed restraints on religious observances, and limited the jurisdiction of the religious courts.[75]

Religious and secular persecution of Jews had been greatly intensified following the Crusades. Though the authorities sought to protect Jews, the Crusades unleashed a wave of devastating pogroms by armies of the poor against Jewish communities in the Rhineland. It was said that whoever killed a Jew who refused baptism was forgiven all his sins, "and there were those who felt unworthy to start on a Crusade at all until they had killed at least one such."[76]

Ruether writes that the Crusades were

> the great turning point of Jewish status in the Western middle Ages, a turning point itself expressive of the Church's indoctrination of popular religious hatred for the Jew. . . . The canonical legislation of the Church in the thirteenth century effected a systematic social degradation of the Jew . . . the Church's basic position was that the Jew should occupy no place of eminence or power in Christian society which would ever put him in a position of authority over a Christian, however modest. . . . Any social contact, living together, eating together, sexual relations, personal conversation, especially in religious matters, was to be prevented, lest Jewish "unbelief" contaminate Christian faith.[77]

Clerical vituperation was already present in the laws of the Christian emperors. The Jews were referred to as a group hated by God, to be regarded by Christian society as contemptible and even demonic. The epithet "Satanic" was applied to the Synagogue. It became common to speak of Judaism in the language of pollution, contagion, disease.[78] This imagery of Jewishness as a contagion was highly developed in the period following the Crusades, receiving its final expression in the segregation of the Ghetto, and the wearing of distinctive Jewish dress (the conical hat and the "Jew badge," usually a yellow circle). There was also a demonization of Jews. They were presented as children of the devil, employed by Satan to combat Christianity, and accused of murdering Christian children, torturing the consecrated wafer, and poisoning wells. And there was talk of a secret Jewish government, directing an underground war against Christians.[79]

The four centuries that followed were centuries of religious persecution in Europe with the systematic humiliation and degradation of Jews. Many Jewish communities were annihilated in large-scale massacres or decimated in pogroms. Jews too experienced the torments of the Holy Inquisition against heretics. Following charges of having desecrated a sacramental wafer, perhaps as many as a hundred thousand Jews were massacred and a hundred and forty communities completely destroyed.[80] Jews were expelled from many countries of Europe or ruthlessly exploited.[81] Disasters such as famines and the Black Death were particularly threatening for Jewish communities, as were periods of religious effervescence, such as the Crusades, or the Easter pogroms following on charges of ritual murder. These Easter pogroms were still being perpetrated in Russia in the nineteenth century.

When set against the long history of Christian vilification and persecution of Jews, the emancipation of Jews is relatively recent. And Ruether comments that there is an uncomfortable proximity between medieval vilification and Nazi anti-Judaism.[82] Indeed many of the images and forms of medieval vilification and persecution recall the Nazi victimization of Jews in the 1930s, suggesting a continuity between them.

Nazi propaganda deliberately exploited the medieval portrayal of Jews, with its obscene fantasies, and its imagery of pollution, contagion, and disease. It played upon the fears and frustrations of the German people, by exploiting the demonic threat of secret world conspiracy. Nurtured in the medieval period, and "documented" in the Russian forgery of the *Protocols of the Elders of Zion*, this combined "ancient demonological terrors" with typically modern anxieties and resentments.[83]

At the legislative level, there are many parallels between the Nazi measures and the canonical laws against Jews, as Hilberg demonstrates.[84] These included the elimination of Jews from public office, the systematic elaboration of prohibitions against contact (sex relations, employment of Germans, schooling, residence, public transport) and distinctive dress (the yellow badge).[85] Hitler, when confronted by two bishops on the issue of Nazi racial policy, is reported to have replied that he was only putting into effect what Christianity had preached and practiced for over 2,000 years.[86]

While the many centuries of Christian anti-Judaism translated into social practice, and while the historical proximity of European and Nazi persecution of Jews and the parallelism of laws and imagery are strong arguments for continuity between Christian inspired anti-Semitism and the Holocaust, the issue is controversial. The contrary view emphasizes the independent development of "scientific" racism, elaborated by the Nazis into a racial doomsday hierarchy, defining the right to survive and the conditions for survival. It lays particular stress on the traumatic aftereffects of the First World War and the crises of modernization; and it minimizes, or indeed dismisses, the religious input by reference to the Nazi rejection of Christianity.

Perhaps too much can be made of the parallelism between the canonical laws and the Nazi measures against Jews. There is, for example, an appreciable correspondence between the canonical laws and the legal dispensations in South African apartheid. Nazi doctrines and the neo-Fichtean romantic idealization of the *Volk* certainly contributed to its development. However, the roots of apartheid are deeply embedded in Afrikaner society, and the Dutch Reformed Church was a major influence in the structuring of Afrikaner race relations and its systematic elaboration into apartheid. Moreover, it consistently provided biblical sanctification for the ideology as in the parable of the Tower of Babel and the predestination of the children of Ham to servitude. This moral and theological justification of apartheid was declared by the General Council of the World Alliance of Reformed Churches to be a travesty of the Gospel, and, in its persistent disobedience to the Word of God, a theological heresy.[87] But notwithstanding the declaration, and notwithstanding the manifest mass atrocities of apartheid over three decades, the South African Dutch Reformed Church, at the meeting of its Synod in October 1986, could only commit itself to a mild disavowal of its biblical justification of apartheid as an error and as incompatible with Christian and ethical principles.[88]

In this case, the link between the theology of the Dutch Reformed Church and apartheid is hardly controversial, though analysts may differ in the weight they attach to the religious component. But some basic principles informing the canonical laws, the Nazi measures and apartheid are common in systems of racial, ethnic, and religious domination. These include the prohibition against intermarriage, sex relations and commensality, and the insistence on the maintenance of hierarchical relationships in a wide range of social contacts. Concepts of pollution are also common enough, reinforcing the restraints on social relations.

Clearly, the parallelism of laws taken in isolation is by no means a conclusive argument for continuity. Moreover, some weight must certainly be attached to the influence of "scientific" racism. Alan Davies, in a critique of Ruether's analysis, argues that an inquiry "into the Christian materials and their social incorporation in the Christian nations" should be balanced by an inquiry into the intellectual and spiritual pathology of European society since the nineteenth century, and its supreme expression in genocide.[89] Yehuda Bauer draws a distinction between traditional anti-Semitism, with such varied components as the romantic movement contributing to an increasingly exclusive nationalism, the exaggerated role attributed to Jews in the initiating of capitalism, the theory of social Darwinism, and the "biologization" of anti-Semitism.[90]

However, there is no inherent logic in social Darwinism or in racist theories that would explain why European Jews were specially targeted for total annihilation, and why there was so much widespread support for their destruction. Nor do their traumas and alienation of the postwar years explain why it was the Jews who were selected as the sacrificial victims. The theory that there was appreciable continuity, whether direct or indirect, between the many centuries of Christian anti-Judaism and the Nazi Holocaust seems more persuasive.

A necessary qualification is that the teachings of the Church provided no specific warrant for genocide. The Church wanted the Jews to be physically preserved to the end of time, although in misery and in a pariah status, to testify to the present election of the Church and to witness its final triumph.[91] But the hatred the Church inculcated served as warrant for many of the pogroms perpetrated by the populace, and at the very least provided the psychological preconditioning for wide participation in the Holocaust. Ruether writes that in Christendom, violence had always come from the mob, while the state had been the protector of Jewish continued existence: now anti-Semitism came from the state itself. "Master of its own eschatology and creator of its own millennium, the Third Reich took in hand the Last Judgment which Christianity had reserved for the coming Christ."[92]

The relationship of the old Christian anti-Judaism to the modern racial anti-Semitism may be viewed as a transformation. Thus Reuther observes that the same stereotypes and the same set of psychological attitudes were preserved in the change of theoretical grounds, with the antithesis between Judaism and Christianity being translated into an antithesis between Jews and Europeans or Jews and Germans.[93]

Lewis argues to similar effect that when religiously expressed anti-Judaism came to be regarded as reactionary and outmoded, it gave way, in more modern and secular circles, to racially expressed anti-Semitism; and that when racial anti-Semitism became discredited, it was succeeded, for some "by an anti-Zionism in which politics takes the place previously occupied first by religion and then by race." The change is one of expression and emphasis rather than of substance, since all these elements have been and still are present. Even now, if one wishes to attack or discredit a Jew as such, one may call him an unbeliever, a Semite or a Zionist, depending on whether the atmosphere and prevailing ideology of the society in which one operated is religious, ethnic, or political.[94] In effect, the argument is that the initial cultivated religious hatred now seeks out its appropriate contemporary ideology. Anti-Zionism, however, is not to be equated with anti-Semitism, but may derive from quite different ideological grounds. And, conversely, support for Zionism, as for example, by Christian fundamentalists, does not exclude anti-Semitism.[95]

As an alternative approach to the theory of transformation, is to view the relationship of the theological and racist rejection of Jews as a fusion, with, for example, modern German anti-Semitism described as "the bastard child of the union of Christian anti-Semitism with German nationalism."[96]

JUDAISM, ISLAM, AND CHRISTIANITY

It must be clear from the previous discussion that the role of the sacred texts in genocidal conflict is variable and appreciably indeterminate. This indeterminacy is certainly evident in the controversy over the significance of traditional Christian anti-Semitism in the Holocaust, which is probably one of the most intensely researched subjects in the history of human societies.[97]

Contributing to this indeterminacy are also curious anomalies in the relationship of the sacred texts to genocidal conflict. The central teachings of Christianity are the very antithesis of anything that could conceivably offer a theological warrant for genocide. Still, the hostile characterization of Jews in the dichotomies between church and synagogue and the charge of deicide legitmated their victimization. The policy of the Catholic Church was never directed to the annihilation of Jews, in contrast to its systematic destruction of heretics and of deviant Christian sects. This is sometimes explained by reference to the concern for purity of doctrine, reaching back to the Council of Nicaea (AD 325). But struggles for power in religious movements often take the form of controversy over doctrine, so that it becomes increasingly difficult to assess the significance of religious motivation.

In Islam, a combination of elements might provide a theological warrant for genocide. These included the belief in Islam as the absolute, final, and perfect revelation; the mission to extend Islam throughout the world; and above all the acceptance of the *jihad* as a means to that end. Practice, however, was less threatening than precept; and within Islam itself, Muslims were allowed considerable freedom of belief, the minimal requirements for doctrinal and ritual conformity being by no means onerous. At the present time, Islamic imperialist expansions and the incorporation of "Peoples of the Book" are hardly contemporary reality. But the continuing vitality of the *jihad*, particularly in relation to Israel, carries a genocidal threat. And this may also be present in certain forms of theocratic fundamentalism, as manifested, for example, in the Iranian government's campaign to eradicate the Baha'i religion.

For Judaism, some of the sacred texts have an intrinsic contemporary relevance, as in God's promise to Abraham that "all the land which thou seest, to thee will I give it and to thy seed forever." And the return to Jerusalem, the Land of Israel, was readily perceived as the fulfillment of a promise—a divine promise which sustained Jews over millennia of exile, homelessness, and persecution. Other texts, however, have a specific historic reference, with no obvious prophetic implication for the future. Thus, the annihilation of the Amalekites in fulfillment of God's commandment would have represented the final event in a historical episode. The selection of this text as a paradigm for contemporary action, and the identification of the descendants of Amalek with the Arabs must surely be impelled by other motivations than theological warrant or divine injunction.

Then, too, the motivational power of the theological warrants must be influenced appreciably by the religious culture. This includes the sacred texts which might serve as warrants for genocide, or shape the hostile attitudes that encourage commission of the crime. They vary in emphasis: thus one cannot read the Pentateuch without being aware of the anathema directed against idol worshippers as "an abomination unto the Lord," or the special reprobation of Jews in the Christian Testament. They vary also in form, whether expressed as awesome and peremptory divine commandments, or as threatening dichotomies, or as parables with potentially destructive implications for other groups.

The religious culture includes also the commentaries, the authoritative declarations of religious councils on matters of doctrine and ritual, and the regulation of daily life and relations with other groups. Account must be taken of religious teaching and services, religious festivals and the events they commemorate, religious music, theater, art, literature, and polemic. And then there are the relations between church and state, and the contemporary contributions of religious culture to civil religion.

The existential situation in the period analyzed must surely be of major significance. Secularization would diminish the significance of the sacred texts, while the fundamentalist reaction to secularism, modernism, Western technology, and civilization would lend them compelling significance. The establishment of the Kingdom of Israel in the Holy Land may be perceived as re-creating the world of the Bible and enhancing the revelatory and prophetic significance of the sacred texts, while the same event evokes in some Islamic circles resentment at this change in the traditional status of religious groups, tolerated as *dhimmis*.

The sheer complexity of the societal context must surely be a major factor in accounting for the indeterminacy of the religious element in genocide. In the Armenian genocide, as in the Holocaust, there is controversy over the role of religious difference. It is generally accepted that the leaders in the Armenian genocide were not motivated by religious intolerance. But this is by no means decisive. The significant factors are the social forces they activated by the policies they pursued, and the declaration of a *jihad* certainly inflamed religious fanaticism in the populace. Moreover, the motivation of the leaders is not easily determined. It is shaped not only by the political philosophy espoused, but also at a deep and unconscious level, by the intangible influences of conditioning in a cultural milieu with a long history of discrimination against a religious minority.

In both the Armenian and the Jewish case, the religious status was a generalized status in the plural divisions of the society. The Turks, in many centuries of rule, did not attempt to integrate Armenians. On the contrary, under the *millet* system, religious affiliation was emphasized and elevated into a basic principle of administrations. Christians were organized in separate units under a patriarch, with appreciable autonomy in spiritual matters, schooling, and the exercise of limited judicial functions, but they were also subject to discriminatory measures. Moreover, the treatment of Christians in the Ottoman Empire had become an international issue in the nineteenth century, precipitating large-scale massacres of Armenians with religious atrocities less than a generation before the final genocide. In the Jewish case, the discrimination against European Jews was much more intense; and it extended over very many centuries. There were long periods in which Jews were pariahs in the host society, and victims of periodic annihilatory attacks. They were subjected also to an accumulated vocabulary of derogatory epithets and obscene imagery.

These cultural heritages are not readily effaced. Indeed, in working in the comparative field of the relations between racial, ethnic, and religious groups, I have always been impressed by the depth of historic memory, and the way in which ancient events, seemingly long consigned to oblivion, suddenly become part of the contemporary conflict. The tenacity of historic memory in some arguments for the continuity of religious passion in the genocides against Jews and Armenians remains.

A generalized religious status is by no means the usual case. There are often religious differences without the superimposition of other differentiating factors. And a surprising element in genocide is the frequency with which the perpetrators and their victims are of different religions, suggesting that even in these cases, the religious differentiation may be significant.

Even where there is a generalized religious status, the theological warrants for genocide are not self-fulfilling, but are activated in particular circumstances. Given the complexity and diversity of the social forces involved, it would seem hardly possible to assess the religious contribution to genocide, whether as motivation, justification, or rationalization, without taking account more generally of the genocidal context.

In the genocidal context, I include the structure of the society, its religious composition and relations with the political institutions, its social classes and other social strata, and some aspects of its international relations. It is clear from the preceding case studies of genocidal conflict that the theological warrants for genocide, or other religious beliefs that might facilitate genocide, do not operate in isolation from the societal context. They interact. Thus the religious dispensations of the Catholic Church in medieval Europe created a social status for Jews that became a significant element in the genocidal massacres of the Peoples' Crusades and in later persecutions, including the Holocaust, if Rosemary Ruether's analysis is accepted.

The fusion of the political and religious structures of power offers a particularly favorable context for the perpetration of religiously motivated genocide.

Contemporary Iran exemplified this destructive potentiality of a theocratic structure in its threatened genocide of the Baha'is. The historical experience of Shi'ite Muslims as a beleaguered, self-righteous minority and the commitment to Islam as the final revelation, absolute, unchanging, and exclusive, did not encourage toleration for the Baha'is. Viewed as apostates for whom the traditional punishment was death, they were subjected to genocidal massacres in 1852, only a few years after the beginnings of the religious ferment which challenged the structure of power and traditional beliefs.

NOTES

1. Rosemary Radford Ruether and Herman J. Ruether, *The Wrath of Jonah—Crisis of Religious Nationalism in the Israeli-Palestinian Conflict* (New York: Harper & Row, 1989), xvii.

2. Ibid., 87, citing Richard Slotkin, *Regeneration through Violence: The Mythology of the American Frontier* (Middletown, Conn.: Wesleyan University Press, 1973), 55 and 84.

3. See the discussion by Norman Cohn, *Warrant for Genocide: The Myth of the Jewish World Conspiracy and the Protocols of the Elders of Zion* (London: Eyre & Spottiswoode, 1967), 53ff.

4. See, for example, Richard L. Rubenstein, *The Age of Triage* (Boston, Mass.: Beacon Press, 1983), 146ff. and Robert E. Eriksen, *Theologians under Hitler* (New Haven, Conn.: Yale University Press, 1985), 19.

5. Robert J. Lifton analyzes this ideology in detail. See *The Nazi Doctors: Medical Killing and the Psychology of Genocide* (New York: Basic Books, 1985), 16–18 and 476–93.

6. Ibid., ch. 6.

7. Professor David Lieber comments that this generalization, made popular by Toynbee, has to be qualified particularly in the case of Judaism. He writes that to the best of his recollection, "it was the Maccabees who engaged in forced conversion in their war against the Idumeans and, it is interesting to note, only that the rabbinical tradition was critical of them for that."

8. F. Rahman, in Mircea Eliade (ed.), *The Encyclopedia of Religion*, Vol. 8 (New York: Macmillan, 1986), 305.

9. *Encyclopedia Judaica* (Jerusalem: Keren Publishing House, 1971), 346.

10. The following brief comments on Judaism in biblical times are extracts from Leo Kuper and Gary Remer, "The Religious Element in Genocide," *Journal of Armenian Studies*, IV (1 and 2): 1992.

11. Ibid.

12. Ibid., 350.

13. D. J. Elazar and J. Aviad, "Religion and Politics in Israel" in Michael Curtis (ed.), *Religion and Politics in the Middle East* (Boulder, Colo.: Westview Press, 1981), 163–96.

14. Ibid.

15. Ibid., 174.

16. Charles J. Liebman and Eliezer Don-Yehiya define the civil religion in Israeli society in these terms. *Civil Religion in Israel: Traditional Judaism and Political Culture in the Jewish State* (Berkeley: University of California Press, 1983).

17. Ibid., 155 and 226.

18. See the discussion by Sammy Smooha of the extreme discrimination against Arabs in *Israel: Pluralism and Conflict* (Berkeley: University of California Press, 1978), 102–3 and *passim*, and his analysis of the policy of domination pursued by the Israeli government, *Existing and Alternative Policy Towards the Arabs in Israel* (Fernand Braudel Center, State University of New York at Binghamton, 1981).

19. See E. Gutman, "Religion and Its Role in National Integration in Israel," in Curtis, op. cit., 197–206.

20. See Liebman and Don-Yehiya, op. cit., 138–39 and 223–24.

21. Ibid., 9.

22. Ibid., 136; see also 145–54.

23. Ibid., 156–59.

24. See the discussion by Liebman and Don-Yehiya, op. cit., 201.

25. See U. Tal, "Foundations of a Political Messianic Trend in Israel," *Jerusalem Quarterly*, No. 35 (1985), 36–45.

26. See the discussion by Liebman and Don-Yehiya, op. cit., 201.

27. Ibid., 36–45.

28. See Tal, op. cit., 42–43.

29. For references to Gush Emunim, see the following: K. A. Avruch, "Gush Emunim: Politics, Religion, and Ideology in Israel," in Curtis, op. cit.; D. Biale, "Mysticism and Politics in Modern Israel: The Messianic Ideology of Isaac Ha-Cohen Kook," in Peter Merkl and Ninian Smart (eds.), *Religion and Politics in the Modern World* (New York: New York University Press, 1983), 170–90; E. Sprinzak, "Gush Emunim, the Tip of the Iceberg." *Jerusalem Quarterly*, No. 21 (1981), 28–47 and Tal.

30. Tal, op. cit., 42–43.

31. Editor's Note: Kahane was an Orthodox-ordained rabbi and extremist in his intensely Jewish nationalistic views. He is also remembered as the founder of the Jewish Defense League (JDL) in New York, a self-appointed militant response "to protect Jews" in light of Black-Jewish tensions during the late 1960s and early 1970s, and the far-right Israeli political party Kach ("Strength"). An Arab later assassinated him in New York after a speech urging American Jews to immigrate to Israel.

32. See E. Sprinzak, "Kach and Kahane: The Emergence of Jewish Quasi-Fascism," in Arian Asher and Michal Shamir (eds.), *The Elections in Israel, 1984* (New Brunswick, N.J.: Transaction Press, 1986), 175 and 181. See also R. I. Friedman, "The Sayings of Rabbi Kahane," *New York Review of Books* (13 Feb. 1986), 15–20.

33. Kahane does envisage non-citizen status for a limited number who recognize total Jewish sovereignty over the land of Israel and the absolute and exclusive right of the Jewish people to it.

34. Rabbi Meir Kahane, *They Must Go* (New York: Grosset & Dunlop, 1981), 7, 99–100, and 121.

35. Ibid., 267–76.

36. Sprinzak, op.cit., 1986 and Friedman, op. cit., 1986.

37. Bernard Lewis, *Semites and Anti-Semites* (New York: Norton, 1986), 118. See generally his discussion of "The Muslims and the Jews," ch. 5, ibid.

38. Lewis, op. cit., 120.

39. Ibid., 122.

40. Rahman, op. cit., 320–21. Rahman cites the following Qur'anic invitation to Jews and Christians: "O people of the book! Let us come together on a platform that is common between us, that we shall serve naught save God."

41. See Rahman, op. cit., 321, and E. Tyan in *The Encyclopedia of Islam* (1965), under "Djihad," 539.

42. R. Peters points out that the concept of *jihad* has a wider connotation than "holy war," and "that all wars between Muslims and unbelievers and even wars between different Muslim groups would be labeled *jihad*, even if fought—as was mostly the case—for perfectly secular reasons" (Eliade, *Encyclopedia of Religions*, Vol. 9, 89). See my paper for wider connotations of the term.

43. Tyan, op. cit., 539.

44. Bernard Lewis, *The Jews of Islam* (Princeton, N.J.: Princeton University Press, 1984), 40.

45. Ibid., 52. See also Norman A. Stillman, *The Jews of Arab Lands* (Philadelphia: Jewish Publication Society of America, 1979), 77.

46. Stillman, op. cit., 57–59 and 211–25.

47. See Johannes Lepsius, *Armenia and Europe* (Paris/London: Hodder & Stoughton, 1897), 253–331, and *Le Rapport Secret sur les Massacres d'Armenie* (Paris: Payot, 1919), 281–88; Lord Bryce, *The Treatment of Armenians in the Ottoman Empire, 1915–1916* (London: His Majesty's Stationery Office, 1916), documents 7, 11, 12, 57, 59, 76, and Arnold Toynbee, *Armenian Atrocities: The Murder of a Nation* (London: Hodder & Stoughton, 1915), 104–5.

48. Lepsius, *Le Rapport Secret*, 1919, 177–81 and 284ff.

49. See Tyan, op. cit., 539.

50. See Emmanuel Sivan, *L'Islam et la Croisade* (Paris: Librarie d'Amerique et d'Orient, 1968).

51. Norman Cohn, *The Pursuit of the Millenium* (New York: Oxford University Press, 1970), ch. 3. See also Steven Runciman, *A History of the Crusades*, Vol. 1 (London: Cambridge University Press, 1951), 265–88.

52. Rudolph Peters, *Islam and Colonialism: The Doctrine of Jihad in Modern History* (The Hague: Mouton Publishers, 1979), 53–62.

53. Majid Khaddurie, *War and Peace in the Law of Islam* (Baltimore, Md.: Johns Hopkins Press, 1955), 54–57. See also the comments on the concept of Jihad in Bernard Lewis, *The Political Language of Islam* (Chicago, Ill.: University of Chicago Press, 1988), 72ff.

54. Peters, op. cit., 135–39, 159, 165.

55. "The Return of Islam," in Curtis, 1981, op. cit., 15–16.

56. See T. Smith, "Iran—Five Years of Fanaticism," *New York Times Magazine* (12 Feb. 1984), and J. Kifner, "Iran Obsessed with Martyrdom," *New York Times Magazine* (16 Oct. 1984).

57. Ibid.

58. Editor's Note: This spelling "anti-Semitism" has since been replaced in scholarly writing by the now more commonly accepted "antisemitism."

59. Lewis, op. cit., 132.

60. Ibid., 209–10.

61. Ibid., 208.

62. Ibid., 256.

63. Ibid., 195. A curious development in Japan is the publication of anti-Semitic literature, also drawing on the Christian thesaurus. See C. Haberman, "Japanese Writers Are Critical of Jews," *New York Times* (12 March 1987), Y22. and D. Goodman, "Reasons for Concern in Japanese Anti-Semitism," *New York Times* (25 March 1987), Y22.

64. Lewis, 1986, op. cit., 206.

65. See G. Baum, in Rosemary Radford Ruether, *Faith and Fratricide: The Theological Roots of Anti-Semitism* (New York: Seabury Press, 1974), Introduction, 1.

66. Ruether, 1974, 64.

67. Ibid., ch. 3, *passim*.

68. Baum, op. cit., 4.

69. Ruether, 1974, 228. The thesis that anti-Judaism, and indeed anti-Semitism, are inherent in Christology is challenged by T. Idinopulos and R. B. Ward. See their "Is Christology Inherently Anti-Semitic? A Critical Review of Rosemary Ruether's *Faith and Fratricide*," *Journal of the American Academy of Religion*, 45(2) (June 1977): 193–214.

70. Rubenstein, op. cit., 132–33.

71. Ruether, 1974, 124–25.

72. Ibid., ch. 5, *passim*.

73. Baum, op. cit., 12–13.

74. Ruether, 1974, 184–95.

75. See Raul Hilberg, *The Destruction of the European Jews* (Chicago, Ill.: Quadrangle Books, 1961), ch. 1.

76. See Cohn, *The Pursuit of the Millennium*, op. cit., 70.

77. Ruether, 1974, 205 and 209.

78. Ibid., 194–95.

79. Cohn, 1967, op. cit., 22–23.

80. Abram Leon Sachar, *A History of the Jews* (New York: Alfred A. Knopf, 1967), 198.

81. Ibid., ch. 15.

82. Ruether, 1974, 214–15.

83. Cohn, 1967, op. cit., 23. Ruether describes the Protocols as providing a clear link between Christian anti-Judaism and modern anti-Semitism, op. cit., 223.

84. Hilberg, *The Destruction of the European Jews*, 5–6, and ch. 4.

85. Ibid., 5. Decision of the 4th Lateran Council 1215, Canon 68, copied from the legislation by Caliph Omar 11 (643–644), who had decreed that Christians wear blue belts and Jews yellow belts.

86. Ruether, 1974, op. cit., referring to an incident cited in *Hitler's Table Talk*.

87. For a discussion of these issues, see D. J. Bosch, "The Roots and Fruits of Afrikaner Civil Religion," in J. W. Hofmeyr and W. S. Vorster (eds.), *New Faces of Africa* (Pretoria: University of South Africa, 1984), 14–35, and N. J. Smith, "Apartheid in South Africa as a Sin and Heresy: Some of Its Roots and Fruits," also in *New Faces of Africa*, 143–52.

88. Pat Sidley, *Press Report*, 22 Oct. 1986.

89. See "Myths and Their Secular Translation," in Alan T. Davies (ed.) *Anti-Semitism and the Foundations of Christianity* (New York: Paulist Press, 1979), 203.

See also Reuther's rejoinder "Old Problems and New Dimensions," in the same volume, 246–50.

90. Jehuda Bauer, *A History of the Holocaust* (New York: Franklin, 1982), 40–48.

91. Ruether, 1974, op. cit., 185–86, 205–6.

92. Ibid., 224–25.

93. Ibid., 215 and 220.

94. Lewis, 1986, op. cit., 252–53. See also his discussion of the same issue in *Islam in History* (London: Alcove Press, 1973), 139–40, and his comment (142) that "Anti-Semitism in its modern form is the response of the secularized Christian to the emancipated Jew—but with theological and psychological roots going back to the very origins of Christianity."

95. I am indebted for this qualification of the argument to Professor Sammy Smooha.

96. See Lucy Dawidowicz, *The War against the Jews, 1933–1945* (New York: Bantam Press, 1986), 123. See also the conclusions of Tal, op. cit., 1975, to somewhat similar effect.

97. See, for example, the different interpretations of the origins of anti-Semitism and its impact on the Holocaust in Helen Fein (ed.), *The Persisting Question: Sociological Perspectives and Social Contexts of Modern Anti-Semitism* (New York: Walter de Gruyter, 1987), and her analysis of social conditions variously affecting the participation of European countries in the Holocaust, *Accounting for Genocide* (New York: Free Press, 1979).

BIBLIOGRAPHY

Bauer, Yehuda (1982). *A History of the Holocaust*. New York: Franklin.

Bosch, D. J. (1984). "The Roots and Fruits of Afrikaner Civil Religion," in J. W. Hofmeyr and W. S. Vorster (eds.), *New Faces of Africa*. Pretoria: University of South Africa, 14–35.

Bryce, Lord (1916). *The Treatment of Armenians in the Ottoman Empire, 1915–1916* London: His Majesty's Stationery Office.

Cohn, Norman (1967). *Warrant for Genocide: The Myth of the Jewish World Conspiracy and the Protocols of the Elders of Zion*. London: Eyre & Spottiswoode.

—— (1970). *The Pursuit of the Millenium*. New York: Oxford University Press.

Curtis, Michael (ed.) (1981). *Religion and Politics in the Middle East*. Boulder, Colo.: Westview Press.

Davies, Alan T. (ed.) (1979). *Anti-Semitism and the Foundations of Christianity*. New York: Paulist Press.

Dawidowicz, Lucy (1986). *The War against the Jews, 1933–1945*. New York: Bantam Press.

Elazar, D. J., and J. Aviad (1981). "Religion and Politics in Israel," in Michael Curtis (ed.), *Religion and Politics in the Middle East*. Boulder, Colo.: Westview Press, 163–96.

Eriksen, Robert E. (1985). *Theologians under Hitler*. New Haven, Conn.: Yale University Press.

Fein, Helen (1979). *Accounting for Genocide*. New York: Free Press.

—— (ed.) (1987). *The Persisting Question: Sociological Perspectives and Social Contexts of Modern Anti-Semitism.* New York: Walter de Gruyter.

Friedman, R. I. (1986). "The Sayings of Rabbi Kahane," *New York Review of Books,* 13 February: 15–20.

Gutman, E. (1981). "Religion and Its Role in National Integration in Israel," in Michael Curtis (ed.), *Religion and Politics in the Middle East.* Boulder, Colo.: Westview Press, 197–206.

Hilberg, Raul (1961). *The Destruction of the European Jews.* Chicago: Quadrangle Books.

Hofmeyr, J. W., and W. S. Vorster, (eds.) (1984). *New Faces of Africa.* Pretoria: University of South Africa.

Idinopulos, Thomas, and R. B. Ward (1977). "Is Christology Inherently Anti-Semitic? A Critical Review of Rosemary Ruether's *Faith and Fratricide,*" *Journal of the American Academy of Religion,* 45(2): 193–214.

Kahane, Meir (1981). *They Must Go.* New York: Grosset & Dunlop.

Khaddurie, Majid (1955). *War and Peace in the Law of Islam.* Baltimore: Johns Hopkins University Press.

Lepsius, Johannes (1897). *Armenia and Europe.* Paris and London: Hodder & Stoughton.

—— (1919). *Le Rapport Secret sur les Massacres d'Armenia.* Paris: Payot.

Lewis, Bernard (1973). *Islam in History.* London: Alcove Press.

—— (1984). *The Jews of Islam.* Princeton, N.J.: Princeton University Press.

—— (1986). *Semites and Anti-Semites.* New York: Norton.

—— (1988). *The Political Language of Islam.* Chicago: University of Chicago Press.

Liebman, Charles J., and Eliezer Don-Yehiya (1983). *Civil Religion in Israel: Traditional Judaism and the Political Culture in the Jewish State.* Berkeley: University of California Press.

Lifton, Robert J. (1985). *The Nazi Doctors: Medical Killing and the Psychology of Genocide.* New York: Basic Books.

Merkl, Peter, and Ninian Smart (eds.) (1983). *Religion and Politics in the Modern World.* New York: New York University Press.

Peters, Rudolph (1979). *Islam and Colonialism: The Doctrine of Jihad in Modern History.* The Hague: Mouton Publishers.

Rahman, F., and Mircea Eliade (eds.) (1986). *The Encyclopedia of Religion.* New York: Macmillan.

Roth, Cecil (ed.) (1972). *Encyclopedia Judaica.* Jerusalem: Keter Publishing House, Ltd.

Rubenstein, Richard L. (1983). *The Age of Triage.* Boston, Mass.: Beacon Press.

Ruether, Rosemany Radford (1974). *Faith and Fratricide: The Theological Roots of Anti-Semitism.* New York: Seabury Press.

Ruether, Rosemary Radford, and Herman I. Ruether (1989). *The Wrath of Jonah: Crisis of Religious Nationalism in the Israeli-Palestinian Conflict.* New York: Harper & Row.

Runciman, Steven (1951). *A History of the Crusades.* London: Cambridge University Press.

Sachar, Abram Leon (1967). *A History of the Jews.* New York: Alfred A. Knopf.

Shamir, Asher, and Michal Shamir (eds.) (1986). *The Elections in Israel, 1984.* New Brunswick, N.J.: Transaction Press.

Sivan, Emmanuel (1968). *L'Islam et la Croisade.* Paris: Librarie d'Amerique et d'Orient.

Slotkin, Richard (1973). *Regeneration through Violence: The Mythology of the American Frontier.* Middletown, Conn.: Wesleyan University Press.

Smith, N. J. (1984). "Apartheid in South Africa as a Sin and Heresy: Some of Its Roots and Fruits," in J. W. Hofmeyr and W. S. Forster (eds.), *New Faces of Africa.* Pretoria: University of South Africa, 143–52.

Smooha, Sammy (1978). *Israel: Pluralism and Conflict.* Berkeley: University of California Press.

Sprinzak, Ehud (1981). "Gush Emunim, the Tip of the Iceberg," *Jerusalem Quarterly,* 21: 28–47.

Steiner, George (1971). *Bluebeard's Castle.* New Haven, Conn.: Yale University Press.

Stillman, Norman A. (1979). *The Jews of Arab Lands.* Philadelphia: Jewish Publication Society of America.

Tal, Uriel (1985). "Foundations of a Political Messianic Trend in Israel," *Jerusalem Quarterly,* 35: 36–45.

Toynbee, Arnold (1915). *Armenian Atrocities.* London: Hodder & Stough.

2

The Last Uncomfortable Religious Question? Monotheistic Exclusivism and Textual Superiority in Judaism, Christianity, and Islam as Sources of Hate and Genocide

Steven Leonard Jacobs

INTRODUCTION: A STUDENT'S TROUBLING PAPER

Among the courses I teach at the University of Alabama, Tuscaloosa, in my capacity as Associate Professor of Religious Studies and holder of the Aaron Aronov endowed Chair of Judaic Studies is "Religion 224: Introduction to the Judaic Experience." Therein we survey the historical experience of the Israelites/Jews from the Biblical period to the present moment, the dominant philosophical and theological motifs of Judaism, the festival and life-cycle calendars as they historically and contemporarily manifest(ed) themselves, and issues of contemporary Jewish concern (e.g., the Holocaust and anti-Semitism, and Israeli and American Jewish survival). In addition to attendance and class participation, the students' graded responsibilities include a paper reacting to any book of their own choosing that addresses the Judaic experience, a take-away final examination, and a brief (7–10 page) research paper, again on a topic of their own choosing addressing the Judaic experience. While, in the aggregate, the overwhelming majority of my undergraduate students are not Judaically knowledgeable or sophisticated, they continue to be fascinated by Jews and Judaism (primarily, I believe, because of the more "public face" of a conservative fundamentalist-oriented Christianity in the American South).

In the fall semester of 2003, one of my students turned in a research paper entitled "Judaism and Anti-Semitism: A Cycle of History." With his permission and agreement (but without identification), I quote from his work:

[T]he persecution of Jews has occurred more often than not as a result of Jewish action or change. . . . The faith of Judaism in itself, with its dogmatically
distinct views and beliefs, sparked religious persecution that spilled over into
a multitude of varying degrees and forms throughout history. . . . The key
dogmas of Judaism would lay the foundation for a chain reaction that would
birth a multitude of beliefs which wholly [sic] define anti-Semitism. . . . It
seems that, before and after the Holocaust, anti-Semitism is rooted in the same
illogical roots—the myths and fear spread by Christianity, and, unfortunately,
the beliefs of the Jews themselves. . . . Judaism has been the ultimate victim
throughout history as its own faith and practices seem to work against the
Jewish people. It is not exactly fair to say that the Jewish people created the
system of hate which has caused them turmoil for thousands of years; [but]
Judaism, with its unique practices and frequent inter-faith conflicts, has led to
the creation of many forms of persecution and prejudice that haunt its followers throughout time.

While it would, perhaps, be too easy to dismiss this writing as the work
of a naive undergraduate falling into the all-too-common contemporary
manifestation of "blaming the victim," or, worse, someone with an anti-
Jewish or anti-Semitic agenda, his reference to such solid sources as Joshua
Trachtenberg's classic (1983) work *The Devil and the Jews: Medieval Conceptions of Anti-Semitism*; Peter Schaffer's important (1997) text *Judeophobia:
Attitudes toward the Jews in the Ancient World*; and Marvin Perry and Frederick M. Schweitzer's recent (2002) book *Antisemitism: Myth and Hate from
Antiquity to the Present* bespeaks otherwise, therefore raising for me the
troubling question of whether there is something inherent in Judaism and
the historical experiences of the Jewish people that has thus engendered
this ongoing anti-Semitic thought and response of the larger communities
wherein Jews have lived and continue to live.[1]

For example, the ancient minority Hebraic understanding of monotheism must have incurred the wrath of the dominant religio-political power
structures and the plurality of their deities. The very creation of the Hebrew
and later Judaic distinctiveness of a seemingly uncompromising dietary
system, thus setting Israel apart from its neighbors in this most intimate
of social interactions, must equally have evoked a distaste for this same
minority. The biblical concepts of both "chosenness" and "election," refer-
enced throughout the Hebrew Torah, if and when shared with others, must
have evoked a similar disdain, and while it must be noted that there is no
biological or racial component to this understanding (which is nevertheless
consistent with a sociological understanding of how groups behave, valu-
ing insiders while devaluing outsiders), it could not have fostered positive
intergroup interactions. Added to this is Israel's own understanding of the
land of its birth not only as holy but as granted to them by their God who
has named them the *only* true and legitimate residential overlords—even

when exiled from it—which must also have strained Israelite/Hebrew/Jewish interactions not only with neighbors but with other host communities as well; it remains, even today, at the root of Middle Eastern tensions. Whether such drives for distinctiveness and difference are, arguably, the sole or primary reasons for anti-Semitism, these differences, coupled with the psychological malady or affliction of xenophobia (i.e., fear of the different, unknown, and that person or group who is not me/us) have played a part over the centuries.

Finally, groups in power, be they political, military, economic, and/or religious seemingly require scapegoating of others, who usually are in the minority, to explain away current and/or future problems and failures; thus the powerful retain whatever power they possess and feel threatened about the possibility of its surrender. This latter explanation goes a long, long way toward understanding the journey of the Jews over the last 2,000 years. Uncomfortably, then, the question remains whether or not Jews themselves by their very distinctiveness and difference have contributed to the enmity the world bore and continues to bear toward them both before and since the Holocaust and the ever-present tensions in the Middle East.

Because I am trained in reading, analyzing, and interpreting classical Jewish texts (Torah, Midrash, Talmud, etc.) and work in the cross-disciplinary and interdisciplinary field of religious studies with a specialization in Holocaust and genocide studies and post-*Shoah* biblical reinterpretation (Hebrew Bible and New Testament), I wonder whether this question of distinctiveness and difference, with the accompanying perceptions of in-group superiority and out-group inferiority, is equally applicable, however modified, to both Christianity and Islam as monotheistic religious traditions, both of which exist in tension rather than harmony with Judaism. Additionally, is monotheism itself a troubling, foundational underpinning to the seeming inability of these three traditions and their adherents to live in even quasi-harmony with one another? Monotheism itself seemingly remains part of the difficulty rather than part of the solution, as it continues to be read and understood textually by its expositors and adherents and translated into behavioral practices to the ongoing detriment of all three religious traditions.

MONOTHEISTIC EXCLUSIVISM IN JUDAISM, CHRISTIANITY, AND ISLAM: REPRESENTATIVE PASSAGES

While continually disharmonious and divisive amongst and between themselves, the one thing that unites the religious traditions of Judaism, Christianity, and Islam is their *public* expression of and commitment to the One God, announced either as Adonai (by Jews hesitant to speak the Ineffable

Name of the Tetragrammaton), Father/Son (Christ)/Holy Ghost or Spirit, and Allah. We know this from the sacred or holy texts each tradition regards as central to its identity, also understood as the very revelation of that same Deity not only to its own community but to all humanity: the Torah or Hebrew Bible of the Jews, the Old and New Testaments of the Christians, and the Qur'an of the Muslims. While each community has raised serious questions regarding the full authenticity of the others' texts, each affirming the *Oneness* of its God, while at the very same time dismissing (or worse) any other understanding of what I choose to call the "divine-human encounter," and therefore by extension dismissing (or worse) *any* group presenting an alternative view.

Judaism

The Torah's rejection of other gods, or, better, the "gods of others," for the people of Israel, occupies a prominent position in the two places where the misnamed and misunderstood *Aseret Ha-Dibrot* (the so-called euphemistically named "Ten Commandments") occur: Exodus 20:3 and Deuteronomy 5:7 "You shall have no other gods in My Presence!" Earlier, in the "Song of Moses" or "Song at the Sea" in Exodus 15:11, the very superiority of the God of Israel to all other gods is affirmed: "Who is like You, O Lord, among the gods?" The late renowned Israeli biblical scholar Yehezkel Kaufmann (1889–1964) reminds us here that the movement in the thought of Ancient Israel, reflected in the texts themselves, was from monolatry (i.e., the acceptance of the reality of other nations' gods but the superiority of Israel's own) to that of monotheism (i.e., the understanding that the One God of Israel is, in fact, the only existent god). (Kaumann, 1960)

Thus, we find the idea of the One God affirmed in Psalms 50:1 ("The Mighty One, God the Lord, speaks and summons the earth from the rising of the sun to its setting"), and that God's unique and special relationship with Zion/Israel in verses 2 ("Out of Zion, the perfection of beauty, God shines forth") and 4 ("His people"), 5 ("My faithful ones, who made a covenant with Me"),[2] and 7 ("My people"). According to the prophet Malachi, that same One God is, indeed, God over all, according to 2:10: "Have we not *all* One Father? Has not One God created us?"

That the God of Israel is ultimately the only god, is also reflected in the text. For example, Psalm 86:10 affirms this same God of Israel as the Only True Divine Reality ("For You are Great and do wondrous things, You Alone are God"), though two verses prior a seeming recognition of other divine realities is expressed ("There is none like You, among the gods, O Lord, nor are there *any* works like Yours"). Might we not see in this apparent contradiction a not-so-subtle lip service to the false understanding of others?

According to the prophet Jeremiah, 18:15, for example, when the people of Israel deviate from their covenantal responsibilities and obligations, they do so in response to a delusion ("But My people have forgotten Me, they burnt offerings to a delusion")—in defiance of the Only True God who exists, 10:10: "But the Lord is the True God, He is the Living God and the Everlasting Ruler. At His wrath the earth quakes, and the nations cannot endure His indignation."

Thus, summarily, these few representative examples, and there are many, many others, paint a portrait of the God of Israel—the God of the Jews—who is the Only Existent God, Alone and True, the One who will *not* tolerate *any* semblance of *other* divine realities, be they *false* or *delusionary*, on the part of His selected and elected and chosen covenantal community. How Jews (and others) have responded to this understanding will be addressed below.[3]

Christianity

The controversies surrounding the moment (2004) of Mel Gibson's movie epic *The Passion of the Christ* notwithstanding, the "translation" of the "Word" of the Parent God into the human person of the Son God, Jesus the Christ, *textually* displaces the Parent and makes the Son the central bridge and connection back to the Parent, and, in so doing, equally displaces the original covenantal relationship of the Jews with their God from its initially perceived first position into a demeaned second position, and, for some, a now-abrogated if not nullified nonexistent position as well (e.g., John 14:6: "I am the Way, the Truth, and the Life. *No one goes to the Father except through Me.*" John 10:9: "I am the Gate. Whoever enters *by Me* will be saved.")

This same Gospel account affirms the Onlyness of God (5:44: "How can you believe when you accept glory from one another and do not seek glory that comes from the One who Alone is God?"), as does I Timothy 1:17 ("To the King of the Ages, Immortal, Invisible, the Only God. . . .") and Jude 1:25 ("to the Only God our Savior *through* Jesus Christ our Lord, be glory, majesty, *power*, and *authority*, before all time and now and forever").

Only this God *though* this Christ, then, possesses the *power* to grant eternality: John 17:3. ("And this is eternal life that they may know You, the Only True God, and Jesus Christ whom You sent"), and Romans 16:27 (". . . the Only Wise God, *through* Jesus Christ.")

This same God, according to I Thessalonians 1:9, is a "Living and True God," equally and importantly affirmed in I John 5:20–21: "And we know that the Son of God has come and has given us understanding so that we may know Him who is True; and we are in Him who is True, in His Son Jesus Christ. He is the True God and Eternal Life."

As is the case with the Hebrew Bible, there are many, many texts through-out which could be cited in support of this understanding of the Onlyness of this Parent God and the path to "salvation" and eternality *through* His Only Son Jesus the Christ. The uses to which these texts have been put—how they have been read, understood, interpreted, and used—will also be discussed below.

Islam

Whatever else the tragedy of September 11, 2001, and this country's questionably labeled ongoing "war on terrorism," has done, particularly in Iraq, it has focused our ignorance on the third great monotheistic religious tradition, Islam, its history and its texts. More courses are presently being taught, more experts and nonexperts are benefiting from the various media spotlights, and a plethora of publications, creditable and suspect, are being issued and/or republished on a regular basis. My focus here, however, is on the texts of the Qur'an rather than, at the outset, on socio-political or religio-theological realities. (Parenthetically, I would urge, however, a seri-ous study not only of relevant and related history and politics, but of the Qur'an as well. An excellent place to start would be 'Abdullah Yûsuf 'Ali's (1991) *The Meaning of The Holy Qur'an: New Edition with Revised Translation and Commentary* or Michael Sell's (1999) *Approaching the Qur'an: The Early Revelations.*)

Like its predecessors the Hebrew Bible/Torah and New Testament, the Qur'an, too, equally affirms both the Onlyness and the Oneness of the God/Allah in its various *suras*. 3:62 (The Family of Imran): "Most surely this is the *true* explanation, and there is *no god but Allah;* and most surely Allah—He is the Mighty, the Wise." 37:35 (The Rangers): "Surely they used to behave proudly when it was said to them: There is *no god but Allah.*" 38:65 (Suad): "Say: I am only a warrior, and there is *no god but Allah,* the One, the Subduer (of all)." 47:19 (Muhammad): "So know that there is *no god but Allah,* and ask protection for your fault and the believing men and the believing women; and Allah knows the place of your returning and your abiding."

God's Oneness is explicitly stated in 2:133 and 2:163 (The Cow): ". . . One God Only, and to Him do we submit"; and "And your God is One God! There is *no god* but He; He is the Beneficent, the Merciful." 4:171 (The Women): "Allah is the Only One God; far be it from His glory that He should have a son, whatsoever is in the heavens and whatever is in the earth is His, and Allah is Sufficient for a Protector." 5:73 (The Dinner Table): "Certainly they disbelieve who say: Surely Allah is the third person of the three; but there is *no god* but the One God, and if they desist not from what they say, a painful chastisement shall befall those among them who disbelieve." 16:51 (The Bee): "And Allah has said: Take not two gods. He is [the] Only One God; so of Me Alone should you be afraid."

So, too, other relevant *suras* could be cited. Also central and fundamental to our understanding are two of the "Five Pillars of Islam": Faith and Prayer (the other three being *Zakat* or charity, fasting during Ramadan, and *Hajj* or Pilgrimage to Makkah).[4] The *Shahada* or "Declaration of Faith" of the pious Muslim is the simple formula "There is *no god* worthy of worship except God [Allah], and Muhammad is His messenger." The *Salat* or "Call to Prayer" (dawn, noon, mid-afternoon, sunset, and nightfall) offered by the *muezzin* is:

> God is most great. God is most great.
> God is most great. God is most great.
> I testify that there is no god except God.
> I testify that there is no god except God.
> I testify that Muhammad is the messenger of God.
> I testify that Muhammad is the messenger of God.
> Come to prayer!
> Come to prayer!
> Come to success (in this life and the Hereafter)!
> Come to success!
> God is most great!
> God is most great!
> There is no god except God.[5]

THE UNFORTUNATE AND TRAGIC USES OF SACRED TEXTS

Depending on whose ox is doing the goring—an allusion to Exodus 21:28–32—*the* fundamental question, at least initially, is *not* that of the religio-theological and socio-political (and militarily violent) uses to which a text is put secondarily, but, rather, how one, either individual or group, reads or understands or analyzes a text, and then and only then, the behaviors or actions that flow from those readings and affirmations.

Judaism, Christianity, and Islam are all what I call *literate religious traditions*, regardless of whether their own communities are themselves everywhere and at all times themselves literate. By this I both mean and understand that each attributes to its sacred texts *power superior* to that which might be ascribed to other writings even by adherents and leaders of their respective traditions. And because these sacred texts, both oral and written, at least initially, are perceived and affirmed as coming directly from God/Allah—what all three regard as the act of "revelation" (the Divine *revealing* [making known] Himself to His specially related human communities)—their initial reception, however these texts are presented to us (original language *or* translation), are accepted *literally*, that is, the texts are read, comprehended, analyzed, *and accepted* based upon a supposedly accurate reception of the words themselves and their grammatical constructions. That is to understand, a text says what it says and means what it means and *not* what we would wish it to say or mean. And, coupled with the turn from oral to written transmission (scribal, printing, computer-generated), and our psychological too-easy acceptance of that which is written down and presented to us (i.e., the all-too-common "fallacy of the printed word"—that which is written is obviously *true*, for were it not true it would *not* be written), sacred texts, perhaps more than any other literary genre, leave other texts far, far in the distance.[6]

Thus, Judaism, Christianity, and Islam continue to do harm to themselves and to others stemming from their *literal* views of their understandings of God based upon their relationships to their sacred texts. *Some* Jews have taken a hard-line and, at times, violent position with regard to settlements throughout the Land of Israel and against those who would oppose them and settle in the same spaces or present alternative understandings, out of their literalist readings of the Hebrew Bible. *Some* Western Christians have, at times, violently evolved a theology of *triumphalist supercessionism* with regard to Jews over the last 2,000 years, tragically successful because of the collusion of Christianity with the various governmental structures that have made their appearances throughout Europe and elsewhere, out of their literalist readings of the Old and New Testaments. Some Muslims have justified violence against non-Muslims—suicide bombers in Israel, September 11th attacks in the United States—based upon a literalist understanding of jihadism external to the personal struggles within oneself to become worthy of Allah, out of their literalist readings of the Qur'an. Thus, the very sacred texts of all three monotheistic religious traditions continue to be used to justify hateful and pregenocidal acts and behaviors based upon those readings and consequent understandings.[7] Indeed, one could cite many other examples within each of these three monotheistic religious traditions.

WHAT, THEN, IS TO BE DONE?

At this moment on the world scene, the voices of the literalists appear to be shouting the loudest, to the disadvantage of us all. In addition, calls for calmness, civil and reasoned discourse, tolerance and respect for diverse and divergent points of view and perspectives result in hateful and violent, if not pregenocidal, acts across and within these three religious communities. Israel and world Jewry have yet to come to grips with the religious significance of the tragedies of Orthodox Jew Baruch Goldstein's murder of Muslims at prayer at the mosque in Hebron, and of the assassination of Prime Minister Yitzhak Rabin by Orthodox Jew Yigal Amir. While the Roman Catholic Church has made significant and important strides and admissions in its relationship with Jews, and the Lutheran Church also has begun the always-painful task of self-examination, too many, both officially and otherwise within the various Protestant Christianities, have yet to truly begin the task of discerning whether both historical and contemporary teachings continue a pattern of denigrating the other who is not like themselves. Within the different strains of Islam, the urgent need to re-examine both teachings *and texts* as to whether those who do violence can and do derive their justifications for their behaviors from their readings/ comprehensions/analyses appears to be too-slowly forthcoming. Indeed, Jonathan Kirsch writes in his (2004) book *God against the Gods: The History of the War between Monotheism and Polytheism:*

> When Arab suicide bombers carried out "martyr operations" in Haifa, Tel Aviv and Jerusalem, and when a Jewish physician opened fire on Muslims at prayer at the Tomb of the Patriarchs, each one was acting out a kind of zealotry that was inspired by a tragic misreading and misapplication of ancient texts.[8]

When, then, is to be done? Specifically, for all three great monotheistic religious communities, is there another way (other than literally) to read, comprehend, and analyze these sacred and holy texts of each tradition and still accord them the power and authority historically ascribed to them, as well as to acknowledge their primary position as the interconnection between the human and the Divine? At the very same time, can such a different reading espoused by others within these communities empower those who wish to both remain within and reach out beyond, religio-theologically as well as socio-politically, to begin the arduous journey toward curbing the hate and the violence? Intellectually, I do believe that can be the case, drawing upon the long-honored though too-often ignored Judaic reading tradition of what I now call "The Midrashic Way," that is, a 2,000-year-old nonliteral interpretive commentary tradition and conversation of and by the rabbis with the Hebrew Scriptures and now encompassing both New Testament and Qur'an.[9] The idea is not initially mine, but rather that of Orthodox Jewish feminist and author Blu Greenberg, though her specific frames of reference were the *Shoah* or Holocaust and only the Gospels.

In her (1989) article "The Holocaust and the Gospel Truth: Christian Confrontations with the Holocaust," published in the journal *Holocaust and Genocide Studies*, Greenberg wrote:

> In as much as I believe, like many others, that the *Shoah* is not a freak event vis-a-vis Christian Gospels but, rather, the expressed culmination of a suppressed

rage against the Jews *embedded within its words,* I shall proceed to take the liberties that ecumenism vests in us.

The conclusion I draw from the Holocaust and from the four decades following it, is that Christianity needs a Talmud and a Midrash that deal with the foundation documents of its faith; that Christians of the next two thousand years ought not to be able to read or teach or understand first century Christianity without these hermeneutical texts of quasi-canonical status. . . .

Why do I use terms such as Talmud and Midrash, so particular to the Jewish tradition? In order to precisely convey *the notions of power, authority, and sacredness,* as Talmud and Midrash have done for Jews for so many centuries unto this very day. Or, to present this in a more ironic fashion—it is not too late, eighteen hundred years later, for Christianity to do what Judaism of the other Jews did in the first century: to become a religion of the "two Torahs."[10]

Ms. Greenberg's radically innovative idea for the Christianities, and my expansion of it to include the Islams as well, to rethink the various manifestations of Judaism given the passages cited and others as well, has not yet been given the attention it now needs in our increasingly violent world. Nor have the calls for more "midrashic readings" of the Hebrew biblical text been heard or affirmed in Israel by her non-Orthodox political leadership, or here in the United States (or elsewhere) by those who are among Israel's most vocal supporters and willing defenders. I would also add that, for this process to succeed—and here I am indebted to German Catholic thinker Johannes Baptist Metz and the late French Jewish philosopher Emanuel Levinas—the time has now come for all three great religious traditions to begin to read their own sacred scriptures *in the presence of the other.* That is to say, given not only the horrors of the twentieth century—aptly named the "Century of Genocide"—but past centuries as well, true textual dialogue, or, in this case, "trialogue," requires, at the outset, that these texts be read, interpreted, and understood in the presence of others for whom *they* are not wholly sacred but who are knowledgeable in their ability to read and understand them as well as their historic and contemporary commentaries. Each community separately and all three communities collectively, out of their own enlightened self-interest, would benefit from the midrashic, non-literalist readings of others and the filtering down of those readings as well into their larger constituencies. Using the midrashic way as the model, let Jews begin to appreciate the problematics of their own texts as seen through the eyes of Christians and Muslims. Let Christians reexamine their own texts and the pains they have caused by listening and truly hearing them given voice by Jews and Muslims. Let Muslims as well benefit from Jews and Christians, conversant with both the Qur'an and the Hadith, and how these outsiders react to and reflect upon such equally problematic texts. Such models do yet exist other than randomly here and there, like scattershot hopefully hitting a target but, more often than not, missing the same.

How fitting, then, in conclusion, to paraphrase the words of the second century Talmudic sage Rabbi Tarphon in the Jewish ethical tractate known as *Pirkei Avot*/Sayings of the Fathers:

> The day is short and the task is great and the workers are sluggish, and the reward is much, and the Master of the house is urgent. It is not incumbent upon you to finish the task, but neither are you free to desist from it. (2:19)

NOTES

1. His full bibliography consists of Marvin Perry and Frederick M. Schweitzer, *Antisemitism: Myth and Hate from Antiquity to the Present* (New York: Palgrave-Macmillan, 2002); Peter Schaffer, *Judeophobia: Attitudes towards the Jews in the Ancient World* (Cambridge, Mass.: Harvard University Press, 1997); Michel Selzer, *Kike!* (New York: Strait Arrow Books, 1972); Joshua Trachtenberg, *The Devil and the Jews: Medieval Conceptions of Anti-Semitism* (New Haven, Conn.: Yale University Press, 1983); John Weiss, *The Politics of Hate* (Chicago: Ivan R. Dee, 2001); and Robert S. Wistrich, *Antisemitism* (London: Methuen, 1991).

2. A most serious and important study of this question is to be found in David Novak, *The Election of Israel: The Idea of the Chosen People* (Cambridge/New York: Cambridge University Press, 1995).

3. It is important to note at the outset that no parity whatsoever is implied regarding the various uses and abuses of these texts by the Jewish, Christian, and/or Muslim communities and those who chose to read and understand them literally and act upon their understandings.

4. Significant Jewish parallels here are *Tzedakah* or "righteous fiscal and other obligations"; fasting, primarily on Yom Kippur or the Day of Atonement; and the three *Sh'losh Regalim* or "Pilgrimage Festivals" of *Pesach* (Passover), *Shavuot* (Weeks), and *Sukkot* (Booths). The *Shahada* may be said to parallel Deuteronomy 6:4: "Listen, Israel: Adonai is our God, Adonai alone"; and the notion of obligatory prayer is incumbent upon religiously devout Jews three times a day (morning, afternoon, and evening, the latter two usually combined).

5. www.islamcity.com/mosque/pillars.shtml.

6. A fascinating discussion of this whole question of literality is found in Vincent Crapanzano, *Serving the Word: Literalism in America: From the Pulpit to the Bench* (New York: New Press, 2000).

7. For an assessment of the genocidal potential possible as a result of such readings, see Leo Kuper (1990), "Theological Warrants for Genocide: Judaism, Islam and Christianity," *Terrorism and Political Violence*, 2(3): 351–79; and Leonard B. Glick (1994), "Religion and Genocide," in Israel W. Charny (ed.), *The Widening Circle of Genocide/Genocide: A Critical Bibliographic Review—Volume 3* (New Brunswick, N.J.: Transaction Publishers), 43–74.

8. Jonathan Kirsch, *God against the Gods: The History of the War between Monotheism and Polytheism* (New York: Penguin Group, 2004), 283.

9. The brevity of this essay does not permit a further fleshing out of this idea, complete with "midrashic readings" of Hebrew Bible, New Testament, and Qur'an, but only its introduction in this context. Two interesting examples of this midrashic approach are Henry F. Knight, *Confessing Christ in a Post-Holocaust World: A Midrashic Exploration* (Westport, Conn.: Greenwood Press, 2000); and James F. Moore, *Christian Theology after the Shoah* (Lanham, Md.: University Press of America, 1993).

10. Blu Greenberg (1989), "The Holocaust and the Gospel Truth: Christian Confrontations with the Holocaust," *Holocaust and Genocide Studies*, 4(3): 281–82. Emphases not in original.

BIBLIOGRAPHY

Anzulovic, Branimir (1999). *Heavenly Serbia: From Myth to Genocide.* New York: New York University Press.

Bartov, Omer and Phyllis Mack (eds.) (2001). *In God's Name: Genocide and Religion in the Twentieth Century.* New York: Berghan Books.

Charny, Israel W. (2002). "A Passion for Life and Rage at the Wasting of Life," in Samuel Totten and Steven Leonard Jacobs (eds.), *Pioneers of Genocide Studies.* New Brunswick, N.J.: Transaction Publishers, 429–78.

Glick, Leonard (1994). "Religion and Genocide," in Israel W. Charny (ed.). *The Widening Circle of Genocide. Genocide: A Critical Bibliographic Review. Vol. 3.* New Brunswick, N.J.: Transaction Publishers, 43–74.

Huntington, Samuel P. (1996). *The Class of Civilizations and the Remaking of World Order.* New York: Simon & Schuster.

Huttenbach, Henry (2004). "Religion and Genocide: The Unexplored Nexus." *The Aegis Review on Genocide*, 1(3): 22–23.

Jacobs, Steven Leonard (2003/2004). "Religion and Genocide: The Last Uncomfortable 'Religious' Question? Monotheistic Exclusivism and Textual Superiority in Judaism, Christianity, and Islam, as Sources of Hate and Genocide." *Journal of Hate Studies*, 3(1): 133–43.

Kaufmann, Yehezkel (1960). *The Religion of Israel: From Its Beginnings to the Babylonian Exile.* Chicago: University of Chicago Press.

Rittner, Carol, John K. Roth, and Wendy Whitworth (eds.) (2004). *Genocide in Rwanda: Complicity of the Churches?* St. Paul, Minn.: Paragon House.

Sells, Michael A. (1996). *The Bridge Betrayed: Religion and Genocide in Bosnia.* Berkeley: University of California Press.

Tinker, George E. (1993). *Missionary Conquest: The Gospel and Native American Cultural Genocide.* Minneapolis, Minn.: Fortress Press.

Totten, Samuel and Steven Leonard Jacobs (eds.) (2002). *Pioneers of Genocide Studies.* New Brunswick, N.J.: Transaction Publishers.

3

A Sweet-Smelling Sacrifice: Genocide, the Bible, and the Indigenous Peoples of the United States, Selected Examples

Chris Mato Nunpa

One of the rationales used to kill the indigenous peoples of the United States was the Biblical justification. Bible verses were quoted many times by Euro-Americans, either before, during, or after a genocidal incident, atrocity, or massacre of native peoples. Specific scriptures related to specific historical events are highlighted in this essay. These include: Columbus and his men and their killing of native peoples, circa 1500; an incident involving Wingina and Ralph Lane in the 1580s; the Pequot Holocaust of 1637; and an example of the use of "Manifest Destiny," which was derived from the "Chosen People and Promised Land" notion of the Old Testament or Hebrew Bible.

Various translations of the Bible, in addition to the use of the King James version, are quoted in this essay. These translations include a Catholic version and the Torah. Also, commentaries on these verses from various selected theologians are utilized. What these verses meant, according to the commentaries and to our common sense, are related to how these verses were used by the perpetrators of genocide.

I. "IN HONOR OF CHRIST OUR SAVIOUR AND THE TWELVE APOSTLES": THE COMING OF COLUMBUS

When Columbus stumbled on these shores, this began what Linda Tuhiwai Smith calls "a huge legacy of suffering and destruction" for the indigenous peoples of the Americas, a 500-year legacy (Smith, 1999, 20).

David Stannard in his book, *American Holocaust*, details the gore, horror, and terror that Columbus inflicted upon the native peoples. When Columbus made the statement that "we shall make war against you in all ways and manners," he was deadly serious (Stannard, 1992: 66). The "ways and manners" included: the slaughtering and massacring of millions of natives; mutilating native peoples by cutting off their hands if they did not bring in their three-month's tribute of gold; using ferocious armored dogs that had been trained to kill and disembowel native peoples when they fled; and just the general stealing, killing, raping, terrorizing, and the torturing of indigenous peoples. Stannard says that, in a twenty-one-year period of time, from 1492 to 1513, nearly *eight million* native people, primarily noncombatants, "had been killed by violence, disease, and despair" (Stannard, 1992: x). In this same statement informing the indigenous peoples of the truth of Christianity and the necessity to swear immediate allegiance to the Pope and to the Spanish Crown, the "requerimiento," Columbus, also, said, ". . . we can, and shall subject you to the yoke and obedience of the Church and of Their Highnesses" (Stannard, 1992: 66). We see no separation of church and state here.

In the course of Columbus' making of war, what the Spanish called "pacification" to describe their campaign of terror, against the native peoples of the Caribbean, Bartoleme de Las Casas, a Catholic missionary, witnessed an event in which the:

> Spaniards found pleasure in inventing all kinds of odd cruelties, the more cruel the better, with which to spill human blood. They built a long gibbet, low enough for the toes to touch the ground and prevent strangling, and hanged thirteen (natives) at a time in honor of Christ our Saviour and the twelve Apostles. (de Las Casas, 1971: 94; Stannard, 1992: 72)

de Las Casas mentioned that the Spaniards hanged, tortured, and mutilated the natives "in honor of Christ our Saviour." There are a number of Biblical references to Christ as "Saviour" in the New Testament. One is found in Luke 2:11, a familiar passage because it is usually read at Christmas time, "for unto you is born this day in the city of David a Saviour, Which is Christ the Lord." John 4:42 says, "And said unto the woman, now we believe, not because of thy saying: for we have heard him ourselves, and know that this is indeed the Christ, the Saviour of the world."

Every Christmas season, the Protestant and Catholic branches of Christianity read Luke 2:11. The various translations show clearly that Jesus Christ is the "Saviour," i.e., the Savior of the world, he who "makes safe, delivers, preserves, to make alive," according to Adam Clarke (*Bethany Parallel Commentary*, 1983: 358). Apparently, in the thinking of Columbus's men, to hang thirteen native people at one time, to kill thirteen indigenous human beings, is to honor their Savior, the one who saves, preserves, and delivers.

As to the idea and action of "honoring" "Christ our Saviour," there are a number of New Testament references which refer to "honoring" Christ. One is found in John 5:23, "That all men should *honour* (my emphasis) the Son, even as they honour the Father. . . ." A second reference to honoring Christ is in I Timothy 1:17 which says, "Now unto the King eternal, immortal, invisible, the only wise God be *honour* (my emphasis) and glory for ever and ever. Amen." Another is found in Revelation 5:13, "And every creature which is in heaven, and on the earth, and under the earth, and such as are in the sea, and all that are in them heard saying, Blessing, and *honour* (my emphasis), and glory, and power, be unto him that sitteth upon the throne, and unto the Lamb for ever and ever."

According to Biblical teachings, Jesus Christ is "the Son of God" (Matthew 17:5, the Transfiguration), the King of Kings (I Timothy 6:15), and "the Lamb of God which taketh away the sin of the world" (John 1:29, 1:36).

There are a number of questions that the reader can legitimately ask: "Are these men who killed other human beings, the native peoples, really Christians?" Is de Las Casas, the Roman Catholic missionary, who provided us this account of hanging thirteen native people at one time a Christian? Did de Las Casas mention at any time, "Hey guys, one of the ten commandments is 'Thou shalt not murder'?" (Exodus 20:13). If there were any "true" Christians there among Columbus and his men, why did they not speak up? Did Columbus and his men think of indigenous peoples as human beings? Or did they think of them as subhumans, or as animals, wild beasts, and, therefore, worthy to be killed, to be slaughtered? In fact, de Las Casas wrote, at another time, ". . . they pitilessly slaughtered everyone like sheep in a corral. It was a general rule among Spaniards to be cruel; not just cruel, but extraordinarily cruel so that harsh and bitter treatment would prevent Indians from daring to think of themselves as human beings or having a minute to think at all . . ." (de Las Casas, 1971: 94).

Did Columbus and his men really use the Bible teachings in a legitimate manner, i.e., hanging thirteen native people at one time? Or, were they, indeed, being true Christians by doing exactly what they did, killing indigenous peoples?

It is worth making several comments regarding de Las Casas. de Las Casas is often lauded by Euro-American scholars as a defender of indigenous peoples. However, I would like to quote two indigenous academics, who reflect and provide a different perspective on de Las Casas. One, "de Las Casas wrote tomes criticizing the atrocities committed by his countrymen against Indian people in the Caribbean, Mexico, and the rest of Latin America. . . . Yet, he was the author of the infamous 'reduction' system which dislocated Indian people from their families and from their culture and inculturated them into European values and social systems" (Tinker,

1993: viii). Secondly, "Though de Las Casas argued for the humanity of indigenous peoples and defended them against physical extermination, like Bishop Whipple, he still believed they needed 'saving.' Thus, while not an advocate of physical extermination, he was an advocate of cultural extermination, guilty of participation in a massive campaign of ethnocide, which many intellectuals consider to be a form of genocide. Indigenous peoples would be no better off under de Las Casas' religious imperialism than under campaigns of physical extermination. . . ." (Wilson, 2003).

II. "CHRIST OUR VICTORY": RALPH LANE AND WINGINA

This incident occurred in the 1580s in North Carolina. The native player is Wingina. The English player is Ralph Lane. Lane discovers that Wingina planned to drive the English out by force with the help of native allies from the south who were hired as mercenaries. Lane, a military man with experience from the Irish campaign, learned of Wingina's plans. Lane mounted a night assault on Wingina's village, but was discovered by the sentries. Both sides now knew the other was plotting each other's destruction. Ralph Lane, good English Protestant that he was, told Wingina he would like to meet with him and his major advisors to discuss peace. When Wingina and his unarmed men came to meet in the open field, they were unaware of Lane's ambush. Lane had instructed his musketeers to shoot down Wingina when he whispers their battle cry. As Wingina approached, Lane whispered the battle cry, the musketeers fired, and Wingina was hit but ran into the woods. One of Lane's men chased him into the trees and returned with Wingina's head. As Dr. Robert Venables said of Lane and this incident, "who would have thought that an Irish prisoner of war, being used as a servant by those who had slaughtered his countrymen just a few years before, would attempt to prove his loyalty by bringing Wingina's head to his captors. We know these details because Lane wrote it down in his diary" (Venables, 1992: 4). What was the battle cry that was uttered to assassinate Wingina? Ralph Lane's battle cry, used to betray the peace negotiations was "Christ Our Victory!" As Dr. Venables further says, "English Christianity, like Spanish Christianity, is off to the same horrible start" (Venables, 1992: 4).

The Biblical reference used by Ralph Lane to kill Wingina and the other native peoples is found in I Corinthians 15:57. This scripture reads, "But thanks be to God, which giveth us the victory through our Lord Jesus Christ" (KJV). The New American Bible, a Catholic version, says, "But thanks be to God who has given us the victory though our Lord Jesus Christ" (NAB). There is no significant difference between the two versions. One version (the KJV) uses "giveth" and the other (NAB) use "has given," a modern usage.

What is the victory that Jesus Christ has given? According to Matthew Henry, the victory is over "the power of death" (*Bethany Parallel Commentary*, 1983: 1046). Jamieson, Fausset, and Brown say the victory is over "death and Hades ('the grave')" as well as over "the law and sin" (*Bethany Parallel Commentary*, 1983: 1046). Adam Clarke writes, "He ('our Lord Jesus Christ') has given us the victory over sin, Satan, death, the grave, and hell" (*Bethany Parallel Commentary*, 1983: 1046).

Ralph Lane, by his use of the phrase "Christ Our Victory," added Wingina and his men, and native people generally, to the above-mentioned list of sin, Satan, death, the grave, and hell over which Jesus Christ has given the victory. Apparently, Jesus Christ had given him, Ralph Lane, justification to kill Wingina and his men, and to cut off Wingina's head.

Again, the question can be asked, "Was Ralph Lane a Christian?" Is this a good Bible verse to justify lying to and killing native peoples? Did Ralph Lane pervert the use of the Bible? Or, did Ralph Lane consider himself part of the "Chosen People" of God and, therefore, had an imperative to exterminate the godless Canaanites, in this case, the indigenous peoples, viz., Wingina and his people? Was Ralph Lane a good Christian, merely fulfilling the word and will of God?

III. "A SWEET-SMELLING SACRIFICE": THE PEQUOT HOLOCAUST OF 1637

Another historical incident from the early seventeenth century vividly illustrates the extensive use of the Bible to justify genocide of the indigenous peoples. In 1637, the English made a stealthy night attack on a stockaded Pequot town near the Mystic River in Connecticut, burned the town, and slaughtered its approximately 600 inhabitants. This event was a literal "holocaust," according to the *Merriam Webster's Collegiate Dictionary* (Tenth Edition): "1. a sacrifice consumed by fire, 2. a thorough destruction involving extensive loss of life, esp. through fire . . . a mass slaughter of people; esp. genocide." John Mason, a man who believed in massacring noncombatants, was the commander of the Connecticut troops. Stannard writes that John Mason had engaged in many assaults upon the native peoples, and "more often than not Indian women and children were consumed along with everyone and everything else in the conflagrations that routinely accompanied the colonists' assaults" (Stannard, 1992: x). At the conclusion of one especially bloody combat, John Mason declared, "the Lord was pleased to smite our Enemies in the hinder Parts, and to give us their Land for an inheritance" (Psalm 78:66). As the reader can plainly see, John Mason was comparing himself and his people to the "Chosen People" of the Old Testament, the Israelites, or Jews. In addition, Mason was comparing the land of the Pequots to the "Promised Land" of the Old Testament, and that the same God of the Old Testament was giving this "Promised Land" as "an Inheritance" to Mason and his people. In Mason's mind, God, right way, and truth were on his side. To dispossess, to remove, and to kill the Pequots and the other indigenous peoples would merely be fulfilling God's will and command.

An incidental comment—the term "conflagrations" means "fire, a large disastrous fire" (*MWC Dictionary*). These burnings, or fires, "routinely accompanied," according to Stannard, the attacks of the English, of the western Europeans, and/or of the Euro-Americans upon the indigenous peoples in the four centuries, from 1500 to 1900. Therefore, the term "holocaust" is not inappropriate to apply to the genocide of the indigenous peoples of the United States—the Indigenous Holocaust!

Continuing with the description of the night attack on the Pequots, some Narragansetts, who long had been at odds with the Pequots, accompanied Mason's troops. However, the Narragansetts found out that Mason was planning nothing less than a wholesale massacre; they dissented and withdrew to the rear. Mason, at the head of one party, and John Underhill, leading the other party, under cover of darkness attacked the unsuspecting Pequots from two directions at once. The British swarmed into the native village, slashing and shooting at anything that moved. Caught off guard, and apparently few warriors in the village at the time, some of the Pequots fled, "others crept under their beds," while still other fought back "most courageously," but this only drove Mason and his men to greater heights of fury. "We must burn them" (Stannard, 1992: 113). Mason later recalled himself shouting, whereupon he set fire to the mats and wigwams, and then wrote a description of the scene of the conflagration,

> And indeed such a dreadful Terror did the Almighty let fall upon their spirits, that they would fly from us and run into the very Flames, where many of them perished. . . . (And) God was above them, who laughed at his Enemies and the Enemies of his People to Scorn, making them as a fiery Oven: Thus were the Stout hearted spoiled, having slept their last Sleep, and none of their Men could find their Hands: Thus did the Lord judge among the Heathen, filling the Place with dead Bodies! (Stannard, 1992: 113–14)

Again, note the references to the Chosen People of the Old Testament and how God was on John Mason's side against the godless Canaanites, viz., the Pequots, the "enemies" of John Mason and "his people," God's people. Since God was on their side, then they, the Christian English, had God's approval of their burning to death the Pequot people. In perpetrating this genocidal massacre, the killers were merely fulfilling God's will, just as the Israelites, the Chosen People, were obeying the Old Testament God's commands to exterminate the Canaanites, Hittites, etc.

Of the many references to the Bible used in this genocidal incident, there is one, in particular, to which I would like to direct the attention of the reader. This is found in a writing of William Bradford, the governor of Plymouth Colony. Bradford describes the British/Euro-American reaction to this holocaust:

> It was a fearful sight to see them thus frying in the fire and the streams of blood quenching the same, and horrible was the stink and scent thereof; but the victory seemed a sweet sacrifice, and they gave the praise thereof to God, who had wrought so wonderfully for them thus to enclose their enemies in their hands and give them so speedy a victory over so proud and insulting an enemy. (Underhill, 1638: 39–40)

Willam Bradford's phrase "but the victory seemed a sweet sacrifice," in referring to the burning and "frying in the fire" of the flesh of the Pequot people, can be derived from a number of Old Testament verses in which rams or lambs were offered up to the Old Testament God for the sins of the people. One is found in Leviticus 8:21, ". . . and Moses burnt the whole ram upon the altar: it was a burnt sacrifice for a sweet savour, and an offering made by fire unto the Lord, as the Lord commanded Moses."

In the Catholic version, Leviticus 8:21 reads thusly, "then having washed the inner organs and the shanks with water, he also burned these remaining parts of the ram on the altar as a *holocaust* (emphasis mine), a sweet-smelling oblation to the LORD, as the LORD had commanded him to do" (NAB, 1970: 107). The same verse in the Torah reads this way, "the entrails and the legs having been washed with water. Moses turned all of the ram into smoke on the altar: that was a burnt offering for a pleasing odor, an offering by fire to the LORD—as the LORD had commanded Moses" (*The Torah*, 1962 and 1967: 192).

Another verse that refers to "a sweet sacrifice" is found in Exodus 29:18, "And thou shalt burn the whole ram upon the altar: it is a burnt offering unto the Lord: it is a sweet savour, and offering made by fire unto the Lord" (KJV). In the Catholic version, this reads, "The entire ram shall then be burned on the altar, since it is a *holocaust* (emphasis mine), a sweet-smelling oblation to the LORD." From the Torah, this same verse reads, "Turn all of the ram into smoke upon the altar. It is a burnt offering to the LORD, a pleasing odor, an offering by fire to the LORD."

A third Old Testament reference, among more than three dozen such references, is Numbers 15:3, "And will make any offering by fire unto the LORD, a burn offering, or a sacrifice in performing a vow, . . . , to make a sweet savour unto the LORD, of the herd or of the flock" (KJV). The Catholic version reads, "if you make to the LORD a sweet-smelling oblation from the herd, or from the flock, in *holocaust* (emphasis mine), in fulfillment of a vow. . . ." The same verse from the Torah reads, "and would present an offering by fire to the LORD from the herd or from the flock be it burnt offering or sacrifice, . . . producing an odor pleasing to the LORD."

The following are various comments from different theologians in regard to the above-mentioned three verses:

Leviticus 8:21—"By this they gave to God the glory of this great honour which was not put upon them, and returned him praise for it, as Paul thanked Christ Jesus for putting him into the ministry, I Timothy 1:12" (*Bethany Parallel Commentary*, 1983: 236).

"a token of their entire dedication to the service of God" (*Bethany Parallel Commentary*, 1983: 236).

Exodus 29:18—"There must be a burnt-offering, a ram wholly burnt, to the honour of God, in token of the dedication of themselves wholly to God and to his service, as living sacrifices, kindled with the fire and ascending in the flame of holy love" (*Bethany Parallel Commentary*, 1983: 204).

Matthew Henry's phrase "in the flame of holy love" is in stark contrast to the actions of these Christian zealots as they burned alive the Pequot town and its people. Could one really characterize the holocaust of the Pequot people as "a flame of holy love"?

"the ram was to be wholly burnt, in token of the priest's dedication of himself to God and His service" (*Bethany Parallel Commentary*, 1983: 204).

Protestants were taught that they, as Christians, were "a holy priesthood." Every Christian was a priest, according to I Peter 2:5, which reads, "Ye also, as lively stones, are built up a spiritual house, an holy priesthood, to offer up spiritual sacrifices, acceptable to God by Jesus Christ." Apparently, the Christian Englishmen, William Bradford, John Mason, et al. were merely exercising their godly function as priests to "offer up spiritual sacrifices," viz., the Pequots, "acceptable to God by Jesus Christ."

The idea of "praising God" in Bradford's words "and they gave the praise thereof to God" is found in numerous verses both in the Old Testament and in the New Testament. One is found in II Chronicles 20:22, "And when they began to sing and to praise, the Lord set ambushments against the children of Ammon, Moab, and Mount Seir, which were come against Judah, and they were smitten." Here, the Israelites are praising God for his help and deliverance from their enemies. Another verse is taken from the New Testament in I Peter 2:9, "But ye are a chosen generation, a royal priesthood, a holy nation, a peculiar people; that ye should shew forth the praises of him who hath called you out of darkness into his marvelous light."

The Christian English knew the Bible well and would have been familiar with these verses. These verses are illuminating for they give the reader insight into the Christian English mentality. By applying to themselves terms such as "chosen," "royal," "a holy nation," or people, the Christian English elevated themselves to a superior position of morality and spirituality in contrast to that of the Pequots and to all other indigenous peoples, who, then, were uncivilized, barbaric, savage, and "in darkness."

Brandon writes of the wholesale massacres by the Christian English of noncombatants that could scarcely be credited if not for the fact that it is the Puritans themselves who recorded them, often with relish. For example, the shrieks of several hundred victims, mostly women and children, dying then in the burning of a large Narragansett community in the winter of 1675, another *holocaust* (emphasis mine), "greatly moved some of our soldiers. They were much in doubt and afterward inquired whether burning their enemies alive could be consistent with humanity and the benevolent principles of the gospel" (Brandon, 1974: 207). It could be said that this twinge of conscience by the Christian English would be of little consolation to the Narragansett dead. All in all, the Pequot Holocaust of 1637 was, from the point of view of the colonizers, the perpetrators of genocide, in addition, to the Lord helping His people, an act of worship to God by the Christian English. The sacrifice by fire of the Pequots was a "sweet smelling sacrifice," a "sweet-smelling savour," unto the Lord.

IV. "CHOSEN PEOPLE" AND "PROMISED LAND": MANIFEST DESTINY

Manifest Destiny was the racist philosophy which fueled the expansion of the United States by invasion and expropriation (or stealing) of indigenous lands during the 1800s. Under this philosophy, the Euro-Americans believed that "through divine ordination and the natural superiority of the white race, they had a right (and indeed an obligation) to seize and occupy all of North America" (Morris, 1992: 67). After the War of 1812, the U.S. had consolidated its power considerably, to the extent that many indigenous nations were now vulnerable to military invasion by U.S. forces, "pre-emptive strikes," if you will. The Indian Removal Act (an official policy of "ethnic cleansing") had been passed in 1830 by the U.S. Congress, and was most enthusiastically implemented by presidents Andrew Jackson and James Buchanan. Thus, the removal, extermination, expropriation, and exploitation of native peoples and their lands began in earnest. This led to what white historians refer to as "the winning of the West" or "westward expansion" in the second half of the 1800s, and to what indigenous peoples refer to as the losing of the West.

The phrase, "Manifest Destiny," was first used by John L. O'Sullivan, a lawyer, a journalist, and ardent Jacksonian Democrat. O'Sullivan believed that the United States had an almost sacred obligation to spread over all of North America. These words, "manifest destiny," appeared in an article, "Annexation," in the *Democratic Review* in July 1845. O'Sullivan wrote that those who were opposing the annexation of Texas into the United States were "limiting our greatness and checking the fulfillment of our manifest

destiny to overspread the continent allotted by Providence for the free development of our yearly multiplying millions" (O'Sullivan, 1845). O'Sullivan
capitalized the term "Providence," and so this would be "God conceived as
the power sustaining and guiding human destiny" (*MWC Dictionary*, 1993:
940), in particular the destiny of Euro-Americans in North America.

Senator Thomas Hart Benton wrote in 1846, one year after O'Sullivan
coined the term, "It would seem that the White race alone received the
divine command, to subdue and replenish the earth, for it is the only race
that has obeyed it—the only race that hunts out new and distant lands, and
even a New World, to subdue and replenish" (Johansen, 1995: 10). Senator Benton used the term "manifest destiny" to refer to the notion that the
United States was ordained to expand westward. The native peoples were to
be eradicated or drastically changed to make way for civilization. Benton's
reference to "subdue the earth and replenish" is found in Genesis 1:28,
"And God blessed them and God said unto them be fruitful, and multiply
and replenish the earth, and subdue it . . . " (KJV).

In the writer's home state of Minnesota, Charles Bryant, a Euro-American
historian of the Dakota-U.S. War of 1862, also, used the phrase, "subdue
the earth." Bryant smugly and arrogantly writes that the conflict of Indian
and white was "a conflict of knowledge with ignorance, of right with
wrong," since the Indian (i.e., the Dakota people of Minnesota) did not
obey "the divine injunction to subdue the earth," he was "in the wrongful
possession of a continent required by the superior right of the white man"
(Meyer, 1993: 116). Generally, since the native peoples, including the Dakota people, did not farm (use of planting sticks) in the same way as the
western European did (use of metal plows), then the native peoples were
not "subduing the earth."

From where did this phase "manifest destiny" come? It came from
the "chosen people/promised land" notion of the Old Testament. There
are many verses from which this idea is derived. Concerning the "chosen
people" notion, one verse is found in Deuteronomy 7:6, "For thou art an
holy people unto the Lord thy God: the Lord thy God hath chosen thee to
be a special people unto himself, above all people that are upon the face
of the earth." Another reference is found in the same book, Deuteronomy
14:2, "For thou art an holy people unto the Lord thy God, and the Lord
hath chosen thee to be a peculiar people unto himself, above all the nations
that are upon the earth."

The Catholic version of Deuteronomy 7:6 reads, "For you are a people
sacred to the LORD your God; he has chosen you from all the nations on
the face of the earth to be a people peculiarly his own." The Torah, regarding the same verse, reads, "For you are a people consecrated to the LORD
your God: of all the people on earth, the LORD your God chose you to be
His treasured people."

One commentator says, "The choice which God had made of this people for his own" (*Bethany Parallel Commentary*, 1983: 345). Other commentators say that the Israelites were "set apart to the service of God, or chosen to execute the important purposes of His providence" (*Bethany Parallel Commentary*, 1983: 345). Another commentator writes that the Israelites "therefore should have no connection with the workers of iniquity" (*Bethany Parallel Commentary*, 1983: 345).

The Catholic version of Deuteronomy 14:2 reads, "For you are a people sacred to the LORD, your God, who has chosen you from all the nations on the face of the earth to be a people peculiarly his own." The Torah states, "For you are a people consecrated to the LORD, your God: the LORD your God chose you from among all other peoples on earth to be His treasured people."

One commentator refers to the Israelites as "the people of God" (*Bethany Parallel Commentary*, 1985: 353). Another says, "Ye are the children of the Lord. The very highest character that can be conferred on any created beings" (*Bethany Parallel Commentary*, 1983: 353). Matthew Henry writes, "a holy people, separated and set apart for God, devoted to his service, . . ." (*Bethany Parallel Commentary*, 1983: 353).

It would appear that the Old Testament God has chosen the Israelites to be a superior people, above all the peoples of the earth. Ironically, this thinking is similar to Hitler, who thought the Aryan race was the superior race, above all the races of the earth. It is doubly ironic that the "superior race" of the Old Testament should encounter, several millennia later, another "superior race" in Nazi Germany in the 1940s, and that the perpetrator of genocide is now the victim of genocide.

The "promised land" idea, also, is found in a number of Old Testament books. For example, one such reference is in Genesis 12:6–7, "And Abram passed through the land unto the place of Sichem, unto the plain of Moreh. And the Canaanite was then in the land. And the Lord appeared unto Abram and said, Unto thy seed will I give this land." Another is found in Genesis 13:12 and 13:15, "Abram dwelled in the land of Canaan. . . . For all the land which thou seest, to thee will I give it, and to they seed for ever." A third reference is found in Leviticus 20:24. "But I have said unto you, Ye shall inherit their land, and I will give it unto you to possess it, a land that floweth with milk and honey: I am the Lord your God, which have separated you from other people." One more reference, which is found in Numbers 14:8, "If the Lord delight in us, then he will bring us into this land, and give it us: a land which floweth with milk and honey."

The *St. Joseph Edition of the New American Bible* (a Catholic version) renders the above-mentioned verses this way, Genesis 12:6–7, "Abram passed through the land as far as the sacred place at Shechem, by the terebinth (a great tree) of Moreh. (The Canaanites were then in the land.) The Lord

appeared to Abram and said, 'To your descendants I will give this land.'"
Genesis 13:12 and 13:15, reads, "Abram stayed in the land of Canaan, . . . ,
"all the land that you see I will give to you and your descendants forever."
Leviticus 20:24 says, "But to you I have said: Their land shall be your possession, a land flowing with milk and honey. I am giving it to you as your
own, I, the LORD, your God, who have set you apart from the other nations." Numbers 14:8 reads, "If the LORD is pleased with us, he will bring
us in and give that land, a land flowing with milk and honey."

The Torah quotes Genesis 12:6–7 in this way, "Abram passed through
the land (Canaan) as far as the site of Shechem, at the terebinth of Moreth.
The Canaanites were then in the land. The LORD appeared to Abram and
said, 'I will give this land to your offspring.'" Genesis 13:12 and 13:15 reads
as follows, "Abram remained in the land of Canaan, . . . , for I give all the
land that you see to you and your offspring forever." Leviticus 20:24 in the
Torah reads, ". . . You shall possess their land, for I will give it to you to
possess, a land flowing with milk and honey. I the LORD am your God who
has set you apart from other peoples." Finally, Numbers 14:8 reads, from
the Torah, "If the LORD is pleased with us, He will bring us into the land,
a land that flows with milk and honey, and give it to us."

One other dimension I would like to mention is the extermination concept, which called for the extermination by the Israelites of the "godless"
Canaanites and Hittites, and was so commanded by the Old Testament God.
One such verse is found in Deuteronomy 20:16–17, ". . . , thou shalt save
alive nothing that breatheth: But thou shalt utterly destroy them: namely,
the Hittites, and the Amorites, the Canaanites and the Perizzites, the Hivites, and the Jebusites: as the LORD thy God hath commanded thee" (KJV).
Another is found in the same book, Deuteronomy 7:2 and 7:16, "And when
the LORD thy God shall deliver them before thee: thou shalt smite them,
and utterly destroy them; thou shalt make no covenant with them, nor shew
mercy unto them: . . . And thou shalt consume all the people which the
LORD thy God shall deliver thee; thine eye shall have no pity upon them;
. . . " (KJV). One more commandment by the Old Testament. God to engage
in a genocidal extermination is found in I Samuel 15:3, "Now go and smite
Amalek, and utterly destroy all that they have, and spare them not; but slay
both man and woman, infant and suckling, ox and sheep, camel and ass"
(KJV). These and other such verses in the Old Testament make quite clear
that the Old Testament God is advocating genocide to be perpetrated upon
the Canaanites and other peoples by the Israelites, the Old Testament God's
"chosen people." Furthermore, since they are commanded to kill all the
Canaanites, they need not feel guilt or remorse about the killing since they
would merely be obeying God and fulfilling his commandment.

Euro-Americans took these verses and applied them to themselves and
to the indigenous peoples and their lands. The Euro-Americans saw them-

selves as God's chosen people. They saw the indigenous peoples of the Americas as the Canaanites and Hittites who needed to be exterminated or driven out of the "promised land," which consisted of the lands of the Pequot in Connecticut, of the Narrangansetts of northeastern United States, of the Tsalagi of North Carolina and Georgia; and of the lands of the Dakota in Minnesota, etc. This "promised land," or the lands of the indigenous peoples of the United States, God had given to the symbolic Israelites, the Christian English and the other Euro-Americans, at least, in their thinking. It did not make any difference to the Euro-Americans that the native peoples had been living in these lands for thousands upon thousands of years. It did not make any difference that the Creator had given these lands to the indigenous peoples, according to their origin stories. The indigenous peoples had no rights that a white man needed to respect! Thus, if God's chosen people kill the "Indians"/Canaanites, who resist the Euro-Americans invading their lands, they, the Euro-Americans/"Israelites" are merely fulfilling God's purpose and following God's will. This type of thinking, or mind-set, of course, provided the basis for the concept which received a name in the nineteenth century and is now known in Euro-American/colonial academia as Manifest Destiny. Note this mind-set at the highest levels of U.S. government, in the United States Congress:

> Congress must apprise the Indian that he can no longer stand as a breakwater against the constant tide of civilization. . . . An idle and thriftless race of savages cannot be permitted to stand guard at the treasure vaults of the nation which hold our gold and silver . . . the prospector and miner may enter and by enriching himself enrich the nation and bless the world by the result of his toil. (Congressional Record, 1846)

Note the "arrogance" of the colonizers, of the invaders, and of the "chosen people," as they refer to the land and natural resources of the indigenous peoples as "our gold and silver."

The concept and trail of Manifest Destiny continued to leave in its wake the genocidal destruction of indigenous peoples, beginning with the arrival of Columbus, into the nineteenth century. In fact, by the mid-nineteenth century, U.S. policy-makers and military commanders were stating—openly, frequently, and in plain English—that their objective was no less than the "complete extermination" of any native people "who resisted being dispossessed of their lands, subordinated to federal authority, and assimilated into the colonizing culture" (Stiffarm, 1992: 34). The country was as good as its word on the matter (in contrast to its word on treaties with indigenous peoples), perpetrating literally hundreds of massacres or cruel removals of native peoples by military and paramilitary formations at points all over the United States, in particular the western United States. A bare sampling of some of the worst must include the "Trail of Tears" in the 1838 removal of the Tsalagi. Half of the people died, 8,000 out of approximately 17,000 (Thornton, 1987: 117–18), on the death march from North Carolina to Oklahoma, which march "was almost as destructive as the Bataan Death March of 1942, the most notorious Japanese atrocity in the II World War" (Stannard, 1992: 123); the 1854 massacre of perhaps 150 Lakota at Blue River (Nebraska); the 1863 Bear River (Idaho) Massacre of some 500 Western Shoshones; the Sand Creek Massacre of 1864, in Colorado, in which approximately 500 Cheyenne, mostly women, children, infants, and old men, were massacred and butchered by the Rev. Colonel John M. Chivington, a Methodist minister, and his troops; the 1868 massacre of another 300 Cheyenne at the Washita River (Oklahoma); the 1857 massacre of about 75 Cheyenne along the Sappa Creek (Kansas), the 1871 massacre of still another 100 Cheyenne at Camp Robinson (Nebraska); and the 1890 massacre of more than 300 Lakota at Wounded Knee, South Dakota, by the U.S. Seventh Cavalry, which event is characterized by Russell Thornton as "perhaps the best-known genocide of North American Indians" (Thornton, 1987: 107).

In the writer's home state of Minnesota, the Dakota people experienced the most traumatic and tragic event in their history, the Dakota-U.S. War of 1862. Charles Bryant, mentioned above, wrote that the Dakota did not obey the divine injunction to "subdue the earth." Therefore, it would be God's will to either "exterminate or remove" (Meyer, 1993: 139) the Dakota so that "the chosen people" (i.e., Euro-Americans) could "possess" the rich and beautiful land that was and is now the state of Minnesota. In this period of time, the Dakota, in addition to warfare, experienced bounties, $25, then $75, and, finally, $200 (Meyer, 1993: 139). They experienced two concentration camps, one at Mankato, and the other at Ft. Snelling near the present-day twin cities of Minneapolis and St. Paul (Meyer, 1993: 135). The Dakota experienced the largest mass execution in the history of the United States when thirty-eight Dakota men were hanged at Mankato, Minnesota, on December 26, 1862. That year, Minnesota out-Texased Texas in death penalty executions. They experienced a forced march on November 7–13, 1862, when 1,700 Dakota people, primarily women and children, were force-marched 150 miles from the Lower Sioux community, in southwestern Minnesota, to the concentration camp at Ft. Snelling. My mother, Elsie Two Bear Cavender, an oral historian, referred to this forced march as "a death march." Then, the Dakota people either fled or were removed by boat from their traditional homelands in Minnesota. Minnesota and the U.S. government conducted their own "ethnic cleansing."

Stannard makes a comment which applies to the preceding massacres and to the genocide over the centuries as the "chosen people" possessed and occupied the land of milk and honey, the lands of the Canaanites, viz.

the lands of the indigenous peoples of the United States. The comment is, "massacres of this sort were so numerous and routine that recounting them eventually becomes numbing, and, of course, far more carnage of this sort occurred than ever was recorded. So, no matter how numbed—or even, shamefully, bored—we might become at hearing story after story of the mass murder, pillage, rape, and torture of American's native peoples, we can be assured that, however much we hear, we have heard only a small fragment of what there was to tell" (Stannard, 1992: 126).

At the turn of the twentieth century, only 237,000+ native peoples were alive in the United States, according to the U.S. Bureau of Census (Stiffarm, 1992: 37). This would be a depopulation or extermination rate of 98.4 percent if we estimate the figure of 16,000,000 for the native population within the continental United States at the time of contact (1492) (Stiffarm, 1992: 27). Stannard writes, "The worst human holocaust the world had ever witnessed, roaring across two continents non-stop for four centuries and consuming the lives of countless tens of millions of people, finally had leveled off. There was, at last, almost no one left to kill" (Stannard, 1992: 146).

CONCLUSION

In conclusion, I am reminded of what Elie Wiesel said regarding the perpetrators of the Jewish genocidal experience:

> All the killers were Christian. . . . The Nazi system was the consequence of a movement of ideas and followed a strict logic; it did not arise in a void but had its roots deep in a tradition that prophesied it, prepared for it, and brought it to maturity. That tradition was inseparable from the past Christian civilized Europe. (Abrahamson, 1985, 33)

In regard to the perpetrators of the genocide of the indigenous peoples of the United States, I, too, say, "All the killers were Christian." The use of Bible verses to justify killing indigenous peoples would certainly indicate, at most, that the perpetrators of genocide against the native peoples considered themselves Christian, and that, at the least, the killers were favorably inclined to Christianity, as opposed to other religions. This writer is inclined, also, to agree with Stannard when he says that Wiesel's observation "is an equally apt beginning for those who would seek to understand the motivations that ignited and fanned the flames of the mass destruction of the native peoples" (Stannard, 1992: 153) of the Americas, generally, and of the United States, specifically. I am beginning to understand why Vine Deloria, Jr., a prominent Dakota educator, lawyer, and philosopher, says, "the track record of individual Christians and Christian nations is not so spectacular as to warrant anyone seriously considering becoming a Christian. From pope to pauper, Protestant to Catholic, Constantinople to the United States, the record is filled with atrocities, misunderstandings, persecutions, *genocides* (emphasis mine), and oppressions so numerous as to bring fear into the hearts and minds of non-Christian peoples" (Deloria, 1992: 189).

The Biblical injunctions of the Jewish and Christian traditions were an integral part of what Wiesel calls "a movement of ideas" and of Deloria's "track record" of Christianity. The "chosen people" and "promised land" notions of the Old Testament were used by the western Europeans and by the Euro-Americans to justify the destruction of indigenous peoples and the dispossession and expropriation of native lands and resources. These scriptural verses were a significant contributor to the perpetration of genocide of the indigenous peoples of the United States.

BIBLIOGRAPHY

Abrahamson, Irving (ed.) (1985). *Against Silence: The Voice and Vision and Elie Wiesel.* New York: Holocaust Library.

Bethany Parallel Commentary on the New Testament: from the Condensed Editions of Matthew Henry, Jamieson/Fausset/Brown, and Adam Clarke: Three Classic Commentaries in One Volume (1983). Minneapolis, Minn.: Bethany House.

Brandon, William (1974). *The Last Americans: The Indian in American Culture.* New York: McGraw-Hill.

Casas, Bartolome de las (1971). *History of the Indies.* New York: Harper & Row.

Congressional Record, 2642 (1846). 46th Congress, 2nd Session. Washington, D.C.: U.S. Government Printing Office.

Deloria, Jr., Vine (1992). *God Is Red: A Native View of Religion.* Golden, Colo.: North American Press.

Grinde, Donald A., and Bruce E. Johansen (1995). *Ecocide of Native America: Environmental Destruction of Indian Land and Peoples.* Santa Fe, N.M.: Clear Light.

Johansen, Bruce E. (1995). *Ecocide of Native America: Environmental Destruction of Indian Lands and Peoples.* Santa Fe: Clear Light Books.

Merriam-Webster Collegiate Dictionary (1993). Springfield, Mass.: Merriam-Webster.

Meyer, Roy W. (1993). *History of the Santee Sioux: United States Public Policy on Trial.* Lincoln: University of Nebraska Press.

Morris, Glenn T. (1992). "International Law and Politics," in M. Annette Jaimes (ed.), *The State of Native America: Genocide, Colonization, and Resistance.* Boston, Mass.: South End Press, 55–86.

New American Bible (1990). New York: Oxford Publishing Company.

O'Sullivan, John (1845). *Democratic Review.* [Cited in Richard N. Freidel (1960), *A History of the United States to 1876.* New York: Alfred A. Knopf; and Howard Zinn (1980), *A People's History of the United States.* New York: HarperCollins.]

Smith, Linda Tuhiwai (1999). *Decolonizing Methodologies: Research and Indigenous People.* London: Zed Books.

St. Joseph Edition of the New American Bible. Translated from the original languages, with critical use of all the ancient sources by members of the Catholic Biblical Association of America (1970). New York: Catholic Book Publishing Co.

Stannard, David E. (1992). *American Holocaust: Columbus and the New World.* New York: Oxford University Press.

Stiffarm, Lenore A., with Phil Lane Jr. (1992). "The Demography of Native North America: A Question of American Indian Survival," in M. Annette Jaimes (ed.), *The State of Native America: Genocide, Colonization, and Resistance.* Boston, Mass.: South End Press, 23–53.

Thornton, Russell (1987). *American Indian Holocaust and Survival: A Population History since 1492.* Norman: University of Oklahoma Press.

Tinker, George E. (1993). *Missionary Conquest: The Gospel and Native American Cultural Genocide.* Minneapolis, Minn.: Fortress Press.

The Torah: The Five Books of Moses (1962). Philadelphia, Pa.: Jewish Publication Society of America.

Underhill, John (1638). *Newes from America.* [Cited in Richard Drinnon (1980), *Facing Westward: The Metaphysics of Indian-Hating and Empire-Building,* New York: New American Library; and David E. Stannard (1992), *American Holocaust: Columbus and the Quest for the New World.* New York: Oxford University Press.]

Venables, Robert (1992). "Lecture #7" [as taught in] Rural Sociology 100. Ithaca, N.Y.: Cornell University.

Wilson, Angela Cavendar (2003). Private e-mail communication.

4

The Accountability of Religion in Genocide

James Fraser Moore

INTRODUCTION

The genocide in Rwanda began just four days after Easter. Was this merely coincidental or in some way planned? This essay will use the case study of Rwanda to explore the relationship between religion and genocide, particularly the way that religious events can become a means for reinforcing political ideologies and motivating people to either stand to the side and watch or become involved in mass killing. My thesis is that the specific liturgical theology of the Christian, even more specifically the Roman Catholic, worship for Easter can be easily manipulated to support the genocidal mind, suggesting that important empirical research that needs to be done to investigate whether this was the case in Rwanda. In fact, the use of religious myth and practice to stir up people to support genocide might be a far more common occurrence than we might presume, and the Rwanda case may show us how this happens.

This study is a part of a larger work of exploring how the texts of Christian worship—hymns, prayers, scripture, and liturgy—continue to promote feelings and images of violence despite our efforts to alter the teaching of the churches toward a theology of respect.[1] A brief examination of two hymns that are commonly part of Protestant Christian hymnals and are often chosen to be sung on Good Friday and Easter can show some of what my ongoing study is trying to expose. The sequence of Good Friday and Easter (which I will explore more fully below) links the symbol of the crucifixion (the death of Jesus by hanging on a cross) and the belief in the resurrection of Jesus from the dead. Even more, we can see in these hymns the various images and the basic theology that is central to the Good Friday and Easter observances.

First, we can look at a hymn for Good Friday, "Ah, Holy Jesus":

    I. Ah, holy Jesus, how hast thou offended, That man to judge thee hath in hate pretended? By foes derided, by thine own rejected, O most afflicted.

    II. Who was the guilty? Who brought this upon thee? Alas, my treason, Jesus hath undone thee. 'Twas I, Lord Jesus, I it was denied thee: I crucified thee.

    III. Lo, the good Shepherd for the sheep is offered; The slave hath sinned, and the Son hath suffered; For man's atonement, while he nothing heedeth, God intercedeth.

    IV. For me, kind Jesus, was thine Incarnation, Thy mortal sorrow, and thy life's oblation; Thy death of anguish and thy bitter passion, For my salvation.

    V. Therefore, kind Jesus, since I cannot repay thee, I do adore thee, and will ever pray thee, Think on thy pity and thy love unswerving, Not my deserving. Amen

Hymns such as this one might have as much impact as any of the texts of worship. The images of the verses of the hymn show the range of hate, guilt, violence, deserved death, innocence, anguish, and pain. The Christian is led to see him/herself as guilty and deserving only pity while gaining salvation through being a slave to the Lord in ongoing adoration. The latter image is clearly one of hierarchical power and obedient service. The link between the images of violence and guilt with the position of obedient service produces a clear potential for manipulation of the masses into action they perceive to be in the interests of God.

A second hymn from the Easter setting is "Christ the Lord Is Risen Today":

    I. Christ the Lord is risen today; Allelulia! Christians, haste your vows to pay, Allelulia! Offer ye your praises meet, Allelulia! At the Paschal Victim's feet; Allelulia!

    II. For the sheep the Lamb hath bled; Allelulia! Sinless in the sinner's stead; Allelulia! Christ is risen, today we cry; Allelulia! Now he lives no more to die; Allelulia!

    III. Christ, the victim undefiled; Allelulia! God and man hath reconciled; Allelulia! Whilst in strange and awful strife; Allelulia! Met together death and life, Allelulia!

    IV. Christians, on this happy day, Allelulia! Haste with joy your vows to pay, Allelulia! Christ is risen, today we cry, Allelulia! Now he lives no more to die, Allelulia!

    V. Christ who once for sinners bled, Allelulia! Now the first born from the dead, Allelulia! Throned in endless might and power, Allelulia! Lives and reigns for evermore, Allelulia!

   VI. Hail, Eternal Hope on High! Allelulia! Hail, thou King of Victory! Allelulia! Hail, thou Prince of Life adored! Allelulia! Help and save us, gracious Lord! Allelulia!

The hymn seems to be a hymn of praise and hope, but it easy to see that all of this is mixed with reminders of the violent scene of Good Friday. The hopeful images are mixed with sorrow about the death of Jesus and are clearly connected to our guilt and lack of any merit. Hope can be found only in a strict following of the triumphant Lord who, again, as a king is enthroned with all power and might. Such a text can also be used to motivate people to leave worship with a sense of obligation to act for causes that are justified as godly. The link between Good Friday and Easter creates a narrative structure that heightens the emotions of the followers to a fever pitch and creates the opportunity to translate those emotions not only as hope and praise but also as spontaneous violence against those who could be labeled as responsible or guilty.

The two hymns I have selected are among many possible choices for Good Friday and Easter worship. They are Protestant hymns, though they are also found in Catholic hymnals. The point is that an examination of these texts can reveal an important component in a genocidal context, specifically that they provide a foundation for the strong emotions of hatred and obedience that are required for mass participation in genocide. While the hymns found in American churches (especially those sung in English and/or translation) may not be used in this exact form in churches in Central Africa, the selections shown here do represent the typical themes of any hymns that might be used during this part of the church year, which would likely promote the same themes, paint similar images, and reinforce the same emotions even if in ways more in keeping with a different culture.

The case of Rwanda is interesting because Good Friday and Easter in 1994 occurred on April 2 and 4, just days before the beginning of the genocide. On Good Friday and Easter, the nearly 95 percent of the Rwanda population that is Christian would have been worshipping in the churches of Rwanda.[3] Almost two-thirds of the population practices Roman Catholicism, first introduced to the area by the White Fathers missionary group and made even more a permanent factor by the ruling Belgian authority, which received a League of Nations mandate over the whole territory of Central Africa after World War I.[4] There are also a number of Protestant groups in Rwanda, notably the Seventh-Day Adventists, whose leadership was involved in one of the most troubling massacres of the genocidal period in 1994.[5] Still, the dominance of the Roman Catholic Church in

Rwanda means that we can be assured that the biblical texts read in the churches for Good Friday and Easter that year would have followed the common lectionary accepted worldwide by the Catholic Church. Thus, we can learn something about what Christians who were involved in worship at that time would have heard prior to the beginning of the killing. Of course, this, too, requires research, and we would gain much by knowing more details about how these services were constructed and what topics were the foci of sermons.

IDEOLOGY AND MYTH

The myth of Ham, taken from the Genesis account and developed in many different ways by different Christians over the centuries, does not directly identify either the Tutsis or the Hutus. Still, the details of the story of Ham are applied to the Rwandan context by the Belgians in order to construct a narrative useful for separating various people, thus making it easier to govern.[6] We can assume that the narrative also shaped the way that Christians attending services thought about their neighbors and gave the Rwandan case a particular twist. First, the regular patterns of Christian worship and teaching activity had become a dominant feature of many areas of Central Africa by the late twentieth century. Of course, the high level of violence found during the Rwandan genocide has been repeated in some ways in neighboring territories, but there is also evidence that we cannot make a direct connection between religious activity and violence. Many places do not produce such violence even with similar patterns of Christian activity. In addition, the two groups, Tutsis and Hutus, apparently did manage a tense but reasonably peaceful coexistence for many decades after Christianity was introduced and became a dominant force in colonial Africa. Other factors appear to be necessary to gain a full sense of the causes of the genocidal violence. My point is that we need to look closer at the religious climate as one contributing factor despite taking seriously these cautionary facts.

The issue derives, in part, from the story of Ham as it was shaped into a Hamitic ideology does not seem to be part of the pre-Christian Rwandan past (Deforges, 1999; Gourevitch, 1998). Christians, particularly Christian missionaries, introduced the ideas of this view of the world. Of course, the Belgian missionaries saw the myth most clearly as a justification of white superiority over and against black Africa. This arrogant approach to the Rwandan people is surely obvious to us now, but the clear military and technological superiority of the Belgians led the Rwandans to accept some elements of this belief. And the hierarchical nature of the racial theory brought in by Europeans does lend itself to further application to whatever power structures already existed among the people as well.

However, there is a difference between social class structures based on power and racial theory based on presumed racial superiority, and then upon mythic narrative that functions as an offshoot of religious authority. They can be brought together but it is likely to work only if the institutions that promote these ideas wed them together in some effective way. That is, the religious institutions must give support to the pattern of power and the myth of superiority, which is unsurprising since it is the way that religion often functions within societies.

The point is that when religion functions to preserve such structures of power it also functions to reinforce political ideologies of hate and fear when such ideologies are linked to the authority of religion. The form of this kind of link is possible only after the ideological pattern has been established clearly: that the other is dangerous and to be feared, and the right to exist and to dominate is given by divine authority (Ham, according to Genesis, is condemned to be the slave of his brothers). The Belgians used this narrative as a presumption that they had a divine right of authority over the Rwandan people. In addition, the particular group singled out as Tutsis were believed to come from the north (from Ethiopia, perhaps, or in the Biblical narrative, the land of Cush). Strangely, this association with Ethiopia, which a number of Christians through the years had identified as Cush from the lineage of Ham the son of Noah, meant that these "Tutsis" were descendents of Ham and thus of a lineage closer to the Europeans and "higher" than the other racial groups of Africa. Whatever the actual legitimation of this claim, the association of the Tutsis with Ham led the Belgians to give them most of the leadership roles, that is, places of political power. Even so, the link to the story of Noah's sons from Genesis, particularly Ham, also gave this mythic view a religious reinforcement that justified the subversion of Africans (even the Tutsis) to the Belgians. Finally, were not only the rights of the other limited by this religious justification, but even the right to exist was put into the hands of the Belgians and could be taken away by fiat or simply ignored. In other words, religious authority was used to rationalize the killing of the other. In many circumstances where the story of Ham is used, the presence of this myth of domination and control of life and death does not produce views that lead people to commit mass killing. But in Rwanda people were led to kill their neighbors, family members, and other members of their churches.

The argument is, however, further, that the myth is more than just a convenience for the genocidal power. The myth is seen as reality, and we can assume that this reality was reinforced not just with political ideology but with religious instruction. The pattern among Christians included—as Jules Isaac showed years ago (1964)—a "teaching of contempt," which in European Christian teaching was aimed explicitly at the Jews. Moreover, the teaching was not an overt teaching against Jews, but rather part and parcel of the teaching of Christianity itself, what Rosemary Ruether (1974) argued made anti-Semitism the left hand of Christology. This teaching of contempt sets a pattern in Christian teaching (such contempt for groups seen as "others" is surely not found just among Christians) that makes being Christian a case of "us against them," and the attitude has been taught in this way from the pulpit as well as in the classroom by Christians through the centuries.

In various places the Hamitic myth was taught from the pulpit and in the classrooom so as to give a religious justification for slavery and support Christians who acted as slave masters. Today this seems extreme, but we all know that it was normalized in America from the colonial period on. Yet slavery is not genocide, even if it can lead to massive suffering and death. The form this teaching took in Rwanda was fundamentally genocidal because it merged the religious justification of white superiority brought in by the Belgians with ethnic difference and hatred imposed as a social structure by the Belgians. Ham is not only to be enslaved (the Genesis narrative makes this belief in the slavery of the descendents of Ham into an inevitable command of God) but to be hated (in Rwanda the descendent of Ham was made to be the elite and became the focus of ethnic hatred). Since the regular patterns of Christian teaching in Europe produce a form of contempt aimed at the Jewish people, it is enough to recognize that the Belgians linked a specialized development the Hamitic mythic tradition in Rwanda with this implicit teaching of contempt in Christianity. Despite the fact that this teaching has been rather specifically focused on the Jews, it can be successfully applied to any group considered to be contemptible. It is possible that Christianity is unique in this potential.

Of course, evidence is scant that the teaching within the churches was manipulated in order to create this merger of the teaching of contempt with the Hamitic myth. That research needs to be done; indeed, what I am suggesting here ought to be done in order to help us understand more clearly the role that religion (in this case, specifically Catholicism) plays in shaping the genocidal mind. The experience of the Holocaust shows that this potential for hatred is always present in the teaching of the churches, and the Rwandan situation was a particular convergence of factors that made genocide a realistic component of a religious vision.

REGULAR WORSHIP: THE EASTER EFFECT

Various scholars have noted that religious leaders became involved or were somehow otherwise complicit in genocide, and arguing as well that the violence often occurred at churches and religious schools.[7] And though the question is frequently asked about why and how this could be, research is still needed to explore the ways that regular patterns of Christian teaching and worship might have fed and justified the genocide.

My analysis is purely suggestive and cannot be determined fully without an actual investigation into the practices at the various churches during the week prior to the beginning of the genocide.[8] Nevertheless, far more striking to me than the strange use of the Hamitic myth is the realization that the genocide began on 7 April 1994, the Wednesday after Easter. On the one hand, it is nearly incomprehensible that neighbors and fellow worshippers could carry out a genocide immediately following the Christian celebration of the resurrection (a symbol of hope). It is also quite difficult to imagine that people would gather in worship on Sunday for Easter and again the following week in a continuation of the Easter theme while contemplating mass killing and as time proceeded, knowing that killing was happening. This coincidence, at the very least, is another evidence of the massive failure of the churches to act even at a time when they should have been prepared to be fully mobilized. The case of Rwanda may also lead us to see the need to broaden the investigation in order to discover how often and in what ways specific religious holidays are occasions for the beginning of mass killing, and how such holidays have been manipulated in other situations to stir up people's emotions so that they are ready to accept or even participate in such killing. What seems specifically true about Christianity may be more generally true about the relation between religions and genocide. I can begin this process by suggesting how an analysis of texts that might be read during the Good Friday and Easter worship services in the churches of Rwanda could be a source for such manipulation.

We may not be so surprised by this conjoining of events if we are made more aware of the actual function of the whole preparation for Easter, most especially the Good Friday observance, and the theological message that is at least implicitly conveyed through these worship settings. While I cannot present a full analysis in this chapter, I can hint at the issues that emerge if we assume that patterns of worship were made to be consistent with genocidal thinking and acting. Much more could be revealed if we had access to the additional liturgical texts that were used that day (hymns, prayers, common readings), but we can see much by looking at chapters 18 and 20 in the Gospel of John, which are foundational texts for Good Friday and Easter. We need both to grasp what these texts present as a narrative that shapes how Christians (we assume also the Rwandan Christians) view the world, especially those who are "other," and to account for the liturgical theology that is constructed by the rhythm of the liturgical year within which the specific worship events like Easter and Good Friday are embedded.

THE LITURGICAL THEOLOGY

The flow of a theological narrative in standard Christian worship in the calendar year is set between the two great feasts of Christmas and Easter, perhaps the two most theologically important Christian festivals. The Christmas component clearly announces the coming of a saving event in the person of Jesus, and through succeeding weeks unfolds the intended meaning of this religious belief. This event, which has been prepared for since ancient times, is an intervention by God to redeem all humanity from sin. Without this salvation, according to this telling of the narrative, all humanity, which is sinful, is condemned by God. The implied theological claim of the Christmas narrative sets up the season of Lent, which is designed to prepare all Christians for the actual saving event of Easter through a pattern of personal confession, meditation, and sacrifice. There is no way to assess just how fully any Christian group is drawn into the activities that are implied by this Lenten meditation period, but the theology presented is clear enough if we read in detail the sequence of texts that are read during this time for worship. The point is to humble, or possibly even humiliate, oneself because none of us are worthy of salvation, or even of the life that God alone has given us. That is to say, the normal pattern is to conclude that all deserve only death.

This period of contemplation and sacrifice culminates liturgically in Holy Week as the full narrative of the last days of Jesus is read with special focus on the death of Jesus, including the strong language of the various texts that condemns the religious leaders for hypocrisy and obtuse rejection of the salvation, that is said to be obviously prophesied from ancient times. While the Holy Week readings do not extend blame as such to all who reject Jesus, it is obvious that the flow of meaning in these texts leads inevitably to a conclusion that only those who fully accept Jesus as the savior can escape the sentence of death, and that those who appear to intentionally reject and especially those who do so with "full knowledge" of the historical prophecies are condemned to eternal death. They are not worthy of life. Of course, one result of this teaching can be that those who know the "truth" have the task of spreading the news to the ones who have not yet believed (the basic themes of the Easter season that lasts for six or seven weeks after Easter). On the other hand, if used to construct the "evil" other, these texts can be used to target groups for elimination justified by the authority of God. It is this theological narrative that would have been heard by regular worshippers in churches during the week preceding the Rwandan genocide, the theology that Jules Isaac labeled a "teaching of contempt."

It is important to recognize that there is no necessary flow from textual condemnation to actions of contempt, even genocide, but the history of Christianity shows all too clearly that contempt generated by the "liturgical theology" does result quite often in violent behavior. In fact, the impact of the passion narrative (what Christians have called this story of Jesus' last days) is so clear that no matter what texts are actually used among the options for telling the story, the theology remains intact. That is, it is conveyed by the flow of the liturgical year. Even so, we can learn even more by examining at a couple of actual, exemplary texts for Good Friday and Easter. My point is that these texts set in a liturgical theology already are heard in the way described, but even more than that, the texts are peopled by various violent actors of both those who support and justify violence and those who act violently.

One more point must be inserted as we turn to specific texts. We should recall that the full narrative is seldom read in the actual worship setting. Instead, biblical texts are used in Christian worship as pericopes, that is, selections extracted from the full texts in order to construct even more clearly an intended meaning. It is this "constructed narrative" that worshippers hear (year after year, Sunday after Sunday).

I am giving only two examples and only portions of texts at that, to help assess the actual content of texts that are heard in worship. The sequence of Good Friday and Easter texts is determined by a pattern in most churches (especially in Catholic churches, to which most Rwandans belong). This pattern is three cycles of texts repeated every three years. If this is taken for 1994, the texts would include John 18:1–19:42 on Good Friday and John 20:1–18 on Easter. The text is structured around stereotypes that function as characters in the story. Judas is the insider who betrays Jesus. The Jewish officials (especially the chief priests) are clearly described as accountable for the death of Jesus. They are even given several chances to change their intent, but plainly choose to have Jesus killed. Peter is the insider who remains silent (though the actual narrative makes it a lesson within the lessons that whereas Peter was one of the important followers, he was weak and said nothing to save Jesus—though the narrative also displays him using his sword to cut off the ear of a slave), the bystander. The narrative culminates with the death of Jesus, which the text explicitly shows happens according to God's plan (so that the scriptures would be fulfilled), and with the resurrection narrative, which also is presented as a prelude to the ascension to the Father, the assumption of power.

Thus, the narrative reads like a story of unjust accusation and innocent sacrifice that is rewarded with new life and with power and glory. Within this narrative is the violence of Peter's sword, the piercing of Jesus' side, the casting of lots for Jesus' clothes, the nailing of Jesus to the cross, and the agony before death. Judas is identified in an earlier text in the gospel as the one who would betray Jesus, while in John alone, we hear that Satan enters Jesus. In addition, when Judas comes to betray Jesus, in John he is said to stand with the ones arresting Jesus. All of this is played out with the priests and the Pharisees as the unambiguous culprits who plot the death of Jesus and choose to make sure it happens.

These human types become a fixture in the way that Christians see the world, even if they are rethought and remade to fit current experience and not left as only part of a past event. Thus, we have a clear picture of the treacherous insider gone bad, the ones who plot the death of Jesus, the divine judgment on the betrayer, and the divine justification of the holy one. This is a morality play with evident meaning for how life is to be understood and lived out. Thus, we cannot be surprised that a basic element of a Christian worldview is a stereotypical construction of us against them, of vigilance against the evil ones and those who would betray who are logically standing with the evil one(s). This is not a call to bring justice, but it is a justification for hatred of those perceived to be standing with the evil one. Such a stance lends itself freely to conspire with the sort of political ideology built on the Hamitic myth. It is shocking but, finally, not so surprising that Christians could be at worship on Easter and four or five days later be killing their neighbors, their relatives, even their compatriots in the Christian community. The one sitting next to us at a table, or in the pew, can be Judas.

Most who explore this relation between fundamental Christian belief and genocidal violence are not prepared to argue that Christianity alone is sufficient to produce genocide, even if the case is the Holocaust. We should assume similar caution in this case of Rwanda even though the situation makes complicity by Christians all the more obvious and disturbing. It is more likely that the Christian narrative liturgical theology, especially the Good Friday-Easter component, can frame an attitude of indifference, placing the "other" completely outside of divine protection and inclusion. That is, the Christian story reinforces any tendency to assume that the other deserves its fate and fosters a willingness to stand to the side and let things take their course. The troubling feature of Rwanda is that so many actually were moved from the sidelines to participate in the violence.

WHAT LESSONS IF ANY?

This analysis is only hypothetical and surely cannot be conclusive. Further study of the actual evidence will show just how much was actually done to manipulate the texts in the churches to prepare the people for the violence that was to come or even to urge them to participate. Still, if there is any validity in the connection between Christianity and Christian organizations and the eventual genocide in Rwanda, then we learn that any effort to prepare for prevention of genocide must include a careful examination of what is consistently taught by religions in "regular" patterns of worship through the texts of worship. The messages conveyed in this way are sometimes subtle but they are also consistently and persistently reinforced through a multitude of repetitions over the course of many years in the lives of regular worshippers. I would say that genocide prevention requires an effort to transform the texts of worship in such a way that Christian worship more explicitly conveys messages that support compassion, respect, and nonviolent solutions rather than narratives that can be used to justify contempt, even hatred, for the other.

NOTES

1. This study is intended, then, as a theological analysis with the aim of showing how the theology of the churches needs to be analyzed and rethought, not only at the scholarly level, but also at the level of the ordinary worship in the churches. Its primary aim is to challenge the churches to begin the process of rethinking so as to more directly uncover and alter genocidal elements that lurk in the liturgies. The essay, however, also urges that such a theological analysis is likely to show areas of social scientific research that can, even must, be pursued. As a theologian I do not contend that this analysis will or even should do this empirical research. My hope is that others with the relevant skills and capacities will follow its lead.

2. The hymns are taken from the *Lutheran Book of Worship* (1978), numbers 123 and 128. My choice to take hymns from the *Lutheran Book of Worship* provides a general example of the way hymns function in a liturgical theology. I am not suggesting that these particular hymns have anything to do with the Rwandan case except that they generally represent the sort of themes that are present in many hymns for Easter, ones that may have been sung that Sunday in 1994 in the Rwandan churches.

3. The statistics in this essay are taken from the official Rwandan government website, www.rwanda.net. My sense from speaking with those Rwandans and others who can know about matters firsthand is that the sort of research I am suggesting might be done has not yet been done. Thus, my essay uses Rwanda as a case study example for the sake of pointing to the theological issues at stake more generally and does not pretend to be speaking about the actual details of the Rwandan setting except where those details are clear.

4. The historical material in this essay is dependent on various sources but primarily on the research found in Alison Des Forges, *Leave None to Tell the Story* (1999).

5. A revealing account of one of the most significant episodes of the genocide can be found in Philip Gourevitch, *We Wish to Inform You That Tomorrow We Will Be Killed with Our Families* (1998). The story gives the name to Gourevitch's book.

6. Both Gourevitch and Des Forges acknowledge that this mythic distinction is introduced by the Belgians, but they do not link the narrative to the Genesis text, and thus to a religious context. Instead, they suggest that this represents a part of the racial ideology that was part of European thinking in the nineteenth century. This is surely true, but the particular story of Ham has a much longer history of use and application to racial and class differences. Claude Rawson gives an effective account

of the use of the Hamitic myth and its link to genocide, even though he does not include an analysis of Rwanda as part of his study in *God, Gulliver, and Genocide* (2001), 298ff. My point is not that it is clear exactly how the churches were involved in promoting this mythic picture that ultimately played a central role in creating the divides of hate that erupted in genocide. It is hard to imagine that the myth could have been promoted without at least the tacit acceptance of religious leaders, if not direct involvement. My point, however, is to point to the notion that the teaching of contempt embedded in the history of Christian teaching has a broader importance than explaining just Christian attitudes about the Jews, and should be seen as basically genocidal as well as anti-Judaic.

7. Note especially the firsthand accounts in Gourevitch.

8. I emphasize that the point of this essay is not primarily to demonstrate that the Rwandan genocide was in central ways impacted directly by the theology of the churches in Rwanda. The conclusion seems one possible hypothesis, and I urge that it should be investigated by social scientists. That empirical evidence is, as far as I can determine, not currently available. The point of this essay, however, remains fundamentally theological; a challenge to the way theology is done in the churches, and does not pretend to be doing an actual empirical study of the Rwandan situation. Rwanda is used for my purposes as a case example that raises heuristic questions about the function of liturgical theologies in shaping the views of Christians.

BIBLIOGRAPHY

Des Forges, Alison (1999). *Leave None to Tell the Story: Genocide in Rwanda*. New York: Human Rights Watch.

Gourevitch, Philip (1998). *We Wish to Inform You That Tomorrow We Will Be Killed with Our Families: Stories from Rwanda*. New York: Picador.

Isaac, Jules (1964). *The Teaching of Contempt: Christian Roots of Anti-Semitism*. New York: Holt, Rinehart and Winston.

Lutheran Book of Worship (1978). Minneapolis, Minn.: Augsburg.

Rawson, Claude (2001). *God, Gulliver and Genocide: Barbarianism and the European Imagination, 1492–1945*. New York: Oxford University Press.

Ruether, Rosemary Radford (1974). *Faith and Fratricide: The Theological Roots of Anti-semitism*. New York: Seabury Press.

5

More Than the Jews . . . His Blood Be Upon All the Children: Biblical Violence, Genocide, and Responsible Reading

Gary A. Phillips

> But every living Turk we killed in Tzrmnitza
> And Bèsatz Fort we leveled to the earth
> And now for thee throughout our parts
> Is not a trace of e'en one single Turk—
> At least thou'lt find not any Turkish ear—
> Bodies headless, ruins, ashes view man here!
>
> —*Mountain Wreath*

THE MASSACRE OF THE DELIJAJ INNOCENTS

In July 1998, regular Yugoslavian army troops aided by Serbian police and irregular forces began a summer offensive directed against the Kosovo Liberation Army (KLA). At the time, the KLA was in loose control of approximately a third of Kosovo. By mid-September, virtually all KLA forces had been driven from villages into neighboring forests leaving the police and army in control of the ethnic Albanian civilian population. By month's end, 200 villages were destroyed, nearly 2,000 civilians were dead, and 300,000 persons were displaced. With seemingly little to be gained militarily, and running the risk of inviting Western military intervention, Slobodan Milošević's forces set their sights on the village of Gornje Obrinje in the Drenica region, home to some 300 families, a KLA stronghold near where guerrillas had previously mounted stiff resistance and government forces had taken substantial casualties (Human Rights Watch, 1999a).

The massacre of the Delijaj family took place Saturday, 26 September. As reconstructed by Human Rights Watch observers and international journalists from the *London Times* and *Guardian* who interviewed family members and other eyewitnesses on the following Monday, the assault on the Delijaj family compound began in the early morning hours on Friday, 25 September (Krieger, 72). Intermittent heavy mortar and artillery fire throughout the day drove nearly all of the inhabitants into the nearby forest. Among the Delijaj family, only twenty-one-year-old Bashkim Delijaj remained behind to care for his invalid father, Fazli Delijaj. The next morning approximately three-dozen tanks firing ground-to-ground missiles and supported by scores of ground forces, many sporting large knives and small axes, advanced on the compound. It is very likely the troops included members of the *Jedinica za Specijalne Operacije* (JSO), an elite special forces unit of the Serbian State Security Office under the command of Franko "Frenki" Simatović, long suspected of perpetrating atrocities against civilian populations. In May 2003, Simatović was indicted by the United Nations International Criminal Tribunal for the former Yugoslavia for war crimes and crimes against humanity "committed against Croats, Bosnian Muslims, Bosnian Croats and other non-Serb civilians from Bosnia and Herzegovina and Croatia between 1991 and 1995" (ICTY, 2008).

Ninety-four-year-old patriarch Fazli Delijaj died in the family compound, his body burned beyond recognition. The bodies of fifteen other family members were found scattered in the nearby woods where they had fled advancing government troops. Two men, Pajazit and Ali, were 60 and 69, respectively; six women—Hava, Hamide, Zahide, Luljeta, Mehane, and Lumnije—ranged in age from twenty-five to sixty-two; and seven children—Jeton, Gentjana, Donjeta, Menduhije, Valmir, and Diturije—were as young as six weeks and as old as nine years; one child, Malsore, was days from being delivered. All received gunshot wounds to the head; several had their throats slit; a number were eviscerated by axe blows.

The following Monday Imer Delijaj, a KLA partisan, returned with Bashkim Delijaj to the compound in search of his family. Imer Delijaj provided this account to journalists (Steele, 1998) and Human Rights Watch observers on the scene, who confirmed the deaths from photographs of the bodies (Human Rights Watch, 1999b):

> I continued up the gully, and saw my nine-year-old son Jeton. He had a wound from his left ear to his mouth. I hope it was from a bullet and not a knife [so he would not have suffered]. It is the only body which I am not sure how he was killed. One shoe was on and one shoe was off.
>
> Five meters away was my sixty-year-old mother, Hamide, lying on her left side. She had a wound on the right side of her head and a small wound on her chest. I think she was killed with a "warm weapon" [a gun] from a close distance. I think she was shot in the face, not killed with a knife.

Nearby was the body of Luljeta, the pregnant wife of my brother, about to give birth any day. We had even decided on a name for the baby, Malsore, which means "mountain girl" and relates to our suffering in the mountains. Luljeta was the same as Hamide. Their legs were together. She was lying on her right side and she had wounds on the left side of her face. She was hit a little more on the back of the head, and there was a small wound on her nose. A smaller wound was on her left shin.

The other body was that of Valmir, the eighteen-month-old son of Adem. He had a wound on the right side of his face near his jaw, and on his right hand he had a hole but not from a bullet, and other small wounds on his body. His pacifier was hanging on his chest.

I next found the body of my wife, Lumnije. She was lying on her right side, and the two girls were next to her, one in front and one behind. The mother's hand was on the baby [six-week-old Diturije].

Four other Delijaj family members—Habib, Hysen, Antigona, and Mihane Delijaj—also perished, their mutilated and decomposed bodies later found along the main road and at a distance from the village. Altogether eighteen family members died that weekend. Of the group who initially sought refuge in the woods, four children—five-year-old Besnik, three-year-old Liridona, thirteen-month-old Arlinda, and two-year-old Alber—miraculously survived. Five-year-old Besnik would later provide a description of the axe murder of his grandfather, Ali, at the hands of a policeman whose "black face" is thought to have been concealed either by a ski mask or camouflage paint, signature markings of the Simatović-led JSO. It is believed the child also witnessed both his mother's and grandmother's execution, although he was unable to provide any details. According to a psychologist who later treated Besnik, post–traumatic stress disorder had rendered him mute.

RELIGION AND GENOCIDE

A voice was heard in Ramah,
Wailing and loud lamentation,
Rachel weeping for her children;
she refused to be consoled,
because they are no more

—Matthew 2:18/Jeremiah 31:15

What possibly explains the brutality, both physical and psychological, visited upon these Muslim innocents? Elderly women and men bludgeoned, burned, or shot to death; children eviscerated or made witnesses to horrific violence; bodies and minds mangled and mutilated (Human Rights Watch, 2001). The authors of the Human Rights Watch 1999 Report suggest that the Gornje Obrinje massacre was carried out to avenge the deaths of comrades who died defending Yugoslavian territorial integrity and to send a clear message to ethnic Albanians seeking an independent Kosovo that all such efforts would be opposed by any and all means necessary. Yet even the report's authors acknowledge "the underlying motives for the brutality of the Yugoslav offensive remain difficult to discern" (Human Rights Watch, 1999b). Curiously, nowhere in the report do the authors mention a link between the violence and the deep religious animosities that fueled Milošević's nationalist aspirations (Sells, 1996). In light of the Bosnian genocide (1992–1995), perhaps it was obvious and needed no elaboration. But the disturbing details of the Delijaj massacre call for analysis, one that presses for a clearer understanding of the complex ties between ethnic identity, religious texts and traditions, and genocide that might shed light on the Gornje Obrinje violence (see Rummel, 1997; Selengut, 2003). The goal is not merely to satisfy the need for analytical clarity, as valuable as that is. It is a responsible first step toward interrupting the violence and a protection of the innocents that was nonexistent on that July weekend for the Delijaj family, a protection demanded by International Law and ethical principle espoused by Western legal and religious traditions.

Leonard Glick and Michael Sells offer two contrasting approaches for understanding the relation between religion and violence. Glick asserts broadly that "[r]eligions cannot liberate humanity from genocide, for they are part of the problem" (Glick, 1999: 496). Since religion, Glick argues, is integral to personal and cultural identity, "it is something of a pointless academic exercise to try to disentangle religious motives and sanctions from the totality of considerations that may impel people of one ethnic group to perpetrate genocidal crimes against another." (Glick, 1994: 61). In arguing this position, Glick posits two broad categories of religion. The first he labels inherently ethnocentric, "localized" religions. Localized religions —Judaism counts as one—express "proto-genocidal" tendencies. He points to the biblical accounts of Israelite massacres of Canaanite peoples in the Book of Joshua (e.g., 6:17–21, 10:28; 10:36–42, and 11:10–11). These narratives of violence imprint Jewish scripture and psyche in a profound way, providing learning and license for believers to repeat divinely sanctioned genocidal violence against others in ever new settings. Glick labels the second type "universalist" religion. Universalist religions—for instance, Christianity and Islam—are both ethnocentric and knotted up by a major, internal contradiction. Glick explains: "on the one hand, ethnic identity presumably does not matter, since the universal truths of the religion override worldly categories; on the other hand, one must try to convert other people, even though that may mean severely disrupting their societies and cultures—and may even lead to their individual deaths" (Glick, 1999: 495). In short, religion is inherently ethnocentric and violence-generating. Glick then draws the somber conclusion: "if we are ever to reach the point where

genocidal massacres will have become a thing of the past, it will not be owing to religions: they are part of the problem" (Glick, 1994: 61). On Glick's
reading we are to conclude not only that religion is a source of the problem,
but that it is a "pointless academic exercise" to give careful scrutiny to the
issue. In the case of the Delijaj massacre, we should be satisfied with the
silence of the Human Rights report or Glick's confident assertion that critical reflection is beside the point.

But the silence and Glick's sweeping claims rather than settle matters
invite further reflection, one that attends to particulars. As examples of
universalist religion, we might ask if Christianity, Islam, Buddhism, and
Hinduism are so easily lumped together? Are they prone to or do they incite
ethnocentric and genocidal violence in the same way, to the same degree,
with the same deadly effect? Is the past history of Christian contempt for
Judaism, authorized in part by its scriptures (notably the Matthean Gospel
depiction of Jews as the "Killers of the Christ," 27:26), religious destiny for
every believing Christian? By Glick's standards, religious genocide is genetic, bound up inextricably in the DNA of theological tradition and texts.
And yet, those very texts of terror that appear to legitimate Holy War stand
side-by-side with other narratives that would appear to counter, critique,
and interrupt the wholesale permission to act violently not only against the
innocent but also the enemy: Isaiah's transmuting of swords to plowshares
(Isaiah 2:4) and Matthew's injunction against returning violence against the
evildoer (Matthew 5:39) in favor of peacemaking (5:9) are two examples.
According to Glick, universalist religions are inherently contradictory, but
contradiction is no stranger to ethnocentric local religions. Contradiction
and paradox perfuse the traditions and texts of Judaism and Christianity in rhetorical, logical, and imagistic ways that, one could argue, work
to destabilize ethnocentric impulses and thus subvert the tie to violence.
Even conceding Glick's general point that Christianity as an instance of
universalist religion has been historically "part of the problem," there is
more to be said and done. It is imperative that we clarify the specific ways
Christian religious texts, symbols, and mythologies inspire, instrumental-
ize, and legitimate violence. Equally, it is incumbent upon us to clarify
the specific ways religious texts, symbols, and mythologies also serve to
critique, subvert, and interrupt the violence. For Christians, unraveling the
entanglements amounts to a critical and moral imperative in light of their
specific history with Jews. Such work promises a thicker understanding of
the mechanisms at work in the Delijaj massacre. Moreover, the need for
such critical work is a moral response to the victims themselves: it was not
a general category of persons murdered at Gornje Obrinje on 26 July, 1998,
but eighteen particular individuals leading concrete lives with specific identities—Jeton, Gentjana, Donjeta, Menduhije, Valmir, and Diturije Delijaj,
among others—not figures but faces who, to invoke Emmanuel Levinas,

impose upon us the moral burden both of understanding and interrupting the violence (Phillips, 2002; Fewell and Phillips, 1998).

Michael Sells advances this work by framing the Serbian genocide in Bosnia in historically concrete terms. Sells analyzes the way a certain reading of the Christian passion narrative, amplified by Serbian epic and folk literature, undergirds a violent Serbian nationalist and racial ideology (Sells, 1996). He labels this religious ideology "Christoslavism," namely "the belief that Slavs are Christian by nature and that any conversion from Christianity is a betrayal of the Slavic race" (Sells, 1996: 36; cf. Velikonja, 1999: 2). According to this ideology, Christianity lies at the core of nation, faith, and race; Serbs are inherently Christian. Serbian converts to Islam, it follows, are by definition national, religious, and race traitors. Betrayal of one's nature and identity, it should come as no surprise, invites and incites the most forceful response, all in the name and spirit of Christian religious purity (Velikonja, 1999: 2).

The historical roots of Christoslavism lie in a specific fourteenth-century national trauma: the unstoppable Ottoman conquest of the Balkans that climaxed in the decisive defeat of the Serbs and the death of Prince Lazar Pribic Hrebeljanovic (1329–1389) at the Battle of Kosovo on 15 June, 1389. The defeat and death of Prince Lazar became the subject matter of Serbia's most important and influential medieval folk literature (Matthias and Vuckovic, 1987) and came to symbolize the loss of Serbian political independence and religious purity. Allegedly betrayed to the Turks by Vuk Branković (d. 1397), a trusted Serb compatriot, Prince Lazar is elevated to Christ-figure status and becomes the quintessential symbol of Serbian politico-religious identity. Branković and the Ottoman Turks are forever identified as the enemies and "killers of the Christ" (Redep, 1991).

Nineteenth-century Christoslavism expressed itself ethically most dramatically as "religious cleansing." *The Mountain Wreath* (Petar II, 1978, vii), a nineteenth-century epic poem and the crown jewel of Serbian national literature, recounts a legendary seventeenth-century Christmas Eve campaign to exterminate Slavs who had converted to Islam. An "expression of the highest union between [Serbian] art and soul" (Petar II, 1978: 5), the poem depicts the conflict between Serbian Christian and Turkish Muslim as the age-old cosmic conflict between good and evil. Within this dualistic perspective, the death of Lazar and the "spirit" of religious outrage against Turks acquire transhistorical, mythological status. When mapped against the contemporary national crisis of loss of Yugoslavian territorial integrity and identity and the Western military intervention in the Balkans, one can see how *The Mountain Wreath* served to validate and valorize the deadly violence visited on Muslims all across the Balkans and the Delijaj innocents in particular.

The poem opens with Bishop Danilo in Job-like fashion lamenting the day the Turks, "that accursed breed," despoiled Serbian land and religion:

"O cursèd day!—may God blot out thy light—
That thou didst bring me forth upon the world!" (ll. 84–85)

The poem climaxes with the news of a battle decisively won in which the Serbs have

"Put them [Turks] all unto the sword
All those who would not be baptiz'd" (ll. 2599–2600)
"But every living Turk we killed in Tzrmnitza
And Bèsatz Fort we leveled to the earth
And now for thee throughout our parts
Is not a trace of e'en one single Turk—
At least thou'lt find not any Turkish ear—
Bodies headless, ruins, ashes view man here!" (ll. 2720–24)

Bloody victory over an ancient enemy expressed in the most graphic terms serves to enflame the national and religious spirit. A student excitedly reports to Abbot Stephen that Muslim men, women, and children are among the dead:

"Slaughter there is, and bloody slaughter too;
For one whole hour I joyously have heard it. (ll. 2575–76)

As for the slaughter of women and children, Abbot Stephen festively responds:

"Smoke curls at Yuletide, is that any wonder!—
Were a whole people being sacrificed,
That could not be without great clouds of smoke!
. . .
"For joyous news comes in from every side." (ll. 2580–82, 2724)

One hears echoes of disturbing Hebrew Bible conquest accounts in which Israel eradicates Canaanite men, women, and children at Yahweh's behest or, at minimum, permission, voiced by a Christian Holy Man with a glee that far matches the wholesale triumphalism of the biblical narrative. Ancient Israelite notions of Holy War (*herem*) and burnt offering (*holocaust*) are poetically overlaid with the Christian Gospel announcement of "Good News." At once ecstatic and eschatological, Abbot Stephen gives prophetic witness to the deaths of the innocents.

Buttressing Serbian epic mythology is the Gospel passion story. "The genocide in Bosnia," Sells explains, "was grounded in a particular version

of the Good Friday story" (Sells, 1996: 144) and the vilification of Jews as
the "killers of the Christ." This construction, fortified by a centuries-old
theology of contempt for Jews, weaponizes Christoslavism by targeting a
different victim. The tradition of Christian anti-Jewish violence dramatized
in the Medieval passion play is now made Muslim-specific through Serbian folk literature and biblical narrative. A virulent tradition of violence
against Jew morphs into violence visited upon Muslims now located in the
cross-hairs. In *The Mountain Wreath*, Prince Lazar's betrayer, Vuk Branković,
becomes the Judas, the turncoat Serb, who is at once the "Christ-killer"
Jew and every Slav who has turned his back upon his true (i.e., Christian)
faith. The ancient Matthean charge of Jewish deicide—"And all the people
answered 'His blood be upon us and our children'" (Matthew 27:25)—is
thus transposed into a modern passion story with Muslims recast in the role
of both the "Christ-killers" and "Judases" (Petar II, 1978: 19–20). Historical
and narrative differences are effaced: Serbian Christoslavism for Matthean
Christology, Muslim crowd for Jewish crowd, blood libel against Muslim
children as against Jewish children, with no distinction. Lazar's blood is
literally upon all the children.

In the passion story pronouncement we catch overtones of the darker side
of advent. The Christmastime massacre of Muslims reenacts Herod's wholesale massacre of the unnamed innocents in Matthew's gospel: "And he sent
and killed all the male children in Bethlehem and in all that region who
were two years old or under" (Matthew 2:16). An understated but central
aspect of the advent spectacle is the violence inflicted upon children. The
wholesale violence announces the arrival and survival of Jesus, for within
Matthew's careful constructed narrative plot the unnamed children are the
necessary collateral damage that leads to Jesus' eventual passion and the
subsequent birth of Christianity. What the Gospel writer Matthew provides
as good theater is taken as terrible history (Crossan, 1996). Thus the "joyous news" of Emmanuel in Matthew 1:23, the one who is born amidst mass
politico-religious trauma and violence in first–century Roman-controlled
Palestine, in *The Mountain Wreath* becomes the "joyous news" of politico-
violence directed *against* seventeenth-century Muslim innocents in Kosovo
(l. 2724). Christoslavism, in effect, erases the differences between story and
history, past and present, Jew and Muslim, Palestine and Kosovo, the innocent and the guilty. It "efface[s] the boundaries between notions of religion
and race" and "turns religious nationalism into the most virulent form of
racialist ideology" (Petar II, 1978: xv). Scripture now becomes script.

Historical trauma, Christian sacrament and scripture, and a nationalist/
racist ideology and mythology combine to form a toxic mix. On the occasion of the 600th anniversary of the Battle of Kosovo, Slobodan Milošević
orchestrated a public reading of *The Mountain Wreath* before an estimated
crowd of one million Serbs. Sells describes this as an occasion where

"[r]eligious symbols, mythologies, mythos of origin (the pure Serb race), symbols of passion (Lazar's death), and eschatological longings (the resurrection of Lazar) were used by nationalists to create a reduplicating Miloš Oblilić, avenging himself on the Christ-killer, the race traitor, the alien" (Sells, 1996, 89). In the epic poem, Lazar's avenger, Miloš Oblilić, succeeds in assassinating the Turkish Sultan Murad I. The fourteenth-century heroic Miloš readily becomes the twentieth-century heroic *Miloš*-evic. By reading and rewriting himself into the epic poem, Milošević identifies with both the avenger and Prince Lazar, and becomes at once historical victim, Christ-figure, bloody avenger, and mythical national leader. Every Serb is invited to make the imaginative identification of Miloš Oblilić with Milošević and of themselves with those biblical and epic narrative heroes who avenge the death of the "Christ figure" upon the guilty.

Viewed in this light, we may begin to see the Gornje Obrinje massacre as a complex, biblically scripted, and ideologically grounded cleansing of *all things Muslim*. The first-century Advent murder of the innocents by Herod, the seventeenth-century Advent murder of Muslim men, women, and children on Christmas Eve, and the July 1998 massacre of the Delijaj children become types of one another. Gospel narrative, epic poem, and Serbian cleansing plans elide. Narrative characters, epic figures, and real children become interchangeable, indistinguishable, expendable. The danger in thinking in terms of types and universals, whether it is about a passion experience or the religious tie to genocidal violence, is that particularity disappears and with it the capacity to draw distinctions, moral and otherwise: "All the male children in Bethlehem" becomes "every living Turk" becomes "all Slavic Muslims." Typologizing and generalization impede understanding and moral action. In response, we must *interrupt the narrative and action by attending to specifics: not only the particular texts and traditions in play but the specific names and faces of the specific innocents who are victims of the violence*—Fazli, Pajazit, Ali, Hava, Hamide, Zahide, Luljeta, Mehane, Lumnije, Jeton, Gentjana, Donjeta, Menduhije, Valmir, Diturije, Malsore (Fewell, 2003; Greenberg, 1989).

THE SUBVERTING BIBLE AND SUBVERTING BIBLICAL VIOLENCE: RESPONSIBLE READING

Human cruelty took the form of a pact with the deity.
A solemn oath was made to kill everything. . . .

—Ernest Renan, *Histoire du people d'Israel*

The massacre of the Delijaj family and a Serbian Christoslavism that employs biblical narratives of violence present us with disturbing questions: What is the relationship between unholy violence and the Holy Bible? Is the biblical text fundamentally and forever genocidal? Have Serbian murderers distorted the Bible, or, lamentably, read it all too well? What can believers do to subvert the link between sacred text and the violence it seems both to inspire and authorize, whether it takes the form of anti-Semitic or anti-Islamic brutality? These are profound and pressing questions that demand a grasp of the complex relationship of religion and violence and of the specific ways scripture functions as script for good and ill (Wallace and Smith, 1994). In brief, with an eye upon Jewish and Christian scriptures, let me offer three provisional observations, intended not to resolve these questions but to open up space for further concrete reflection with the aim of understanding and interrupting the violence.

First, there is an absolute need to deal with textual realities: *Genocidal violence is portrayed and justified in Jewish and Christian scriptures.* Gerd Lüdemann speaks of this as the Bible's "dark side" (Lüdemann, 1997), its "ruinous" features. First and Second Testament narratives inscribe all manner of violence: violence directed against children, violence against other peoples, violence against creation itself. At times readers are confronted with an unimaginable, totalizing violence, breathtaking in its scope and mind-numbing in its impact. Responsible readers and citizens, therefore, cannot easily dismiss murderous appeals to biblical murder narratives as simple misreading. Extermination is biblical; anti-Judaism is biblical; violence against the unprotected and innocent is biblical. Nor can we easily overlook the fact that God is portrayed as indiscriminately wielding violence through Israel directed against Canaanite men, women, and children, among other peoples (cf. Numbers 21:1-3, Deuteronomy 2:30-35 and 3:3-7, Joshua 6:17-21, 10:28, and 11:10-11). Holy War is biblical, and God ordains it; it is war for the "sanctification of God's name" (*Kiddush Hashem*) (Selengut, 2003, 25). Jews and Christians who take their texts seriously cannot be too careful when dealing with these narratives and this God, because their own children are not immune to divinely inspired and authorized violence as Job all too well discovered (Job 1:18-19). Unless we confront sacred texts with eyes wide open, reading for what they say, we will not understand with requisite specificity how scripture in the name of religion scripts violence, and how it can be subverted.

Such reading must be historically grounded. Responsible readers must understand the historical origins of the scriptures read and lived with and the forces at work that brought them into being. Specific biblical texts of terror, indeed the wider canon itself, arose out of cultural conditions and in response to human experiences marked by tragedy and suffering. What the post-exilic formation of the Pentateuch (Genesis through Deuteronomy) and the post-Second Temple emergence of the Gospels and Acts share in common are settings of sociopolitical violence; the First and Second Testaments both reflect and refract the experiences of displacement, destruction, and despoliation. It is therefore hardly surprising that religious texts and genocidal violence are bedfellows. By this reading, the traumatic suffering experiences written into Jewish and Christian scriptures in one age lend themselves to be read out by those suffering in another. The key to responsible reading and acting is to know whether or not one has grasped the ethical centrality of these texts, and that centrality cannot be grasped apart from an understanding of the counter experiences and critique also reflected and refracted within the body of scripture taken as a canonical whole.

Second, there is an absolute need to deal with the full textual and historical reality: *The biblical text subverts claims to absolute, totalizing understanding, action and belief, religious or otherwise.* As a library of texts, the Bible is a subverting, self-undermining artifact as much aimed at the religious—at times even more so—as the nonreligious: "By its very nature, by the stand it takes against the conventions of its world," writes Jonathan Magonet, "[the Bible] subverts the power structures or gender definitions or religious presuppositions of its own times" (Magonet, 1991: 6). Despite certain narrative invitations, the Bible resists identification with and reduction to a specific ethnicity, ideology, or religious nationalism. Through its narrative, poetic, and rhetorical strategies readers are invited to interrupt easy isomorphic identification and effacement of differences. Over against Joshua's narratives of war-frenzied ethnocentrism stand Isaiah's universal covenant and injunction to beat swords into plowshares; over against calls for racial and religious purity in Ezra and Nehemiah we encounter the story of Ruth; over against a God who kills first-born Egyptians is a God who perceives the suffering of Israel and has compassion; over against a Deuteronomic logic that systematizes good and evil must be read Qoheleth who ridicules any effort to rationalize either God or human life; over against Matthean and Johannine anti-Judaism must be read the Markan privileging of Jewish and Gentile women as passion heroines; over against Gospel anti-Pharisaic denunciations stands Jesus' radical embrace of Judaism's Torah. Paradox and contradiction are central to the "logic" of the Bible and its articulation of truth. "[The multiple dimensions of the Hebrew Bible] are not inconvenient complications to our finding 'the truth,' they are of the very essence of that 'truth'" notes Jonathan Magonet (Magonet, 1991: 23). What Glick identifies as Christianity's "ethnocentric contradiction" is, therefore, not a weakness, a knot to be unraveled and dispensed with, but an enduring potency that can empower the *religious* effort to subvert the ugly tie between religion and violence encountered in scripture and expressed in totalizing and totalitarian ideology. Christoserbianism may claim biblical grounding, but it fails miserably, violently, to live the central inconvenient truth of the prophets and the gospels.

Third, there is an absolute need for concretion: *Genocidal acts and readings that script violence are more likely to occur when victims are stripped of their name, face, and individuality; conversely, a moral and critical response that interrupts violence is more likely to occur when particular names and faces are attached to individual victims.* Generalization is an enabling condition of bigotry, hate, and murder. The wholesale construction of "the Jews" in John's gospel as the enemy of the Light works to reinforce a dualistic mythology and the association of Jews and Judaism with the perverse and the murderous (8:44). Medieval pogroms against "the Jews" relied heavily upon John's and Matthew's gross characterizations to script violence and thus reify the dualism. However, reading for the face and the contours, for the concrete particulars, counters the move toward dehumanization that makes violence imaginable. Careful attention to John's presentation of the Samaritan woman (4:7–42), for instance, reveals an interlocutor who steadfastly refuses to yield to Jesus' stereotyping and generalizations. She teaches the one identified with the Light what it means to deal with specificity and difference: to expose the concrete experiences that have been her life; to go to those rejected by Israel (the Samaritans). This particular Samaritan woman stands in the text and tradition as a corrective to Jesus' and John's facile generalizations. The rejected other becomes visible, particular, a woman with a face, a human being who invites a moral and religious acceptance and respect.

As Primo Levi powerfully described, the Nazis succeeded in dehumanizing concentration camp victims by systematically stripping them of every aspect of their individuality: work, family, clothes, hair, language, name, and moral choice (Levi, 1986: 27). Ironically, the maintenance of the death camp as a killing machine required a deliberate neutralization of the moral response on the part of perpetrators as a practical necessity in order to enact the violence. The erasing of particulars allowed the human to become subhuman in the eyes of the perpetrators. "Musselman" (the Muslim) was Levi's term for the human being stripped of all discernible features—soul, body, and belief—now characterized by vacant eyes, the look of living death. That all-too-familiar haunting face staring from behind barbed wire fence would appear in Serbian concentration camps in Bosnia a half-century later. Serbian perpetrators of genocide against Bosnians and Kosovars frequently camouflaged their faces with paint or ski masks. Was this an implicit acknowledgement that perpetrators, too, must sacrifice name, face and humanity—soul, body, and belief—in order to subvert the moral response evoked by the face of the victim? Might this explain why so many victims in Gornje Obrinje died of facial and head wounds?

Samuel Bak, child-artist and survivor of the liquidation of the Vilna ghetto, has captured the faces of his murdered friend Samek Epstein, the Gornje Obrinje victims, and indeed every child in his haunting *Crossed Out II*, the image we confront on the cover of this book. Bak's painting evokes memory of an unnamed child in the famous 1943 photograph of the boy from the Warsaw Ghetto as well as connotes the christological iconography of the Western artistic and religious tradition; he is Everychild who has ever been the target of hatred however inspired. Bearing the wood that will incinerate his remains, the boy in *Crossed Out II* awaits the executioner's gunfire, his death hood doubling as burial shroud and, perhaps trebly, the executioner's mask. Criss-crossed wooden beams sandwiching his torso mark him as the intended target. But more incongruous doublings give us pause. We catch sight of a purported prisoner in the cross-hairs moments before his execution, and a child posed for a photographer's shooting in some commercial studio equipped with its standard nondescript backdrop, a jarring juxtaposition of the penal and the domestic. We envision yesterday's innocent child held at gunpoint but also today's child soldier bearing a rifle-like weapon and sporting a bandolier across his chest. The frame slips, and we can see ourselves in the sentenced boy's space, uncomfortably wearing the shoes of photographer, executioner, bystander, indifferent spectator. Bak's painting asks us: What sense does this make? How are we to respond? And we answer: By grasping the ways narrative and nationalism, image and ideology can dangerously inflect and infect one another; also by taking the place of this innocent boy and interrupting the violence (Fewell and Phillips, 2008: 93–124; Fewell and Phillips, 2009).

When pondering the relationship of religion to the violence of the Delijaj massacre and the wider Muslim genocide, we must inquire about the specific ways biblical narratives and Serbian national epic inform and texture historical trauma, past and present. Of equal importance, we must recognize the self-subverting features of biblical texts and traditions that oppose the imposition of violence upon the innocent and the accompanying totalitarian impulses. Of greater importance still is the need to attend to Imer Delijaj's actual words; to view the Human Rights Watch photographs; to track Franko Simatovi 's war crimes trial; to attend to the particularities of those individual human beings, the innocents, who were murdered, lost to the world, never to be redeemed or restored to life and whose suffering and death—in stark contrast to the innocents of the Biblical plots—lacks all purpose and meaning. We must move from the general to the particular, from ethnic category to actual child. Specificity and concretion alter the way we read and respond responsibly when the historical victims of the Gornje Obrinje massacre are not just Kosovar Muslims but the Delijaj family. How differently the event registers when we learn that it's not just a nine-year-old Muslim child, but a little boy named Jeton Delijaj. How urgent and different the call to interrupt the violence becomes when those acts are directed not against a generic *all the children* but Jeton and his mom, baby brother, and little sister; and his cousins, Gentjana, Donjeta, Menduhije, Valmir, Diturije, and Malsore.

BIBLIOGRAPHY

Crossan, John Dominic (1996). *Who Killed Jesus? Exposing the Roots of Anti-Semitism in the Gospel Story of the Death of Jesus.* New York: Harper.

Fewell, Danna Nolan (2003). *The Children of Israel: Reading the Bible for the Sake of Our Children.* Nashville, Tenn.: Abingdon Press.

Fewell, Danna Nolan and Gary A. Phillips (2008). "Bak's Impossible Memorials: Giving Face to the Children" in Danna Nolan Fewell, Gary A. Phillips, and Yvonne Sherwood (eds.), *Representing the Irreparable: The Shoah, the Bible, and the Art of Samuel Bak.* Boston, Mass.: Pucker Art Publications.

—— (2009). *Icon of Loss: The Haunting Child of Samuel Bak.* Boston, Mass.: Pucker Art Publications.

Glick, Leonard (1994). "Religion and Genocide," in Israel W. Charny (ed.), *The Widening Circle of Genocide. Genocide: A Critical Bibliographic Review. Vol. 3.* New Brunswick, N.J.: Transaction Publishers, 43–74.

—— (1999). "Religion and Genocide," in Israel W. Charny (ed.), *Encyclopedia of Genocide. Vol. 2.* Santa Barbara, Calif.: ABC-CLIO, 494–96.

Greenberg, Blu (1989). "Christian conversations with the Holocaust: The Holocaust and the Gospel Truth." *Holocaust and Genocide Studies,* 4(3): 273–82.

Human Rights Watch (1999a). *A Week of Terror in Drenica: Humanitarian Law Violations in Kosovo.* New York: Human Rights Watch. Available through the Internet at: http://hrw.org/reports/1999/Kosovo/index.htm

—— (1999b). *Gornje obinje: Massacre in the Forest.* New York: Human Rights Watch. Available through the Internet at: http://hrw.org/reports/1999/Kosovo/Obrinje6-02.htm#P279_32193.

—— (2001). *Memorandum on Charges against Indictees Currently Living in Serbia. April 1, 2001.* New York: Human Rights Watch. Available through the Internet at: www.hrw.org/backgrounder/eca/icty-bck-0401.htm.

International Criminal Tribunal for the Former Yugoslavia (2008). "Stanišić & Simatović Trial Scheduled to Begin 10 March 2008." Available through the Internet at: http://www.icty.org/sid/8915.

Krieger, Heike (2001). *The Kosovo Conflict and International Law: An Analytical Documentation, 1974–1999.* Cambridge: Cambridge University Press.

Levi, Primo (1986). *Survival in Auschwitz: The Nazi Assault on Humanity.* New York: Collier.

Lüdemann, Gerd (1997). *The Unholy in Holy Scripture: The Dark Side of the Bible.* Translated by John Bowden. Louisville, Ky.: Westminster John Knox.

Magonet, Jonathan (1997). *The Subversive Bible.* London: SCM Press.

Matthias, John and Vladeta Vukovic (trans.) (1987). *The Battle of Kosovo: Selected Poems.* Athens: Ohio University Press.

Petar II (1978). *The Mountain Wreath.* English translation, notes, and commentary by James W. Wiles. Serbian notes and commentaries by Vido Latkovic. Edited by Zviko Apic. Toronto, Ont.: Jugoslavica.

Phillips, Gary (2002). "The Killing Fields of Matthew's Gospel," in Tod A. Linafelt (ed.), *A Shadow of Glory: Reading the New Testament after the Holocaust.* New York: Routledge, 232–47.

Phillips, Gary with Danna Nolan Fewell (1997). "Ethics, Bible, Reading as If." *Semeia*, 77: 1–22.

Redep, Jelka (1991). "The Legend of Kosovo." *Oral Tradition*, 6/2–3: 253–65. Available through the Internet at: http://journal.oraltradition.org/files/articles/6ii-iii/11_redep.pdf.

Rummel, R. J. (1997). *Death by Government.* New Brunswick, N.J.: Transaction Publishers.

Sells, Michael (1996). *The Bridge Betrayed: Religion and Genocide in Bosnia.* Berkeley: University of California Press.

Steele, Jonathan (1998). "Kosovo—Women, Children Massacred." *Guardian (London)*, 30 September 1998.

Selengut, Charles (2003). *Sacred Fury: Understanding Religious Violence.* Lanham, Md.: AltaMira Press.

Velikonja, Mitja (1999). "Historical Roots of Slovenian Christoslavic Mythology." *Religion in Eastern Europe* 19(6): 1–5. Available through the Internet at: http://www.georgefox.edu/academics/undergrad/departments/socswk/ree/art_list99.html.

Walker, Tom (1998). "Hidden Horror Betrays the Butchers of Kosovo." *Times (London)*, 30 September 1998.

Wallace, Mark and Theophus Smith (eds.) (1994). *Curing Violence.* Sonoma, Calif.: Polebridge Press.

II

RELIGION AND MASS VIOLENCE: EMPIRICAL DATA AND CASE STUDIES

6

Religion and Genocide

Leonard B. Glick

INTRODUCTION

The people known as Apa Tanis live in a cluster of villages in the mountainous Subansiri district of northern Assam, just south of the Chinese border. Their world has changed dramatically over the past two or three decades, but until quite recently they were living much as their ancestors had lived for generations. The anthropologist Christoph von Fürer-Haimendorf conducted ethnographic studies among them in 1944–1945 and several times thereafter through 1978, and his accounts of their culture (1962) provide an appropriate point of entry into the subject. We begin with them not because traditional Apa Tani culture was exceptionally violent or otherwise distinctive in this regard, but simply because they may be taken as representative of innumerable peoples living in small-scale ("tribal") societies throughout the world.

The Apa Tanis are agriculturalists, dependent on their rice and other crops for subsistence. Each year in March, just prior to the planting season, they perform a communal ritual, called Mloko, when priests representing the various Apa Tani clans perform sacrifices and recite chants intended not just for their own group but for "the general welfare of the people." These events serve "to give ritual expression to the unity of the tribe," "to cement friendly relations across village boundaries and to counteract tensions and jealousies between the inhabitants of different villages" (1962: 141, 143). In short, applying terms familiar to our own experience we may say that the ritual affirms and maintains ethnic solidarity. To participate is to acknowledge that one experiences personal identity as an Apa Tani, and that one's individual welfare and that of the entire community are inseparable.

Consistent with this intense and virtually exclusive identification with their own tightly defined social world, traditional Apa Tanis defined morality solely in terms of that world. "All relations with members of other societies," we are told, stood "outside the sphere of morally prescribed action," and people were able to "conceive of right or wrong conduct" only in connection with the values and expectations of their own immediate social environment (1962: 150).

As one might expect, Apa Tani religion is congruent with this moral perspective. The local deities divide into three main categories, one of which comprises deities associated with warfare and raiding. In past years, when such activities were still an integral part of their lives, Apa Tani men invoked the blessing and protection of their deities before setting off on raids against ethnically alien neighbors (1962: 136; 1980: 169–71). The raids were not of a sort that would earn a rating on our scale of atrocities, but in the very small world of the Apa Tanis and their neighbors these were devastating assaults with significant numbers of casualties. Fürer-Haimendorf describes one raid conducted by a man he knew, a clan leader and "a balanced and reasonable person insofar as the conduct of affairs inside the Apa Tani valley was concerned." This man "once led a raid on the Dafla village of Dodum which resulted in the killing of thirteen men and the sale into slavery of seventeen captive women and children" (1962: 129).

LOCALIZED ROOTS AND THE ROOTS OF ETHNOCENTRISM

I have focused briefly on these aspects of traditional Apa Tani life not because they seem especially unusual or remarkable but for just the opposite reason: because they may tell us something fundamental about all human culture and behavior. The first and perhaps most obvious point is that for these people, as for people everywhere who adhere to their own local religions, the distinction between "religion" and "culture" is essentially meaningless. What we identify as religious beliefs and rituals are inseparable components of a total way of life, symbolic expressions of the recognition that a people, their land, and their culture are ineffably linked. I call religions of this kind "localized," because sacred places, sacred times and sacred beings must find realization in the lives of particular people living in particular locations. Conversion to a localized religion is possible only by becoming one of the people; obviously one could not convert to the Apa Tani religion without becoming part of that small community.

Ethnocentrism—broadly defined as preference for one's own sociocultural group and conviction that it is superior to all others—is an intrinsic feature of localized religions. As we have seen for the Apa Tanis, rituals have as one of their foremost (if unstated) purposes the affirmation of internal bonds and celebration of collective identity. By their very performance rituals enhance the conviction that the gods look upon one's own people with particular favor—and implicitly, that they care less or not at all about outsiders. To put this somewhat differently, the message of localized religions is love not for humanity but for one's own people exclusively. Caring only as they do for the welfare and survival of the local community, the deities are readily enlisted in battles against outsiders, and they are not given to making fine-tuned judgments about the fairness or morality of particular military decisions. In conflicts with alien peoples, whether defensive or offensive, it is entirely logical to expect that the deities, if properly supplicated, will bless the local community with a bloody victory. After all, why should they not be pleased by the destruction of those who serve strange gods?

Behavior of this sort is often called "warfare," but obviously it does not compare in scale or duration with what we ordinarily understand by that term; rather, we are talking about episodic raiding with what I shall call *proto-genocidal intent*. Typically, the goal in such raids is to destroy an entire village or settlement, the common intention being to kill everyone, perhaps excepting a few of the younger women and children who are carried off for incorporation into the home group. Actions of this sort have been recorded well into the twentieth century in parts of the Amazon, New Guinea, the Philippines and elsewhere. (See, e.g., Harner, 1972: 182–87, on the Jivaro of eastern Ecuador; Godelier, 1986: 103–4, on the Baruya of Papua New Guinea.)

But lest I be misunderstood to be trying to create an unflattering portrait only of people unenlightened by the world's great religions, let me now extend our perspective. It may come as a surprise to say that perhaps the most familiar of all localized religions is Judaism, but a moment's thought will reveal that this is the case. Conversion to Judaism is impossible, a contradiction in terms, without entry into Jewish ethnic identity, and the "Gentile" who converts to Judaism literally becomes a Jew. Judaism is the religion of the Jewish people; it celebrates their history, their identity, their covenantal relation with a God who is conceived to be at one and the same time the creator of the universe and the particular deity of a single people—a theological problem that need not detain us. The ancient Hebrews were distinguished from their contemporaries by their conviction that there was only one God; but like their contemporaries, all of whom adhered to localized religions of their own, they were certain that their God, ineffably alone though he might be, was attached to them, and only to them, in the kind of firm contractual relationship that one finds in localized religions everywhere. He was well prepared, of course, to support them in war as in peace, and indeed He looked with favor on what we may fairly call their proto-genocidal destructiveness. The Book of Joshua provides us with one of the earliest texts in which a deity quite plainly promotes the destruction of a people. As the Hebrews, under Joshua's leadership, undertake the conquest of Canaan, they massacre everyone who stands in their way. Here, in a representative passage, we learn what happened immediately after the complete destruction of Lachish and Eglon:

> From Eglon Joshua and all the Israelites advanced to Hebron and attacked it. They captured it and put its king to the sword together with every living thing in it and in all the villages; as at Eglon, he left no survivor, destroying tin and every living thing in it. Then Joshua and all the Israelites wheeled round towards Debir and attacked it. The captured the city with its king, and all its villages, put them to the sword and destroyed every living thing; they left no survivor. They dealt with Debir and its king as they had dealt with Hebron and with Libnah and its king. So Joshua massacred the population of the whole region—the hill-country, the Negeb, the Shephelah, the watersheds—and all their kings. He left no survivor, destroying everything that drew breath, as the Lord the God of Israel had commanded. Joshua carried the slaughter from Kadesh-barnea to Gaza, over the whole land of Goshen and as far as Gibeon. All these kings he captured at the same time, and their country with them, for the Lord the God of Israel fought for Israel. (Joshua 10:36–42; *New English Bible*; Old Testament, 1970: 301)

It is instructive (and distressing) to note that contemporary Jewish ultra-nationalists in Israel root their politics in the Book of Joshua and equate their territorial aspirations with the will of God. Here, for example, is Shlomo Aviner, a prominent theorist for the Gush Emunim ("Bloc of the Faithful") movement in a 1982 article entitled "The Moral Problem of Possessing the Land": "From the point of view of mankind's' humanistic morality we were in the wrong in (taking the land) from the Canaanites. There is only one catch. The command of God ordered us to be the people of the Land of Israel." Others have identified the Palestinians as "Canaanites" who are engaged in a "suicidal" struggle opposing God's own intentions; hence the Jewish people must be prepared to destroy them if they persist in pursuing their collective "death-wish" (Lustick, 1988: 76–78).

We can only speculate about how deeply such patterns of thought and behavior are embedded in the human psyche, but there is good reason to surmise that everything I have discussed so far—*ritual affirmation of communal unity and ethnocentric sentiments, belief in deities that belong exclusively to the home group, proto-genocidal attacks on neighboring groups identified as alien or "other," conviction that one's own deities approve of such attacks and promote their success*—have been intrinsic components of the human condition since the emergence of our species, late in the Pleistocene epoch, some fifty thousand or more years ago.

Judging from what has been learned in recent decades about human evolution, individuals in the earliest human societies must have been subjected to powerful selective pressures for intelligence, cooperativeness, effectiveness as communicators, and capacity for coordinated action and interaction with members of the home community. In line with this went pressures for the development of qualities conducive to group survival: people who were capable of understanding and promoting collectively created behavioral rules and expectations, shared values and goals, sentiments and beliefs congruent with communal survival. The unfit—those who were too unintelligent, aggressive, greedy, or otherwise unqualified to contribute to the collective welfare—must have been rigorously eliminated, either by murder, expulsion, or, at the very least, ostracism.

UNIVERSALIST RELIGIONS

I have characterized *localized* religions as those in which religious expression is deeply rooted in ethnic or communal identity, such that conversion to the religion without incorporation into the ethnic community is a logical impossibility. In contrast, the two religions that qualify least ambiguously for the label "world religions," Christianity and Islam, are manifestly *universalist*: first, because they explicitly reject ethnic limitations in their claims to having originated in revelations that utterly transcended all historical and geographical boundaries; second, because propagation of the faith and conversion of the unredeemed are among their definitive purposes. Adherence to such a belief system requires an inescapably paradoxical stance on ethnocentrism. On the one hand, ethnic identity is presumably of no real significance, since the universal truths of the religion transcend such worldly categories; on the other hand, possession of such truths not only justifies but indeed requires extraordinary effort to convert others—even though that may entail the undermining of their individual societies and cultures, and even though it may lead to their individual deaths.

Localized religions characteristically define moral behavior in terms of local norms, values, and purposes: moral behavior is that which sustains the group and promotes its welfare. Universalist religions appear on first acquaintance to present a loftier definition of morality, one that emphasizes adherence to relatively abstract standards of love and fellowship. In striking contrast to the pragmatic ethnocentrism of localized morality, universalist morality declares that human beings should be benignly disposed toward others, and that selfish or aggressive behavior is a manifestation of wickedness or evil. In effect, it endeavors to repress, perhaps even to deny, the undeniable: the sinister aspect of human nature that finds expression in readiness to oppress those who are defined as Other (cf. Charny, 1982: 188–91; Staub, 1989: 58–62). But the histories of Christianity and Islam are of course replete with evidence that those who profess universalist doctrines are ready and willing to engage in egregious crimes of genocidal or near-genocidal dimensions, not only against people whose religions differ radically from their own but also against anyone perceived as posing a challenge or threat to orthodoxy.

CHRISTIAN PERSECUTION OF THE JEWS

Nowhere has this been more evident than in the history of Christian persecution of the Jews. The subject has been examined over the years by so many writers that one hesitates to add yet more commentary, but the matter is too central to our subject to be overlooked. Obviously the problem is complex, but its foundations can be laid out in a few words. In the Christian worldview, Judaism is not just another erroneous religion, and Jews are not just another people in need of revelation and conversion. To the contrary, Judaism has always been *the* other religion, the one from which Christianity had to disengage itself, and against which Christianity had to define itself, in order to come into being and to endure. Likewise, Jews have always been *the* other people, those against whom Christians positioned themselves, and in contrast to whom they identified themselves. For Christianity was a revolutionary religion, a departure of immense proportions from the world of localized religions, a reinterpretation of Judaism so radical that the two could not possibly coexist peacefully as equally "correct" interpretations of human history and destiny. Most importantly, the Jewish Messiah, envisioned by Jews as a fully human descendant of King David who would restore them to the glory of the Davidic past, was wholly transformed into a divine redeemer who accepted suffering and death for the salvation of all humanity. And of course Jews were the descendants of the very people among whom the redeemer had appeared and preached, only to be scorned and condemned to death (Ruether, 1974; Davies, 1979).

Considering the magnitude of their crime, why had Jews been spared at all? Why had God not willed complete destruction as their only appropriate punishment? Pondering this question in his *City of God*, Augustine explained that although the Jews were spared, they were dispersed, not only to punish them but also so that they might fulfill their destined purpose as "testimony," or "witness," to Christian truth:

> They were dispersed all over the world—for indeed there is no part of the earth where they are not to be found—and thus by the evidence of their own Scriptures they bear witness for us that we have not fabricated the prophesies about Christ . . . for we recognize that it is in order to give this testimony, which, in spite of themselves, they supply for our benefit by their possession and preservation of those books, that they themselves are dispersed among all nations, in whatever direction the Christian Church spreads. . . . For if they lived with

that testimony of the Scriptures only in their own land, and not everywhere, the obvious result would be that the Church, which is everywhere, would not have them available among all nations as witness to the prophecies which were given beforehand concerning Christ. (Bettenson, 1972: 827–28)

Thus does Augustine explain why a people with a localized religion came to be located everywhere in the known world!

This statement provided foundations for papal policy toward Jews right up to our own time: they were to be restrained, as befitted their deplorably rebellious and intractable nature; but they were to be tolerated, in accordance with God's will that they be permitted to live as "testimony" until he would reveal to them the light of Christian truth and restore them to favor.

But subtle theological arguments and papal pronouncements were of no concern to the people who perpetrated crimes against Jews throughout the later medieval period, often in the name of Christian zeal. Beginning in the late eleventh century, the emergence of a new class of Christian merchants and steady increase in Christian clerical influence created an ideological climate that was increasingly unfavorable to Jews, and that led first to their relegation to the role of despised moneylenders, then to their being identified as embodiments of evil, literally the devil's own people, appropriate objects for extortion, persecution, and destruction (Chazan, 1973; Hsia, 1988; Jordan, 1989; Little, 1978, chap. 3; Parkes, 1976; Trachtenberg, 1943). The harbinger of all that was to follow came in 1096, when armies participating in the First Crusade made their way to the Rhineland cities of Speyer, Mainz, Worms, and Cologne, where they perpetrated a series of massacres that resonate in Jewish memory to this very day. Jonathan Riley-Smith, an authority on the crusades, challenges the customary view of these armies as "undisciplined hordes of peasants" under the command of incompetent or irresponsible leaders. To the contrary, he argues, they were well organized, well-equipped units commanded by "experienced knights" of noble birth who knew quite well what they intended to accomplish. Thus, he concludes, it is no longer possible "to adhere to the comforting view that the massacres were perpetrated by gangs of peasants" (Riley-Smith, 1984: 54–56; 1986: 51–52). Moreover, he continues, although crusading armies were chronically impoverished, and given to extortion and pillage whenever opportunity presented, this is not an adequate explanation for the Rhineland massacres; rather, the crusaders were motivated primarily by religious fervor. They wanted to avenge the Crucifixion: sometimes by forcibly converting Jews and killing those who resisted; more often, perhaps, by killing them outright. Many crusaders were probably unable even to distinguish between Moslems and Jews, "and could not understand why, if they were called upon to take up arms against the former, they should not also persecute the latter" (Riley-Smith, 1984: 67–69; 1986: 54–55).

The deepest irony in this story attaches to the relationship between Jews and bishops. In the most complete contemporary account of the massacres, the *Chronicle of Solomon bar Simson*, we read of Jews turning repeatedly to these foremost representatives of the Church, and we learn that these men consistently did their best to defend and protect Jews, even when this meant no inconsiderable danger for themselves (Eidelberg, 1977: 21–72; Chazan, 1987: 90–95). We envision Jews huddling terrified in cathedral courtyards, crowding for days on end in rooms of an archbishop's palace (surely a place they had never expected to see from the inside), racing for their lives into a cathedral sacristy filled with priestly robes and crucifixes. We see them bringing their wealth and valuables for safekeeping to a cathedral treasury, and on at least one occasion bringing even Torah scrolls to the bishop's palace to save them from the mob. The bishops themselves behave for the most part with commendable, even astonishing, sympathy and generosity. True, they often urge conversion as the only way out, but under benefit of hindsight it can be said that had more Jews been willing to go through the motions of conversion, they would have lived to return to Judaism within a year, for that was explicitly permitted by a decree of Emperor Henry IV. To put this in contemporary terms, considerations of social class and economic welfare seem to have outweighed religious differences when a bishop was acting in his role as a political authority. For in the final analysis most Jews were respectable people, industrious merchants who contributed substantially to the local economy; and despite all religious obligations, the bishop's overarching priority was to maintain "law and order" and to protect people of this kind—even Jews steeped in blindness. That they failed for the most part was not due to want of effort.

Although medieval popes were intent on degrading Judaism and Jews at every opportunity, they adhered nevertheless to the principle that Jews, provided they conducted themselves with appropriate humility, were not to be subjected to inordinate oppression or physical harm (Grayzel, 1966, 1989; Stow, 1988). Interestingly enough, it was not Jews but heretical Christians against whom medieval popes were prepared to direct violence of genocidal proportions, as witnessed by the Albigensian Crusade of the early thirteenth century, in which a French army, assembled in response to a call from Pope Innocent III, invaded the southern French territory of Languedoc to destroy the dualist heresy known as Catharism or Albigensianism. The historian Walter Wakefield explains why medieval Christians viewed heretics with such loathing:

> Heresy could not be a casual matter when religion was so vital an element in life. It had to be regarded as the most grievous sin and crime into which man could fall, for by denying the magistracy of the church which Christ had established, over which His vicar in Rome presided, the heretic became a traitor to God himself. Moreover, he imperiled others by his words and example,

medieval writers were fond of likening heresy to a loathsome and contagious disease. . . . So noxious was the crime that unless it were resolutely dealt with many other souls might be gravely endangered. Secular officials put heretics to death in the conviction that one faith in one church was the indispensable cement of Christian society. (Wakefield, 1974: 16–17)

The Cathars viewed the world as a battleground between a spiritual domain created by God and a material domain created by Satan. In defiance of the Nicene Creed they taught that Jesus did not share in God's divine nature but was His spiritual emissary, a spirit in the form of man who had never assumed a truly material body. The essential elements of Christian sacraments—communal wafers, wine, baptismal water—were nothing more than evil matter, they maintained; even the sacrament of marriage should be condemned, because it led to the entrapment of spiritual souls in material bodies subject to sin and wickedness.

Catharism found widespread acceptance in much of western Europe, but especially in northern Italy and southern France, where it had attracted adherents from every social class and encouraged widespread defections from the Church. The town of Albi was among the first places where Cathars were identified and condemned as heretics—hence the name Albigensians for adherents in Languedoc (*ibid.*, 30–33).

In 1208 a papal legate in southern France was murdered. Blame naturally fell on the Albigensians, and with this as the ostensible provocation, Innocent preached a crusade to liberate the region from heresy. In 1209 a vast army assembled at Lyon and made its way southward, killing heretics and faithful Christians alike; the record of brutality matches that for the Rhineland in 1096. The most dreadful massacre occurred in Béziers, a town near the Mediterranean coast southwest of Montpellier. Having forced their way into the town, the troops "cut the inhabitants down mercilessly." A local church, crowded with terrified townspeople (many no doubt with no connection to Catharism) was burned, as were many other buildings, all this accompanied by the usual pillage. A gratified archbishop, one of the crusade leaders, reported (probably with exaggeration) that his army had killed some 15,000 people, "showing mercy neither to order nor age nor sex," and characterized the victory as "miraculous." The miracle had its desired effect: "A shock of horror," says Wakefield, "spread across Languedoc," and eventually Catharism disappeared as a challenge to the Church (*ibid.*, 102).

CHRISTIANS IN THE NEW WORLD

Since the onset of the colonial era in the fifteenth century, missionizing has been so intimately connected with colonizing that one cannot readily separate their adverse effects on non-European peoples—and at times those effects have reached proportions that qualify readily as genocidal. Perhaps the grimmest example is the Spanish invasion of Mexico, in which colonists espousing Christian sentiments but motivated primarily by lust for gold were accompanied by missionary friars whose foremost purpose was to win savage souls for Christ. To the friars, says the historian Charles Gibson,

> America offered a larger and more challenging stage than Europe. The non-Christian peoples of America were not simply to be converted. They were to be civilized, taught, humanized, purified, and reformed. To the humanist friars, America appeared as Christian obligation writ large. Its vast populations were to be set on new paths of Christian virtue and godliness. (Gibson, 1966: 71–71)

That most of these missionaries had essentially benign intentions can hardly be doubted, but the harsh reality was that an inescapable corollary of their efforts was relentless destruction of Mexican Indian religions and cultures—a process that went hand in hand with the more explicitly oppressive practices of the colonists. Conversion often meant little more than the most superficial formalities—two Franciscan friars are said to have baptized 15,000 Indians in one day (Hanke, 1970: 20)—but even that was enough to promote the cultural dissolution that was already under way. In the eyes of the missionaries Indians were either childlike innocents or degenerate savages, but in either case it was axiomatic that their only hope for eternal life lay in Christian enlightenment and conversion. Unfortunately for the vast majority of Indians, eternal life was the only kind remaining to them. Massive disease epidemics, exhaustion from forced labor and other forms of egregious mistreatment, despair over the disappearance of traditional community life and culture—all these combined to produce a demographic decline of awesome proportions: from an original native Mesoamerican population of some twenty-five million to about one and one-half million by 1650 (Wachtel, 1984: 212–13; Wolf, 1982: 134).

Among the Spanish clergy were some who questioned the legitimacy of forcefully subduing people for the ostensible purpose of bringing them into the Christian fold. The outstanding spokesman in this regard was Bartolomé de las Casas (1474–1566), the Dominican friar whose *History of the Indies*, based on his own observations and reflections, is renowned as one of the earliest indictments of colonial oppression. In 1550 Las Casas participated in an event that may be said to have epitomized both aspects of the relationship between religion and genocide in the Americas: on the one hand, an appeal to human decency as the foundation of virtue; on the other, insistence that the demands of revealed religious truth override all other considerations. The occasion was a public disputation staged in Valladolid, Spain, before a council of theologians and public officials. The contestants were Las Casas and Juan Ginés de Sepúlveda (1490–1573), a prominent humanist scholar whose reputation rested in particular on a distinguished translation of Aristotle's *Politics*. The two men were to address their arguments to a single question: "Is it lawful for the king of Spain to wage war on the Indians before preaching the faith to them in order to subject them to his rule, so that afterwards they may be more easily instructed in the faith?" Sepúlveda defended the affirmative, grounding his position in the Aristotelian doctrine of natural slaver (*Politics*, book 1, chapter 5), and arguing that subjugation of Indians was both necessary and just: necessary in order to spread the Christian faith, and just because Indians were a sinful and idolatrous people. Las Casas replied that, to the contrary, warfare and subjugation were "iniquitous, and contrary to our Christian religion," and argued that nothing justified decimation of a people and complete destruction of their way of life (Hanke, 1970: 38–41 and *passim*). Not surprisingly, no clear decision or resolution emerged from the learned council members; nor, we may safely assume, did ordinary Spanish colonists or missionaries much concern themselves with the intricacies of philosophical reasoning over the justice or injustice of their way of life. In effect, Spanish colonialism in the Americas had arisen on foundations of pious religiosity coupled with unbridled greed, and their ultimate product was genocide.

THE ARMENIAN GENOCIDE

But Christians have certainly not been the only perpetrators of genocide, and indeed they themselves have been subject to severe oppression. The suffering of early Christians under Roman persecution is common knowledge. The most infamous case in modern times is undoubtedly the Armenian genocide of 1915–1917, an atrocity that only recently has begun to receive the attention it deserves (Hovannisian, 1967, 1986; Housepian, 1966; Charny, 1984; Walker, 1987; Lang and Walker, 1987; Institut für Armenische Fragen, 1987; Kuper, 1981). Since the subject has been covered authoritatively in the first volume of this series (Hovannisian, 1988), it will not be considered in detail here, but it merits our attention for several reasons. First, the sheer magnitude and extensiveness of the mass murder was exceeded in our time only by the destruction of the Jews of Europe. Second, it was initiated not by religious fanatics or narrowly educated reactionaries, but by the so-called Young Turks, whose emergence to power in 1908–1909 might have been expected to herald a new era of acceptance and integration for the beleaguered Armenian minority. Ironically, the result was precisely the opposite. "One of the most unanticipated and for the Armenians most tragic developments in modern history," observes Richard Hovannisian, "was the process from 1908 to 1914 in which the seemingly liberal, egalitarian Young Turks became transformed into xenophobic nationalists bent on creating a new order and eliminating the Armenian Question by eliminating the Armenian people" (1988: 94).

Third, it is not without significance that the Armenians, like the Jews of Europe, the Chinese of Southeast Asia, the Tamil of Sri Lanka, and to some extend the Ibo of Nigeria, differed not only religiously from the surrounding population but also occupationally, being prominent as merchants, shopkeepers, and office workers in predominantly agricultural societies (Dadrian, 1975; Tambiah, 1986: 38; Kuper, 1981: 74–75).

Should the Armenian genocide be attributed primarily to religiously based antagonism, or would it be more accurate to say that the Christian identity of the victims was incidental to their situation? The answer returns us to the propositions on religion, culture and identity introduced at the beginning of this paper. No matter what their personal religious convictions may have been, the Turkish perpetrators looked upon Islam as an integral element in their collective identity; likewise, Christianity was an equally definitive element in the identity of their victims, who could have "become Turks" (if ever) only by converting to Islam. It is instructive to note that apologists for the Turks cited the need for "Turkification and Moslemization" as an essential precondition for establishment of a modern republic (Hovannisian, 1986: 124). Thus, the "Armenian question" was an irreducible compound of ethnic and religious identity; and the Armenian genocide was an effort—successful, in the final analysis—to purge a people whose crime was ethnic and religious distinctiveness.

NEAR-GENOCIDAL ETHNIC-RELIGIOUS CONFLICTS

During the past several decades, religious differences have been salient in a number of ethnic conflicts that have reached near-genocidal dimensions. In some cases the antagonists, although at times unequally matched, generated enough violence on each side to suggest that we should characterize the conflicts as ethnic warfare but not genocide. I have in mind such situations as the civil war in Sudan between Islamic Arabs living mainly in the northern part of the country and black Africans in the southern provinces who adhere either to traditional religions or to Christianity (Johnson, 1988; Young, 1976: 489–501); the Algerian War, which pitted an indigenous Muslim population against French Christian colonial settlers (Horne, 1977); the Catholic-Protestant conflict in Northern Ireland and the Chinese campaign against Tibetan Buddhist monasteries and monks. (The last named is perhaps the most subject to debate about its nature and severity; see especially Mullin and Wangyai, 1983.)

These are all "plural societies," that is, societies characterized not just by the presence of diverse ethnic groups but by "persistent and pervasive cleavages," often in conditions of social-economic stratification and political inequality (Kuper, 1981: 57–59); thus, the ethnic-religious identities of the contestants have been inseparable in effect from the political and economic contexts of their conflicts.

The most dramatic of such situations in recent times, and almost certainly the most destructive of human life and property, were the violent conflicts associated first with the separation of Pakistan from India and later with the separation of Bangladesh from Pakistan. In 1947, when independence for India and Pakistan was accompanied by massive ethnic warfare, the slaughter and destruction were especially severe in the Punjab, the northwestern province of India that was home not only to a thoroughly mixed population of Hindus and Moslems but also to millions of Sikhs, for whom partition of the region into Indian and Pakistani segments meant political dismemberment of their homeland. Hindus and Sikhs were pitted against Muslims in vicious fighting that reached levels of unspeakable brutality on both sides. The intentions of the combatants clearly qualify as genocidal, but they were well enough matched in numbers and destructive capacity to inflict immense suffering in both directions (Kuper, 1981: 63–68; Collins and Lapierre, 1975, chapter 13).

This was not the case in 1971, when East Pakistan seceded from West Pakistan and became Bangladesh; there the contestants were not equally matched, and it was only the intervention of the Indian army that enabled the Bengalis to gain their independence. East Pakistan had a 1970 population of about seventy-five million, the great majority of whom were Muslims; but the population included some eleven million Hindus and more than a million Muslim immigrants from India known at Biharis. The independence movement created complex alignments that do not correlate well with religious groupings. The response by West Pakistan was a sickeningly brutal military reprisal that caused probably two million or more deaths and left the country in a shambles. The murder, torture, and rapine were not limited to any segment of the Bengali population, and the fact that their victims were fellow Muslims seems to have made no difference to Pakistani troops on the rampage. There is evidence, however, that Hindus suffered disproportionately, having been regularly singled out by West Pakistanis and at times assaulted also by Bengali Muslims and Biharis (Mascarenhas, 1971: 116–17). Bengali militants, probably both Muslim and Hindu, retaliated when they could against West Pakistanis, and against Biharis who were accused of collaborating with the invaders, in crimes of essentially equal cruelty (Aziz, 1974; Levak, 1974: 219), but the genocidal balance sheet appears to be tilted heavily in the other directions (Kuper, 1981: 76–80; 1988: 166; Mascarenhas, 1971, chapter 9).

More recently in Bangladesh, Muslim Bengalis have been responsible for oppression of near-genocidal dimensions perpetrated against predominantly Buddhist hill-dwelling peoples of the Chittagong district, in the isolated southeastern corner of the country. These people differ from the rest of the population not only in religion; they resemble Burmese physically and possess distinctive cultures and languages with Southeast Asian affinities. Those who are not Buddhist are mostly either Hindu or Christian, or adhere to their own localized religions. Bengalis have been moving into their region in ever-greater numbers for the past several decades; by 1980 immigrants numbered about 225,000 in a total population of 815,000, and they were increasingly disposed to force their way into territory occupied by the hill peoples. A local resistance movement formed in the 1970s, and the Bangladesh government responded with military intervention, mass arrests, destruction of villages and forced resettlements. In March 1980, soon after a conflict with resistance fighters in which some soldiers were killed, 200 to 300 Chittagong people were massacred by troops joined by armed Bengali civilians. Following an initial assault, the violence spread: people were forcibly converted to Islam; Buddhist temples were attacked, "monks and nuns were mercilessly killed or wounded," and villages were burned (Anti-Slavery Society, 1984: 75). Further attacks involving even worse massacres, rape, torture, and destruction took place repeatedly during the 1980s (Amnesty International, 1986; Anti-Slavery Society, 1984: 77); and the situation has continued to deteriorate into what one writer has called a "programme of systematic extermination of indigenous nationalities of the Chittagong Hill Tracts because they are ethnically, religiously, and culturally different from the Muslim Bengalis" (cited in Kuper, 1988: 166).

An especially grim situation has also developed during the past decade in Sri Lanka, where a Tamil independence movement, accompanied by considerable violence, has evoked severe retaliation by the Sinhalese majority. Murderous riots and vendetta killings have almost destroyed the frail social fabric of a nation that had experienced premonitory outbreaks of ethnic conflict ever since independence. The Tamils are largely Hindu; the Sinhalese are Theravada Buddhists, and the more militant among them declare this to be central to their personal identity but to Sri Lankan national identity. In a penetrating study of the historical background and contemporary socioeconomic context of the conflict, the anthropologist Stanley Tambiah points out that religious rituals and cults derived from syncretic blending of Buddhist and Hindu elements are not gaining great popularity as expressions of doctrinaire Sinhalese Buddhist nationalism that is militantly anti-Tamil and anti-Hindu (1986: 57–63). Ironically, forms of religious expression that owe their existence to cultural pluralism are not being invoked in support of monocultural nationalism.

CLERGY AND GENOCIDE:
CHRISTIAN CLERGY AND THE HOLOCAUST

We have reviewed a number of situations in which atrocities of genocidal proportions were generated, at least in part, by religious motives or religiously sanctioned antagonism. But have religious leaders, particularly of the universalist religions, demonstrated any capacity beyond the ordinary to oppose actions leading toward genocide? Have they pointed the way toward a pan-human consciousness that might counteract parochialism, chauvinism, and ethnic antagonism?

The answer seems to be that with rather few exceptions they have not. Nor should that surprise us. People who achieve positions of religious leadership may be precisely those who are certain that they possess absolute Truth. That such individuals can be exceedingly dangerous is evident when one considers the actions of contemporary religious fundamentalists in such places as Iran, Israel, and Northern Ireland.

But most religious leaders are not "true believers" of the sort who are prepared to sweep away all obstacles from the path to redemption; they are intelligent people who want orderly, purposeful lives for themselves and for others. How do such individuals respond when confronted with prospects of imminent destruction, not of their own people but of another? Are they able to transcend religious parochialism? Do they take a stand on behalf of those who differ, or do they follow the more expedient path of looking out for one's own and accommodating to the world as it is?

Probably the best-documented answers to such questions are to be found in the many studies of the responses of German clergymen, Protestant and Catholic, to the persecution and massacre of the Jews of Europe between 1933 and 1945. The Holocaust was indisputably the pre-eminent genocide of our time, but the subject has already been accorded detailed consideration in the first volume of this series (Berger, 1988). Here we shall consider only studies of how the clergy responded to Nazi persecution of German Jews in the 1930s and later to information that massacres of genocidal proportions were probably taking place in Eastern Europe. (See especially Conway, 1968, 1980; Ericksen, 1985; Gutteridge, 1976; Helmreich, 1979; Kulka and Mendes-Flohr, 1987; Lewy, 1964; Littell and Locke, 1974; Zahn, 1962; Zerner, 1983.) Their conclusions are quite consistent: although a significant minority of German clergymen resisted what they perceived as a threat to fundamental Christian values, most adopted attitudes ranging from passive acceptance (characteristic of the great majority) to enthusiastic endorsement of the Nazi regime and its policies, including aggressive chauvinism and expansionism. Moreover, clerical resistance and protests, such as they were, focused almost entirely in issues connected directly with the welfare and survival of the churches, not the persecution of Jews or other victims of the Nazi regime.

Most instructive in this regard was their response to the so-called Aryan Clause, issued by a Protestant synod in Berlin, in September 1933, ordering that pastors of Jewish descent, or married to Jewish women, be dismissed: a number of clergymen protested, although most adopted the more prudent course of saying nothing. In addition, many clergymen and Christian laity made an effort, sometimes at serious risk to themselves, to assist and encourage "non-Aryan" converts to Christianity, acting in the conviction that faith was the sole determinant of status as a Christian; but of course, as they saw it they were supporting Christians, not Jews.

When it came to persecution of Jews as such, far fewer clergy—only a deservedly remembered handful—spoke out, and even they sometimes qualified their statements with references to Jews as people burdened with an inescapable curse. A statement issued in 1936 by the Bishop of Baden was representative of a view expressed time and again, by Protestants and Catholics alike:

> When the Jews crucified Jesus, they crucified themselves, their revelation and their history. Thus the curse came upon them. Since then that curse works itself out from one generation to another. This people has, therefore, become a fearful and divinely ordained scourge for all nations, leading to hatred and persecution. (Gutteridge, 1976: 71)

Even the two pastors most often cited as opponents of Nazism, Dietrich Bonhoeffer and Martin Niemöller, both accepted publicly the dictum that the Jews were destined to suffer as punishment for the Crucifixion (Zerner, 1983: 63–64; Gutteridge, 1976: 103–4).

Perhaps the most outspoken and least ambivalent public statement was issued in October 1943 by a Prussian synod of liberal Protestant pastors. Taking note of all victims of the regime, including "the people of Israel," the synod took a firm (if obviously belated) stand against mass murder: "Concepts such as 'elimination,' 'liquidation,' and 'unworthy life' are not known in the divine order. Extermination of people solely because they are related to a criminal, or old or mentally disturbed, or because they belong to an alien race, is not a sword granted by God to be wielded by the state" (Translation modified from Helmreich, 1979: 336 and Bracher, 1970: 385).

Such statements were the exception, and we know how much effect they had. But in fairness to those clergymen who might have resisted had they dared, we must remember that overt resistance to a fascist dictatorship meant, at best, exposure to ostracism and public condemnation, at worst, incarceration in a concentration camp or assassination. The well-documented life of Dietrich Bonhoeffer is a case in point (Bethge, 1970), as is the fate of the brave priest Bernard Lichtenberg, who prayed publicly in Berlin for the Jews (Hilberg, 1961: 299–300; Lewy, 1964: 293). In November 1938, a Lutheran pastor, Julius von Jan, preached a sermon condemning the infamous *Kristallnacht* attacks on Jews; he was beaten nearly to death by a mob, then carried off to prison (Conway, 1968: 375–76). As the historian Karl Dietrich Bracher has observed, "the decision to resist was reached in terrible loneliness in the midst of a mass society," and retrospective judgments of the German clergy (as of all ordinary Germans) should be tempered with appreciation of the price of resistance (1970: 379). One may feel less charitably disposed, however, when it is remembered that many clergymen moved well beyond necessity in expressing support for the Nazi regime and its policies.

Although the Catholic clergy, generally speaking, were somewhat less overtly chauvinistic, their overall record was essentially like that of their Protestant counterparts. Guenter Lewy's definitive study of the subject shows that although Catholic priests also tried to protect converts, they paralleled the Protestant clergy in passive acquiescence, taking no significant stand on behalf of Jews (1964, chapter 10). Gordon Zahn supports this conclusion in his study of the Catholic clergy: "at no time was the individual German Catholic led to believe that the regime was an evil unworthy of his support" (1962: 73). Commenting specifically on the Catholic clergy's response to the realization that persecution had reached the stage of genocide, Lewy says:

> The word that would have forbidden the faithful, on pain of excommunication, to go on participating in the massacre of the Jews was never spoken. And so Catholics went on participating conscientiously, along with other Germans. (1964: 293)

Lewy and others have pointed to instructive contrasts with France, Italy, Belgium, Holland, and elsewhere in Western Europe, where many Christian clergy hid and otherwise assisted Jews on a scale quite beyond anything reported for Germany. It would appear that most clergy everywhere followed in the path of general public sentiment and were not significantly affected one way or the other by their religious professions; when it came to the difficult decisions, being German or French mattered more than being Christian (Lewy, 1964: 293–94; Marrus and Paxton, 1981: 270–79; Zuccotti, 1987: 207–17).

With regard to the much-discussed question of papal actions during the Holocaust, it seems evident that although the two popes, Pius XI (1922–1939) and Pius XII (1939–1958) adhered to the traditional papal principle that Jews were not to be physically oppressed, they followed the path of political expediency, recognizing that some 40 percent of the German population was Catholic and not wanting to risk placing them in danger with the Nazi regime. Moreover, Hitler's touted determination to destroy Bolshevism resonated with the Church's deepest political aspirations. Thus, Pius XI's 1936 encyclical *Mit brennender Sorge* (With Profound Concern) rejected racist ideology as contrary to Christian doctrine but said nothing about anti-Semitism as such and did not mention the persecution of Jews. And when the Germans evacuated the Jews of Rome in October 1943, obviously for the purpose of dispatching them to extermination centers, Pius XII said nothing publicly, although he appears to have given tacit approval to Italian priests and nuns who assisted Jews (Lewy, 1964: 295–308; Zuccotti, 1987: 128–35).

The conduct of Christian clergy and their congregations in the United States is tersely summed up by David Wyman in his study of American responses to the Holocaust: "At the heart of Christianity is the commitment to help the helpless. Yet, for the most part, America's Christian churches looked away while the European Jews perished" (1984: 320). Wyman provides a few pages of well-documented commentary on the indifference and ineffectiveness of all but a handful of Christian clergy during the critical years. A "Day of Compassion" sponsored in May 1943 by the Federal Council of Churches (with substantial Jewish support) was supposed to raise awareness through appropriate sermons and services, but despite heavy publicity very few churches paid any attention. "Perhaps more significant in retrospect than the slight impact of the "Day of Compassion," observes Wyman, "is the fact that this modest effort turned out to be the Christian church's main attempt during the entire war to arouse an American response to the Holocaust. And even it came only after months of prodding by Jewish friends of the Federal Council's leaders" (*ibid.*, 102).

Writing after the war, Martin Niemöller's brother Wilhelm, "an assiduous apologist in nearly all respects" for the liberal wing of German Protestantism, passed judgment on his church in terms that might well have been extended to others, and we may leave the final word on this subject to him:

> The picture as a whole is dismal. One of the most glorious opportunities to make proof of Christian profession through Christian action was, taken as a whole, missed and unexercised. (Gutteridge, 1976: 167)

CONCLUSION

Western thought has been shaped by Christianity, a universalist religion that has always aimed to transcend ethnic or national boundaries; Christianity is understood to be a revelation that can be adopted by any people anywhere. Hence, we are inclined to distinguish "religion" from the totality implied by such terms as culture and ethnicity. But for many people, including Christians, religious beliefs and practices are an integral element of identity and experience, and every ethnic group—with all the bonds of shared history, physical type, language, and values that the term entails—possesses a religion as an essential feature of its identity. In a sense, then, it is something of a pointless academic exercise to try to disentangle religious motives and sanctions from the totality of considerations that may impel people of one ethnic group to perpetrate genocidal crimes against another. Did Turks massacre Armenians solely for "religious" reasons? Did the armies of West Pakistan clearly distinguish between Bengali Hindus and Muslims? I have suggested that we face here a complex problem, centering, unfortunately, on what appear to be universal human dispositions, rooted in our evolutionary heritage, to dislike, to mistrust, and, with relatively little provocation, to attack people perceived to differ from one's own reference group; and more often than not, religious differences are part of a larger picture.

If we accept this to be the case, it comes as no surprise and no disappointment to learn that religious leaders, whether they be shamans, priests, pastors, mullahs, or rabbis, appear on the average to demonstrate neither more nor less compassion for aliens than anyone else. If a few men and women of strong religious faith and moral fiber have indeed taken a stand against genocidal oppression, so have an equal number of people with no particular attachment to religious or "spiritual" concerns. It appears that if we are ever to reach the point where genocidal massacres will have become a thing of the past, it will not be owing to religions: they are part of the problem.

BIBLIOGRAPHY

Alexander, Richard D. (1979). *Darwinism and Human Affairs.* Seattle and London: University of Washington Press.
Almog, Shmuel (ed.) (1988). *Antisemitism through the Ages.* Oxford and London: Pergamon Press.
Anti-Slavery Society (1984). London.
Aristotle (2009). *Politics.* Oxford: Oxford University Press.
Augustine (1972). *The City of God against the Pagans.* Hammondsworth: Penguin.
Aziz, Qutubuddin (1974). *Blood and Tears.* Karachi: United Press of Pakistan.
Barnett, Victoria (1992). *For the Soul of the People: Protestant Protest against Hitler.* London and New York: Oxford University Press.
Berger, Alan L. (ed.) (1988). *Genocide: The Critical Bibliographic Review.* New York: Facts on File.
Bettenson, Henry (ed.) (1972). *Documents of the Catholic Church.* Oxford: Oxford University Press.
Bethell, Leslie (ed.) (1984). *The Cambridge History of Latin America.* Cambridge and New York: Cambridge University Press.
Bethge, Eberhard (1970). *Dietrich Bonhoeffer: Man of Vision, Man of Courage.* New York and Evanston: Harper & Row.
Bracher, Karl Dietrich (1970). *The German Dictatorship.* New York: Praeger.
Braham, Rudolph H. (ed.) (1983). *Perspectives on the Holocaust.* Boston and The Hague: Kluwer-Nijhoff.

Chadhuri, Kalyan (1972). *Genocide in Bangladesh.* Bombay: Orient Longman.

Charny, Israel W. (1982). *How Can We Commit the Unthinkable? Genocide, The Human Cancer.* Boulder, Colo.: Westview Press.

—— (1988). *Genocide: A Critical Bibliographic Review.* London: Mansell Publishing Co.

—— (1991). *Genocide: A Critical Bibliographic Review,* Volume 2. London: Mansell Publishing Co.

—— (ed.) (1984). *Toward the Understanding and Prevention of Genocide.* Boulder, Colo.: Westview Press.

Chazan, Robert (1973). *Medieval Jewry in Northern France: A Political and Social History.* Baltimore: Johns Hopkins University Press.

—— (1987). *European Jewry and the First Crusade.* Berkeley and Los Angeles: University of California Press.

Cochrane, Arthur C. (1962). *The Church's Confession under Hitler.* Philadelphia: Westminster Press.

Collins, Larry, and Dominique Lapierre (1975). *Freedom at Midnight.* New York: Simon and Schuster.

Conway, John S. (1968). *The Nazi Persecution of the Churches, 1933–1945.* New York: Basic Books.

Dadrian, Vahakn N. (1975). "Common Features of the Armenian and Jewish Cases of Genocide," in Drapkin, Israel, ed., *Victimology: A New Focus/Volume 4: Violence and Its Victims* (Lexington: D.C. Heath), 99–120.

Davies, Alan (ed.) (1979). *Anti-Semitism and the Foundations of Christianity.* New York: Paulist Press.

Drapkin, Israel, and Emilio Viano (eds.) (1975). *Victimology: A New Focus.* Lexington: D. C. Heath.

Eibl-Eibesfeldt, Irenäus (1979). *The Biology of Peace and War.* New York: Viking Press.

Eidelberg, Shlomo (ed.) (1977). *The Jews and the Crusaders: The Hebrew Chronicles of the First and Second Crusades.* Madison: University of Wisconsin Press.

Eriksen, Robert P. (1985). *Theologians under Hitler: Gerhard Kittel, Paul Althaus, and Emmanuel Hirsch.* New Haven, Conn. and London: Yale University Press.

Falconi, Carlos (1970). *The Silence of Pius XII.* London: Faber and Faber; and New York: Little, Brown.

Faulhaber, Michael (1934). *Judaism, Christianity, and Germany.* New York: Macmillan.

Fein, Helen (1979). *Accounting for Genocide: National Responses and Victimization During the Holocaust.* New York: Free Press.

Fleischner, Eva (ed.) (1977). *Auschwitz: Beginning of a New Era? Reflections on the Holocaust.* New York: Ktav.

Friedlander, Henry, and Sybil Milton (eds.) (1980). *The Holocaust: Ideology, Bureaucracy, and Genocide.* Millwood: Kraus International Publications.

Friedlander, Saul (1966). *Pius XII and the Third Reich: A Documentation.* New York: Knopf.

Friedman, Philip (1978). *Their Brothers' Keepers.* New York: Holocaust Library.

Fürer-Haimendorf, Christoph von (1962). *The Apa Tanis and Their Neighbors.* London: Routledge and Keegan Paul; and New York: Free Press of Glencoe.

Gallin, Mary Alice (1961). *German Resistance to Hitler: Ethical and Religious Factors.* Washington, D.C.: Catholic University of America Press.

Gibson, Charles (1966). *Spain in America.* New York: Harper & Row.

Godelier, Maurice (1986). *The Making of Great Men: Male Domination and Power among the New Guinea Baruya.* Cambridge and New York: Cambridge University Press.

Grayzel, Solomon (1966). *A History of the Jews.* Philadelphia: Jewish Publication Society of America.

—— (1989). *The Church and the Jews in the XIIIth Century, Volume II: 1254–1314.* New York: Hermon Press.

Gutman, Yisrael, and Efraim Zuroff (eds.) (1977). *Rescue Attempts during the Holocaust.* Jerusalem: Yad Vashem.

Gutteridge, Richard (1976). *Open Thy Mouth for the Dumb! The German Evangelical Church and the Jews.* Oxford: Blackwell; and New York: Barnes and Noble.

Haas, Peter J. (1988). *Morality after Auschwitz: The Radical Challenge of the Nazi Ethic.* Philadelphia: Fortress Press.

Hallie, Philip P. (1979). *Lest Innocent Blood Be Shed.* New York: Harper & Row.

Hanke, Lewis (1959). *Aristotle and the American Indians: A Study of Race Prejudice in the Modern World.* Bloomington: Indiana University Press.

—— (1970). *Tears of the Indians: Includes the Life of Las Casas by Sir Arthur Helps.* New York: John Lilburne.

Harner, Michael J. (1972). *The Jivaro: People of the Sacred Waterfalls.* Garden City, N.J.: Natural History Press.

Helmreich, Ernst Christian (1979). *The German Churches under Hitler: Background, Struggle, and Epilogue.* Detroit, Mich.: Wayne State University Press.

Hilberg, Raul (1961). *The Destruction of the European Jews.* Chicago: Quadrangle.

Horne, Alistair (1977). *A Savage War of Peace: Algeria, 1954–1962.* London: Macmillan; and Hammondsworth: Penguin.

Housepian, Marjorie (1966). *Smyrna 1922: The Destruction of a City.* New York: Farber and Farber.

Hovannisian, Richard G. (1967). *Armenia on the Road to Independence.* Berkeley and Los Angeles: University of California Press.

—— (ed.) (1988). *The Armenian Genocide in Perspective.* New Brunswick, N.J.: Transaction Books.

Hsia, R. Po-chia (1988). *The Myth of Ritual Murder: Jews and Magic in Reformation Germany.* New Haven, Conn. and London: Yale University Press.

Institut für Armenische Fragen (1987). *The Armenian Genocide: Collected Documents about the Armenian Genocide.* 3 Volumes. Munich: Institut für Armenische Fragen.

Johnson, Douglas H. (ed.) (1988). *Vernacular Christianity: Essays in the Social Anthropology of Religion.* New York: Lillian Barber Press.

Jordan, William Chester (1989). *The French Monarchy and the Jews: From Philip Augustus to the Last Carpetians.* Philadelphia: University of Pennsylvania Press.

Kershaw, Ian (1987). *The "Hitler Myth": Image and Reality in the Third Reich.* Oxford and New York: Oxford University Press.

Koonz, Claudia (1987). *Mothers in the Fatherland: Women, the Family, and Nazi Politics.* New York: St. Martin's Press.

Kukla, Otto Dov, and Paul R. Mendes-Flohr (eds.) (1987). *Judaism and Christianity under the Impact of National Socialism*. Jerusalem: Historical Society of Israel.

Kuper, Leo (1981). *Genocide: Its Political Use in the Twentieth Century*. New Haven, Conn. and London: Yale University Press.

——— (1988). *Race, Class, and Power*. New York: Aldine Publishing Company.

Lang, Berel (1990). *Act and Idea in the Nazi Genocide*. Chicago and London: University of Chicago Press.

Lang, David Marshall, and Christopher J. Walker. (1987). *The Armenians*. London: Minority Rights Group.

Levak, Albert E. (1974). "Provincial Conflict and Nation Building in Pakistan," in Wendell Bell and Walter E. Freeman, eds., *Ethnicity and Nation Building: Comparative, International, and Historical Perspectives* (Beverly Hills: Sage).

Lewy, Guenter (1964). *The Catholic Church and Nazi Germany*. New York: McGraw-Hill.

Lifton, Robert J. (1986). *The Nazi Doctors: Medical Killing and the Psychology of Genocide*. New York: Basic Books.

Littell, Franklin H., and Hubert G. Locke (eds.) (1974). *The German Church Struggle and the Holocaust*. Detroit, Mich.: Wayne State University Press.

Little, Lester (1978). *Religious Poverty and the Profit Economy in Medieval Europe*. Ithaca, N.Y.: Cornell University Press.

Lustick, Ian S. (1988). *For the Land and the Lord: Jewish Fundamentalism in Israel*. New York: Council on Foreign Relations.

Marrus, Michael R., and Robert O. Paxton (1981). *Vichy France and the Jews*. New York: Basic Books.

Mascarenhas, Anthony (1971). *The Rape of Bangladesh*. Delhi: Vikas Publications.

Matheson, Peter (1981). *The Third Reich and the Christian Churches*. Grand Rapids, Mich.: William B. Eerdmans.

Mullin, Chris, and Phuntsog Wangyai (1983) *The Tibetans*. London: Minority Rights Group.

Parkes, James (1976). *The Jew in the Medieval Community*. New York: Hermon Press.

Poliakov, Leon (1979). *Harvest of Hate: The Nazi Program for the Destruction of the Jews of Europe*. New York: Holocaust Library.

Reynolds, Vernon, et al. (eds.) (1986). *The Sociobiology of Ethnocentrism: Evolutionary Dimensions of Xenophobia, Discrimination, Racism, and Nationalism*. London: Groom Helm; and Athens: University of Georgia Press.

Riley-Smith, Jonathan (1984). *The First Crusade and the Idea of Crusading*. London: Athlone.

——— (1986). *The First Crusade and the Idea of Crusading*. Philadelphia: University of Pennsylvania Press.

Ross, Robert (1980). *So It Was True: The American Protestant Press and the Nazi Persecution of the Jews*. Minneapolis: University of Minnesota Press.

Rubenstein, Richard L., and John K. Roth (1987). *Approaches to Auschwitz: The Holocaust and Its Legacy*. Atlanta, Ga.: John Knox Press.

Ruether, Rosemary (1974). *Faith and Fratricide: The Theological Roots of Anti-Semitism*. New York: Seabury Press.

Sereny, Gita (1974). *Into That Darkness: From Mercy Killing to Mass Murder*. London: Andre Deutsch.

Snoek, Johan M. (1970). *The Grey Book: A Collection of Protests against Anti-Semitism and the Persecution of the Jews Issued by Non-Roman Catholic Churches and Church Leaders during Hitler's Rule.* New York: Humanities Press.

Staub, Ervin (1989). *The Roots of Evil: The Origins of Genocide and Other Group Violence.* Cambridge and New York: Cambridge University Press.

Stow, Kenneth (ed.) (1989). *Solomon Grayzel: The Church and the Jews in the Thirteenth Century.* Detroit: Wayne State University Press.

Suhrke, Astri, and Leila G. Noble (eds.) (1977). *Ethic Conflict in International Relations.* New York and London: Praeger.

Tal, Uriel (1975). *Christians and Jews in Germany: Religion, Politics, and Ideology in the Second Reich, 1870–1914.* Ithaca, N.Y. and London: Cornell University Press.

Tambiah, S. J. (1986). *Sri Lanka: Ethnic Fratricide and the Dismantling of Democracy.* Chicago and London: University of Chicago Press.

Tec, Nechama (1986). *When Light Pierced the Darkness: Christian Rescue of Jews in Nazi Occupied Poland.* Oxford and New York: Oxford University Press.

Trachtenberg, Joshua (1943). *The Devil and the Jews: The Medieval Conception of the Jew and Its Relation to Modern Antisemitism.* New Haven, Conn.: Yale University Press.

Wachtel, Nathan (1984). *The Vision of the Vanquished: The Spanish Conquest of Peru through Indian Eyes, 1530–1570.* New York: Harper and Row.

Wakefield, Walter L. (1974). *Heresy, Crusade, and Inquisition in Southern France, 1100–1250.* Berkeley and Los Angeles: University of California Press.

—— (1987). *Armenia: Survival of a Nation.* New York: St. Martin's Press.

Whitaker, Ben (ed.) (1972). *The Fourth World: Victims of Group Oppression.* London: Sidgwick & Jackson; and New York: Schocken.

Wilson, Edmund O. (1978). *On Human Nature.* Cambridge, Mass. and London: Harvard University Press.

Wolf, Eric R. (1982). *Europe and the People without History.* Berkeley and Los Angeles: University of California Press.

Wright, J. R. C. (1974). *"Above Parties": The Political Attitudes of the German Protestant Church Leadership, 1918–1933.* Oxford: Oxford University Press.

Wyman, David (1984). *The Abandonment of the Jews: America and the Holocaust, 1941–1945.* New York: Pantheon.

Young, Crawford (1976). *The Politics of Cultural Pluralism.* Madison: University of Wisconsin Press.

Zahn, Gordon C. (1962). *German Catholics and Hitler's Wars: A Study in Social Control.* London: Sheed & Ward; and New York: E. P. Dutton.

Zerner, Ruth (1983). "Holocaust: A Past That Is Also Present," in *Society* 20: 31-35

Zuccotti, Susan (1987). *The Italians and the Holocaust.* New York: Basic Books.

—— (1993). *The Holocaust, the French, and the Jews.* New York: Basic Books.

7

Jihad and Genocide: The Case of the Armenians

Richard L. Rubenstein

By virtue of their capacity to define a target group as a radically evil, unrepentant enemy of God, the great monotheistic religions have the potential to provide a singularly powerful and effective legitimation for genocide. When this happens, unremitting mass murder can become an essential condition for the imagined realization of an ideal world of true fraternity and felicity. Mass murder ceases to be a crime and becomes instead a sanctified defense of truth, goodness, and civilization. It should, nevertheless, be recognized that under normal circumstances these same religions contain mitigating restraints that have limited their potential destructiveness.

The destructive potential of Christianity and Islam has been heightened by the fact that each tradition claims that it alone possesses the full measure of the divinely revealed truth, and that, throughout much of their respective histories, each has had the power and the numbers effectively to enforce their respective definitions of reality within the territory in which they were dominant. Of crucial importance is the fact that each tradition claims that the divine revelation was fundamentally concerned with real events that took place at identifiable moments in history. Moreover, Christianity and Islam have each been responsible for the creation of an entire civilization. Each tradition has engendered a world of art, architecture, seasonal and life-cycle rituals, music, literature, philosophy, law, a calendar of sacred and profane time, and distinctive conceptions of political legitimacy.

Nevertheless, each of the respective claims to divinely revealed truth rests upon an empirically insecure foundation. Testimony concerning purported historical events is, in any event, subject to challenge, falsification, and multiple interpretations. For example, Christianity rests on the proposition that the crucifixion of a Galilean Jew was the prelude to his resurrection and ascension to Heaven as the one who saves humanity from death. The vast majority of Christian believers throughout history have accepted this proposition as indubitably true. Nevertheless, there are large numbers of people for whom this corpus of belief stretches the limits of credibility.

Similarly, non-Muslims are hardly likely to find credible the views of Muslim scholars such as the Pakistani Abu A'la Mawdudi, also known as Syed Abul 'Ala Maudoodi (1903–1979). Mawdudi rejected the historical chronology that locates the beginnings of Islam in the seventh Christian century. Instead, he and others made the claim that Islam is the eternal and original divinely revealed religion of humanity, and that both the Hebrew Scriptures and the New Testament are imperfect distortions of God's original revelation. According to Mawdudi, "The entire creation obeys the laws of God, the whole universe, therefore literally follows the religion of Islam—for Islam signifies nothing but obedience and submission of [sic] Allah, the Lord of the Universe . . . everything in the universe is 'Muslim' for it obeys God by submission to His laws" (Mawdudi, 1997: 10; also, Bat Ye'or, 2002: 196).

Such assertions inevitably raise the issue of the nonbeliever who must be viewed as either hopelessly ignorant of, or in willful rebellion against, God. In a multireligious, secular society, the nonnegotiable truth claims of each tradition can be "bracketed" in the public sphere, and no distinctive theological claim need be regarded as privileged. Such societies were rarely, if ever, to be found before the French and American Revolutions. Instead, both Islam and pre-Enlightenment Christianity claimed a cognitive monopoly in religious matters in those areas in which they were politically and socially dominant. In the case of Christianity, the Roman Catholic Church's cognitive monopoly was preserved by means of a partnership between church and state that entailed visiting bitterly harsh punishments, not excluding torture and death, upon heretics, and degraded, segregated status upon dissenting minorities such as the Jews. Having derived its legitimacy from the church, the state shared a common interest in the suppression of heresy and the degradation of dissidents.

Until the twentieth century, the military and political boundary between the world of Christianity and that of Islam could also be characterized as a cognitive frontier (Berger, 1967: 48). While there were Christians domiciled within Islam from its inception, save for the influence of colonial powers in the nineteenth and twentieth centuries, such domicile was permitted only on the basis of conditions defined by Islamic authorities. Initially, a strictly Muslim cognitive monopoly was unattainable. In view of the rapidity of the Muslim conquests in the early years, it was neither possible nor prudent to convert or eliminate all of the conquered peoples. Their talents were often indispensable to the creation of the vast Islamic empire. The Muslims solved the problem by the *dhimma*, the pact of submission and protection, they imposed upon defeated Jews and Christians—the "Peoples of the Book"—as well as on Zoroastrians, by means of which these groups were granted toleration within Islamic lands. The dhimma resembled the *b'rith* or covenant treaty prevalent in the ancient Near East, used by the Hittites and other peoples to define the relationship between a stronger power and its weaker client states. As a suzerainty treaty, the covenant was a pact imposed by the more powerful suzerain upon a vassal king. It was, in essence, an asymmetrical power relationship in which the sovereign lord spelled out the conditions under which the weaker client and his successors could receive his protection. The weaker party had the choice of either accepting the conditions or attempting to reverse the power relations by military action. The imposition of a covenant was usually consequent upon the defeat of the weaker party. As in the case of the dhimma, the covenant was a device that enabled the incorporation of subject peoples of different religions and culture within the empire of a dominant overlord (Mendenhall, 1955; Eichrodt, 1996; Gaffney, 1984: 144; Hillers, 1972; Lowe, n.d.; McCarthy, 1972).

The dhimma was, in turn, the outcome of jihad. As formulated by Muslim jurists, on the basis of the Qur'an and the hadiths (sayings or actions attributed by tradition to the Prophet Muhammed) the concept of jihad is fundamental to the relationship between Muslims and non-Muslims, especially the "People of the Book." Islam envisioned the world as divided into two irreconcilable realms, *dar al-Islam*, the realm of Muslim dominance where, theoretically, justice and peace prevailed; and *dar al-Harb*, the region of war, characterized by heedlessness, disorder, internal strife, and unbelief. As such, the latter realm constituted a threat to true religion. Consequently, its inhabitants were either to be converted to true religion or to be defeated militarily (Kelsay, 1993: 34–35). Nevertheless, the purpose of jihad is less the conversion of the nonbeliever than the endeavor to enlarge the domain of justice and peace that is thought to be possible only where Islam prevails. For strict Muslims, there is no neutral domain that is neither dar al-Islam nor dar al-Harb, although the latter's disorders can be partly mitigated in regions governed by a scriptural religion such as Christianity (Lewis, 1993: 50). Such an arrangement is, nevertheless, unsatisfactory since Muslims hold that Jesus, like all of the prophets, was a Muslim. Hence, for Muslims, Christianity does not correspond to the true religion of Jesus, and peace and justice cannot truly prevail until all peoples are united under the aegis of a truly Islamic state (Kelsay, 1993: 34). Jihad thus becomes a relationship "constructed within an ideology of territorial expansion and world domination" (Bat Ye'or, 2002: 42–43).

According to Ibn Tamiyah (1263–1328), a highly influential Muslim thinker regarded as the source of Wahhabism, the strictly traditionalist movement founded by Muhammad ibn 'Abd al-Wahhab (1703–1792) and strongly supported by the Saudi monarchy, Muslims alone have the right to the possession of the world's material wealth. Concerning territory conquered by Islam, Ibn Tamiyah comments:

> These possessions received the name of fay [booty taken in war from infidels that became the property of the umma and administered by the caliph] since Allah had taken them away from the infidels in order to restore them to the Muslims. In principle, Allah has created all things of this world in order that they may contribute to serving him, since he created man only in order to be ministered to. Consequently, the infidels forfeit their persons and their belongings which they do not use in Allah's service to the faithful believers who serve Allah and unto whom Allah returns what is theirs; thus is restored to a man the inheritance of which he was deprived, even if he had never before gained possession of it (Laoust, 1948: 34–35; Bat Ye'or, 2002: 429, n32).

Andalusian jurist Ibn Hazm (994–1064) took a similar position: God has established the infidels' ownership of their property only for the institution of booty for Muslims (Arnaldez, 1962: 457).

It is obvious that, for strict Islamic traditionalists, unconverted infidels dwelling in the dar al-Harb have no inherent right either to life or property. War, sanctified as jihad, is the umma's appropriate relationship to such infidels. At least theoretically, and often in practice, a permanent state of war existed between the dar al-Islam and the dar al-Harb that excluded the possibility of genuine peace, although provisional pacts of truce were permitted when they offered some advantage to the umma. Moreover, the state of permanent war continued even after the defeat of the infidel. The options available to conquered Jews, Christians, and Zoroastrians were harsh in Islam's early years and became harsher over time. Infidels who rejected conversion were given the choice of savage destruction, enslavement, or expulsion on the one hand, or of submission as dhimmis to humiliating, second-class subject status that included payment of the *jizya*, the obligatory poll tax payable to the Muslim state, on the other. It is beyond the scope of this essay to enter into details, save to observe that dhimmi status entailed permanent degradation of status for both the individual and his or her religious tradition. Above all, it is important to recognize that the dhimmi had no inherent human rights and depended for his or her security on the conditional protection bestowed upon him or her by the Muslim overlord. In a sense, the dhimmi was regarded as a captive in a never-ending war. Any infraction of the conditions imposed upon him or her entailed the total withdrawal of protection. The dhimmi then became an outlaw with neither human rights nor protection.

Too little has been written about the genocidal potentiality of Islam, yet an early genocide of the twentieth century and a precursor of the Holocaust was inflicted by a Muslim country on its Christian Armenian population:

the 1915 genocide of Turkey's Armenian minority. That genocide was preceded by an earlier near-genocidal massacre of between 100,000 and 200,000 Christian Armenians under Sultan Abdul Hamid II (1877–1909) in 1894–1896, and the slaughter of an additional 30,000 in the Adna region in 1909. The earlier violence was carried out under the Sultan's traditionalist leadership in what he and his circle believed to be the defense of the Ottoman Empire. The more thorough-going massacre during World War I was carried out by the modernizing Young Turks in what they believed to be the defense of the Turkish nation.

The difference in regime and objective has led to a disagreement by at least two major scholars on the question of relation of the massacres of 1894–1896 and 1915. Vahakn N. Dadrian (2003) holds that the earlier massacres were part of an ever-intensifying series of assaults that culminated in the 1915 genocide. Ronald Grigor Suny holds that Abdul Hamid was a traditional imperial monarch who was prepared to use murderous violence to "keep his Armenian subjects in line." Nevertheless, "he did not consider the use of mass deportation to change the demographic composition of Anatolia" (Suny, 2001: 44). While not denying that religion played a part in both 1894–1896 and 1915, Suny argues that the ideology that motivated the Young Turk perpetrators in 1915 was primarily ethnic and nationalistic. Moreover, he holds that the genocide would, in all likelihood, not have occurred had it not been for the war and the "foreign policy blows" that led to the loss of much of European Turkey in the years immediately preceding the Great War" (Suny, 2001: 50–52; Bat Ye'or, 1996: 195).

It is beyond the competence of this writer to evaluate the differences between these eminent scholars. Yet there are sufficient areas of agreement to suggest that religion played a significant role in both the massacres of 1894–1896 and the genocide of 1915. The case for the role of religion in genocide is more readily apparent in 1894–1896, when the Ottoman polity was, at least in theory, a sacred society ruled by the sultan-caliph who, as caliph, was widely recognized among Sunni Muslims as the head and successor to the Prophet. According to Dadrian, the fundamental common law principle governing the relations in the Ottoman Empire between the Muslim elite and non-Muslim subjects was a quasi-legal contract, the *Akdi Zimmet* (contract with the ruled nationality), in which the sovereign guaranteed the safety of "their persons, their civil and religious liberties, and, conditionally, their property in exchange for the payment of the poll and land taxes, and acquiescence to a set of social and legal disabilities" (Dadrian, 2003: 4). In essence, the Akdi Zimmet was, in spirit and in substance, the dhimma, the Muslim pact of submission that terminated the state of war and stipulated the conditions under which Christian, Jewish, and Zoroastrian subject peoples or dhimmis were permitted domicile in Islamic lands (Bat Ye'or, 2002: 37–38).

To repeat, strictly speaking, Islamic tradition envisages no such thing as genuine peace between faithful Muslims and infidels. There can be a truce when combat appears unlikely to succeed. There could also be conditional toleration in a multinational, multireligious empire based on the hierarchical gradation of status, such as the Ottoman Empire, in which the distinctions of rulers and ruled, Muslims and non-Muslim, were maintained (Suny, 2001: 30–31). Nevertheless, there are no inalienable human rights for non-Muslim subject peoples. Prior to modernization, their rights were contractual and conditional based strictly upon fulfillment of the dhimma. Whenever a dhimmi or a dhimmi community failed to do so, the contract of submission and protection became ipso facto null and void and the state of war would be resumed.

During the nineteenth century, a crisis arose in the relations between the subject communities and the Ottoman Empire as a result of the modernizing *Tanzimat* (reorganization) reforms and the resulting dissonance between traditional common law and the newly formulated public law. The reforms were initiated in 1839 by Sultan Abd al Majid (1823–1861) under the prodding of the Western powers and Russia. They guaranteed honor, life, and property for all Ottoman subjects, regardless of race or religion. In 1856, a second, expanded edict of reform asserted the equality of all Ottoman subjects, Muslim and non-Muslim. Given the religiously legitimated, traditional subordination of non-Muslims to Muslims, the decree, known as the *Hatt-I Hümayun* of 1856, was bitterly resented by the overwhelming majority of Muslims, especially in view of the role of foreign pressure in bringing about what amounted to the formal abolition of dhimmi status.

The reactions of both the Muslim and non-Muslim populations was recorded by Cevet Paþa, an astute observer and a high Ottoman official:

In accordance with this *ferman* [edict] Muslim and non-Muslim subjects were to be made equal in all rights. This had a very adverse effect on the Muslims. Previously, one of the four points adopted, as basis for peace agreements, had been that certain privileges were accorded to Christians on condition that these did not infringe on the sovereign authority of the government. Now the question of [specific] privileges lost its significance; in the whole range of government, the non-Muslims were forthwith to be deemed the equals of the Muslims. Many Muslims began to grumble: "Today we have lost our sacred national rights, won by the blood of our fathers and forefathers. At a time when the Islamic millet was the ruling millet, it was deprived of this sacred right. This is a day of weeping and mourning for the people of Islam."

As for the non-Muslims, this day, when they left the status of *raya* [dhimmi] and gained equality with the ruling millet, was a day of rejoicing. But the patriarchs and other spiritual chiefs were displeased, because their appointments were incorporated in the ferman. Another point was that whereas, in former times, in the Ottoman state, the communities were ranked, with the

Muslims first, then the Greeks, then the Armenians, then the Jews, now all of them were put on the same level. Some Greeks objected to this, saying: "The government has put us together with the Jews. We were content with the supremacy of Islam."

As a result of all this, just as the weather was overcast when the ferman was read in the audience chamber, so the faces of most of those present were grim. Only on the faces of a few of our Frenchified gentry dressed in the garb of Islam could expressions of joy be seen. Some notorious characters of this type were seen and heard to say: "If the non-Muslims are spread among the Muslims, neighborhoods will become mixed, the price of our properties will rise, and civilized amenities will expand." On this account they expressed satisfaction (Braude and Lewis, 1982: 30).

In 1876, a liberal constitution was proposed by Midhat Pasha (1822–1883) during his brief second tenure as grand vizier. At first the new sultan, Abdul Hamid II (1876–1909), was inclined to accept the constitution, but he quickly changed his mind and effectively terminated the period of Tanzimat reforms. The rest of his reign was a period of conservative reaction. The likely negative consequences of reform were already understood in 1856 by an earlier grand vizier, Mustafa Reşid Pasha (1800–1858), a brilliant diplomat. In a memorandum addressed to the sultan in the wake of the reforms of that year, Reşid foresaw the possibility of a "great slaughter" as a result of the efforts to establish the civic equality of all Ottoman subjects through legal enactment (Hurewitz, 1956: 154; Dadrian, 2003: 37, n3).

Reşid's views were prescient. Muslim traditionalists regarded emancipation of Jews and Christians as profoundly offensive. They believed that emancipation voided the dhimma. Before emancipation, payment of the jizya, the poll tax imposed upon all male dhimmis, symbolized their subjection, inferior status, and termination of jihad. By voiding dhimmi disabilities, traditionalists believed the dhimma had been rendered null and void. In their eyes, dhimmi emancipation did not mean an end to civic disabilities but the restoration of the state of war against the dhimmis. Under the circumstances, the traditionalists believed that, at least in theory, the umma, the Muslim community, once again, had the right to seize dhimmi property, kill adult male dhimmis, and if they chose, to enslave dhimmi women and children. Moreover, these actions were regarded "not only as justified but also as mandatory and even as praiseworthy" (Bat Ye'or, 1985: 101).

In the 1880s, Armenian exiles in Europe, influenced by Western ideas about national self-determination and the "people" as the source of political legitimacy, began to campaign for Armenian national autonomy. The Armenians did not initially seek full political independence, but nationalism provided a powerful legitimation for separation from the multinational Ottoman Empire. As such, it was profoundly subversive of the imperial order. Armenian rebels in the Caucasus also organized raids into Ottoman territory. The vast majority of Armenians sought amelioration of their situation within the empire, but by 1890 an Armenian Revolutionary Federation was established in Tiflis that demanded Armenian freedom "with gun in hand" (Kinross, 1977: 556–57). In 1891, the sultan responded by raising a force of Kurdish Muslim irregulars and sanctioning their predatory attacks on Armenians. Within a year, the Kurds had formed cavalry units totaling 15,000 men. Assured of legal immunity, the Kurds attacked and spread terror among Armenians in the capital and the hinterland. In 1893, Armenian revolutionaries posted placards in many towns and cities calling on Muslims to rise up against the sultan's oppression. Since the sultan was also the caliph, combining the traditional functions of political and religious leadership, the Armenian action was seen by traditionalists as a radical breach of the dhimma.

Another source of Turkish resentment stemmed from the fact that the Armenians were a "market dominant minority" (Chua, 2003). Very frequently, discriminated minorities, barred from service in the military or the state bureaucracy and subject to other forms of social and vocational discrimination, rely on education and training for their economic survival and well-being to a much greater extent than do indigenous majorities. Such minorities are also likely to be concentrated in urban centers and to specialize in urban trades and crafts, finance, and the professions. Their capital consists in what is in their heads and cannot be taken from them. Often subject to expulsion, they form diaspora networks that are intrinsically advantageous in both finance and commerce. This has been the case with the European Jews before World War II, the Chinese in Southeast Asia, the Lebanese in West Africa, and the Armenians in the Ottoman Empire.

During the nineteenth century, Armenians tended to become economically superior to the Turks. The more affluent sent their sons abroad to receive their education in a rapidly modernizing Europe. As Christians, they had links to Europe that were not possessed by the Muslim majority. Diaspora Armenians sent home remittances and brought back new machines and technology to their families in the empire. When the sale of Muslim lands to non-Muslims was permitted by the reforms of 1856, Armenians had the resources to buy up large landholdings, especially after 1870 (Suny, 2001: 39). This resulted in a reversal of status in a world newly oriented toward industry and commerce. In the traditional world of Islam, the Armenians suffered status inferiority as dhimmis. In the new world, the status of the Muslims was in fact inferior, although not in their own self-perceptions. Resentment was bitter and fed on itself so that Abdul Hamid II's efforts to undo the reforms received widespread Muslim support.

Actual massacres first broke out in the summer of 1894 in Sasun in southern Armenia. Turkish authorities used Armenian resistance to Kurdish aggression as a pretext for indiscriminate rape and slaughter. News of the outrages quickly spread to Europe, and Britain, France, and Russia demanded a commission of inquiry. These same powers also sought to persuade the Ottoman government to adopt reforms in those provinces where most of the Armenians were domiciled. The sultan made an empty show of accepting some reforms, although he had no intention of implementing them. In September 1895, Armenians demonstrated in Constantinople in order to pressure the sultan and the European powers to implement the reforms. The police and radical Muslim elements in the capital city responded with ten days of massacre and terror. About the same time, an unprovoked, premeditated massacre began in the city of Trebizond on the Black Sea (Adalian). The massacres then spread through almost every town with a significant number of Armenian inhabitants. There was nothing spontaneous about the massacres. They were, in fact, military operations that began and ended daily with the call of a bugle (Kinross, 1977: 559).

The worst massacre occurred in the city of Urfa, known to the ancient world as Edessa, where Armenians constituted about a third of the population. After a two-month siege of the Armenian quarter, in December 1895, Armenian leaders gathered in their cathedral and requested official Turkish protection. The Turkish commander agreed, then surrounded the cathedral, permitting Turkish troops and the mob to rampage through the Armenian quarter, burning, looting, and killing all adult males. Dadrian comments that, wherever possible, the killing was done in such a way as to emphasize the religious nature of the deed (Dadrian, 2003: 147). Lord Kinross describes the way in which the slaughter was assimilated to a sacrificial ritual: "When a large group of young Armenians were brought before a sheikh, he had them thrown down on their backs and held by their hands and feet. Then, in the words of an observer, he recited verses of the Koran and 'cut their throats after the Mecca rite of sacrificing sheep'" (1977: 560).

The mosques were places of incitement; the Christian churches were slaughterhouses. Some 2,500 Armenians were burned alive in the Cathedral of Urfa; Murderous mobs were urged on by their imams. The worst butchery often followed Friday services. Dadrian also comments on the importance of local religious authorities in the implementation of the massacres. The sultan in distant Constantinople could issue orders for the massacres, often framed in covert language, but the interpretation of those orders, as well as local planning and implementation, required the leadership of local authority figures. Because of the empire's theocratic nature, local religious leaders used their authority to assure the mob that the massacres were in accordance with the *Seriat* (shari'a) (Dadrian, 2003: 149). With very few exceptions, the *muftis* (jurisconsults who dispensed formal legal opinions), *kadis* (magistrates and guardians of law and order), *ulemas* (Muslim theologians), and *mullahs* played a crucial role in conferring religious legitimacy on the slaughter (Dadrian, 2003: 150).

In many locations, after the men were killed, the mob sought to force surviving widows and children to convert. Those who refused were murdered (Hartunian, 1968: 12–14). The massacres constituted an unprecedented level of violence on the part of the Ottoman Empire against one of its subject peoples. Abdul Hamid II was clearly determined to frustrate Armenian hopes of reform in spite of pressure from the Great Powers. He also worked to crush any Armenian attempt to organize politically. Estimates of the number of dead range from 100,000 to 300,000. Tens of thousands emigrated; thousands were forcibly converted to Islam. The sultan understood that he could deal with his subjects as he pleased because the relations of the Great Powers with his empire trumped all other considerations. From his point of view, the Armenians got what they deserved. By seeking to overcome their subordinate status, and by seeking the help of foreign rulers, they had broken their contract and placed themselves in a state of war with his realm in which no violence, expropriation, or violation was out of bounds. Nevertheless, the massacres of 1894 were not genocidal in act or intent. Abdul Hamid's policies were traditionalist and restorationist. Although he employed extreme violence against the Armenians, he had no interest in the demographic homogenization of his realm and had no intention of eliminating any major religious or ethnic group from his empire. Full-scale genocide and ethnic uniformity had to await the modernizing twentieth-century regime of the Committee of Union and Progress, the Young Turks.

THE YOUNG TURKS

The Young Turks' political agenda was different from the sultan's. They were a Turkish nationalist reform party that responded to the weakness of the Ottoman Empire as manifested by Austria-Hungary's annexation of Bosnia-Herzegovina in 1908, Italy's seizure of Libya and the island of Rhodes in 1912, the independence of Albania in 1912, and the Ottoman defeat in the First Balkan War of 1912–1913 that led to the loss of much of the Ottoman Empire in Europe. Moreover, as noted, in the empire itself, Muslims had been losing ground to dhimmi minorities—the Greeks, Jews, and Armenians—who dominated the world of commerce and the professions. According to S. N. Eisendrath, an internationally recognized authority on modernization, "the Turkish Revolution completely rejected the religious basis of legitimation and attempted instead to develop a secular national one as the major ideological parameter of the new collectivity" (cited in Suny, 2001: 44). The Young Turks were modernizing, rationalizing "progressives" who understood, as did the Japanese elites at the time of the Meiji Reformation of 1866–1869, that absent modernization, the independence and territorial integrity of their respective empires would be in peril. In 1908, the Young Turks effectively overthrew Abdul Hamid II's traditionalist regime. In their initial enthusiasm, many Armenians made an understandable but deadly miscalculation. They assumed that the overthrow of an inefficient and corrupt regime by one that was less corrupt and more rational augured well for their own community. The Young Turks had given public assurances of equal treatment of the empire's non-Muslim minorities, but the logic of their modernizing revolution made ethnic homogenization rather than diversity the almost inevitable political outcome.

The first generation of Turkish revolutionaries were divided on the issue of working with the Armenians, as was evident at the First Congress of the Ottoman Opposition that met in Paris in February 1902. Some of the more liberal Young Turks thought that an alliance with the Armenians would elicit a favorable response from the Europeans. Armenian activists declared that cooperation with the Turkish revolutionaries was conditional on the implementation of reforms in the six Anatolian *vilayets* (provinces) with significant Armenian populations, to be guaranteed by the European powers. The conditions were acceptable to the majority attending the congress but were vehemently rejected by the nationalist minority. The latter regarded European support as wholly at odds with their fundamental objective, the creation of a strong, independent Ottoman realm in which the traditional status hierarchy would be more or less intact. The views of the minority ultimately carried greater weight as they represented the dominant tendency among most Young Turk organizations and newspapers (Suny, 2001: 46–47).

According to Suny and other authorities, in the first decade of the twentieth century the Young Turks shifted from what he characterizes as an "Ottomanist orientation" that emphasized the equality of the millets in a multinational society to a more Turkish nationalist position that stressed the predominance of the ethnic Turks over the subordinate communities consisting of "the protected flock of the Sultan," Armenian, Catholic, Jewish, and Orthodox (Suny, 2001: 47). Until World War I, loyalty to the empire remained part of Young Turk rhetoric, but it was increasingly supplanted by nationalist ideology. The shift placed the Armenian political leaders in a difficult position. Their community was to be found on both sides of the Ottoman-Russian border. In addition, the Armenians were split into two factions, largely along socioeconomic lines. The *Dashnak*, members of the Armenian Revolutionary Federation (*Hai Heghapokhakan Dashnaksutiun*), represented the Armenian petty bourgeoisie of Anatolia; the patriarchate represented the wealthy commercial class of the capital and other larger cities (Braude and Lewis, 1982: 418). The Dashnak ultimately sought autonomy if not complete Armenian independence. The patriarchate and its allies sought a restoration of their traditional privileges as dhimmis in the millet system that was threatened by the centralizing tendencies of government.

When the war began, the Dashnak urged Armenians to volunteer in the Ottoman army. In Tsarist Russia, the Dashnak urged Armenians to enlist in the Tsarist army. As a result, both the Tsarist and the Ottoman governments suspected the Armenians of disloyalty. The situation was aggravated by the dangers confronting the Ottoman Empire in 1914 and 1915. In November 1914, over the objections of field commanders, Turkish forces led by Enver Pasha, Minister of War and one of the ruling Young Turk triumvirate, attempted to regain land in the Caucasus lost to the Russians in 1878. Enver's effort ended catastrophically at Sarikamis, a Turkish town in the Caucasus. In the west, Djemal Pasha led an attack in February 1915 on the Suez Canal that also ended in defeat. In March 1915, in response to a Russian request for aid, allied naval forces under Admiral Sir John de Robeck, Commander of the Aegean Squadron, made preparations to force a passage through the Dardanelles Strait. The evacuation of Constantinople began and the state archives and the empire's gold reserves were sent away. Most observers anticipated the empire's collapse. However, on 18 March 1915, as a result of an unsuspected Turkish minefield in the Dardanelles, five Allied warships were destroyed and the Allied attempt to force the strait ended in disaster.

When the Young Turks contemplated evacuating from Constantinople to the Anatolian heartland, they could not ignore the issue of security. Anatolia's population was mixed. In addition to Turks, it was inhabited by Greeks, Armenians, and Kurds whose loyalty was suspect in Turkish eyes. Some Greek civilians were deported from the coastal areas, but the deportations were not genocidal in intent. The defeat at Sarikamis intensified Turkish suspicions of Armenian loyalty. In the first months of 1915, Ottoman authorities demobilized Armenian soldiers, who were then forced into labor brigades and compelled to dig their own graves before being shot. Rumors of the slaughter spread in the Armenian villages (Suny, 2001: 52). On 20 April 1915, the Armenians of Van rose up in self-defense, an action depicted by the Turks as a revolutionary uprising. The Armenians held out in Van until 14 May 1915, when the city was captured by the Russians with the aid of some Armenian guerrillas who proclaimed Van the capital of an independent Armenian republic. The Turks recaptured the city in July. They were infuriated by what they regarded as Armenian treason and launched a massacre, butchering the men and robbing, raping, and leaving the women to die. Dr. Clarence B. Ussher, an American medical missionary in Van, reported that 55,000 Armenians were killed there in May. On 24 April 1915 the Ministry of the Interior ordered the arrest of Armenian parliamentary deputies, former ministers, and some intellectuals. Thousands were arrested, including 2,345 in the capital, most of whom were subsequently executed (Dadrian, 2003: 421).

On 27 May 1915, a new emergency law was promulgated, the "Temporary Law of Deportation." The law authorized military leaders to order the deportation of population groups on suspicion of espionage or treason, and in cases of military necessity. With this sweeping authorization and without explicitly naming the Armenians, the Turkish government arrogated to itself the genocidal deportation of its Armenian population. Shortly thereafter, Enver Pasha's brother-in-law Djevet Bey recently appointed governor of the Van vilayet, gave an order to "exterminate all Armenian males of 12 years and older" in that border region (Mazower, 2001). Actual genocide began in April 1915, with the rounding up and deportation of Armenian men in one population center after another. The men were usually imprisoned for several days, after which they were marched out of town and massacred. Later women, children, and older men were also deported. The women were often raped and mutilated before being killed. Thousands of the female deportees were given the choice of conversion to Islam or death. Having lost their men and completely at the mercy of hostile Turks and Kurds, many of the women converted. We return to that subject below.

In June 1915, the government began to use the railroads to expedite deportation and extermination. Freight cars were employed to deport thousands to remote areas where they were left to starve to death while being assaulted by the ravages of nature and human malice. Many were murdered outright. The Armenian deportees were among the first men and women in the twentieth century to learn that human rights are inseparable from political status. Having been deprived of all political status save that of outlaw by the Ottoman government, there was no abuse that could not with impunity be inflicted upon them.

The extermination project was thoroughly modern in spirit and implementation from its initial planning stages to its thorough-going execution. Mass extermination was advocated in the planning sessions as the appropriate "scientific" response to the universal struggle of the races for survival. Like other modernizing elites of the period, the largely European-trained Young Turk elite interpreted the relations between races and nations in Social Darwinist terms. Above all, the Young Turks had a reliable, centralized bureaucratic network. Taalat Bey, one of the ruling triumvirs and Minister of the Interior, did not entrust the assignment to old-fashioned provincial bureaucrats but sent Young Turk bureaucrats to act as his personal representatives and, when necessary, to punish governors and local governors who, out of compassion or greed, failed to carry out orders. In other words, there was a special organization with responsibility for organizing the massacres. At the local level, there were death squads who were given the name of "Butcher Battalions" (*Dekmejian*).

Taalat Bey spelled out the objectives of his government in a telegram to the Police Office in Aleppo, Syria, dated 15 September 1915:

It has been reported that by order of the Committee [of Union and Progress]
the Government has determined completely to exterminate the Armenians
living in Turkey. Those who refuse to obey this order cannot be regarded as
friends of the Government. Regardless of the women, children or invalids, and
however deplorable the methods of destruction may seem, an end is to be put
to their existence [i.e., the Armenians] without paying any heed to feeling or
conscience.
    Minister for the Interior, Taalat (Sarkisyanz, 1975: 196)

The Young Turks characterized their aggression as "deportations" and
insisted that they were acting in the interests of national security. However,
it was quickly apparent that something very new had taken place, and that
the number of victims far exceeded that of the nineteenth-century massacre.
Moreover, deportation had acquired a new and sinister meaning (Mazower,
2001). In 1915, deportation became an instrument of extermination in
which no fewer than one million Armenians perished.
    Many volumes have been written about the Armenian genocide. One of
the earliest was also one of the most comprehensive, the report assembled
by Viscount James Bryce in 1916 in partnership with Arnold Toynbee and
presented to Sir Edward Grey, the British Foreign Secretary. The authors
concluded the report with an observation concerning the slaughter: "It
was a deliberate, systematic attempt to eradicate the Armenian population
throughout the Ottoman Empire and it has certainly met with a very large
measure of success" (Toynbee, 1916: 648).
    To this day, Turkish authorities deny that genocide ever took place and
insist that their actions were necessary defensive measures against a disloyal
minority (Turkish Foreign Minister's Defense of Armenian Massacres, 1916). The
vast majority of responsible scholars have refuted that claim. Nevertheless,
the Turkish government has used every threat in its diplomatic arsenal to
prevent any friendly government from officially taking issue with its genocide
denial (Mazower, 2001).
    As noted above, there is little reason to doubt that Abdul Hamid's mas-
sacres were in large measure religiously motivated. The sultan-caliph wanted
to put the Armenians in their place as a dhimmi component in his multinational empire. He did not want to exterminate them. Not so, the Young
Turks. Within months after Turkey's entrance into the Great War, the decision
to exterminate the Armenians had been taken. When the deed was done, the
justifications the Young Turks offered were largely political and economic.
    When I first wrote about the Armenian genocide, I stressed the modernity
of the enterprise and its economic, political, and military motives (Rubenstein, 1983: 12–19). I did not consider the possibility that the perpetrators'
motives might have included a very important religious component. The
modernizing Young Turk elite was largely dismissive of their own religious
inheritance. Today, I would argue that religion was a necessary but not a

sufficient cause of the genocide. I would further argue that the crimes perpetrated against the Armenians were regarded by the Turks as legitimate defensive methods of dealing with dhimmis who had violated the conditions of the dhimma and hence were outlaws, for whom everything, including life, property, freedom from slavery, and family, was forfeited. I would further argue that the persistent Turkish genocide denial—so different from the German way of dealing with their genocide—is due, at least in part, to the belief that they did no wrong in exterminating the Armenians, a belief that rests ultimately on the traditions of jihad and the dhimma. In the massacres of 1894–1896, Turkish authorities were quite open about the religious legitimations. In 1915, there was no comparable frankness, but that did not mean that the old traditions did not give most yet-to-be-secularized Turks a relatively easy conscience about the slaughter of the Armenians and the expropriation of their property (Dadrian, 2003: 422–24).

In any event, there is one aspect of the genocide in which the religious element was indubitably present. According to Ara Sarafian, in addition to the killings and general massacres, a large number of Armenians were "'abducted,' 'carried off,' or 'converted to Islam'" (Sarafian, 2001: 210). Sarafian further argues that "the fate of this latter class of Armenians was part of the same genocidal calculus as those who were murdered." It is estimated that between 100,000 and 200,000 Armenians, most of who were women and children, escaped death by converting to Islam in 1915–1916. The absorption of these converts into the Muslim community had the same objective as outright genocide, the elimination of the Armenian community as a demographic presence in the Ottoman Empire. In addition to killing a very large number of Armenians through forced marches and starvation, the deportations served to weaken and terrify women and children who had lost their male protectors before or during the deportations. According to Sarafian, "young women and children were rendered prime candidates for absorption into Muslim households after they were isolated from their families and terrorized during the forced marches and execution of their elders" (2001: 210).

Sarafian contends, with considerable justice, that the authorities were implementing a "single policy of destruction" in both the outright murder of adult males and in the absorption of Armenian women and children. The same Ottoman bureaucrats who controlled the deportations were also in charge of the conversion program. In the initial stages of the assault on the Armenian community, there were "voluntary" conversions. Some individuals were selected by individual Muslims for absorption into their households. In addition, government agencies distributed Armenians to Muslim families. Children in government-sponsored orphanages were converted and directly absorbed into the Muslim community. Events in Trebizond are illustrative of how the program functioned. Between 1 July and 18 July

1915, five deportation convoys left Trebizond. Oscar Heizer, the American consul, reported that their guards killed most of the deportees shortly after leaving (Heizer, 1915; Dadrian, 2003: 421–37). Approximately 3,000 children—girls up to fifteen years old and boys no older than ten—were placed in a number of houses designated as "orphanages" by the Turks. Another 300 were housed in the American missionary school, which was turned into an orphanage. An official sent from Constantinople to supervise the extermination of the Armenians subsequently closed down both orphanages. The Turks drowned some children; others were distributed to Muslim households where, according to Heizer, they were assimilated as Muslims within weeks (Sarafian, 2001: 212–13). Elsewhere, U.S. Consul Leslie Davis reported on the passage of thousands of deportees through Harpoot, which was situated on a principal route to the deserts of Syria. Davis wrote that hardly any men had survived among the deportees. Subject to constant beatings, given little or no food or water, the victims were rapidly dying. The gendarmes guarding the Armenians refused to permit them to leave the convoy or to receive aid from American missionaries. They did, however, permit Turks to visit the convoys with doctors to select "the prettiest girls" for their own purposes. Davis further reported that the Turks were not only seeking to exterminate the Armenians; they were also seeking to absorb a large number of them as Muslims. Sarafian concludes that there was a mass transfer of Armenians into Muslim households in 1915. By destroying the Armenian social structure in the early stages of the genocide through the murder of young men, heads of families, and community leaders, the Turks were able to garner "the ideal candidates for absorption" into Muslim households and the general Muslim population (Sarafian, 2001: 217).

As cruel as this program was, it differed fundamentally from the Nazi Final Solution. Suny observes that "to a considerable degree, religious differences were transmuted by both the Armenians and the Turks into racial and national differences, far more indelible and immutable than religion" (Suny, 2001: 50). Nevertheless, Suny's qualifier "to a considerable degree" is important. For the Nazis, the racial difference between the so-called Aryan and non-Aryan was unbridgeable and immutable. In the National Socialist universe, there was absolutely no room for an absorption program for non-Aryans. Some Poles and others with the appropriate physical characteristics could be absorbed, but not Jews. By contrast, even in genocide, religion made a difference in the Ottoman Empire. Conversion could and did save some Armenians even as it destroyed their community. Moreover, as noted, both the extermination and the conversion process were fully consistent with Islamic tradition in the eyes of the Turks.

The Turks also eliminated Christian minorities besides the Armenians, albeit by somewhat gentler means. In January 1923, after Greece's failed invasion of Turkey's Anatolian mainland and Turkey's repudiation of the 1920 Treaty of Sèvres, at Turkey's insistence, both countries agreed to an exchange of populations. Between 1923 and 1930, 1.25 million "Greeks" were "repatriated" from Turkey to Greece; a smaller number of "Turks" departed from Greece to Turkey. However, as Bernard Lewis points out, the exchanges did not imply acceptance of the European principle of nationality in which Greeks and Turks, "unwilling or unable to live as national minorities among aliens," elected to return to their homeland and live among their own people. In reality, the great majority of Anatolia's "Greeks" spoke little or no Greek, speaking Turkish among themselves although writing in the Greek script. Similarly, many of the "Turks" in Greece and Crete spoke Greek among themselves and knew little or no Turkish. In actuality, the expulsions were based on religion. Turkish-speaking Christians faithful to the Greek Orthodox Church were expelled to Greece, a "homeland" they had never known, while Greek-speaking Muslims were expelled to Turkey (Lewis, 1993: 142–43). The Armenian genocide, the absorption-conversion program, and what was, in effect, the expulsion of Turkey's "Greeks" all shared a common objective, the elimination of a significant Christian demographic presence from Turkey. The methods varied, but all three events can be seen as religiously motivated state-sponsored programs of population elimination.

Finally, I take note of an authoritative report, based entirely on Arab sources, entitled "Contemporary Islamist Ideology Authorizing Genocidal Murder" by Yigal Carmon. It demonstrates that today's radical Islamists regard genocide as a legitimate weapon against those they regard as enemies of Islam. Holding that Islam is now under attack, they see unremitting jihad as defensive and holds it to be the single most important Muslim religious obligation. It is obligatory for Muslims without restriction or limitation. No weapons or types of warfare are to be excluded. Without exception, all infidels are to be fought and, barring conversion, are to be exterminated (MEMRI, 2004). I must, however, stress that these are the views of the most radical elements within contemporary Islam. We do not know the extent to which the extremists can persuade or compel the Islamic mainstream to share their views.

BIBLIOGRAPHY

Adalian, Rouben Paul (1999). "Hamidian (Armenian) Massacres" in Israel W. Charny (ed.) *Encyclopedia of Genocide*. Vol. 1. Santa Barbara, Calif.: ABC-CLIO, 287–88. Also available through the Internet at: www.armeniangenocide.org/ hamidian.html.

Arnaldez, Roger (1962). *Etudes d'Orientalisme dediees a la memoire de Levi-Provencal*. Paris: G. P. Maisonneuve et Larose.

Bat Ye'or (1996). *The Decline of Eastern Christianity under Islam: From Jihad to Dhimmitude.* Rutherford, N.J.: Fairleigh Dickinson University Press.

—— (1985). *The Dhimmi: Jews and Christians under Islam.* Translated from the French by David Maisel, Paul Fonton, and David Littman. Rutherford, N.J.: Fairleigh Dickinson University Press.

—— (1996). *The Decline of Eastern Christianity under Islam: From Jihad to Dhimmitude—Seventh–Twentieth Century.* Translated from the French by Miriam Kochan and David Littman. Rutherford, N.J.: Farleigh Dickinson University Press.

—— (2002). *Islam and Dhimmitude: Where Civilizations Collide.* Madison, N.J.: Fairleigh Dickinson University Press.

Berger, Peter L. (1967). *The Sacred Canopy: Elements of a Sociological Theory of Religion.* Garden City, N.Y.: Doubleday.

Bostom, Andrew G. [no date]. "The Armenian Genocide Was a Jihad." Available through the Internet at: www.secularislam.org/articles/genocide.htm.

Braude, Benjamin, and Bernard Lewis (1982). *Christians and Jews in the Ottoman Empire: The Functioning of a Plural Society.* New York: Holmes & Meier.

Chua, Amy (2003). *World on Fire: How Exporting Free Market Democracy Breeds Ethnic Hatred and Global Instability.* New York: Doubleday.

Covenant (1972). In Cecil Roth (ed.) *Encyclopedia Judaica, Vol. 5.* New York: Macmillan, 1012–22.

Dadrian, Vahakn (2003). "Children as Victims of Genocide: The Armenian case." *Journal of Genocide Research,* 5(3): 421–37.

Eichrodt, Walter (1966). "Covenant and Law." *Interpretation: A Journal of Bible and Theology,* 20: 302–21.

Gaffney, Edward M. (1984). "Of Covenants Ancient and New: The Influence of Secular Law on Biblical Religion." *Journal of Law and Religion,* 2 (1): 117–44.

Hartunian, Abraham H. (1968). *Neither to Laugh Nor to Weep: A Memoir of the Armenian Genocide.* Boston, Mass.: Beacon Press.

Heizer, Oscar. (20 July 1915). "Report on the Treatment of Children in Trebizond." [Correspondence from Ambassador Henry Morgenthau to the Secretary of State.] Available through the Internet at: www.armeniangenocide.org/us-7-20-15-text.html.

Hillers, Delbert R. (1972). *Covenant: The History of a Biblical Idea.* Baltimore, Md.: Johns Hopkins University Press.

Hurewitz, J. C. (1596). *Diplomacy in the Near and Middle East: A Documentary Record.* Princeton: Van Nostrand.

Kelsay, John (1993). *Islam and War: A Study in Comparative Ethics.* Louisville, Ky.: Westminster/John Knox Press.

Kinross, Lord (1977). *The Ottoman Centuries: The Rise and Fall of the Turkish Empire.* New York: William Morrow.

Laoust, Henri (1948). *Le Traite de droit public d'Ibn Taimya.* Traduction annotee de la `Siyasa sar 'iya. Beirut: Institut Francais de Damas.

Lewis, Bernard (1993). *Islam and the West.* New York: Oxford University Press.

Lowe, David [no date]. "The Old Testament Covenant as a Form of Treaty." Available through the Internet at: http://pweb.jps.net/-davejen/covenantastreaty.htm.

McCarthy, Dennis J. (1972). *Old Testament Covenant: A Survey of Current Opinions.* Richmond, Va.: John Knox Press.

Mawdudi, Abul Ala (1997). *Towards Understanding Islam*. New York: Message Publications.

Mazower, Mark (2001). "The G Word". [Book review of Arnold J. Toynbee (ed.) *The Treatment of Armenians in the Ottoman Empire, 1915–1916: Documents Presented to Viscount Grey of Fallodon, Secretary of State for Foreign Affairs by Viscount Bryce*. Uncensored ed. Princeton, N.J.: Gomidas Institute, 2000.] *London Review of Books*, 23(3), 8 February 2001. Available through the Internet at: http:/l.lrb.co.uv23/nO3/mazoOl.html.

MEMRI (Middle East Research Institute) (27 January 2004). *Contemporary Islamic Ideology Authorizing Genocidal Murder*. *Special Report No. 25*. Available through the Internet at: http://memri.org/bin/articles.cgi?Page=archives&Area=st&ID=SR 2504# edu2.

Mendenhall, George E. (1955). *Law and Covenant in Israel and the Ancient Near East*. Pittsburgh, Pa.: Biblical Colloquium.

Rubenstein, Richard L. (1983). *The Age of Triage: Fear and Hope in an Overcrowded World*. Boston, Mass.: Beacon Press.

Sarafian, Ara (2001). "The Absorption of Armenian Women and Children into Muslim Households as a Structural Component of the Armenian Genocide," in Omer Bartov, and Phyllis Mack (eds.) *In God's Name: Genocide and Religion in the Twentieth Century*. Providence, R.I.: Berghahn Books, 209–21.

Sarkisyanz, Manuel (1975). *A Modern History of Transcaucasian Armenia*. Nagpur, India: Udyama Commercial Press.

Suny, Ronald Grigor (2001). Religion, Ethnicity, and Nationalism: Armenians, Turks, and the End of the Ottoman Empire," in Omer Bartov, and Phyllis Mack (eds.) *In God's Name: Genocide and Religion in the Twentieth Century*. New York: Berghahn Books, 23–61.

Toynbee, Arnold J. (ed.) (1916). *The Treatment of Armenians in the Ottoman Empire 1915–1916: Documents Presented to Viscount Grey of Fallodon, Secretary of State for Foreign Affairs by Viscount Bryce*. London: H. M. Stationery Office, 21–47. 2nd ed. Beirut: G. Doniguian & Sons.

Turkish Foreign Minister's Defense of the Armenian Massacres (1916). *Current History Magazine*, December. Available through the Internet at: www.cilicia. com/arolOc-nyt191612.html.

8

Islam and Genocide: The Case of Bangladesh in 1971

Mohammad Omar Farooq

INTRODUCTION: GENOCIDE IN EAST PAKISTAN

In 1971, the West Pakistani army carried out genocide in East Pakistan. Adam Jones reflects on his Internet site that "the mass killings in Bangladesh (then East Pakistan) in 1971 vie with the annihilation of the Soviet POWs, the holocaust [sic] against the Jews, and the genocide in Rwanda as the most concentrated act of genocide in the twentieth century" (Jones, n.d.). Unfortunately, it remains relatively unknown and studied.

The genocide lasted nearly nine months, during which Muslims, Hindus, and other non-Muslim minorities were killed indiscriminately. Ten million refugees fled to India. Ruling West Pakistani elites abused Islam to subjugate and punish East Pakistanis for seeking justice, regional autonomy, and freedom from being treated as a colony. Western countries supported Pakistan in general, albeit sometimes chiding its military regime. The United States went much further, supporting the army both politically and militarily, despite vehement protest from its diplomatic staff in East Pakistan (Hitchens, 2001). Meanwhile, Pakistan claimed to be the first Islamic republic of the postcolonial twentieth century. The Muslim world mostly supported its propaganda, both internationally and domestically, while remaining ignorant or silent about the genocide.

This was probably the only modern genocide in which a so-called Islamic republic set out to kill Muslims, even though Hindus and other minorities were also targeted. Islam has been utilized to slice Pakistan from British-colonized India, and it was now abused to commit this genocide. In this context, we shall explore some legitimate questions about the abuse of Islam for genocide.

A HISTORICAL OVERVIEW

Two strains of Islam are prevalent in South Asia: the Muslim merchants, saints, and preachers, especially those hailing from the East, and the religion that spread via Arab military expeditions to Sind during the early eighth century, when some Muslim women were taken hostage and all efforts for their release failed (Schimmel, 1980: 4). Various competing and contending Muslim rulers have since been present, including the Mughals (1526–1858), who arrived and settled in India in the sixteenth century. They, along with the British who came afterward, helped shape the new India that some fanatical Hindus may now consider as *akhand bharat* (indivisible India). Notably, these rulers had no Islamic legitimacy, as the Qur'an and the Prophetic legacy call for governance based on *Shura* (mutual consultation) and a representative, participatory, and accountable framework. India, nonetheless, developed and prospered considerably with its Arab/Muslim contacts. Jawaharlal Nehru (1889–1964), the first Indian prime minister, observed that "culturally the contact of the Arabs with the people of India had great results" (Nehru, 1989: 154).

During the strong and virtually incontestable Muslim rule in India, communal problems were marginal, and "beneath the ruffled surface of storm and stress, there flowed a genial current of mutual harmony and toleration in different spheres of life" (Majumdar, et al., 1967: 394). Some Muslim rulers did come to only invade and plunder, however, adding to majority resentment. Regardless, Indian history must record the Muslim rulers' general tolerance toward non-Muslims and their interest in preserving pluralism and tolerance. Amartya Sen, an Indian/Bengali Nobel Laureate economist, comments that "the presence of diversity and variety within a tradition applies very much to Islam as well." The Mughal emperors were generally "not only extremely tolerant, but some even theorized about the need for tolerating diversity" (Sen, 1998: 42; see similar observations by Hodgson, 1974: 334).

Hindu-Muslim relationships, affected by the Muslim minority rule over the Hindu majority, and in some cases by the discriminatory or repressive roles of some Muslim rulers, became strained when the British conquered and colonized India. The British channeled the tension to advance colonial interests, exacerbating it further. During the two centuries of its rule, Britain's politics played an increasingly divisive role, which became pronounced when Gandhi upheld "Hindu-Muslim unity as a prerequisite to true self-determination" or independence from the British (Thursby, 1975:

130, 173). As the British left, India looked forward to its independence as two sections: a primary homeland for Muslims and another one for Hindus.

The 1947 partition occurred amidst Hindu-Muslim hostilities, with massacres and displacement of millions. Islam was a key rallying point for Muslim independence; after the partition, it remained at center-stage for Pakistan. The "Two Nation theory" that is, that Muslims and Hindus are two separate nations and, given the power and other dynamics of the region, Muslims might not secure their rights or expect their fair share in an undivided India was pivotal to polarizing Hindus and Muslims and galvanizing support for a separate Muslim homeland.

The seeds for Pakistan's subsequent split in 1971 were sown in its conceptual framework. The Muslim League began in East Bengal; Bengali Muslims were at the forefront of the movement for autonomy. Politics during 1940–1947 resulted in a major turnabout for Bengali Muslims. Muslim-majority Bengal did not become independent, achieving autonomy as a region as envisioned. Instead, due to communalism, especially of the elite Hindus of West Bengal (Chatterji, 1994: 16), and the machinations of the non-Bengali leadership of the Muslim League, Bengal was split along religious lines to form the eastern wing of Pakistan and West Bengal, a part of India. This contradicted the Lahore Resolution of 1940, which had outlined an independent or autonomous status for Bengal, along with several other contiguous areas with a Muslim majority. Under the resolution, neither was to become a part of Pakistan as a nation-state nor was it to be split.

Thus, the partition of 1947 had this Hindu-Muslim issue at its core, as did the partition of Bengal. Pakistan became a unique independent nation with two wings almost 1,100 miles apart and a large, rather hostile country in between. Cross-migration of Muslims and Hindus due to religion was both voluntary and coerced, marking an ugly, gruesome, and shameful chapter for both. In addition, East Pakistan had a rude awakening from Pakistan's very inception as it met with neglect and contempt from its counterpart-minority in West Pakistan. In language and almost every other aspect, West Pakistani elites followed policies that relegated East Pakistan to the status of a colony (Payne, 1973: 8; Jahan, 1997).

East Pakistan made energetic efforts to reconcile with West Pakistan. Yet the Language Movement of the early 1950s (which was led by Bengali Muslims, including organized groups such as Tamaddun Majlis), its military vulnerability during the India-Pakistan war in 1965, and the neglect of the leadership during the 1970 cyclone that killed 200,000 people served to strengthen the demand for greater regional autonomy.

After a sustained period of military oligarchy, Pakistan seemed to be progressing toward democracy. In 1970, a free and fair general election was held. The Awami League, under the leadership of Sheikh Mujibur Rahman

(1920–1975), won the majority. This would have enabled an East Pakistani party to form a national government for the first time. As it turned out, East Pakistan's jubilation and relief were premature. Ruling military elites of Pakistan, supported by such leading West Pakistani politicians as Zulfikar Ali Bhutto (1928–1979), had decided against transfer of power to the democratically elected government. In the words of Robert Payne: "The People of East Pakistan, by declaring for regional autonomy, had assumed the role of the enemy in the eyes of the military elites in West Pakistan. They must therefore be punished, and the punishment would take the form of a general massacre. It was believed that the shock of a general massacre would bring the East Bengalis to their senses" (1973: 31).

As the show of political games continued, the military proceeded to beef up its presence in East Pakistan. On 25 March 1971, it began a preplanned massacre to suppress East Pakistan's demand for regional autonomy and punish its people for their aspirations. "For month after month in all the regions of East Pakistan the massacres went on. They . . . went about their work mechanically and efficiently, until killing defenseless people became a habit like smoking cigarettes and drinking wine. Before they had finished, they had killed three million people. Not since Hitler invaded Russia had there been so vast a massacre" (Payne, 1973: 29). Rummel's mean estimate is 1,500,000, which includes an estimated minimum of 50,000 "revenge-killings" of non-Bengalis and collaborators with the Pakistani army by agitated Bengali mobs and pro-liberation resistance forces during 1971, and by the first government of the newly independent country (Rummel, 1997: 155). These also, by all definitions, were crimes against humanity.

Beginning on 25 March, the events of 1971 marked the final hours of an ill-fated union, as the people of what is now Bangladesh realized the two Pakistan's marriage was headed for divorce. That it would be so painful and ugly was underestimated. Nonetheless, India was never happy having its adversary Pakistan on both sides of its border. Pakistani ruling elites offered India the excuse it needed to directly and militarily intervene in East Pakistan. On 16 December 1971, the Pakistani army formally surrendered to its Indian counterpart, and, assisted by India's indulgent midwifery (Wheeler, 2000), the struggle and suffering of East Pakistanis ended with the birth of independent Bangladesh.

GENOCIDE 1971: SOME PERTINENT ASPECTS

Modern genocide studies have helped clarify general aspects of the phenomenon. In the context of this genocide, several key aspects can be identified.

Racism or a Sense of Superiority

Almost all genocides reflect forms of racism manifested in the perpetrators' overt display of superiority. In this case, Pakistani ruling elites were evidently condescending toward East Pakistanis. "Blind contempt for the Bengalis has always been a common failing of the colonially minded administration" (Mascarenhas, 1971: 83). Ayub Khan (1907–1974), a military dictator of Pakistan, "thought of [Bengalis] as the conquered people, while the inhabitants of West Pakistan were the descendants of conquerors" (Payne, 1973: 41). Even religiously, the Muslims of East Pakistan were not as good but were considered "half-Muslims" (Mascarenhas, 1971: 18).

Demonization, Deception, and Brutality

It requires considerable indoctrination, including but not limited to demonization of the victims, to instigate otherwise ordinary people to kill indiscriminately. In this case, indoctrination of the West Pakistani military "consisted of a short course on the psychology of the Bengalis, who were depicted as weaklings, traitors, and subversives who loved India more than Pakistan, and who were not true Muslims. Their instructions were to put down a rebellion that was expected to occur in the near future" (Payne, 1973: 13). Pakistani soldiers "had been brought from the West with a 'mission of killing *kafers* (disbelievers),'" only to realize soon "that the military authorities had set them against those who cannot be called religious enemies" (Chaudhury, 1972: 159).

The newly appointed military chief for East Pakistan, General Tikka Khan (1915–2002), seemed determined to carry out the plans of the ruling establishment by teaching all Bengalis a lesson they would never forget. He boasted of "erasing a race of bastards in Bangladesh" by destroying their "Hinduite culture" and teaching them how to be "true Mussalmans" (Chaudhury, 1972: 70).

Dichotomized View Based on Hatred and Prejudice

The environment for genocide is often framed by estrangement of people via a dichotomized view of "us vs. them" (Stanton, 1996; Waller, 2002: 238). Minds are ambushed by a devious psychosis: "either you are with us or against us." Such a perspective can turn airplanes into objects of terror, striking people randomly and indiscriminately. Similarly, by this logic an entire nation can be held hostage through sanctions causing almost a million deaths, including half a million children (Powell, 1998: E01), imposed in order to punish a former friend and ally (like that of Baghdad or Halabjeh).

Despite the disproportionate contribution and sacrifice made by Bengal's Muslim majority to bring about independence from colonial rule, the people of East Pakistan were marginalized and exploited soon after partition and, over time, treated as a colony. They became "them" for the ruling and military elite "us" of (West) Pakistan. In this dichotomy, the core hatred underpinning the subcontinent's Hindu-Muslim relationship affected the ties between Pakistan and India, spilling over to those between East and West Pakistan (Thursby, 1975: 134–35).

Lack of Democracy

R. J. Rummel, a noted genocide scholar, argues that the degree of democratic freedom a people enjoys is strongly correlated in high inverse proportion to the likelihood of a government committing democide. Hardly any domestic genocide has been committed by modern democracies, and totalitarian governments account for the vast majority of genocides. From this perspective, "power kills; absolute power kills absolutely" (Rummel, 1997: 267).

The genocide of 1971 offers a textbook example of what can happen under authoritarianism and lack of democracy. Since its inception, Pakistan had never experienced effective, sustained democracy. As soon as an outcome of democracy appeared to favor the neglected and exploited majority, its military proceeded to kill it (Mascarenhas, 1971: 26).

ISLAM AND CRIMES AGAINST HUMANITY

Since the genocide was carried out under the pretext of defending a united Pakistan, ostensibly created "in the name of Islam," the issue of Islam and genocide deserves greater scrutiny.

The twentieth century has logged numerous genocides, rationalized by explicit or implicit ideological warrants. As Kuper argues "The religious facilitation of genocide is only one of the many available legitimizing warrants" (Kuper, 1990: 353). Nonreligious ideologies, such as Nazism, Communism, ideologies of colonization, or even capitalism, may or may not have explicit warrants but nonetheless contain ingredients for inciting or abetting genocide. Yet religion by itself has not been a common cause for genocides. "It is clear from the . . . case studies of genocidal conflict that the theological warrants for genocide, or other religious beliefs which might facilitate genocide, do not operate in isolation from the societal context. They interact" (Kuper, 1990: 375).

Islam served as a rallying cry to galvanize Muslims' support for Pakistan as their separate homeland, but since its inception, its foundation has not included Islam. Anthony Mascarenhas, the journalist working for the London-based newspaper the *Sunday Times*, who really brought the story of the genocide of the Bengali people to the attention of the international community, covered it from the field throughout 1971 and authored a well-documented book of that period. He wrote: "Pakistan, indeed, did have an ideological basis, but it has certainly not developed into an ideological state in the accepted sense of the term. . . . If the contrary were true, . . . [T]he world would . . . not be witnessing now the horror being perpetrated by a Muslim army from West Pakistan on the Bengali Muslims of the eastern part of the country" (Mascarenhas, 1971: 7–8).

Payne takes a harsh view of Pakistani military elites: "It was against the Muslim creed to drink spirits, but they drank prodigiously. Islam frowns on excess, and demands that all men should live in humble servitude to God, and they were the least humble of men. The essential egalitarianism of Islam, by which the slave becomes the equal of the master, had no meaning for them. They observed the outward formalities of Islam if it pleased them or if it suited them, but did not feel bound to them. They were above the law, even the moral law" (Payne, 1973: 37). Nevertheless, they identified no reason to suspect God would not be on their side simply because they did not follow or uphold Islamic principles or guidance. Indeed, as if to defile Islam's historical legacy, they recruited and organized armed groups of militias named after important events in Islamic history. One such group was Al Badr, named after "the battle of Badr, which Mohammed fought successfully in 624 with 300 of his own followers pitted against a thousand Meccans" (Payne, 1973: 46). With this Islamic veneer they took up the mission: "The green of East Pakistan must be painted red"—that is, drowned in blood (Payne, 1973: 47).

Let us briefly address the four pertinent aspects of the 1971 genocide mentioned above from the Islamic religious perspective. On the subject of racism, it must be stressed that antiracism is one of the pristine aspects of Islam. The Qur'an is categorically against any artificial superiority of a human being over another based on race, language, color, status, age, or gender: "*Verily the most honored of you in the sight of God is (the person who is) the most God-conscious*" (Qur'an/49:13). The Last Sermon of the Prophet included this clarion call to humanity: "O people, Remember that your Lord is One. An Arab has no superiority over a non-Arab nor a non-Arab any superiority over an Arab; also a black has no superiority over white, nor a white any superiority over black, except by piety and good actions. Indeed the best among you is the one with the best character." Yet, just because Islam's message is egalitarian, it does not assert that those claiming to be its adherents would uphold it. Anyone who looks down upon another human being, whether a fellow Muslim or a non-Muslim, defies Islam.

Islam is also against demonization, deception, or brutality. It categorically rejects the human susceptibility to hatred, prejudice, and treating others unjustly. "O you who believe! Stand out firmly for justice, as witnesses to God, even as against yourselves, or your parents, or your kin, and whether it be [against] rich or poor: for God can best protect both. Follow not the lusts [of your hearts], lest you swerve, and if you distort [justice] or decline to do justice, verily God is well-acquainted with all that you do" (Qur'an/4:135).

Regarding cruelty and brutality, Muhammad could not have said it more clearly and emphatically: "God will definitely enforce the settlement of all the dues to those entitled to receive them on the Day of Judgment, even the wrong done to a hornless goat by a horned goat will be addressed" (Riyadus Saleheen, #204). Thus, infliction by anyone of systematic, brutal tortures on Muslims or non-Muslims is a perversion of Islam.

The problem of a dichotomized worldview is endemic, irrespective of its religious or secular interpretations. This is a major vulnerability of Muslims as well. Islamic orthodoxy did develop a worldview based on a dichotomy between *dar al-Harb* (Abode of War) and *dar al-Islam* (Abode of Peace), laying down detailed rules and codes for both war and peace. While genocides do not have rules, a dichotomized worldview, especially one tinged with prejudice, can foster conditions for violence and aggression. Although the *dar al-Harb/al-Islam* dichotomy cannot be used to legitimize crimes against humanity, in the context of India-Pakistan dichotomized sentiments prevailed. Bengali Hindus were dehumanized and demonized, and Bengali Muslims were portrayed as semi-Hindus, half-Hindus, or not genuine Muslims. The outcome was the same for both the Muslims and Hindus of East Pakistan who resisted the colonial, hegemonic rule of West Pakistan and especially for those who participated in, supported, or sympathized with the independence movement after 25 March 1971.

Encouragingly, contemporary Islamic discourse is reassessing classical orthodoxy's worldview as unwarranted, reformulating it to be more inclusive and pluralistic (AbuSulayman, 1993; Ramadan, 2003). The reformulation seeks better harmony with a humanity-oriented vision of the Qur'an as well as the Prophet's legacy. War will always be legitimate for self-defense and, in some cases, to thwart aggression. Acknowledging this long before any multilateral international treaties, Islam had proactively set laws and codes for wars or conflicts (El-Dakkak, 2000). However, unless the Qur'an is analyzed in fragments and used or abused for questionable interests and agendas, the Islamic norm of the relationship with others is based on this unambiguous verse: "Let there be *no hostility* except against those who practice oppression" (Qur'an/2:193).

Though it stands against all racism or demonization/dehumanization, Islam may not sufficiently prevent persecution or genocide by Muslims. Human beings will do what they are bent upon doing; their history manifests this. Even without any "theological warrants," literalists, extremists, and authoritarian power abusers have abused Islam, pitting Muslims against Muslims and non-Muslims alike. The 1971 genocide is a tragic example: major Western powers aside, generally the Muslim world remained silent or ignorant about it; worse, some Muslims in East Pakistan even collaborated with the genocidal army. The contention that Muslims need a collective mechanism and framework to defeat such destructive tendencies seems quite compelling.

The Qur'an is categorically against hatred or prejudice that prevents people from being just. "O ye who believe! stand out firmly for God, as witnesses to fair dealing, and *let not the hatred of others to you* make you swerve to wrong and depart from justice. Be just: that is next to piety: and fear God" (Qur'an/5:8). Regrettably, this Qur'anic clarification did not prevent the 1971 genocide.

In addition to the need for a reformulation of Islamic thought, there seems a critical need for a democratic environment and institution in governance. The 1971 genocide was perpetrated to subvert the democratic process. A powerful, entrenched and maniacal military regime resolved to do anything to deny this democratic governance by the people. Here it is noteworthy that the legacy of Islam during the immediate post-Prophetic era was the foundation of a representative, participatory, and accountable form of governance, which was overthrown in a counterrevolution after the period of the Rightly Guided Caliphs. A system based on *Shura* (mutual consultation) of the people was replaced with hereditary, autocratic rule. Even the Prophet's own grandson and a number of his own family members were brutally massacred. Muslims familiar with this history studying the genocide of 1971 can benefit by learning about the ills of autocratic rule and genocide.

Muslims need to rebuild their societies for representative, participatory and accountable governance, in keeping with Islamic and democratic spirit (Farooq, 2002). Democratic societies are less likely to commit domestic massacre, as Rummel has powerfully argued. Democracy may not stop the genocide of "others," but it may help prevent potential genocides. It should be noted, however, that many authoritarian regimes have been abetted or even patronized by Western democracies. Hence, the Muslims' quest to move toward democracy faces both an internal and external challenge.

CONCLUSION

Genocides from both distant and recent history mark a loss of humanity of the perpetrators. Inhuman treatment of others—Muslims or non-Muslims,

Jews or non-Jews, communists or noncommunists, Armenians or non-Armenians, Bengalis or non-Bengalis—has been rationalized. Should faith, philosophy, ideology, creed, and conviction fail to guide and inspire us to reject parochial, exclusivist views and attitudes and acknowledge humanity above all else, we may not have seen the last genocides.

A Bangladeshi must not care only about genocides against Bangladeshis or Bengalis. A Muslim must not care only about genocides against Muslims. An Asian must not care only about genocides against Asians. As human beings we must care about all genocide, and most especially about the surviving victims.

A crime against humanity is a crime, regardless of the people involved. "If any one slew a person—unless it be for murder or for spreading mischief in the land—it would be as if he slew the whole people: and if any one saved a life, it would be as if he saved the life of the whole people" (Qur'an/5:32). This principle should offer a common ground on which to adopt a resolute stance against all crimes against humanity. Inspired by and anchored in Islam's universalistic principles, and joining hands with all others, Muslims can guard against becoming either victims or perpetrators of human rights abuses and crimes against humanity.

BIBLIOGRAPHY

AbuSulayman, Abdul Hamid (1993). *Towards an Islamic Theory of International Relations: New Directions for Methodology and Thought*. Herndon, Va.: International Institute of Islamic Thought.

Chatterji, Joya (1994). *Bengal Divided: Hindu Communalism and Partition: 1932–1947*. Cambridge: Cambridge University Press.

Chaudhury, Kalayan (1972). *Genocide in Bangladesh*. Bombay: Orient Longman.

El-Dakkak, M. Shokry (2000). *State's Crimes against Humanity: Genocide, Deportation, and Torture from the Perspectives of International and Islamic Laws*. Kuala Lumpur: A. S. Noordeen.

Farooq, Mohammad Omar (2002). "Islam and Democracy: Perceptions and Isperceptions," *Message International*, 27(4/5): 17–19.

Hitchens, Christopher (2001). "The Case against Henry Kissinger." *Harpers Magazine, Part 1: The Making of a War Criminal*. February, 302(1809), 33 (26p.); *Part 2: Crimes against Humanity*. March, 302(1810), 49 (26p.).

Hodgson, Marshall (1974). *The Venture of Islam: Conscience and History in a World Civilization*. Chicago, Ill.: University of Chicago Press.

Jahan, Rounaq (1997). "Genocide in Bangladesh," in Samuel Totten, William S. Parson, and Israel W. Charny (eds.), *Century of Genocide: Eyewitness Accounts and Critical Views*. New York: Garland, 291–316.

Jones, Adam [no date]. *Case Study: Genocide in Bangladesh, 1971*. Available through the Internet at: www.gendercide.org/casebangladesh.html.

Kuper, Leo (1990). "Theological Warrants for Genocide: Judaism, Islam and Christianity." *Terrorism and Political Violence*, 2(3): 351–79.

Majumdar, R. C., H. C. Raychaudhury, and Kalikunker Datta (1967). *An Advanced History of India*. New York: Macmillan.

Mascarenhas, Anthony (1971). *The Rape of Bangladesh*. Delhi: Vikas Publications.

McDowell, Rick (1998). "Iraq: As the People Suffer." *Catholic Worker Magazine*, January/February.

Nehru, Jawaharlal (1989). *Glimpses of World History: Being Further Letters to His Daughter, Written in Prison, and Containing a Rambling Account of History for Young People*. Delhi: Oxford University Press.

Payne, Robert (1973). *Massacre*. New York: Macmillan.

Powell, Michael (1998). "The Deaths He Cannot Sanction: Ex-U.N. Worker Details Harm to Iraqi Children," *Washington Post*, December 17, E01.

Ramadan, Tariq (2003). *Western Muslims and the Future of Islam*. London: Oxford University Press.

Rummel, R. J. (1997). "Statistics of Pakistan's Democide Estimates, Calculations, and Sources," in *Statistics of Democide: Genocide and Mass Murder since 1900*. New Brunswick, N.J.: Transaction Publishers. Also available through the Internet at: http://www.hawaii.edu/powerskills/sod.chap8.htm

——— . (2002). "Genocides," in *Encyclopedia Italiana*. Available through the Internet at: www.hawaii.edu/powerkills/genocide.ency.htm.

Schimmel, Annemarie (1980). *Islam in the Indian Subcontinent*. Leiden: E. J. Brill.

Sen, Amartya (1998). "Universal Truths: Human Rights and the Westernizing Illusion." *Harvard International Review*, 20(3): 40–43.

Simon, Mafoot (2003). "A New Voice in Muslim Europe." *The Straits Times* (Singapore), 6 August.

Stanton, Gregory (1996). "The Seven Stage of Genocides." Available through the Internet at: www.genocidewatch.org/7stages.html.

Thursby, G. R. (1975). *Hindu-Muslim Relations in British India: A Study of Controversy, Conflict, and Communal Movements in Northern India, 1923–1928*. Leiden: Brill.

Waller, James (2002). *Becoming Evil: How Ordinary People Commit Genocide and Mass Killing*. Oxford: Oxford University Press.

Wheeler, Nicholas J. (2000). "India as Rescuer? Order versus Justice in the Bangladesh War of 1971," in *Saving Strangers: Humanitarian Intervention in International Society*. Oxford: Oxford University Press, 55–77.

9

The Genocidal Twentieth Century in the Balkans

Paul Mojzes

INTRODUCTION

Ethnic nationalist, political, and economic reasons were the primary driving force for the series of genocides and ethnic cleansings that took place in the Balkans during the twentieth century; however, religious factors were closely interwoven in a role supportive of genocidal practices. Because the traditionally close linkage between nation and religion found in most of Europe has persisted most tenuously in Eastern Europe, for large segments of the population it is not clearly discernible which factor is *ethnonational* and which *ethnoreligious*. Political and military leaders easily manipulate this situation. In this chapter the history of the genocides and ethnic cleansing in the Balkans will be presented first, followed by examination of the issues of punishment of the perpetrators, cleansing and genocide, and the specific role of religion in these horrors.

Genocides frequently take place in wartime. That was the case in the frequent Balkan Wars. The First Balkan War took place in 1912–1913; the Second Balkan War in 1913. The First World War, 1914–1918, began in the Balkans. The Second World War, 1941–1945, was followed by what some have called the Third Balkan War (Glenny, 1994). I have made a case that this was not a single war but a series of wars, in Slovenia (1991), Croatia (1991–1996), Bosnia and Herzegovina (1992–1995), and the war over Kosovo (1999) (Mojzes, 1994: 97–121). Genocides and ethnic cleansing accompanied all but World War I. I have also argued that, in order to preserve the full shock value of the word genocide, one should distinguish it from a milder form called "ethnic cleansing," which is really a subcategory of genocide (Mojzes, 2002: 51–56).

FIRST AND SECOND BALKAN WAR GENOCIDES

In exploring the literature on genocide, one is unlikely to encounter mention of the First and Second Balkan wars. For one, at the time they were waged the word had not yet been invented. Then World War I came so soon on their heels overshadowing them in importance and devastation, that they were soon neglected. Unlike the genocide of the Armenians, the Balkan genocides were not carried out against a nationality that was later well represented in the West and whose members would be able to bring attention to their case. The Balkan genocides of 1912 and 1913 concerned four ethnic groups, and none made a sustained case that they had experienced genocide because they were not only victims but simultaneously also perpetrators.

Yet these were among the earliest European genocides in the twentieth century—preceding the Armenian genocides—with only the genocides against the African tribes by German colonial forces in 1902 taking place earlier. One would not know it from reading most of the histories of the Balkan Peninsula—they simply narrate the reasons for the wars, the course of military action, the results of the wars, and the peace treaties that followed. With the exception of a comment that the wars were particularly brutal, genocides are not mentioned (Wolff, 1956).

The genocidal nature of the first two Balkan wars is, however, duly underscored in the Carnegie Endowment Inquiry that produced "The Report of the International Commission to Inquire into the Causes and Conduct of the Balkan Wars," issued in 1913 (International Commission, 1993). The inquiry was conducted by a commission of eight members from Austria, France, Germany, Great Britain, Russia, and the United States. The First Balkan War was fought against Turkey by a coalition of Bulgaria, Greece, Montenegro, and Serbia with the purpose of liberating territory held by the Turks in Europe. The Second was fought among the former allies for redistribution of the liberated lands, especially Macedonia. Bulgaria fought Greece, Serbia, and Montenegro, with Turkey and Romania joining in the war against Bulgaria for territorial gains.

These wars were relatively short but, by their very nature, genocidal. For one, the aim was to eliminate the Turks—both soldiers and the population—from areas liberated by the Balkan nations. Second, territories occupied by the army of a nation were to be cleansed of inhabitants of other nationalities in order to establish the right to retain the land. Thus, in areas where the population was mixed—which was frequently the case—the winners drove out or indiscriminately slaughtered the other ethnic populations. Villages were burned down, often with people in them, small babies roasted alive, women raped and usually killed, men rounded up and executed. Large numbers of people were made into fugitives who were hunted down like animals; plunder was commonplace, as was torture. The commission cited details supported by photographs, testimonies of witnesses, letters by soldiers to their families; war posters glorified atrocities carried out against the enemy, who may have been an ally six months earlier. Macedonians had not yet been recognized as a distinct ethnicity, and they suffered from attacks by all who contested parts of Macedonia. As a result of the wars, Albania was created, albeit with undefined borders—thus Albanians became involved in the chaotic war crimes, but in a more or less disorganized manner.

Some of the genocides were spontaneous acts committed by the military and paramilitary or even the local population, but many of the attacks were commanded by higher officers who intended to lead their campaign to victory by impressing upon enemies that the savagery might end if they surrendered and evacuated the territory. A French observer, for instance, reported "atrocities were almost always enjoined by the officers on their men, who, despite their native harshness, hesitated to strike other Slavs, but yesterday their brothers in arms" (International Commission, 1993: 140). There were forcible conversions of Muslims to Christianity, many imposed under the conviction that since Turks had converted Christians to Islam forcibly in the past it was right to bring their descendants back into the Christian fold, by coercion if necessary. It was around this time that someone applied Tzar Alexander III's infamous policy of "thirds" (originally directed toward the Jews of Russia): namely, one-third of Turks (a group that also included the native non-Turkic Muslim population) would be converted, one-third would be deported, and one-third would be killed. That goal was not fully carried out, especially not in regard to conversions, but the number of those driven away from their homes was very large. Objects of worship suffered destruction; in parts of Serbia, Bulgaria, and Greece, few mosques survived.

WORLD WAR I AND BEYOND

World War I broke out in the Balkans, triggered by the assassination of the Hapsburg Archduke Ferdinand and his wife in Sarajevo by a young Serb, and the subsequent attack upon Serbia by Austria-Hungary. Bloody battles with huge casualties were fought in Serbia, Albania, and Greece throughout the war, but so far no evidence has emerged of targeted genocides during this war. Thus, World War I has the distinction of being the only war in the twentieth-century Balkans without having genocidal dimensions.

This was not the case in the war between Greece and Turkey from 1919 to 1921. Strictly speaking, that was not a Balkan but an Asia Minor war in which Greece—on the urging of the Western powers—attempted to retake what in ancient times had been Greek inhabited lands in Asia Minor around the port of Smyrna (Izmir). Misha Glenny points out the scorched-earth nature of the initial Greek attack: eyewitnesses later testified that everyone, Turkish and Muslim, was exterminated on the territories occupied by the Greek army and paramilitary formations. When the fortunes of war turned in favor of the Turkish army led by the founder of the Turkish Republic, Kemal Pasha Ataturk, retaliation was visited mercilessly upon the Christian, i.e., the Greek and Armenian, population (Glenny, 2001: 382–92). This was another instance of mutual or alternating genocide. Glenny concludes that this was the actual ending of the Balkan wars that began in 1912.

THE HOLOCAUST AND
THE GENOCIDES DURING WORLD WAR II

The peak of genocidal destructiveness in the Balkans was reached in World War II, particularly on the territory of Yugoslavia and to a lesser degree in Greece. Yugoslavia was occupied and partitioned by the Axis powers into about ten units, some falling under direct German, Italian, Hungarian, and Bulgarian occupation, others becoming puppet-governments of the Independent State of Croatia and a Serbian ministate, and still others annexed by Albania, which had already fallen under Italian rule prior to the outbreak of World War II. Greece was occupied by Germany, with smaller parts taken by Bulgaria, which had joined the Axis powers. The genocides varied from place to place.

Three groups were especially targeted for genocide: Jews, Serbs, and Roma. The most consistent genocide was carried out against Jews, who were targeted for total extermination. Only Bulgarian Jews managed to escape being surrendered to the death camps. In all lands under German control or influence, anti-Semitic legislation resembling the Nazi Nuremberg laws was passed. The Croatian and Bulgarian legislatures eagerly mimicked the German legislation limiting employment, movement, and property rights, and otherwise discriminating against the Jews living in these lands. Very quickly, Jews were incarcerated in concentration camps and the killing began.

The fate of Jews under Bulgarian control varied significantly, depending on whether they lived in Bulgaria proper or in the lands Bulgaria occupied in 1941. In all Bulgarian-controlled lands, Jews were subjected to humiliating and restrictive anti-Jewish measures as a result of the Bulgarians' alliance with Germany. A high Bulgarian government official was sent to Germany to learn firsthand how to oppress the Jews. According to the 1934 census, there were 48,400 Jews in Bulgaria (four-fifths of 1 percent of the population), of whom 97 percent lived in cities, half of them living in Sofia. Despite official persecution, they were saved due to the courageous resistance of some Bulgarian intellectuals, Orthodox bishops, and parliamentary deputies, in the final instance, convinced King Boris III to resist Nazi pressure and allow the vast majority of Bulgarian Jews to live. Metropolitan Stefan stressed the difference between converts and nonconverts. He also asked that Jews be judged by their actions, not by who they were. A parliamentary deputy, Dimitar Peshev, spoke out courageously and wrote a letter to the National Assembly protesting the Law for the Defense of Nation but was eventually thrown out of the National Assembly for his letter and remarks (Todorov, 2001: 4, 50, 54, 123, 125–31). Yet the trend was established: along with Denmark and Italy, Bulgaria was one of the few countries whose Jews escaped genocide, for which Bulgaria has received rightful recognition.

Unfortunately, the same cannot be said for the Jews of Macedonia and Thrace, two areas that were annexed by Bulgaria during World War II. Bulgarians considered both Macedonia and Thrace to be "newly liberated territories" that were rightfully theirs, and that which they had been unjustly deprived during the Second Balkan War and World War I. All the inhabitants of Macedonia and Thrace became Bulgarian citizens except their Jews, to whom the generally appreciative attitudes in regard to the wartime Bulgarian government do not apply. The Bulgarian army and police arrested and delivered the Jews of Macedonia and Thrace almost in their entirety to the death camp at Treblinka. In late March of 1943, the Jews of Bitola, Štip, Skopje, and other smaller towns of Macedonia were assembled at the "Monopol" Tobacco Factory in Skopje and, in three transports, expeditiously surrendered by Bulgarian authorities to the SS, who delivered 7,358 Jews to their deaths in Treblinka (Lebl, 1990: 325–47; Kolonomos and Veskovik-Vangeli, 1986). The Jews of Pirot (Serbia) and Thrace, about 4,200 of them, were sent north to the city of Lom on the Danube and in March 1943 were shipped first to Austria and from there to Treblinka (Kolonomos and Veskovik-Vangeli, 1986: 355–56). Percentage-wise, Macedonia lost about 97 percent of its Jewish population.

Germany had also occupied much of Greece. For the first year, they did not undertake drastic measures against the 50,000 Jews of Thessaloniki (Salonica) but instead made a thorough inventory of their assets. In July 1942, 9,000 Jewish men were compelled to form a forced-labor brigade that was tormented in order to "soften up" the Jewish community, first for plunder and then for deportation. The Jews, who made up nearly half the city's population, were segregated in ghettos by March 1943 and were then speedily (between March and August) deported to Auschwitz along with

another 9,000 Jews from Athens, Ioannina, Corfu, and the Greek islands
(Glenny, 2001: 511–18; Roth, 2000: 516). Most of them were gassed im-
mediately upon arrival, while about 12,000 remained for forced labor. The
Greek population also suffered terribly, mostly from starvation.

The German occupational authorities were swiftest in eliminating the
Jews of Serbia (including the Banat region of Vojvodina), where they held
full sway. Zeni Lebl described in two of her publications how Serbia had
become practically *"Judenfrei"* even prior to the Wannsee Conference of
January 1942 which affirmed the decision for the "Final Solution" (Lebl,
2001; 2002). The Germans occupied the territory in April 1941. The chief
of the German military command, Turner, issued the following order to all
his commanders in October 1941, well after the extermination of Jews had
already begun:

> In principle it has been determined that Jews and Gypsies represent elements
> of disorder and as such threaten public peace and order. The Jewish intellect
> caused this war and has to be destroyed. Gypsies, by their internal and external
> characteristics cannot be members of human communities. It has been deter-
> mined that the Jewish element to a considerable degree took part in leading
> the [resistance] bands, while the Gypsies are responsible for acts of cruelty and
> intelligence gathering. Therefore, in principle, in case [of reprisals (Levntal's
> note)] all Jews and all Gypsies are to be supplied to our troops as hostages.
>
> In addition there is the intention for the women and children of Jews and
> Gypsies to be first detained in a collection camp and then removed from that
> element by deportation from the Serbian region. For that goal all necessary
> preparations are to take place. (Levntal, 1952: 17)

At first, all Jewish men were arrested and held as hostages, mostly in several
Belgrade detention centers. As guerilla activity began against the German military in July of that year, the German authority exacted revenge by killing 100
Serb or Jewish hostages for every dead German. Since the Jewish males had
already been incarcerated, they were the most frequent shooting victims, but
thousands of Gypsies were likewise terminated, as were many Serbs (Levntal,
1952: 19). By the end of October 1941, all the Jewish men had been shot
(Lebl, 2001: 321). The rest of the Jewish families from Banat were rounded
up during the summer of 1941. After a short stopover in Belgrade between
8 and 12 December 1941, they were taken, together with Belgrade's Jewish
women and children, to the *"Sajmište"* fairgrounds on the other side of the
river, technically on the territory of the independent state of Croatia. There
they lived in miserable conditions, while groups of women and children were
transported back to Belgrade daily in a large truck brought in from Germany,
in which by the time they arrived on the outskirts of the city, they had been
poisoned by carbon monoxide. After the war, survivors nicknamed the truck
"dušegupka" (soul exterminator).

All the Jewish inmates were exterminated by early May 1942, where-upon the Nazis concluded that Serbia was *Judenfrei,* except for some who had contracted mixed marriages (Lebl, 2001: 332). About 90 percent (or 14,500) of the 16,000 Jews of that area perished, making it, along with Macedonia, the site of one of the highest percentages of Jewish victims of the Holocaust. Only those Jews who ran into the woods to join the guerillas (many of whom were killed in action), those who were taken to Germany as Yugoslav army POWs, and those who successfully fled to Italian-occu-pied territories escaped this extermination. Lebl also points out the irony that most Jewish POWs in German POW camps survived the war while their families, as well as those who hid prior to being sent to the camps were killed (Lebl, 1995).

Hungary had occupied Bačka, Baranya, and parts of Medjumurje. Initially Hungary protected its Jewish population, although discriminatory measures were taken against them. An exception happened in Novi Sad and Southern Bačka where a massacre of the Jews and Serbs of the region took the lives of an estimated 3,000 people on 21–23 January 1942. As a pretext it was called *racja*—"raid"—allegedly in response to some minor communist-led sabotage and attacks on Hungarian police and soldiers (Golubović, 1992: 51–149). Golubović provides a total of 3,340–3,809 victims, but the record indicates that whereas some of these victims were killed in the same year, they did not die during the January *racija*. In Novi Sad, for example, the number of killed Jews (809) exceeded that of the Serbs (375) (Golubović, 1992: 141). Then Jews of military age had been conscripted into working battalions and initially were kept in camps such as Bačka Topola, from which they were taken as forced labor to dig trenches and do other hard labor for Hungarian army units fighting in Ukraine and other parts of the Soviet Union, where almost none survived. The rest of the Jewish popula-tion was forced to wear the Jewish star and suffered various types of harass-ment but were not deported until the fall of 1944, when the Nazi German authorities engineered a coup d'etat and installed an extremely right-wing fascist Hungarian government that permitted Adolf Eichmann to carry out extermination of the very sizable Jewish population of Hungary proper as well as all Hungarian occupied territories (450,000) by delivering them to Auschwitz. This sealed the fate of the Jews who lived in Hungarian-occu-pied Yugoslav territories, few of whom survived the deportation.

The most complex and highest in genocidal casualties took place on the territory of the Independent State of Croatia (abbreviated to NDH for *Nezavisna Država Hrvatska*). Hitler and Mussolini rewarded the puppet gov-ernment of Ante Pavelić with large portions of Croat land (except that sig-nificant segments of the Dalmatian littoral were ceded to Italy) plus Bosnia and Herzegovina. Three nationalities became the primary target of genocide in this Croat state: Jews, Serbs, and Roma.

The Croat state took on the anti-Semitic stance of Hitler's *Third Reich*, immediately discriminating against and then exterminating most of the Jews living on that territory. Of the 40,000–60,000 Jews who lived there, only about 5 percent of them survived. The Jews of Bosnia and Herzegovina who came under the control of NDH were also rounded up, and of its approximately 14,000 Jews 12,000 died in camps of Croatia and Auschwitz (Levntal, 1952: 64). While some of them were deported to the large extermination camps in Poland, most of them were destroyed in Croatia's own death camps, primarily in Jadovno near Gospić and Jasenovac. Jasenovac in particular was an effective extermination camp—some claim that, in terms of killings, it was the third largest camp in Europe, right after Auschwitz and Treblinka. The main camp was Jasenovac proper but the name applies also to a complex of about seven camps on a territory of about 100 square miles. A total of twenty-six concentration camps were established on the territory of NDH, such as Drnje, Kruščica, Surovo, Bugojno, Bijeljina, Lepoglava, Rogatica, Vlasenica, Tuzla, Tenje, and Pag, but only Jadovno, Jasenovac, and Stara Gradiška were large extermination camps.

The animosity between Croats and Serbs is of relatively recent origin. There had been some tensions between the Catholic Croats and Orthodox Serbs based on religious rivalry since the eleventh century. There was also some Croat resentment of privileges given by the Hapsburg monarchs to Serbs who had settled in the border region between the Ottoman and Hapsburg empires and were willing to fight for the Hapsburgs. But the animosity increased greatly during the establishment of a common state, the Kingdom of Serbs, Croats, and Slovenes (renamed Yugoslavia in 1929), when many Croats experienced the rule of the Serbian (by then Yugoslav) king as the Serb subjugation of Croats. An extremist reaction to this perception took shape as the supernationalist *ustaša* movement corresponding to the Nazi SS which took on the racist position that Serbs were an inferior people from whom Croats needed to segregate themselves and eliminate from Croat land. Ustaša troops were distinguished from the *domobran*, the less ideological Croat national guard units, but were comparable to the *četniks*, the Serb extreme nationalist paramilitary units who combined with the remnants of the prewar Yugoslav army units consisting of Serbs.

Almost immediately upon taking control in April 1941, the new *ustaše* puppet government passed laws saying that all who dishonored the Croatian people were to be executed. This was followed by racial and ethnic exclusionary laws against Jews and Serbs (Decree "On Racial Affiliation," 1941). While Jews were to be simply eliminated, in regard to the Serbs the old formula of thirds was resurrected by Mile Budak, the Minister of Education of NDH (Lituchy, 1998). One third of about 2.2 million Serbs would be converted to Catholicism, one-third killed, and one-third deported to Serbia. Milan Zanić, another minister in this government, stated that "this must be Croatian and of no one else, and there is no method that we as Ustashe will not use in order to make this country truly Croatian and to cleanse it of Serbs, who would threaten us at the first chance. We do not hide this fact. That is the policy of this state, and when we carry it out we will act only according to the principle of the Ustashe" (Dedijer, 1992: 131).

The perpetrators, mostly *ustaše*, approached the task methodically and cruelly—so cruelly that even some German Nazis were shocked while others were so impressed that they advocated the use of similar brutality by the SS. While most of the *ustaše* units were composed of Croats, who were traditionally Roman Catholic, there were also special formations of Muslims who regarded themselves as Croats but wore the fez as part of the uniform. Later, the Nazis recruited two Muslim Waffen-SS divisions, named Handžar and Kama, that were part of the Axis armies. Thus, at least in some locations in Bosnia and Herzegovina, Croatia, and Montenegro, people who were at least nominal Catholics and Muslims fought against Eastern Orthodox. In the Balkans, religion sometimes played a stronger identity role than ethnicity, though most often the two overlapped. Some of the Catholics regarded one part of the Orthodox population in Croatia as Croat and believed that once they were converted to Roman Catholicism, they would more firmly take on Croat rather than Serb self awareness.

While the complicity of the Catholic hierarchy (especially archbishop Alojzije Stepinac) is a subject of much controversy, a number of Roman Catholic priests participated in coercive conversions of Serbs (Suttner, 2003: 196–202). Some Serbs were thus saved from exterminations, others were killed despite their conversions, and still others were killed because they would not convert. There were also Catholic clergy who strenuously objected to such conversions and advocated a complete moratorium until the coercive pressure of the government ceased. Archbishop Stepinac permitted the clergy to convert Jews and Serbs to Catholicism speedily, allegedly to save them from death, asserting that those who really intended to convert are likely to remain Catholics while those who did it to save themselves will undoubtedly abandon Catholicism after the cessation of the oppressive conditions of life.

Killings of Serbs were far more voluminous than the conversions. The numbers are disputable, but not the brutality. Killings were carried out by knife, rifle butts, mallets, bullets, starvation, fire, drowning, decapitation, hanging, torture, rape, pushing into ravines, and every other conceivable means. Most died after they had been deported to concentration camps, but many were killed in their homes or neighborhoods, or while fleeing their homes. Sometimes only men between the ages 16 and 50 were massacred; at other times, every Serb from infancy to advanced age, were exterminated (Mirković, 1993: 317–32). Sometimes entire villages were completely wiped out, such as Prkos in Kordun, Croatia; at other times, more than one massacre occurred in the same village, such as Glina where a first massacre was followed by the slaughter of about 700 peasants, who were taken to a church, ostensibly to be converted to Catholicism (Mirković, 1993: 324).

One of the first Balkan concentration camps was Jadovno near Gospić. Any of the pits and ravines at the foot of Mount Velebit were filled with bodies, initially of Jews and then largely of Serbs, along with some Roma and Croats (Levntal, 1952: 59). Often the victims were bound to each other in a line, and the first few were killed with rifle butts or other implements (the *ustaše* bragged that they killed without firing bullets); and then the entire row would be pushed into the ravine (Bajić, 1990). Dogs were thrown into the pit to finish off the wounded. It is estimated that 2,500–2,800 Jews and a much larger number of Serbs, as well as a smaller number of other nationals, including many Romas—for a total of about 62,000–68,000 people—were killed in Jadovno. This camp was closed by October 1942 because a larger camp complex had been established in Jasenovac.

Of all of the concentration camps in the territory of the former Yugoslavia, Jasenovac undoubtedly has the worst reputation; some have called it "the Yugoslav Auschwitz" (Dedijer, 1992). Recently the Holocaust Memorial Museum in Washington, D.C., has devoted more attention to it; it is one of the few death camps listed in the Hall of Remembrance, along with Auschwitz, Dachau, Bergen-Belsen, Sobibor, and Treblinka. Opened between August 1941 and February 1942, Jasenovac was actually a complex of five major and three minor subcamps in a territory of about 150 square miles that operated till April 1945, when it was liberated by the *partizans*. It is alleged that about 20,000 children were murdered there, which is simply illustrative of the extraordinary cruelty with which this camp was run (see both www.ushmm.org and Jasenovac Research Institute for representative materials). The *ustaše* did not resort to the industrial-scale killings favored later by the Nazis; the killing methods resembled those used by the *Einsatzguppen* in the early stages of the Holocaust. Rape and even cannibalism took place. The *ustaše* camp commanders and guards excelled in torture and killing too ghastly to describe but perniciously selected a few from the thousands of Roma slated for death whom they ordered to be not only grave diggers but also rapists and executioners (Levntal, 1952: 101–3).

The greatest controversy surrounding the camps is the numbers. Soon after the end of World War II, the Yugoslav authorities claimed that 1,700,000 Yugoslavian citizens had been killed in the war, and that out of that number about 1,100,000 Serbs had lost their lives, 700,000 in Jasenovac. It is now recognized that these figures are exaggerated—they were extrapolations of demographic rather than real losses (meaning they include losses due to emigration, loss of natality, bombing, and disease, as well as death on the battlefield, killing and terror in the camps, etc. (Bogosaveljević, 1996: 159–70). In the prelude to the Balkan wars of the 1990s, namely the period after Tito's death in 1980, and in the course of the wars, the issue of the numbers of victims became part of war propaganda. Both Croats and Serbs reopened the questions of who had been the perpetrators and victims, and of how many were killed. Serbs tended to inflate the number of Serb victims and dismiss the importance of Croats who were killed, blaming the Croats in general for their losses; Croats, for their part, minimized the number of the Serb victims and concentrated on killings they attributed to Serbs. Thus, some Serbs claimed that more than a million Serbs died in Jasenovac alone, while some Croat sources said no more than 20,000 perished there.

While there is very little that is edifying in this shameful contest of maximizing and minimizing fatalities, the outcome is that we have a somewhat more accurate consensus emerging. At Jasenovac, 50,000 Serbs, 13,000 Jews, 10,000 Roma, and about 12,000 Croats and Muslims were killed (Mirković, 1993: 322). One of the reasons why numbers are difficult to establish is that the authorities had three weeks before the camp was captured by the *partizans* to excavate bodies and burn and destroy the material and written evidence, thereby covering up the enormity of the crime (Levntal, 1952: 105). The total number of actual victims (rather than demographic losses) caused by the NDH government are estimated at 350,000–400,000 Serbs, 60,000–65,000 Jews, and 27,000 Roma.

There is a complicated and troubling story of the activities of the Italian occupational forces. A widespread opinion holds that whereas Mussolini's Italy was anti-Semitic in its orientation that it actually protected Jews during the Holocaust. That reputation was believed accurate by Jews and Serbs who tried to reach Italian-held territory in order to be saved and for many it worked. It is fair to say that comparatively individual Italian officials and sometimes governing authorities showed a more humane attitude toward Jews and Serbs. But regretfully, for thousands of Jews and Serbs the experience was quite different. Many of the Jews who were running away from the *ustaše* were returned by a conscious decision of Italian authorities with clear knowledge of what would happen to these victims (Levntal, 1952: 120). Additionally Italian authorities interned Jews from such cities as Dubrovnik, Gorski Kotar, Split, and Sušak in concentration camps in Kraljevica and Rab. Some of these Jews managed to survive; others fell into German hands upon Italian surrender and perished.

The most tragic story is that of the concentration camp on the island of Pag. This island was under Italian supreme control but the *ustaše* was allowed to operate a camp for two months during the summer of 1941 in clear view of the Italian military in which gruesome torture, rape, and killing of Serbs and Jews took place. The dead were buried in shallow graves or thrown into the sea. After the *ustaše* closed the camp Italian soldiers exhumed the bodies and burned the remains (Levntal, 1952: 124–31). Thus, the good reputations both the Italian and Bulgarian enjoy regarding the Holocaust are gravely tarnished in the territory of Yugoslavia.

But it was not only the Nazis and their allies who were genocidal. Concurrently, Serb *četnik* forces carried out a massive genocide in their attempt to form a "greater Serbia" by establishing ethnically pure Serb areas in Bosnia and Montenegro. General Draža Mihajlović, the supreme commander of the *četnik* and Serb royalist forces, gave instructions to his officers to carry out "cleansing of Sandžak [an area of southwest Serbia] of Moslem population and cleansing Bosnia of Muslim and Croat population" (Miletić, 1990: xxv). About 86,000 Muslims were killed. (The number of Croats liquidated by the *četniks* remains unavailable.) Some of these were retaliatory attacks; others were Serb *četnik* forces unprovoked attacks of Croat and Muslim villages and dwellings. Entire villages, together with their inhabitants, were thus wiped out in Montenegro and Bosnia and Herzegovina.

Roma were killed, in camps and elsewhere, almost everywhere in the territory of the former Yugoslavia. Their numbers were not always easily established because some of them were nomads, but they were held in extremely low esteem and treated very poorly before and after the war. They were sometimes assigned the task to bury those who had been executed, only to be destroyed themselves when the job was finished. In a few cases, such as the Novi Sad *racija*, some sources stated that in addition to Jews and Serbs, Romas were also the target of the massacre, but closer investigation did not confirm that (Golubović, 1992: 148).

During the war Italy created a "greater Albania" as an Italian protectorate that also included most of Kosovo. Until Italy's surrender in 1943 Jews were relatively protected. After Italy's surrender Germans marched into these territories. A Waffen-SS division called Skender Beg (the name of a medieval Albanian hero) was formed of Albanians who bought into the Nazi ideology and they turned over the several hundred Jews who were hiding in Kosovo and Albania to the Nazis, who deported them for extermination at Bergen-Belsen. A far more extensive action was undertaken against the Serbs of Kosovo: thousands of them were killed and driven out of Kosovo in an act of ethnic cleansing (Morris, 1996: xviii). It is important to note this as a correction of the common misconception that the government of Slobodan Milosevic was the first to carry out ethnic cleansing in Kosovo in the 1990s. After the end of the war, Tito allegedly discouraged resettling of Serb and Montenegrin deportees in Kosovo in order to avoid additional bloodshed, a decision that Serbs in the 1980s and 1990s bitterly condemned as anti-Serbian. The internal security forces of Tito's government, however, imposed such harsh measures against the Albanian population that those measures assumed a retributive dimension.

The total number of "real casualties" for all of Yugoslavia ranged between 1,014,000 and 1,027,000, a staggering figure for a prewar population of about 18,000,000 (Mirković, 1993: 320). A large number of these deaths were genocidal, though the exact number will never be established with any degree of accuracy. The ravages of World War II left an indelible imprint on the collective and individual memories of its people.

AFTER WORLD WAR II AND BEFORE THE THIRD BALKAN WAR

At the very end of the war, the Croat *ustaše* and *domobran* as well as Montenegrin *četniks* had been withdrawn to Austria along with their family members and others who feared the Communist takeover (both *partizan* and Soviet) and hoped that they could surrender to the Western allies. Many of them perished in battles with the *partizans* but some succeeded in giving themselves up to the British forces in Austria. However, the British decided to turn them over to Tito's *partizans*. Indiscriminate massacres of the captives took place in the Bleiburg forest, Kočevski Rog, and other locations in Slovenia and Croatia. One group of captured endured the *križni put* (the path of the cross), during which they were transported back and forth between Croatia and Macedonia in cattle cars without food or water, with the dead simply ditched by the wayside.

The Yugoslav government kept these events strictly secret. Estimates of these massacre victims vary from 30,000 to 200,000, but the most accurate figures seem to be those of Vladimir Žerjavić, who posits that some 60,000 to 70,000 were killed in May 1945—specifically, 45,000–57,000 Croats and Muslims, 8,000 Slovenes, and over 3,000 Serbs and Montenegrins (Mirković, 1993: 322). Many of the mass graves have recently been excavated and their long-held secret publicized. Croatian nationalists depict them as the remains of Serbian-led massacres, but this is not an accurate portrayal. While it is true that most of the *partizans* were ethnic Serbs, there were among them Croat, Slovene, Muslim, and other nationals, and it is much more accurate to characterize these as massacres by the Communist-led *partizans* against the remnants of forces fighting on the Nazi side rather than genocide. They were clearly war crimes or politicides, but not genocides. Hungarian Nazi sympathizers in the Vojvodina were also massacred by *partizan* forces in the Vojvodina.

More clearly genocidal was the roundup of all German ethnics who had not withdrawn with the retreating German armies, approximately 500,000 of whom were living in Yugoslavia. All ethnic Germans were placed in concentration camps (usually former German villages) where most of them were incarcerated for many years, and in which mortality from disease and malnutrition was very high. An estimated 26,000 Germans perished as the result of the treatment in the camps. In the 1950s the Yugoslav government disbanded the camps and permitted the vast majority of Germans (about 400,000) to emigrate to Germany (Tudjman, 1996: 262). The effect was that Germans who had lived in these lands for centuries were resettled by governmental action with very few remaining. Many people think that the internment and resettlement of the Germans was retaliation for the evil that the Nazi Germans did to other populations and is therefore to be overlooked as an act of genocide, but in my opinion, a genocide is a genocide no matter whether it is allegedly justified. It does not diminish the responsibility of the Nazis or the gravity of the genocides they committed to say that, subsequently, many of the victors carried out genocides of the vanquished Germans. About 10,000 Italians and thousands of Hungarians left Yugoslavia as they were associated with nations that had invaded the country.

When all this horrendous bloodletting and ethnic cleansing ended, it became the policy of President Josip Broz-Tito to implement ethnic reconciliation through a policy named *bratstvo i jedinstvo* [brotherhood and unity] by emphasizing the socialist nature of the new society. Tito curbed further retaliatory bloodshed for the killings and destruction of World War II, though many real and potential enemies of his regime perished or were incarcerated. To quiet the passions and give Yugoslavs a chance for ethnic reconciliation, Tito discouraged both ethnic blaming and exhumation of remains of the victims of genocides. Meanwhile, there were frequent mentions of the victims of fascism, namely of *ustaše* and *četnik* crimes, a concomitant silence shrouded the *partizan* war crimes. War crimes of the foreign forces, particularly the Germans, were emphasized while the ethnicity of the domestic perpetrators was downplayed. Few mass graves were exhumed during Tito's lifetime. While some consider that to be a deliberate attempt to hide the truth, I see it as a necessary period of healing the wounds of war and enabling the reunification of a country that was so severely splintered and destroyed during the war. But after Tito's death in 1980, things took a turn for the worse.

Three other Balkan countries have experienced massive violence since World War II. In Albania, the extremist Communist regime of Enver Hoxha carried out a massive politicide against all real and potential enemies of the regime, instituting the most oppressive government in Europe. That government claimed in its 1976 constitution that Albania was the first atheist country in the world and had eliminated all religious activities and closed all religious buildings of the Islamic community, as well as Orthodox and Catholic churches (Mojzes, 1992b: 119–26). But ethnically and culturally speaking, the regime's targets were all Albanians, and the murders, concentration camps, torture, and so forth do not fall under the 1948 UN Genocide Convention, unless the wholesale attack on all religions by atheistic communism may fall under the genocidal category.

In Greece, a communist insurgency led to a very bloody civil war that lasted from 1945 to 1949, but, here, it was Greek on Greek violence, thus not counting as genocidal.

Bulgaria, however, was another matter. When the Communists took over Bulgaria, they decided to get rid of their Turkish minority (about 10 percent of the population). They did so by forcible deportation in 1950, placing most Turks on trains and taking them to the Turkish border. Turkey was initially unwilling to take the deportees, and the trains stood for days on the border until Turkey relented and accepted them. About 250,000 Turks were deported to Turkey at this time (Wolff, 1956: 476–80). Then the government turned against the *Pomaks*, the Bulgarian converts to Islam. The intent was to Bulgarize them, i.e., to change their culture and customs in conformity with that of the majority. Mosques were destroyed under coercion, and they were forced to take Bulgarian instead of Muslim names, and submit to reeducation aimed at homogenizing them with the majority Bulgarians. This pressure did not relent until the fall of Todor Zhivkov's regime and the collapse of communism in 1990.

THE GENOCIDES OF THE 1990S IN CROATIA, BOSNIA-HERZEGOVINA, AND KOSOVO

The wars of the 1990s were, in some measure, a continuation of the unfinished business of World War II, as genocides and war crimes of that period were "rediscovered" and politicized in the most negative of ways. Memories of the evil that was committed in World War II were reactivated by very public exhumation of victims' mass graves in the glaring light of the press and media. Bone after bone, skeleton after skeleton were brought out of the soil to the crying and wailing of relatives, friends, and onlookers. Serbs accused Croats and insisted that they had not apologized for these crimes; Croats blamed the Serbs in like manner. Old memories were jarred, and young people were nudged into taking on the duty of avenging the losses of their grandparents' generation. Many willingly took on this charge and became fierce national chauvinists ready to confront the new/old enemies, who just a short time ago had been friends and neighbors. Yugoslavia was heading toward violent disintegration.

A series of wars took place. Initial low-intensity violent conflict in Kosovo and Croatia in the 1980s was a prelude to full-scale warfare. The wars were:

in June 1991, a brief war in Slovenia,
in 1991–1996, a long war in Croatia with some periods of cease-fire,
in 1992–1995, the bloodiest war, in Bosnia and Herzegovina (Mojzes, 1995: 87–124),

in 1999, a war in Serbia over Kosovo, and
in 2001–2002, a low-intensity war in Macedonia.

The war in Slovenia did not have genocidal aspects. The wars in Croatia, Bosnia-Herzegovina, and Kosovo did, whereas in Macedonia there were genocidal intentions that were not played out since the conflict was successfully negotiated to an end.

When the political party, the Croatian Democratic Union (*Hrvatska Demokratska Zajednica*, or HDZ), campaigned and won the election in Croatia on a platform of independence, the Serbs in Croatia, organized around the Serbian Democratic Party (*Srpska Demokratska Stranka*, or SDS), strenuously objected to breaking away from the Yugoslav Federation and, upon failing to prevent secession, threatened that Serb-majority areas in Croatia would secede. The war thus pitted Croats (85–90 percent of the population) against Serbs (10–15 percent of the population) with the Yugoslav People's Army first posturing as a buffer between the warring sides but soon supporting the Serbs. Most Croat soldiers having defected from the Yugoslav army, joined the newly formed Croatian military. At first the Serbs controlled significant sections of Eastern and Western Slavonia, Baranja, Kordun, and Lika, organizing a pseudo-state named "Republika Srpska Krajina" that never gained international recognition. Serbs carried out bloody ethnic cleansing in territories under their control, all the while claiming that Croats had engaged in similar activities in the rest of Croatia.

The case of Vukovar, a beautiful, old city on the western banks of the Danube, is a case in point. Vukovar's population had been mixed. The Serbs tried to overrun it while the Croats put up a staunch defense. The artillery of the Yugoslav army pulverized the city and Croats claimed that the defenders had been destroyed by barbarian means, including the slaughter of wounded in the hospital. The Serbs, for their part, pointing to a large number of bodies throughout the city, and claiming that these had been Serbs whom the Croats killed as they withdrew from the city, alleged Croat atrocities. Both sides provided photographic evidence of the slaughter of children as well as adults, but it is often difficult to establish whose bodies were being shown to viewers. Sometimes the very same photographs would be shown on both Serb and Croat television, each alleging that the victims are theirs while the perpetrators were of the enemy group. The paramilitaries of both sides, some recruited locally and others brought in, were usually the ones who carried out the most inhumane massacres.

Significantly, the new Croatian state took on a number of the symbols associated with NDH of World War II, including the revival of paramilitary units that used *ustaše* insignia and banners. Among the Serbs, there was a concomitant revival of *četnik* symbols. The two sides tended to refer to each other derogatorily, mostly as *ustaše* and *četnik*. Villages were burned, people were killed (about 10,000 is the most frequently cited number) or driven from their homes, massive looting and blackmail took place, and some exchange of population was hastily organized—all in order to create ethnically homogenous areas. The issue was ethnoreligious because one of the clear distinguishing marks of the two people was that traditionally the Serbs were Orthodox and the Croats Catholic Christians. The leadership of the two churches manifested solidarity with the political project of their ethnic group and contributed more to division than to reconciliation. United Nations forces were placed to assist with cease-fires, but these were frequently violated. After the war in neighboring Bosnia-Herzegovina was terminated in 1995, the Croatian government, with considerable help from the North Atlantic Treaty Organization (NATO), carried out a successful military operation that drove the Serb armed forces and civilian population out of all but Eastern Slavonia. Formerly majority-Serb areas of the Serbian Krajina became devoid of Serbs in a matter of a few days, bringing about the single largest flow of refugees of these wars (300,000 by some accounts), who fled to Serbia or Serb-held areas in Bosnia. By 1997, the few remaining areas under Serb control in Eastern Slavonia were peacefully turned over to the Croatian government with the assistance of the UN. Thus the Croatian state retained all the territories that the Republic of Croatia had within the federal state of Yugoslavia (Štitkovac, 1995: 147–64; Silber and Little, 1996), but was now almost devoid of Serbs.

The war in Bosnia and Herzegovina was even more complex and costlier (Burg and Shoup, 1999). It was a three-way conflict between Bosnian Serbs (33 percent), Croats (22 percent), and Muslims (44 percent), who later preferred the term *Boshniak* for themselves. After the war broke out in Croatia, there was little hope that Bosnia and Herzegovina would be able to avoid getting sucked in, yet it was not until April 1992 that the war began. Serbs wanted by all means to prevent the secession of Bosnia and Herzegovina, claiming that these were ancient Serb territories. Most Croats desired their annexation to Croatia. Slobodan Milošević (1941–2006) and Franjo Tudjman (1922–1999), the presidents of Serbia and Croatia respectively, sought repeatedly to make secret deals to partition Bosnia and Herzegovina. The Muslims hoped that the issue could be settled but leaned toward independence of a unitary Bosnia. When a referendum was held, Serbs boycotted it; Muslims and Croats voted overwhelmingly for independence and the war broke out. The Serbs, helped by the Yugoslav army (renamed in the course of the war as the Serbian military), controlled up to 75 percent of the land in a short time. The Croats were prepared for the fighting, as were the Serbs, but the Muslims were not and therefore, under duress, had to join the Croats.

Ethnic cleansing commenced at once because the Serbs, seeing that Yugoslavia was lost, tried to create a "Greater Serbia" with contiguous territories.

This was hard to achieve because the three ethnicities were intermingled to a very large degree. There were ethnically homogenous villages, and in some towns one of the three ethnic groups may have been in the majority, but the ethnic maps of Bosnia and Herzegovina resemble an air-sprayed three-color mélange that could be disentangled only by the most violent re-population—which was what the Serbian ethnic cleansing attempted to do. The other two groups responded in kind (Burg and Shoup, 1999: 169–85). Unfortunately one-sided accounts of this struggle have appeared in print, for example the pieces by Roy Gutman and Ibrahim Kajan (Gutman, 1993; Kajan, 1993a: 86–97).

A frequent pattern was that the paramilitary units of one ethnic group would take over a town and first kill those members of their own ethnicity who were known as proponents of pluralistic integration. Having eliminated potential opposition to their plans, they would then start killing the most prominent citizens of the other ethnicities, sometimes detaining those who were real or potential opponents in concentration camps where the most fearsome tortures were common. These included genocidal rape (of women and men), beatings, electric shock, sexual mutilation, forcing the inmates to eat each other's body parts or excrement, and so forth ("Rape as Crime against Humanity," n.d.). The rest of the population would desperately try to flee, and such migration was facilitated by means of ensuring that exorbitant fees would be paid, that property would be transferred without compensa-tion, and that valuables would be turned over. Migrants often left with just a few items packed in plastic bags, relieved that they saved their own lives. As often as not, other members of their families were not so lucky. It is estimated that 200,000 citizens of Bosnia and Herzegovina were killed, two million (out of a population of four million) were deported or fled from their homes, and countless numbers were wounded or maimed through torture, hunger and thirst, and similar. Europe was confronted with pictures it had last seen after the Nazi era: barbed wire, emaciated inmates, corpses lying in streets and byways, cities pounded into rubble, homes and villages burned down, men filming themselves with decapitated heads of enemies.

The alliance of Croats and Muslims did not last. Between the years 1993 and 1994 they fought each other as mercilessly as they had with the Serbs. Now pictures of emaciated Muslim inmates of Croat camps reached the world as somewhere, somehow, Bosnian Muslims themselves retaliated fiercely by attacking Serb or Croat civilians. The woods and ravines of this mountainous country are full of buried and unburied skeletons. What the world saw was limited to where journalists were able to go with their cameras, but at least as much or more took place far from the cameras' eyes. In addition, many of the journalists did not understand the complex issues and allowed themselves to be manipulated and provided heavily biased reports, thereby distorting world public opinion (Burg and Shoup, 1999: 162–63).

The city of Sarajevo was under constant media coverage, and for four years the world was witness to the Serbian artillery and snipers wreaking havoc on a daily basis on a divided and encircled city, leaving practically no building undamaged. Many Serbs stayed in Sarajevo but they were pounded just as mercilessly as the other inhabitants on the supposition that they, as traitors to their ethnic cause, deserved no better. The story of Mostar, the capital of Herzegovina, is equally tragic. At first, Serbs controlled the city and subjugated the members of the other two ethnicities. Then they were driven out, and soon the Croats and Muslims entered a fierce fight that led to the division of the city with the western bank taken over by the Croats and the eastern bank by the Muslims. Each side became ethnically cleansed, and in the fighting the Croats destroyed the bridge built in 1566 that is the trademark of the city. For a long time, even in peacetime, the Croat authorities did not permit open traffic between the two parts of the city, the Croat part having been rebuilt and modernized while the Muslim part was left in tatters.

There were towns and regions where interethnic relations had been very good before the war and the citizens decided not to get involved in the war. However, they were sucked in anyway by means of atrocities engineered on by the Counterintelligence Services (*Kontra Obaveštajna Služba*, or KOS) of the Serbian military. In a city in which, for instance, Serbs and Muslims lived harmoniously, the KOS would secretly pay one or more Muslim criminals to massacre ten to twenty Serb civilians and then give the killers protection or safe haven. That would so traumatize the Serb inhabitants that they could be persuaded by someone to carry out a countermassacre upon the Muslims of the town, and ethnic cleansing would be carried out. At other times, the KOS carried out the initial massacre with its own men and then planted evidence that it had been done by the Muslims (Interview with a former member of the Yugoslav secret police, 17 November 2003).

In Stolac, Herzegovina, the Croat military forces with the help of some of the local Croat population destroyed all of the mosques—including one of the region's most beautiful mosques, built in the sixteenth century—killed and tortured many of the Muslims, detained them in camps, and then deported almost all Muslim inhabitants with the purpose of making Stolac an ethnically homogenous Croat city ("Crimes in Stolac Municipality: 1992–1994," n.d.).

Perhaps the best known tragic story is that of Srebrnica in eastern Bosnia. In September 1995 the Serbian army, under the command of general Ratko Mladić (b. 1942), overran the town, which had been declared a UN protected zone. The Dutch UN force was unequal to the task of protecting the city. After negotiation, women, children, and older men were permitted to evacuate to Tuzla, but about 7,000–8,000 men of fighting age were kept back. Some of them fought their way through the Serb encirclement, but about 7,000 of them were mass murdered despite assurances that they would be safe. The Serbian army subsequently attempted to hide the evidence. The incident—the single largest mass murder in Europe since World War II—energized world public opinion and spurred the United Nations to bring the war in Bosnia to an end with a combination of military threat (aerial bombardment of Serb forces) and negotiation at Dayton, Ohio. But the story is much more complex and tragic than the Serb atrocity alone. Muslim forces had previously taken advantage of the "safe zone" to make raids on Serb villages surrounding Srebrnica in which they killed, burned, and looted indiscriminately, thereby bringing upon themselves the ire of the Serbs who in any case sought to establish a contiguous territory with Serbia as the war was winding down (Honig and Both, 1997).

Even memory itself was destroyed by elimination of the religious and cultural monuments of the enemy ethnoreligious group. Churches, mosques, monasteries, cemeteries, libraries, monuments, museums: all were targeted because they were symbols of the "old," of the presence of the other ethnic groups whose members were to be driven out (Riedlmeyer, 1995). Sometimes, as many as six mosques were dynamited in a single night.

For a while it seemed that Serbia would avoid war in its own territory, but the policies of discrimination and repression imposed by the Milošević regime in view of the unresolved national question in Kosovo gradually led to war. Kosovo (its full name being Kosovo and Metohija, while the Albanians call it Kosova) has a murky history as its two populating nations have entirely different stories about the past. The Serbs regard Kosovo as the cradle of their statehood, and as sacred land because numerous medieval monasteries and churches dot the land. It was there that, in 1389, the Serbs lost a battle to the Ottoman Turks, which subsequently led to overlordship and then occupation that lasted into the twentieth century. In the First Balkan War (1912), Kosovo was finally reintegrated into Serbia. From 1941 to 1945, Kosovo became part of "Greater Albania" under Italian and then German protectorate, only to be returned to Yugoslavia after the war as an autonomous province of Serbia. The Albanians hold that Kosovo is rightfully theirs because, they claim, since the sixteenth century they have constituted the majority of the population. The Serbs claim that the ethnic Albanian numeric preponderance is of recent origin, the result of the ethnic cleansing of Serbs and an Albanian demographic explosion. In the past, of course, when Serbs held the territory they controlled the Albanians, and when the Muslims were the overlords Albanians controlled the Serbs. During World War II, Albanians avenged themselves on the Serbs for the Serb repressions between the two world wars. Then, right after the end of World War II, Serbian secret police carried out fierce repressions of Albanians. Under Tito, greater freedoms had gradually been granted to the Albanians, and by the 1970s they enjoyed considerable privileges and powers, so much so that the

Serbs of Kosovo started bitterly complaining that they were being driven out of the province—allegedly 200,000 Serbs had been "forced" to migrate out of Kosovo. On top of that, a demographic explosion among the Albanian population changed the ratio of the population from perhaps 50-50 to 90-10 in favor of Albanians by the 1980s. The Serbian Orthodox Church began complaining of a genocide of its population. Tito held it all in check, but when he died in 1980 the violent incidents between Serbs and Albanians increased. Neither domestic nor international solutions to their dilemma were found until 1985, when Slobodan Milošević, perhaps unwittingly, bumped into an issue that made him into a hero to the Serbs overnight. He promised protection to the Serb minority, eliminated the autonomy of the province, to put it directly under the government of Serbia, and instituted drastic repressions of Albanians while granting privileges to Serbs.

Initially, the Albanians reacted admirably with peaceful resistance, even when Serbs were engaged elsewhere during the war in Croatia and Bosnia (Clark, 2000). But after these wars ended, Milošević missed the opportunity to find a more equitable resolution to the Kosovo conflict. By 1998, an extremist, terrorist organization was formed that called itself the Kosovo Liberation Army (KLA), which started attacking the Serb army and civilians. Milošević reacted fiercely, and some Albanians were massacred. The international community, led by the United States, proposed first civilian peace monitors then military presence. The Clinton administration, especially Secretary of State Madeleine Albright, used a heavy hand in negotiations at Rambouillet, France, to which Milošević could not and would not yield, and on 6 April 1999—ironically on the anniversary of the Nazi bombardment of Belgrade—NATO began daily aerial bombardment of Belgrade and the rest of Serbia, including Kosovo. Seventy-eight days later, Milošević finally had to submit. The immediate result of the bombardment was the temporary flight of about a million Kosovo Albanians to Macedonia, Albania, and Montenegro. Both Serb forces and NATO bombing destroyed much property. According to NATO, it was the Serbian army and police that forced the Albanians from their homes. The Serbs contend that it was NATO's incessant bombing that made the refugees flee. It was probably both. In any case, it seemed that an Albanian genocide was in the making, one that might clear Kosovo of Albanians. Serbs too were sustaining casualties through collateral damage.

After Milošević's government was forced to seek an end to the bombardment, Kosovo became a United Nations Protectorate, and though it was legally still a part of Serbia, all Serb troops and governing bodies had to leave Kosovo. The Albanian refugees returned relatively quickly in large numbers. But as they returned, the KLA and other Albanian extremists sought to expel almost all non-Albanians (Serbs, Roma, Bosnians, Montenegrins, and even Turks). Some were killed, houses were burned, churches and monasteries destroyed, monks and nuns threatened. Serbs now constituted less than 1 percent of the population of Kosovo, and they were ghettoized in places like Kosovska Mitrovica. The Serbian population dared not travel outside of UN military convoys and rarely left their houses at night. Even as late as 2003, Serb children were shot and killed. All this took place under the watch of United Nations forces which did not halt the reverse genocidal process (Interview with a Russian policeman, 15 October 2003; Skaric and Mohajlovska, 2002). Thus, it is incorrect to say that the NATO intervention prevented genocide. It might have prevented a genocide against part of the majority population of Kosovo, but it completed the process of the genocide of the minority. Initially, claims were made in the media that the Serbs had killed 100,000 Albanians. This figure has been drastically revised to less than 10,000. The number of Serbs killed by Albanians is significantly lower, but mass graves of Serbs have also been discovered, and occasional killing continues to this day. Likewise, briefly the charge of genocidal rape was repeated but was later downplayed, reducing it to a smaller number of rape incidents.

Until 1999, Macedonia seemed to be the only former Yugoslav republic that had seceded without bloodshed. In the first years of their independence Macedonians prided themselves on inhabiting one of the few calm places in the former Yugoslavia. But that calm was interrupted during the Kosovo war. First, there came a huge influx of Albanian refugees that the country was unable to handle, and second came NATO armies that used Macedonia as a staging ground for entry into Kosovo. Most Slavic Macedonians opposed their presence, though the Albanian Macedonians welcomed it. The huge influx of Albanians massively disrupted the population equilibrium of Macedonia, making Slavic Macedonians feel less safe. When the Serbs de facto lost Kosovo to Albanians, the Albanians of Macedonia, particularly their extremist element, felt that this was a golden moment for them to possibly accomplish the same goal in Western Macedonia, where their numbers were significant. Conflicts increased, and an insurgent army, named the National Liberation Army (NLA, consisting at least partly of some of the same fighters that fought in the KLA), struck in 2001, taking over a number of villages and localities, threatening even the capital city of Skopje. About a hundred people died, and in the process, churches, mosques, and monuments were destroyed and desecrated as ethnoreligious symbols, homes were burned, people were driven out of their cities, individuals were assaulted and other ethnically inspired crimes were carried out.

The conflict clearly had an ethnic character. The Albanians (who make up between 20 and 40 percent of the population) are for the most part Muslims; the Macedonians are Orthodox Christians. While not all Albanians favor secession and annexation to either Albania or Kosovo, few explicitly opposed the NLA, which claimed to fight for greater human and ethnic rights. Macedonian extremists responded to NLA's demands, while the majority of the Macedonian population regarded the NLA as a terrorist organization. Fortunately, there were already UN forces on the ground, and these were quickly reinforced. With the assistance of the United States, European Community, and the UN, the government negotiated with the rebels, and in 2002 an agreement was hammered out in Ohrid that led the NLA to disarm and enter the political process. The tension subsided significantly, except that a small number of the insurgents reorganized themselves and continued terrorist attacks into 2003. Macedonia is not assured a nonviolent future as the uneasy truce may give way to new warfare, but greater stability has prevailed.

CENTRAL ISSUES

Many issues arise out of the murderous century. We will briefly look at three, the issue of punishment of the perpetrators, the issue of ethnic cleansing and genocide, and the role of religion.

Justice for Perpetrators

Many (if not most) of the perpetrators escaped judicial processes and were not legally punished. During the first two Balkan wars, there were only a few minor trials in which the Bulgarian army court-marshaled a few of its officers who had encouraged wanton killing of civilians. Other armies have not even conducted inquiries.

After World War II, perpetrators of war crimes that may have been committed by the winners were not prosecuted. The perpetrators among the losers were sometimes tried, but most escaped and hid abroad (mostly in Latin America and the United States) until their death (e.g., Ante Pavelić). Of those who are still alive, some are being investigated while others have successfully evaded discovery (*Philadelphia Inquirer*, 28 November 2003). Examples of those who were tried were the Serb General Draža Mihajlović (tried in 1946) and the Croat Andrija Artuković (in 1988).

The most organized efforts have been made in regard to the wars of the 1990s. An International Criminal Tribunal for the former Yugoslavia was created in 1993, located in The Hague, Netherlands. Slobodan Milošević became the first living head of state ever to be indicted and tried on charges of genocide, crimes against humanity, grave breaches of the Geneva Convention, and violations of the laws and customs of war. After a four-year trial that included charges of genocide, Slobodan Milosevic died of a heart attack in his jail cell in 2006 thereby bringing the pursuit of justice to an unsatisfactory end. Six other Serb civil or military leaders—but no Croats or Muslims—were charged with genocide. Over 160 were indicted on various charges including genocide. Thirty-eight have been convicted and eight acquitted. Some are being tried or are awaiting trial (for details see www .un.org/icty). If Franjo Tudjman (b. 1922) had not died in 2000, and Alija Izetbegović (b. 1925) in 2003, perhaps they too should have faced the tribunal. Radovan Karadžić (b. 1945) and Ratko Mladić (b. 1942), the two worst war criminals, are still in hiding. The leaders of the KLA responsible for atrocities against Serbs also deserve to be tried in The Hague. I believe that the same court should also try the initiators of the NATO bombardment of Serbia, but the world is not yet ready to mete out justice to leaders of the great powers.

In any case, the words of President Theodore Roosevelt seem appropriate in regard to perpetrators: "I feel very strongly that if any people are oppressed anywhere, the wrong inevitably reacts in the end on those who oppress them; for it is an immutable law in the spiritual world that no one can wrong others and yet in the end himself escape unhurt" ("Letter of President," 2003).

Ethnic Cleansing and Genocide

The issue of ethnic cleansing and genocide is more complex than it seems at the outset. The destruction of the Jews during World War II has been clearly assessed as genocidal. But the mass killing of Serbs by Croats and Muslims and Croats by Serbs in the same war is more difficult to judge. The same applies to the wars of the 1990s in regard to the massive extermination of Muslims, Croats, and Albanians by Serbs and the less well-known mass killings of Muslims and Serbs by Croats, of Croats and of Serbs by Muslims, and Serbs by Albanians.

Many people think that ethnic cleansing is a synonym for genocide. Since the number of those who were killed, wounded, exiled, incarcerated, tortured, and raped is so large many would argue that what took place was undoubtedly genocide. I have argued that genocide and ethnic cleansing are not synonymous (Mojzes, 2002: 51–56). Ethnic cleansing is an attempt to homogenize the population of one area by forcibly removing victim populations, usually with accompanying atrocities, so that a claim can be made that the land belongs to the perpetrator. But not every ethnic cleansing amounts to genocide, nor does the scope of killing alone determine the nature of the process. According to the 1948 UN Convention on Genocide, intent to destroy a people must be proven for killings to qualify as genocide.

That ethnic cleansing and accompanying atrocities took place in all of these conflicts is indisputable. But careful analysts have pointed out that it is not equally sure that all of them were genocides. Lord David Owen, one of the chief negotiators of the wars of Yugoslav disintegration on behalf of the European Community, stated, "In the 1990s the specific problem is to distinguish between genocide and ethnic cleansing" (Owen, 1995: 80). He quotes George Kenney, a former U.S. State Department officer: "Bosnia is not the Holocaust or Rwanda; or Lebanon. A relatively large number of white people have been killed in a gruesome fashion in the first European blow-up since World War II. In response the United Nations has set up the first international war crimes trials since Nuremberg. But that does not mean the Bosnian Serbs' often brutal treatment of the Bosnian Muslims is a unique genocide" (Owen, 1995: 80). Owen thinks that this court will determine the issue, because there are indeed those, like the above-cited Ibrahim Kajan, who argue that the Serbs, in regard to the Boshniaks, had violated every single item of the UN Genocide Convention provisions.

Steven Burg and Paul Shoup provide a thorough examination of the charges of ethnic cleansing and genocide. According to them, between one and two-thirds of all inhabitants of Bosnia have been internally or externally displaced, although not all under the same conditions: some were compelled to leave by the enemy, others were coaxed to leave by their own leaders for a variety of reasons—all, however, left due to fear (Burg and Shoup, 1999: 171–72). The three sides had incompatible aims. The Muslims wanted to preserve a unitary Bosnia, while the Croat and Serb nationalists were bent on partitioning it "The cruelties that were committed in the course of Serb ethnic cleansing are significantly better documented than those committed against the Serbs or the Croats, and for this reason, comparisons of the degree or of the nature of the atrocities committed must be made with care" (Burg and Shoup, 1999: 172–73). Massacres were carried out by all three sides, but they were most often carried out by the Serbs.

During World War II, the impact of Croat ethnic cleansing was particularly destructive. In the 1990s, it was the Serb ethnic cleansing that was especially devastating, and "the sum total of atrocities committed by the Serbs was in a category by itself" (Burg and Shoup, 1999: 173). According to Burg and Shoup, "ethnic cleansing thus achieved a two-fold objective: creating largely irreversible facts on the ground," because the traumatized cleansed would be unable to return to their former dwellings, "and enlisting the local population in a cover-up of its operation and consequences" out of fear of retribution (Burg and Shoup, 1999: 174).

The existence of Serbian detention or concetration camps, such as Karakaj in Zvornik, Karaterm-Prijedor, Omarska, and Trnopolje, was made known by Western media, but the Croat camps at Dretelj and Gabela and the Muslim camps at Čelebići and Tarčin received little publicity. One of the reasons for this was that many Western observers and journalists had become convinced that the Serbs were the main culprits, while the Muslims, and to a lesser degree the Croats, were the victims; therefore they scrutinized the Serb misbehavior more intensely. Also journalists exercised caution lest reporting the atrocities of the Croats and Muslims be perceived as a form of "moral equivalency," thereby understating the special responsibility of the Serb extremists. Not believing in the inherently greater cruelty of any of the three peoples, in 1992 I wrote: "The sad truth is that neither the Croats nor the Muslims would have conducted themselves any better than the Serbs. If they had been more powerful, they would have been the ones carrying out 'ethnic cleansing'" (Mojzes, 1992a: 998). This was sharply contested by my Croat and Muslim friends, but not long thereafter revelation of their own ethnic cleansing came to light. "The evidence makes it clear that all three parties—including the Muslims" [who were the most aggrieved community]—were behaving in ways that undermine any claim to moral superiority" (Burg and Shoup, 1999: 181).

But the determination of genocide would depend on how one defines it and there are significant disagreements in that regard despite the wording of the UN Genocide Convention. Central to any definition is that the victim people were to be eliminated in whole or in part *as such*. This was surely the case in certain localities of Bosnia and Herzegovina, where one ethnic group intended to remove the others from the land. That is genocidal. On the other hand, there is no evidence that there were more than some individuals who would have attempted the eradication of the entire other nationality or religion from Bosnia. The fact that exchanges of prisoners had been arranged, or that women and children were being expelled to the adjacent territory controlled by the other side, would indicate less than genocidal intent, comprising an argument that the war was not genocidal. Thus the question of whether it was ethnic cleansing or genocide remains murky, and honest people may disagree about it.

The proceedings of the International Criminal Tribunal for the former Yugoslavia (ICTY) in The Hague contributed substantially to shedding more light (but also heat) on the issue of the genocidal nature of the most recent wars. It revealed many more details of the massacres, torture, concentration camps, rapes, expulsions, and other crimes against humanity (see the details of the various indictments and judgments of the ICTY). The mandate to the tribunal was that the following acts were punishable:

a) genocide
b) conspiring to commit genocide
c) direct and public incitement to commit genocide
d) attempt to commit genocide, and
e) complicity in genocide.

An important legal clarification was made in the case of *Prosecutor v. Ratimir Krstic* in the case of the Srebrenica massacres. The demonstration of the intent to destroy at least a *substantial* part of a group must be "evaluated not

only in absolute numbers but in relation to the overall size or the prominence of people within the group," especially if the victims are representative of or necessary to the survival of the entire group in a particular locale
(rather than the entire group everywhere). In other words, according to the
United Nations, "what needs to be proven is the intent of the perpetrator to
destroy a part of the group as such. . . . The intent can be judged not only
from acts of physical destruction but also from speeches and acts to dis-
perse the targeted group and wipe out its traces from a particular territory."
Based on such criteria it is clear that, indeed, genocides were perpetrated in
all the cases that are surveyed above.

The Religious Factor

The final issue is whether these were religiously inspired ethnic cleansings or genocides. The answer is necessarily ambiguous. They were not, if
one looks only at the primary motivation. These were not classical situations where religion is at the top of the reasons for action; rather, political, economic, and above all, ethnic nationalist reasons were foremost.
However, religion did play a role in supporting, condoning, and even
blessing the conflicts that resulted in ethnic cleansing or genocide. From
a distance or with direct involvement, clergy of all major faiths supported
their warriors, who often used religious symbols as magical amulets—using the Orthodox three-finger salute, the Catholic rosary beads, or the
Muslim prayer rugs. "*Bog čuva Srbe,*" "*Bog čuva Hrvate,*" and "*Allahu akbar*"
("God protects Serbs/Croats" and, in Arabic, "God is Great") were slogans
used as battle cries. God was invoked as protector of the newly formed
state structures, and clergy were given honorary positions at assemblies
and parades. The demolition of sacred objects was frequently top priority.
Clergy blessed arms.

Beyond that there is a more "camouflaged" role of religion that in the Balkans as in many other European situations, creates a symbiosis that I have
called ethnoreligious (Mojzes, 1998: 74–98, esp. 75–80; Mojzes, 1992a).
Lenard Cohen also provides ample evidence of what he calls "the ethnoreligious nexus" (Cohen, 1998: 43–73, esp. 45–47). The case for the closest
relationship between religion and genocides in Bosnia has been made by
Michael Sells (Sells, 1996; 1998: 196–206). Sells considers Serbian Orthodox nationalism uniquely responsible for genocide in the Bosnian war. He
also links it to Serbian experiences in Kosovo, in which case he rejects the
Serbian claim that Kosovo Albanians were carrying out genocide against
Serbs prior to 1985. He coined the term "Christoslavism," later adopted by
some other scholars, to analyze the myth of the 1389 Battle of Kosovo as
one of the sources of the Serbian nation's identification with the suffering
and resurrection of Christ (Velikonja, 2003a).

Indeed, a good strong case can be made linking religion to the ethnic goals of Serb extremists. Yet I am deeply convinced that if a similar extensive study were to be made of the Croat Roman Catholic and Bosnian and Albanian Muslim or Macedonian Orthodox ethnoreligiosity the results would be quite similar. The most prominent Catholic sociologist from Croatia, Željko Mardešić (aka, Jakov Jukić) provides a basis for such an assertion by pointing out that modernity came late to the Balkans, delaying the growth of democracy and civil society. Therefore it was the churches and religious communities, rather than political parties, which became the protectors and promoters of the ethnic identities and human aspirations of their national communities (Mardešić, 2003: 3–4). That being the case it is logical that whenever the promotion of ethnonational interests led to extremes, namely ethnic cleansing and/or genocide, these acts were being carried out "under God."

BIBLIOGRAPHY

Allen, Beverly (1996). *Rape Warfare: The Hidden Genocide in Bosnia-Herzegovina and Croatia*. Minneapolis: University of Minnesota Press.

Ali, Rabia, and Lawrence Lifschultz (eds.) (1993). *Why Bosnia? Writings on the Balkan War*. Stony Creek, Conn.: Pamphleteer's Press.

Bajić, Milorad (1990). "David u jamama Golijata." Available through the Internet at: http://www.srpsko-nazledje.co.yu/sr-1/1990/01/article-7.html.

Bogosaveljevic, Srdjan (1996). "Nerasvetljeni genocide," in Nebojsa Popov (ed.), *Rrpska strana rata: trauma i katarza u istorijskom pamcenju*. Belgrade: Republika, 159–70.

Burg, Steven L., and Paul S. Shoup (1999). *Herzegovina: Ethnic Conflict and International Intervention*. New York: M. E. Sharpe.

Clark, Howard (2000). *Civil Resistance in Kosovo*. London: Pluto Press.

Cohen, Lenard (1998). "Bosnia's 'Tribal Gods': The Role of Religion in Nationalist Politics," in Paul Mojzes (ed.), *Religion and the War in Bosnia*. Atlanta, Ga.: Scholars Press, 43–73.

"Crimes in Stolac Municipality: 1992–1994" [no date]. Available through the Internet at: http://www.haverford.edu/-relg.sells/Stolac/StolacCrimesl(2and3).html.

Decree "On Racial Affiliation" [Document no. 76] (1941). In *The Pavelic Papers: An Independent Project Researching the History of the Ustase Movement, 1929–2003*. Available through the Internet at: www.pavelicpapers.com/documents/jasenovac/text/Ja0001.txt.

Dedijer, Vladimir (1992). *The Yugoslav Auschwitz and the Vatican: The Croation Massacre of the Serbs during World War II*. Buffalo, N.Y.: Prometheus Press and Freiburg, Ger.: Ahriman-Verlag.

Dedijer, Vladimir, and Antun Miletic (eds.) (1990). *Genocid nad Muslimanima, 1941–1945: Zbornik dokumenata i svjedocenja*. Sarajevo: Svjetlost.

Glenny, Misha (1994). *The Fall of Yugoslavia*. New York: Penguin Books.

—— (2001). *The Balkans: Nationalism, War, and the Great Powers, 1804-1999.* London, and New York: Penguin Books.

Golubović, Zvonimir (1992). *Racija u juznoj Backo 1941 godine j.* Novi Sad: Istorijski muzej Vojvodine.

Gutman, Roy (1993a). "Rape Camps: Evidence Serb Leaders in Bosnia OKd Attacks." *Newsday*, April 19. Available through the Internet at: www.haverford.edu/relg/sells/rape2.html.

—— (1993b). *A Witness to Genocide: The 1993 Pulitzer Prize-winning Dispatches on the "Ethnic Cleansing" of Bosnia.* New York: Macmillan.

Harran, Marilyn, et al. (2000). *The Holocaust Chronicle.* Lincolnwood, Ill.: Publications International.

Holocaust Era in Croatia, Jasenovac, 1941-1945. Available through the Internet at: http://1.us.orWmuseuexMbit/onlinejasenovacisto/pfint.hl.

Honig, Jan Willem, and Norbert Both (1997). *Srebrnica: Record of a War Crime.* New York: Penguin Books.

International Commission to Inquire into the Causes and Conduct of the Balkan Wars. (1993). *The Other Balkan Wars: A 1913 Carnegie Endowment Inquiry in Retrospect with a New Introduction and Reflections on the Present Conflict.* Introduction by George F. Kerman. Washington, D.C.: Carnegie Endowment for International Peace.

Jasenovac Research Institute. Available through the Internet at: www.jasenovac.org/whatwasjasenovac/index asp.

Kajan, Ibrahim (1993). "Is This Not Genocide?" in Rabia Ali, and Lawrence Lifschultz (eds.), *Why Bosnia? Writings on the Balkan War.* Stony Creek, Conn.: Pamphleteer's Press, 86-97.

Kolonomos, Zamila, and Vera Veskovik-Vangeli (1986). *Evreite vo Makedonija vo Vtorata svetska vojna, 1941-1945: zbornik na dokumenti* [The Jews in Macedonia during the Second World War, 1941-1945]. Skopje: Makedonska akademija na naukite.

Lebl, Zeni (1990). *Plima i slom: iz istorUe Jevreja vardarske Makedonije.* Gornji Milanovac, Serbia: Decje Novine.

—— (1995). *Jevreji iz Jugoslavije ratni vojni zarob jeniciu Nemackoj—A Memorial of Yugoslavia Jewish Prisoners of War.* Tel-Aviv, Israel: Technosdar.

—— (2001). *Do "Konacnog Resenja": Jevreji u Beogradu—1521-1942* [Until the "Final Solution": The Jews in Belgrade—1521-1942.] Belgrade: Cigoja.

—— (2002). *Do "Konacnog Resenja": Jevreji u Srbyi.* [Until the "Final Solution": The Jews in Serbia]. Belgrade: Cigoja.

"Letter of President Theodore Roosevelt to Jacob N. Schiff, November 16, 1905" (2003). *Heritage: Newsletter of the American Jewish Historical Society*, 1(2): 24.

Levntal, Zdenko (ed.) (1952). *Zlocini fasistickih okupatora i njihovih pomagaca protiv Jevreja u Jugoslaviji.* Belgrade: Savez jevrejskih opstina FNR Jugoslavije.

Lituchy, Barry (1998). "What Is the Vatican Hiding?: The Vatican's Complicity in Genocide in Facist Croatia: The Suppressed Chapter of Holocaust History." Available through the Internet at http://.ccg.orWdomaiolocaustrevealed.orWChurcaticm.

Miletić, Antun (1990). Introductory notes. In Vladimir Dedijer, and Antun Miletić, *Genocid nad Muslimanima, 1941-1945: Zbornik dokumenata I svjedocenja.* Sarajevo: Svjetlost, i-xxix.

Mirković, Damir (1993). "Victims and Perpetrators in the Yugoslav Genocide, 1941-1945: Some Preliminary Observations." *Holocaust and Genocide Studies,* 7(3). 317-32.

Mojzes, Paul (1992a). "The Reign of 'Ethnos': Who Is to Blame in Yugoslavia?" *The Christian Century,* 109(32): 996-99.

—— (1992b). *Religious Liberty in Eastern Europe and the USSR: Before and After the Great Transformation.* Boulder, Colo.: Eastern European Monographs.

—— (1994). *Yugoslavian Inferno: Ethnoreligious Warfare in the Balkans.* New York: Continuum.

—— (1998). "The Camouflaged Role of Religion in Bosnia and Herzegovina," in Paul Mojzes (ed.), *Religion and the War in Bosnia.* Atlanta, Ga.: Scholars Press, 74-98.

—— (2002). "Ethnic Cleansing," in Carol Rittner, John K. Roth, and Stephen M. Smith (eds.), *Will Genocide Ever End?* St. Paul, Minn.: Paragon House, 51-56.

Mojzes, Paul (ed.) (1998). *Religion and the War in Bosnia.* Atlanta, Ga.: Scholars Press.

Morris, Katherine (1996). "Introduction," in *Escape through the Balkans: The Autobiography of Irene Grunbaum.* Translated and edited by K. Morris. Lincoln: University of Nebraska Press, xi-xxiii.

Owen, David (1995). *Balkan Odyssey.* New York: Harcourt, Brace.

Popov, Nebojsa (ed.) (1996). *Srpska strana rata: trauma i katarza u istorijskom pamcenju.* Belgrade: Republika.

"Rape as Crime Against Humanity". Available through the Internet at: haverford .edu/relg/sells/rape.html.

Riedlmeyer, Andras (1995). Killing Memory: The Targeting of Bosnia's Cultural Heritage—Testimony Presented at a Hearing of the Commission on Security and Cooperation in Europe. 4 April 1995. Available through the Internet at: www. haverford.edu/relg/sells/killing.html.

Roth, John K. (2000). *World Philosophers and their Works.* Pasadena: Salem Press.

Sells, Michael (1996). *The Bridge Betrayed: Religion and Genocide in Bosnia.* Berkeley: University of California Press.

—— (1998). "Serbian Religious Nationalism, Christoslavism, and Genocide in Bosnia, 1992-1995," in Paul Mojzes (ed.), *Religion and the War in Bosnia.* Atlanta, Ga.: Scholars Press, 196-206.

Silber, Laura, and Allan Little (1996). *Yugoslavia: Death of a Nation.* New York: TV Books.

Skaric, Svetomir, and Nadica Mihajlovska (2002). *Law, Force and Peace in Kosovo and Macedonia.* Skopje, Macedonia: Tri D.

"Special Prosecutors Racing against Time to Root Out Nazis" (2003). *Philadelphia Inquirer,* 28 November.

Štitkovac, Ejub (1995). *Bosnia and Hercegovina: The Second War.* Chicago: Lawrence Hill Books.

Suttner, Ernst Christoph (2003). "Erzbischof Alois Kardinal Sepinac: Glaubenszeuge in turbulenter Zeit." *Ostkirchliche Studien,* 52(2-3): 196-202.

Titkovac, Ejub (1995). "Croatia: The First War," in Jasminka Udovicki and James Ridgeway (eds.), *Yugoslavia's Ethnic Nightmare: The Inside Story of Europe's Unfolding Ordeal.* New York: Lawrence Hill Books, 147-64.

Todorov, Tzvetan (ed.) (2001). *The Fragility of Goodness: Why Bulgaria's Jews Survived the Holocaust: A Collection of Texts with Commentary.* Princeton, N.J.: Princeton University Press.

Tudjman, Franjo (1996). *Horrors of War: Historical Reality and Philosophy.* Translated from Croatian by Katarina Mijatovic. New York: M. Evans.

Udovicki, Jasminka, and James Ridgeway (eds.) (1995). *Yugoslavia's Ethnic Nightmare: The Inside Story of Europe's Unfolding Ordeal.* New York: Lawrence Hill Books.

Velikonja, Mitja (2003a). *Religious Separation and Political Intolerance in Bosnia Herzegovina.* College Station: Texas A&M University Press.

—— (2003b). "The Role of the Religions and Religious Communities in the Wars in Ex-Yugoslavia" 1991–1999. *Religion in Eastern Europe,* XXIII(4): 1–42. Also available through the Internet at: http://64.233.183.104/search?q= cache: P6598mLxOLgJwww.georgefox.edu/academics/undergrad/departments/socswk/ ree/2003/velikonja03.doc+The+role+of+religions+and+religious+communities+in +the+wars+of+ex-Yugoslavia&hl=en.

"What Is Jasenovic?" (n.d.). Brooklyn, N.Y.: Jasenovich Research Institute. Available through the Internet at: http://www.jasenovac.org/index.asp.

Wolff, Robert Lee (1956). *The Balkans in Our Times.* Cambridge, Mass.: Harvard University Press.

10

"Death Was Everywhere, Even in Front of the Church": Christian Faith and the Rwandan Genocide

Stephen R. Haynes

> When we arrived, I looked at the school across the street, and there were children, I don't know how many, forty, sixty, eighty children stacked up outside who had all been chopped up with machetes. Some of their mothers had heard them screaming and had come running, and the militia had killed them, too. We got out of the vehicle and entered the church. There we found 150 people, dead mostly, though some were still groaning, who had been attacked the night before. The Polish priests told us it had been incredibly well organized. The Rwandan army had cleared out the area, the gendarmerie had rounded up all the Tutsi, and the militia had hacked them to death.
>
> —Brent Beardsley

I remember quite vividly driving along an interstate highway during the summer of 1994 and listening with rapt attention to a National Public Radio report on the tragedy in Rwanda. In just 100 days following a government coup in early April, somewhere around 800,000 Rwandans had been ruthlessly murdered by their countrymen. When I arrived home, I located Rwanda on a map of the world hanging in my daughter's room, and for several weeks I paid close attention to media reports of the refugee crisis that followed the slaughter. But as information on the genocide and its aftermath became harder to come by, I, like most other Westerners, let Rwanda slip from my mental radar. On subsequent occasions, when Rwanda did enter my mind, I had difficulty remembering who had killed whom. Had Tutsis been the victims of Hutus? Or was it the other way around? Unfortunately,

Americans in positions of power were having similar difficulties. General Wesley Clark, Director of Strategic Plans and Policy for the Joint Chiefs of Staff during the genocide, recalls Pentagon staffers asking whether it was "Hutu and Tutsi or Tutu and Hutsi?" (Power, 2002: 330).

In the decade since the end of the Rwandan genocide, the literature of description and analysis has steadily grown and can now be fairly called voluminous (*Holocaust and Genocide Studies*, 2003: 216–19). Among the first to appear were Alain Destexhe's (1995) *Rwanda and Genocide in the Twentieth Century* and Gérard Prunier's (1995) *The Rwandan Crisis: History of a Genocide*. In the late 1990s, scholarly anthologies on genocide began to include chapters on Rwanda. And in the past five years, veteran journalists have written best-selling books that present the horrors of Rwanda—and the West's inaction—in sharp relief. Prominent in this genre are Philip Gourevitch's (1998) *We Wish to Inform You That Tomorrow We Will Be Killed with Our Families: Stories from Rwanda*, and Samantha Power's (2002) *"A Problem from Hell": America and the Age of Genocide*, which devotes a sixty-page chapter to Rwanda.

AN AFRICAN HOLOCAUST?

Despite differences in style, disciplinary perspective, and intended audience, most of these studies evince a compulsion to relate the Rwandan tragedy to the Holocaust. Destexhe's *Rwanda and Genocide in the Twentieth Century* opens with a quote from Holocaust survivor Primo Levi ("It has happened once, and it could all happen again)," and a chapter titled "The Unlearned Lesson of History." A more recent scholarly study—Mahmood Mamdani's (2001) detailed account of the political conditions underlying the tragedy titled *When Victims Become Killers*—repeatedly cites parallels between Rwanda and the Nazi "Final Solution of the Jewish Question."

Popular studies of the genocide are even more prone to establish Rwanda-Holocaust connections. Philip Gourevitch introduces his riveting account of the Rwandan crisis and its aftermath with the observation that "the dead of Rwanda accumulated at nearly three times the rate of Jewish dead during the Holocaust. It was the most efficient killing since the atomic bombings of Hiroshima and Nagasaki" (Gourevitch, 1998: 3; Waller, 2002: 252). Samantha Power, in analyzing the public rhetoric that preceded and paved the way for a genocidal assault against the Tutsis, compares the "Ten Commandments of the Hutu" with the Nazi Nuremberg Laws. According to Power, it is difficult to consider claims that "every Tutsi is dishonest in business" and aims only at the supremacy of his ethnic group, and exhortations that the Hutu "should stop having mercy on the Tutsi" and must engage in preemptive self-defense, without thinking of Nazi anti-Semitism.

Power also likens Kenya's return of a planeload of refugees to Rwanda to the United States' decision to "turn back the USS *St. Louis* during the Holocaust." Indeed, she notes, when they appealed for Western intervention in the genocide, Tutsi rebels in the Rwandan Patiotric Front (RPF) invoked the Holocaust. "When the institution of the UN was created after the Second World War," RPF representative Claude Duisaidi reminded United Nations Security Council members, "one of its fundamental objectives was to see to it that what happened to the Jews in Nazi Germany would never happen again" (Waller, 2002: 338, 357, 370).

Such references are, in part, acknowledgments that the landscape of contemporary genocide is so dominated by the *Shoah* that other tragedies may remain invisible unless they are shown to be "like the Holocaust." Particularly as arguments for the singularity of the Jewish experience have multiplied over the past decade, students of mass death in Armenia, the Americas, the Balkans, and a dozen other places have responded to the uniqueness argument by establishing parallels between the Holocaust and these "other genocides."

Should we dismiss references to the Holocaust in the literature on Rwanda, then, as reflections of fierce competition for the attention and sympathy of atrocity-numbed readers? Or are the tragedies really comparable? Comparable or not, one familiar with the Holocaust cannot help but be struck by the formal similarities: stories of unprovoked cruelty and betrayal, of rescue and gratuitous kindness, of the dilemmas facing "mixed" families, of hiding, passing, and survival; rationalizations on the part of perpetrators and bystanders who traffic in self-exculpating images of entrapment; the refusal of Western governments to strike against the killing apparatus (cf. the "Auschwitz and the Allies" controversy with the decision not to jam Radio Mille Collines, which in 1994 was broadcasting incitements to genocide).

Genocidal Rwanda is reminiscent of Nazi Germany in other ways, too. There are pregenocidal legal persecutions (including quotas and identity cards); there is the essentializing of "race" in which one group is cast as a threat to the other's survival; there is the mystification of a hated minority into a strangely powerful entity against whom the majority must defend itself; there are the same dehumanizing images ("rats" in Germany; "cockroaches" in Rwanda) that make elimination of the victims easier once the genocide is underway. And there is the same slow process of establishing what happened that has dogged attempts to explain the seemingly inexplicable.

GENOCIDE AND CHRISTIAN CREDIBILITY

Rwanda is also a source of all-too-familiar stories of complicit Christian leaders and institutions, stories that challenge the credibility of faith in a postgenocide world. In fact, like Nazi Germany, genocidal Rwanda is an exceedingly unattractive venue for Christian self-examination. There are so many cases where "blood" proved thicker than baptismal water, and so much evidence for religion's inability to transcend loyalties of class or ethnicity. While it has taken decades of scholarship and soul-searching to comprehend the churches' failures under Nazism, these failures have emerged with alarming rapidity in the case of Rwanda. And yet, the Christian world has been no more willing to learn from them. For example, following a line of defense familiar to students of the Holocaust, the Vatican has insisted that the Church should not be held responsible for the acts of individual Catholics.

But, whereas the churches and their representatives escaped serious scrutiny in the immediate aftermath of World War II, within five years of the cease-fire in Rwanda Christian leaders were being arrested and charged with crimes against humanity. In 1994, the UN Security Council established the International Criminal Tribunal for Rwanda (ICTR), which began its proceedings in January 1997. By 1999, those jailed on suspicion of aiding in the genocide included nineteen Rwandan priests, among them Bishop Augustin Misago, whose diocese was the site of an estimated 150,000 murders. The Hutu bishop was accused of refusing to shelter Tutsis from Hutu mobs, and of sending nineteen schoolgirls to their deaths by expelling them from a local high school (Kantz, 1999).

Misago pleaded innocent, likened himself to the falsely accused Jesus, and was supported by the Vatican, which claimed that Rwandan leaders were waging a "defamatory campaign" against the Catholic Church ("Rwandan Bishop," 1999). But as the accusations multiplied, the image of a scapegoated church became harder and harder to sustain. In April 2001, two Benedictine nuns who had escaped to Belgium were tried there on charges of complicity in the genocide. The sisters were alleged to have given killers access to thousands of massacre victims who were seeking refuge at their convent, and to have provided the gasoline used by Hutu militiamen to burn down a garage where 500 Tutsi men, women, and children were hiding. When the women were convicted in June 2001, the Vatican complained that the Rwandan genocide was "being attributed to so few people" (Donovan, 2003). Such protests ring hollow for those concerned with Christian credibility in an age of genocide.

Demonstrating that genocidal apostasy was not a "Catholic problem," in early 2000 a Rwandan pastor in the Seventh-Day Adventist Church who had fled to El Paso, Texas, was extradited for trial before the ICTR. Seventy-five-year-old Elizaphan Ntakirutimana was accused of having joined convoys of armed soldiers and civilians who searched for and attacked Tutsis during the genocide. The pastor's victims, it was alleged, included survivors who had sought refuge in his church and hospital compound ("Pastor Will

Face Charges," 2000). In February 2003, Pastor Ntakirutimana and his phy-
sician son were convicted of genocide, complicity in genocide, conspiracy
to commit genocide, and crimes against humanity (Donovan, 2003).

As if these high-profile trials were not enough for the Christian world
to endure, in July 2000, a seven-member panel operating under the aegis
of the Organization for African Unity (OAU) concluded that Christian
leaders—along with Western governments and the UN—bore partial responsibility for the deaths of several hundred thousand Rwandans. Church
leaders, the panel concluded, failed to use "their unique moral position
among the overwhelmingly Christian population to denounce ethnic hatred and human rights abuses" (Malcolm, 2000). Further, the OAU panel
implied, Rwanda's genocide could be traced to Catholic missionaries and
Belgian and German colonial rulers who helped promote the idea that the
nation's majority Hutu population was inferior to Tutsis ("Churches Called
Complicit," 2000). Finally, the panel condemned the Church's failure to
acknowledge and apologize for its role in the genocide.

WHAT'S THE GOOD NEWS?

Surely the picture of Christian involvement in the Rwandan genocide is
not as uniformly bleak as these accusations and verdicts suggest. Surely the
genocide has also brought to light stories of altruism capable of restoring
our faith in humankind and God. One tale of Rwandan redemption that
has received considerable attention since the release of the feature film
"Hotel Rwanda" (2004) is that of Paul Rusesabagina, a Hutu hotel manager
who harbored desperate Tutsis while the genocide raged. But Rusesabagina
is more Schindler than Bonhoeffer, more champion of interethnic solidarity
than of Christian charity. Alas, the Rwandan Bonhoeffer who resisted evil
unto death out of faithfulness to Christ has yet to be identified. Nor have
we found the Hutu Corrie ten Boom capable of sustaining the evangelical
belief in God's protection of the righteous, or the African Le Chambon-
sur-Lignon where the persecuted were sheltered by simple Christians in a
"conspiracy of goodness."

Precisely because there is so little good news to be gleaned from the
Rwandan killing fields, post-Holocaust Christians cannot afford to ignore
the religious and political questions raised there. A chief issue on the religious side is the nature of human nature, what traditionally has been called
theological anthropology. Although most scholars of the genocide have
assiduously avoided theological questions, Christians cannot help but ask
what this and other episodes of mass killing tell us about the essence and
extent of our fallenness. Reinhold Niebuhr, according to an "oral tradition,"
is reported to have taught that Original Sin is the only Christian doctrine

for which there is empirical evidence. If Niebuhr was correct, there is probably more evidence for original sin in the study of contemporary genocide than anywhere else. And because the killing in Rwanda was extraordinarily low-tech, it is impossible to avoid the anthropological question by taking refuge in impersonal categories such as "bureaucratization" or "modernity." Rwandans were killed not by gas pumped into a sealed chamber by a soldier under orders, but by civilians wielding machetes, knives, guns, and grenades. There were few if any "desk-murderers," and the killing was far from anonymous. The perpetrators were not professional killers "doing their duty," but bands of peasants that included women and children.

Considering the nature of human nature in the light of genocide does not require that we ignore the social and institutional dimensions of evil analyzed by social scientists, but it forces us to acknowledge how easily human beings become complicit in the destruction of others—through abhorrence of difference, self-deception, and the idolatry of race and nation. Combining the language of theology and evolutionary psychology, the anthropological question posed by the Rwandan genocide might be phrased this way: What adaptations or situational factors exacerbate the genocidal potential in our fallen human nature, and how do we keep them from doing so?

Politically, Rwanda confronts Christians with a stark reminder of how little we can count on governments to engage in moral action when this is perceived to conflict with national interest. In the books of Gourevitch and Power and the PBS *Frontline* (1997) documentary "The Triumph of Evil," we are introduced to solid evidence that the Rwandan genocide might have been averted if the UN or its member-nations had acted on information received from a field commander in January 1994. An informant close to Hutu Power extremists in the Rwandan government revealed that the militias he was charged with training had been formed not for protection from the RPF (a guerilla army of Rwandan exiles), but for the extermination of Tutsis. The message sent to the UN peacekeeping mission in New York detailed the Rwandan government's plans: "He has been ordered to register all Tutsi in Kigali. He suspects it's for their extermination. Example he gave was that in 20 minutes his personnel could kill up to 1,000 Tutsis" ("The Triumph of Evil," 1997). Because the informant revealed the location of arms that were to be distributed for the task, the United Nations Mission in Rwanda (UNAMIR) commander requested permission to seize the weapons and protect the informant and his family. This information and request were discussed among key members of the UN staff, and promptly buried. With thoughts of avoiding "another Somalia," his superiors instructed the field commander to take no action ("The Triumph of Evil," 1997).

Three months later, events in Rwanda unfolded just as the Hutu informant had predicted, and the elimination of the Rwandan Tutsis was underway. The morning after President Habyarimana's plane was shot down amid suspicious circumstances, ten Belgian peacekeepers were tortured and mutilated as a warning to the Western democracies. Roadblocks were set up, marauding death squads (*interahamwe*) took to the streets, educated professionals, encouraged and directed by radio broadcasts, massacred their colleagues in churches and hospitals, corpses rotted in the streets and clogged rivers, Tutsis and moderate Hutus attempted to flee or cowered in embassies and hotels protected by foreigners, white citizens of Western nations were evacuated amid heart-wrenching pleas for help by desperate Africans, and UNAMIR troops ignominiously withdrew from their compounds, leaving those who had sought their protection to be hacked to death. The Western response to this maelstrom of genocidal evil was precisely the one for which Hutu Power extremists had hoped: under pressure from Belgium and the United States, the UN Security Council voted to terminate its mission in Rwanda. While American and UN representatives steadfastly refused to utter the word "genocide" in connection with the tragedy, Karel Kovanda, the Czech Republic's ambassador to the UN, was to the point: "When you come from Central Europe, one has a sense of what holocausts are about; you recognize one when you see one" (Power, 2002: 361).

THE WANNSEE "FAX"

All of which raises a troubling question about the "civilized" world's response to genocide during the twentieth century. If one of the Nazi leaders present at the Wannsee Conference in January 1942, had—in a fit of conscience—leaked plans for the "Final Solution to the Jewish Question in Europe" to the Allies, would this information have altered the fate of Jews under Nazi control? To put the question in starker (if more imaginative) terms: If, in 1942, the Wannsee villa had been equipped with a device capable of communicating with similar devices in London, Washington, and Moscow, and this device had been used to transmit detailed information regarding the coming Holocaust of the European Jews, would politicians have reacted any differently than they did when reports of the Final Solution reached them in the following months and years? The Western response to the genocidal crisis in Rwanda suggests that the answer to this question must be "no," that Allied government officials would have treated a leaked Wannsee protocol as irrelevant to their strategic interests, and buried it. If this seems incredible, recall that in 1942 Western democracies had neither the Holocaust as precedent nor the political obligation under the UN's Genocide Convention to intervene.

Rwanda, then, forces us to acknowledge a painful reality. Even though our consciousness of mass death and even our use of the word genocide have been thoroughly conditioned by the Holocaust, it is not at all clear that Holocaust awareness has made Western democracies or their citizens—religious or otherwise—any more sensitive to mass death or any more committed to incur personal risk by intervening to stop it. This conclusion follows inexorably from the fact, so poignantly demonstrated in "The Triumph of Evil," that it was only a few months after ceremonies marking the opening of the United States Holocaust Memorial Museum—ceremonies at which President Clinton vowed on behalf of all Americans "to preserve this shared history of anguish, to keep it vivid and real so that evil can be combated and contained"—that warnings of the Rwandan tragedy reached the White House. On 8 April 1994, at the same State Department press conference at which Prudence Bushnell of the department's Bureau of African Affairs warned of mounting violence in Rwanda, Michael McCurry criticized foreign governments for preventing the screening of *Schindler's List*, and added that "the most effective way to avoid the recurrence of genocidal tragedy is to ensure that past acts of genocide are never forgotten" (Power, 2002: 351–52). Later that month—a few weeks after *Schindler's List* had claimed the Oscar for best picture—Vice-President Al Gore proclaimed that Washington's Holocaust memorial was needed "to remind those who make the agonizing decisions of foreign policy of the consequences of those decisions." Meanwhile, his government was rejecting State Department proposals to impede the genocide and worrying that its refusal to act might hurt the Democratic Party in upcoming midterm elections. If there is a more dramatic example of the yawning gap between rhetoric and reality in contemporary politics, it is difficult to imagine.

This particular gap reflects a stunning irony: while our culture is awash in images of a genocide that ended over fifty years ago, we have trouble remembering the names of the antagonists in a conflict that occurred within the last decade. Is it simply the passage of time that installs international tragedies in our consciousness? More likely, it is a function of what Richard L. Rubenstein has identified in his writings as a fundamental dimension of the Holocaust's "uniqueness": its resonance with biblical and theological motifs in Judeo-Christian civilization. But the failure of Rwanda to penetrate the Western mind has to do with geography and race as well. Indeed, Western Christians perceive the Holocaust not only through a religious grid, but also through the prism of color. Despite the explicit racial dimensions of Nazi ideology, both perpetrator and victim in the Holocaust are perceived as vaguely "white." Even in the Balkans, through the difficult-to-pronounce names and the unfamiliar traditions, we are able to identify victims who "look like us."

But Rwanda is a different story. The mental maps of many Americans simply do not include East Africa. The crises there—even when they reach the threshold of media awareness—remain far away, the historical and political contexts unfamiliar, the "tribes" involved indistinguishable. Unless a conflict pits "white" against "black," as in South Africa or Zimbabwe, it does not hold our attention for long. Alas, it may not be possible for Westerners to establish an enduring connection with victims of genocide unless we can identify with them on the superficial level of ethnicity, religious affiliation, or color. Therein lies another cautionary lesson regarding human nature.

LESSONS FOR CHRISTIANS

Apart from the corruptibility of human nature and the failure of Western democracies to act in accord with their moral rhetoric, what are the specific lessons for Christians who want to remember Rwanda? One is awareness that Christian people and their institutions are deeply implicated in the genocide. Many scholars (e.g., Mamdani, 2001) portray the Rwandan tragedy as an indictment of European colonialism or a metaphor for the dilemmas of post–Cold War foreign policy, but these approaches should not distract us from the Christian dimensions of the disaster. Timothy Longman observes that more people may have been killed in church buildings than anywhere else (Longman, 2001: 139–79). In this regard, Rwanda offers images that not even the Holocaust can match—images of churches becoming killing sites, and of parishioners murdering each other.

Rwanda also presents us with compelling evidence of the role of Christian leaders in creating a genocidal culture. Charles de Lespinay accuses the Rwandan clergy of being "propagators of false information tending to maintain a climate of fear, suspicion and hatred," and of encouraging new onslaughts by denying a genocidal reality. "The exacerbation of past and present rivalries," according to de Lespinay, "is entirely the fault of the missionary-educated intellectual 'elites.'" In particular, he charges, prominent clergy have refused to condemn the killing (characterizing it as wartime self-defense or "double genocide"), or have excused the murders as delayed justice for past wrongs (Lespinay, 2001: 169). Such accusations have come from inside the Rwandan churches as well. According to priest and human-rights activist Andre Sibomana, "there is no doubt that the Roman Catholic Church did not live up to its moral responsibility in the years which preceded the genocide. It's a reality which no one can deny." The Rwandan bishops stood by the government," Sibomana wrote in 1997, even when they were informed that a genocidal assault was in the offing (Sibomana, 1997).

Yet the religious message from Rwanda transcends the genocidal activities of believers in the most Christianized society in Africa (90 percent Christian and 63 percent Roman Catholic, according to a 1991 census). Rwanda also reminds us of the way biblical myths of origins can exercise a pernicious influence in history. As almost every commentator on the genocide has noted, the antagonism between Hutu and Tutsi is based in putative racial distinctions. These distinctions were constructed from a quasi-biblical ideology that was introduced by white explorers in the nineteenth century and reiterated by European colonialists seeking to benefit from inter-African antagonism. The intellectual foundation for this ideology is English explorer John Hanning Speke's 1863 *Journal of the Discovery of the Source of the Nile,* which was reprinted in 1996 (Speke, 1996). Like other nineteenth-century Westerners, Speke assumed that Africans were descendants of "our poor elder brother Ham [who] was cursed by his father, and condemned to be the slave of both Shem and Japheth" (Speke, 1996: xvii). But Speke made an original contribution to white perceptions of Africa with his theory of ethnology "founded on the traditions of the several nations, as checked by my own observation of what I saw when passing through them" (Speke, 1996: 241).

Speke surmised, based on their distinctive physical appearance, that the Wahuma (Tutsi) were descendants of "the semi-Shem-Hamitic of Ethiopia," cattle-herding "Asiatic" invaders who migrated south, lost their original language and religion, and darkened through intermarriage. From his journal, we learn that Speke elaborated this ethnological theory for a Tutsi king using the book of Genesis "to explain all I fancied I knew about the origin and present condition of the Wahuma branch of the Ethiopians, beginning with Adam, to show how it was the king had heard by tradition that at one time the people of his race were half white and half black" (Speke, 1996: 495). Eventually this Hamitic Hypothesis was used to explain how "civilization" came to Africa, and it was adopted in Rwanda as the basis for colonial theories of Tutsi superiority, for missionary education that placed ethnic diversity in European class perspective, and for the Hutu revolutionary image of Tutsis as nonindigenous invaders from the north. While this "biblical" background to the Rwandan genocide has rarely been reported in the West, it was commonly understood among the perpetrators and victims.

Further, stories from Rwanda force us to ask whether we would have acted differently in a similar situation, whether we are so unlike the perpetrators and bystanders who became agents of genocide. Indicating the primeval dimensions of murder, Phillip Gourevitch explains the Rwandan tragedy with reference to Genesis 4: "In the famous story, the older brother, Cain, was a cultivator, and Abel, the younger, was a herdsman. They made their offerings to God—Cain from his crops, Abel from his herds. Abel's portion won God's regard; Cain's did not. So Cain killed Abel" (Gourevitch, 1998: 62). The problem of human nature is faced with disturbing honesty in James Waller's (2002) book *Becoming Evil: How Ordinary People Commit Genocide and Mass Killing.* In offering a unified theory of perpetrator behavior, Waller discredits the various psychological mechanisms we rely upon to distance ourselves from those who commit genocide. Illuminating what he calls "our ancestral shadow," Waller identifies the universal "reasoning circuits" bequeathed to us by natural selection to solve the adaptive problems of intergroup relations faced by our ancestors. Those most relevant for understanding our capacity for extraordinary evil, according to Waller, are ethnocentrism, xenophobia, and the desire for social dominance. These are "powerful, innate, 'animal' influences on human behavior that represent evolved social capacities lying at the core of human nature" (Waller, 2002: 153).

Finally, because it reveals that the world's leading democracy conspired to ignore and deny an ongoing genocide at the very moment when American consciousness of the Holocaust was at its height, Rwanda forces Christians to ask how Holocaust awareness relates to antigenocidal thought and action. Gourevitch concludes from his highly disturbing study of Rwanda that people who take seriously governments' commitment to keep genocide from occurring in other nations are dangerously deluding themselves. If this is the case, it points to the need for a unified Christian approach to the prevention of genocide that is realistic about the moral capacities of nation-states and the institutions they create.

BIBLIOGRAPHY

"Churches Called Complicit in Genocide: Report from International Panel of Organizations for African Unity" (2000). *The Christian Century*, 19 July. Available through the Internet by searching at: www.findarticles.com.

Destexhe, Alain (1995). *Rwanda and Genocide in the Twentieth Century.* Translated by Alison Masschner. New York: New York University Press.

Donovan, Gill (2003). "Pastor, Son Convicted for Roles in 1994 Genocide." *National Catholic Reporter*, 7 March. Available through the Internet by searching at: www.findarticles.com

Gourevitch, Philip (1998). *We Wish to Inform You That Tomorrow We Will Be Killed with Our Families: Stories from Rwanda.* New York: Picador.

Holocaust and Genocide Studies, "Recently Published Works in Holocaust and Genocide Studies: Other Genocides and Crimes Against Humanity," *Holocaust and Genocide Studies*, 17:1 (2003): 216–219.

Kantz, Matt (1999). "Rwandan Bishop Augustin Misago Arrested for Alleged Genocide." *National Catholic Reporter*, 23 April. Available through the Internet by searching at: www.findarticles.com

Lespinay, Charles de (2001). "The Churches and Genocide in East Africa," in Omer Bartov, and Phyllis Mack (eds.), *In God's Name: Genocide and Religion in the Twentieth Century.* New York: Berghahn Books, 161–79.

Longman, Timothy (2001). "Christian Churches and Genocide in Rwanda," in Omer Bartov, and Phyllis Mack (ed.), *In God's Name: Genocide and Religion in the Twentieth Century.* New York: Berghahn Books, 139–79.

Malcolm, Teresa (2000). "Panel Says Church, U.S. Share Blame for Genocide." *National Catholic Reporter*, 28 July. Available through the Internet by searching at: www.findarticles.com.

Mamdani, Mahmood (2001). *When Victims Become Killers: Colonialism, Nativism, and the Genocide in Rwanda*. Princeton, N.J.: Princeton University Press.

"Pastor Will Face Charges of Genocide" (2000). *The Christian Century*, 16 February. Available through the Internet by searching at: www.findarticles.com

Power, Samantha (2002). *"A Problem from Hell": America and the Age of Genocide*. New York: Basic Books.

Prunier, Gerard (1995). *The Rwanda Crisis: History of a Genocide*. New York: Columbia University Press.

"Religion and Genocide: Nuns in Rwanda Convicted of Genocide" (2001). *Commonweal*, 13 July. Available through the Internet by searching at: www.find articles.com.

"Rwandan Bishop [Augusto Misago] Denies Role in Genocide" (1999). *National Catholic Reporter*, 13 October. Available through the Internet by searching at: www.findarticles.com.

Sibomana, Andre (1997). "Never Again: The Church and Genocide." *Commonweal*, 5 November. Available through the Internet by searching at: www.findarticles .com.

Speke, John H. (1996). *Journal of the Discovery of the Source of the Nile*. Chiefly Illustrated from Drawings by James Grant. Originally published in 1883. Minneola, N.Y.: Dover Books.

"The Triumph of Evil: How the West Ignored Warnings of the 1994 Rwanda Genocide and Turned Its Back on the Victims" (1997). A WGBH/*Frontline* Co-Production. Transcript available through the Internet and PBS Online: http://www.pbs .org/wgbh/pages/frontline/shows/evil/etc/script.html.

Waller, James (2002). *Becoming Evil: How Ordinary People Commit Genocide and Mass Killing*. New York: Oxford University Press.

III

ALTERNATIVE READINGS OF TROUBLING TEXTS: RELIGION AS A FORCE AGAINST VIOLENCE

11

Getting Rid of the G-d of Abraham: A Prerequisite for Genocide

David Patterson

"Genocide is horrible, an abomination of our species, and totally unacceptable," says R. J. Rummel in his excellent study *Death by Government*. "It is an obscenity—the evil of our time that all good people must work to eradicate" (Rummel, 1994: 31). Few would disagree. And yet, Rummel's statement contains an incongruity of terms that characterizes much of genocide studies. The incongruity lies in the conjunction of the words *species* and *evil*. Viewed as a species, humanity can commit actions that are repugnant and appalling, but not actions that are evil. For evil is a *religious* category that suggests an action that is not merely repugnant and appalling, but one that opposes the Holy One who, according to the Torah, created the human being in his image and likeness (see Genesis 1:26–27). From the standpoint of Torah-based religion, therefore, a human being is not one species of animal among many. Rather, a human being harbors a trace of what is more than being: a human being is a breach of being. Neither animal, vegetable, nor mineral, a human being is a *speaking* being, what in Judaism is known as a *medaber*, and therefore bears the image of a divine being—not with infinite authority but with infinite responsibility and infinite dearness (Maimonides, 1956: 68). That is why genocide is *evil*, and not just unpleasant or a matter of historical curiosity: it is precisely because a human being is not *part* of a species but is a uniquely holy being, one whose sanctity does not lie in anything that can be weighed or measured, counted or observed. That is what makes genocide evil. And that is what most people, including scholars, do not recognize.

Because most people think of human beings as a species of animal, I am not so sure that Rummel is right when he asserts, "Most people recognize this evil for what it is" (Rummel, 1994: 31). Inasmuch as we take humanity to be a species of animal, we render human beings both nameless and faceless, which is itself a necessary precondition for the mass slaughter of men, women, and children. To put it another way, few scholars, if any, take the Torah to be a revelation from the Holy One; hence, few scholars, if any, have a sense of the holiness of the human being as a child of G-d rather than a product of nature. Scholars who are among these few include not only Orthodox thinkers such as Jonathan Sacks in his book *Crisis and Covenant*, and Bernard Maza in *With Fury Poured Out*, but also Abraham Joshua Heschel in *God in Search of Man*, for example, and Emil Fackenheim, whose 614th Commandment, which he discusses at length in *The Jewish Return into History*, implies the existence of 613 that also come from a commanding Voice. Still, most people, including scholars, do recognize that something is horribly wrong with genocide, and so they cry out for an explanation: How could it happen? But because they do not recognize *why* genocide is evil, most of their explanations, while often partially true, are often misguided. And why is that?

As modern thinkers, we are steeped in an ontological mode of thought that equates thinking with being, that understands freedom in terms of self-legislating autonomy, and that eliminates any notion of an absolute from beyond being that inserts itself into being—all of which is antithetical to the traditional understanding of biblically based religion. In fact, we are so hostile toward the G-d of Abraham and those who embrace biblical monotheism that when we ask how genocidal horror could happen, we go looking for its "theological warrants." Religion, it is supposed, is the cause of genocide. Religion is the cause of war and murder. More often than not, the experts maintain, it is in the name of G-d that people engage in mass murder and megamurder, genocide, and democide (in addition to Glick and Kuper discussed here, see Bartov and Macks, 2001; see also Ellis, 1997). Therefore, says Leo Kuper, "a common characteristic of genocide is the presence of religious difference between perpetrators and victims" (Kuper, 1990: 351).

As Rummel has demonstrated, however, this is simply not the case. Not a single pope or ayatollah can compete with Stalin, Mao, or Hitler. And while power and technology may be part of the reason why they cannot compete, these differences are not definitive. Even Kuper concludes that "the role of sacred texts in genocidal conflict is variable and appreciably indeterminate" (Kuper, 1990: 372). In coming to this conclusion, he demonstrates that he is an honest scholar: it is indeterminate because it does not hold up even under a cursory examination. The real question is not whether there are religious differences between the two parties; the question, rather, is whether, among the perpetrators, there is a divine, absolute prohibition against murder that would limit their actions even if they would like to kill more people. And neither modern nor postmodern thought can determine such an absolute.

Where, then, lies a more fundamental relation between "sacred" texts and genocide? It is to be found in the texts that shape modern thinking. Thus, it is no coincidence that genocide is a distinctly modern phenomenon as will be shown in this chapter. It is distinctively modern due as much to modern philosophy as to modern technology, for philosophical outlook determines the direction of scientific technology.

ONTOLOGICAL THOUGHT AND GENOCIDAL ACTION

Stalin, Mao, and Hitler—the twentieth century's top three mega murderers— do not come from nowhere. Steeped in certain ways of viewing the world and humanity, they emerge from a process of thinking G-d out of the picture, a process that is traceable to the Enlightenment. The philosophical outlook that began with the Enlightenment emphasized the self's autonomy, authenticity, and resolve in such a way that it soon became philosophically necessary to get rid of the G-d of Abraham. One of the giants of the Enlightenment, of course, was Immanuel Kant. Here the intellectuals in the room will balk: How could such a humanistic giant, such a moralist, as Kant possibly have any connection to the "Century of Genocide" now past, to the abomination of our species, to the obscenity and the evil of our time?

This is how: If the Cartesian *cogito* situates being within the thinking ego ("I think, therefore I am," according to René Descartes), the Kantian critique deduces everything from the thinking ego, and, thus, as Franz Rosenzweig astutely points out, "'reduces the world' to the perceiving self" (Rosenzweig, 1999b: 24). Far from glorifying the human being, however, the reduction of the world to the perceiving self is radically dehumanizing. "Corresponding to the Copernican turn of Copernicus which made man a speck of dust in the whole," says Rosenzweig, "is the Copernican turn of Kant, which, by way of compensation, placed him upon the throne of the world, much more precisely than Kant thought. To that monstrous degradation of man, costing him his humanity, this correction without measure was, likewise, at the cost of his humanity" (Rosenzweig, 1999a: 96). Refashioning himself after his own image, the human being loses his humanity, the sanctity of which can be determined only from beyond being; he ends by first dehumanizing and then by murdering the *other* human being. The Nazis are a case in point.

At the June 1939 meeting of the National Socialist Association of University Lecturers, Walter Schultze, the head of the association, declared: "What the great thinkers of German Idealism dreamed of, and what was ultimately the kernel of their longing for liberty, finally comes alive, assumes reality. . . . Never has the German idea of freedom been conceived with greater life and greater vigor than in our day" (Mosse, 1966: 316). And the greatest representative of German Idealism was Immanuel Kant. Insisting, for example, that religion derives from morality, and not the other way around, Kant embraces a rationalist theology that is opposed to anything resembling a revealed religion, such as Judaism, and that therefore reduces human beings to a species—a rational species, yes, but a species nevertheless (Wood, 1992: 394–416). Indeed, in *The Conflict of the Faculties*, Kant insists that "the euthanasia of Judaism is the pure moral religion" (Kant, 1979: 95). (Of course, the euthanasia of Judaism amounts to the elimination of the G-d of Abraham, Isaac, and Jacob!) Kant takes a step in that direction in his *Universal Natural History*, where he asserts that the only thing dependent upon G-d's will is the creation of matter (Beiser, 1992: 39). Once matter is the only thing that comes from G-d, G-d soon becomes superfluous, except as the projection of one's own psyche, as in Ludwig Feuerbach (Feuerbach, 1957: 12–13), or as what one aspires to become in a self-apotheosis, as in Friedrich Nietzsche (Nietzsche, 1966: 154). Contrary to the embrace of anything like a divine will or commandment, the human being is "determinable," says Kant, "only by laws which he gives to himself through reason" (Kant, 1985: 101). Yes, through reason . . . but why exactly should reason enjoy such a status?

Judaism recognizes the precarious reliability of human reason. That is why among the laws of Torah are the *chukim*, those laws that, at first glance, are contrary to reason. That is why the Talmud teaches that it is better to follow a commandment because it is commanded rather than because we desire to follow it or because it makes sense to us (*Avodah Zarah* 3a). If we follow the prohibition against murder only because we wish to follow it, then we are the authority, not G-d. And the day may come—indeed, many days have come—when we no longer wish to follow G-d's authority. To affirm the authority of G-d at the expense of the authority, and, therefore, the autonomy of the human being is to undermine the Enlightenment thinking exemplified in Kant. Hence, Judaism is the opposite of Kantian idealism—which is why Kant wanted to see it eliminated. With the elimination of Judaism, however, we have the elimination of the *absolute* injunction against genocide, the divine injunction that makes genocide more than an abomination or an obscenity—it makes it *evil*.

Like Kant, G. W. F. Hegel was a rationalist who associated freedom with human autonomy. His writings, as Paul Lawrence Rose has noted, "conform to the basic Kantian idealist and moralist critique of Judaism. Judaism is seen as the epitome of an unfree psyche" (Rose, 1990: 109). Unlike Kant, however, Hegel draws on the Christian notion of the Christ as the Incarnation to develop a view of G-d that denies the otherness of the divinity. In Hegel, Emil Fackenheim explains, "divinity comes to dwell, as it were, in the same inner space as the human self" (Fackenheim, 1993: 190–91). Resisting this internalization, Jews live an "animal existence," as Hegel sees it; they are in a "state of total passivity, of total ugliness," and are to blame for refusing to "die as Jews" (Hegel, 1948: 201–5). Resisting this internal appropriation of G-d by the self—and contrary to the philosophers' creed—the Jews insist upon the divine prohibition from beyond being, making genocide an evil within being. With Hegel, however, the perceiving self that had appropriated the world now appropriates the divinity, and within a generation or two becomes the seat of law and not the servant of law.

The philosophical result of the incarnation of G-d in the self and the subsequent deprecation of the Jews can be found in the thinking of atheistic neo-Hegelians such as Feuerbach and Marx, where, says Fackenheim, "divinity vanishes in the process of internalization, to be replaced by a humanity potentially infinite in its modern 'freedom'" (Fackenheim, 1973: 191). Because it is infinite, the human being's "modern freedom" eliminates the Infinite Being, so that men (and women) may now do whatever they have the will to do. Indeed, they are justified by will alone. Proceeding along this line of development, then, Nietzsche determines that the will to power is a will to freedom, where freedom is understood as an autonomy beyond any law, resolute and decisive. To be sure, "the expression 'will to power,'" says the Nazi Martin Heidegger, "designates the basic character of beings; any being which is, insofar as it is, is will to power. The expression stipulates the character that beings have as beings" (Heidegger, 1979: 18). Here Heidegger echoes Nietzsche's assertion that "German philosophers" are "*commanders and legislators*: they say, '*Thus* it *shall* be!'. . . their will to truth is—*will to power*" (Nietzsche, 1966: 136). After Nietzsche's will to power defines the *character* of beings, then, Heidegger's resolve defines the *authenticity* of beings. Resolve, then, is the root of autonomy and freedom.

This thinking that began with Kantian idealism and culminated in Heideggerian postmodernism *has to* seek the elimination of heteronomous Jewish thought, inasmuch as such thought embraces the absolute authority of the Holy One, who is known only through his uncompromising commandment. That embrace is what Heidegger complained of when he complained about the "Jewification" of the German mind (Kissel, 1992: 12). Thus the philosopher Heidegger joined the Nazi Party, which would see to a "Final Solution" to the Jewification problem! One sees why political power and scientific technology can be so deadly: they are employed with the sense that one is judged not from on high but only from within. Conscience, which the Nazis derided as a Jewish invention, is eclipsed by resolve. Thus, G-d as the basis of autonomy and Torah as the ground of freedom are gone. What remains is the human species as an ontological curiosity and human culture as an anthropological phenomenon, both of which have no more than a relative value. Each of them, subsequently, is engaged in a power struggle with other human and cultural phenomena for the authority to assert what is right. And as history has shown, when that power struggle loses the limiting principles of religion, it becomes genocidal.

IMPLICATIONS AND LESSONS

Once G-d is eliminated from our thinking, then power is the only reality and weakness is the only sin, so that the perpetrators are not in error; rather, the victims are in error for being weak. Once G-d is eliminated from our thinking, we need not become more righteous in order to be in the right; we only have to become more dangerous. Once G-d is eliminated from our thinking, then each of us—every culture, society, and ethnic group—is like god, but of no *intrinsic* value, and therefore of equal value. Yes, like god, but not as the G-d of Abraham, who is loving and longsuffering, but as the false god of our egocentric aspirations, the god who can do what he wants and who gets what he wants. Once the G-d of Abraham is thus eliminated from our thinking, what remains is "systems of belief," rather than divine injunctions (Kuper, 1990: 352), so that, no longer the measure of a culture, religion is equated with culture (Glick, 1994: 44). But when a scholar appeals to systems of belief or equates religion with culture, he or she loses all grounds other than expedient grounds for objecting to genocide. Here genocide is not evil—it is merely contrary to my interests.

Emmanuel Levinas accurately states the implications of the ontological thinking that leads to genocide when he says: "A philosophy of power, ontology, is, as first philosophy one which does not call into question the same, a philosophy of injustice. . . . Heideggerian ontology, which subordinates the relationship with the Other to the relation with Being in general, remains under obedience to the anonymous, and leads inevitably to another power, to imperialist domination, to tyranny" (Levinas, 1969: 46–47). As Rummel has shown, tyranny is one of the necessary conditions for genocide; not a single twentieth-century democracy has undertaken a genocidal program (Rummel, 1994: 2). What is the connection between ontology and tyranny? Grounding freedom in the autonomy and authenticity in the resolve of the self, ontologically based thinking situates freedom outside any divine law and therefore is ultimately lawless. The terrible irony is that much of the scholarship on genocide is grounded in ontology as first philosophy. After all, Rummel refers to human beings as a species, and not as children of the G-d who forbids murder, and Leonard Glick equates religion with culture (Rummel, 1994; Glick, 1994).

What comes out in the foregoing is a fundamental hostility of ontological thinking toward religion in general and toward Judaism in particular. Why Judaism? Because Judaism is held to be the first written expression of the absolute commandment from beyond the world, including the prohibition against murder, a prohibition that comes *directly* from G-d and not from some tribal chieftain. Therefore Judaism denies the thinking about freedom, autonomy, and resolve that characterize modern ontological thought. The hostility toward Judaism is tied to the impulse to insist that religion is behind our genocidal actions. It is the same hostility that leads to anti-Semitic tendencies among intellectuals who see localized religions as the source of the "proto-genocidal intent," and Judaism as "the most familiar of all localized religions" (Glick, 1994: 47). The implication is clear: whereas Christians blamed the Jews for the murder of G-d, intellectuals blame the Jews for the murder of humanity. Hence the comparison of Israelis to Nazis by scholars such as Marc Ellis (in an interview on Australia's ABC Radio National, 8 August 2001; also Ellis, 1997: 1–5) and by leaders such as Algerian Ambassador to the United Nations Mohamed-Saleh Dembri (Anti-Defamation League Press Release, 21 March 2002). If genocide "is an obscenity—the evil of our time that all good people must work to eradicate," one wonders what must be done with those who are behind it.

Christians cite Scripture, which they take to be truth, to prove that the Jews killed G-d in the person of Jesus. Similarly, intellectuals cite Scripture, which they regard as myth, to prove that the Jews are behind genocide. Glick, for example, points out that "as the Hebrews, under Joshua's leadership, undertake the conquest of Canaan, they massacre everyone who stands in their way" (Glick, 1994: 46), and Kuper makes a similar observation (Kuper, 1990: 356). What such thinkers fail to realize is that what makes genocide not only horrible but also *evil* is precisely the authority of the G-d who prohibits murder (Exodus 20:13) and commands love for the stranger (Deuteronomy 10:19)—*absolutely*, from beyond all cultural contexts, all ontological contingencies, localized and otherwise. Whether one defends or attacks G-d's commandment to wage war and even wipe out certain tribes, the argument can be made only from adherence to the Covenant between G-d and humanity, that is, only from the Torah: once anyone rejects the divine prohibition against murder, one has no grounds for objecting to the divine commandment to wage war.

Further, in the interest of honesty, one should at least note why certain tribes were so singled out. It was because "even their sons and their daughters do they burn in the fire to their gods" (Deuteronomy 12:31). Thus, they renounce the holiness of human life that is proclaimed in the Torah and that makes genocide evil. Once we get rid of G-d, then passing our children through fire in the interest of power can easily be justified; it is not wrong—it is simply a cultural peculiarity. Once the category of holiness is out of the picture, all that remains is human autonomy and an "authenticity" that is rooted in resolve. And, contrary to the divine commandment, human resolve knows no limiting principle.

Also in the interest of honesty, it should be pointed out that, when they took Jericho under Joshua's leadership, the Hebrews did not massacre everyone who stood in their way: the righteous—Rachav and here family—were spared, *not* because of their culture or their beliefs, but because of their self-sacrificing loving-kindness. In keeping with the concept of the *Chasidei Umot Ha-Olam*, the Righteous among the Nations, the Hebrews do not insist that everyone follow the Hebrew religion in order to have a place with G-d. Thus, the prophet Jonah can go to Nineveh and successfully call the people to repent, and thus bring them salvation without insisting that they convert to Judaism. Had Jonah been a Christian or a Muslim, "saving" the people of Nineveh would certainly have entailed their conversion to the religion of the "savior" or prophet.

Here we do have a key to a possible connection between religion and genocide. Wherever a religion divides humanity into believers and infidels, into the saved and the damned—wherever a religion insists that only the adherents of that religion have a place with G-d, and therefore insists on sameness rather than difference—then there is, indeed, a potential for mass murder, if not for genocide. The histories of Christianity and Islam bear this out. Contrary to those creeds, Judaism does not demand that a person become a Jew in order to have a place with the Holy One. Does it not stipulate that Jews have a special, unique place with the Holy One that is inaccessible to others? From the standpoint of Judaism, one is righteous not in the light of having embraced a certain doctrine, but because of engaging in a certain action. The idea of a righteous and, therefore, redeemed non-Christian or non-Muslim is alien to those traditions.

Nevertheless, revealed religion and ontological thinking display a crucial difference in their contributions to genocide. The difference between the Crusaders' slaughter of Jews and Muslims in the Middle Ages, for example, and the megamurder perpetrated by Stalin, Mao, and Hitler does not lie in the technology at their disposal. Rather, it lies in the limiting principle at work in the religious teaching. At any point during the Christian bloodbath, one could still be a Christian and suggest that the killing was going too far, precisely by invoking Christian teaching. If, as Kuper rightly points out, "the teachings of the Church provided no specific warrant for genocide" (Kuper, 1990: 371), thus is because such a warrant would be contrary to other stated teachings, as for instance, the commandment to love one's enemies (Matthew 5:44). With National Socialism and Communism, there is no going too far, and to suggest that the actions of the Party were excessive would amount to losing membership. What the megamurderers perpetrated, therefore, was not unimaginable—it was everything imaginable.

For the imagination was the only limit, and power was the only reality. For the Christians, reality is constituted not by power but by truth. And where there is truth, there is a limiting principle at work.

With regard to the Muslims, the matter is neither so clear nor so encouraging. Reading through the Qur'an, I do not find a parallel to the Christian insistence upon love for one's enemies, or a view of G-d as a father and therefore as one who is to be understood in terms of love, or the injunction to refrain from condemning one's neighbor and leaving ultimate judgments to G-d. What I do find is a view of a heaven reserved for Muslims, with the fire reserved for the nonbelievers. In modern times, at least, the Muslim world has produced no one comparable to Mahatma Gandhi or Martin Luther King, Jr. What that world has produced is a discourse of rabid Jew-hatred, a notion of martyrdom defined in terms of murder, and an international network of terrorism. This is not to say that there are no righteous people among the Muslims. To be sure, between 1987 and 1993 more than 800 Palestinian Muslims were murdered by the Palestinians themselves for suggesting that their people might have a better future if they were to follow a path of peace with the Israelis (Associated Press report, 2002; the IDF places the figure at 1,000 to 1,200); as of September 2002 that figure stood at 233 for the Intifada that began in September 2002 (Radlaur, 2002). Often these martyrs were tortured and lynched, their bodies butchered and dragged through the streets of Hebron, Ramallah, or Nablus to the cheers of thousands (see Associated Press report, 2002; also Mazen, 2002; see also Huggler and Ghazali, 2003). If otherwise well-meaning Muslims are to avoid playing into the hands of megamurderers, then the cries of those martyrs must be heard above the cheers of those crowds.

CONCLUDING THOUGHTS

If the imperative that "all good people must work to eradicate" genocide is to be categorical, then it must somehow be grounded in an absolute, divine prohibition against murder, such as we have from the G-d of Abraham. Without that absolute prohibition, the human being has no absolute value. Without that commandment from the Holy One, the human being has no holiness. To be created in the image and likeness of G-d is to be commanded by G-d, so that, as the Ten Commandments are laid out on the tablets, the affirmation "I am G-d" parallels the injunction "Thou shalt not murder." Genocide is evil because genocide amounts to the most radical assault against the G-d of Abraham. It is no accident that, more often than not, genocidal regimes are also anti-Semitic regimes. They are anti-Semitic because, in order to pursue the genocidal program, they have to eliminate the divine prohibition against murder that comes to the modern world through the Jews.

If "all good people must work to eradicate" genocide, it is not necessary for these good people to become Jews. But it is necessary for them to assume a Jewish condition: they must take on the precarious task of becoming a light unto the nations. As the Chosen People, the Jewish people are chosen to attest to the chosenness of every human being. And, for every human being, to be chosen is to affirm, in word and in deed, the infinite dearness of the *other* human being. That is what makes good people good. That is what elevates us beyond the status of species. And that is what makes genocide evil.

BIBLIOGRAPHY

Anti-Defamation League (2002). "ADL Deplores Algerian Comparison of Israelis to Nazis at UN Meeting, Calling It 'Blatant Anti-Semitism.'" Press release, 21 March 2002. Available through the Internet at: http://www.adl.org/PresRele/ASInt13/4058_13.asp.

Associated Press (2002). "Palestinians Face Internal Violence." News report, 16 May 2002.

Bartov, Omer and Phyllis Mack (eds.) (2001). *Genocide and Religion in the Twentieth Century.* New York: Berghahn Books.

Beiser, Frederick C. (1992). "Kant's Intellectual Development: 1746–1781," in Paul Guyer (ed.), *The Cambridge Companion to Kant.* Cambridge: Cambridge University Press, 26–61.

Ellis, Marc H. (1997). *Unholy Alliance: Religion and Atrocity in Our Time.* Minneapolis, Minn.: Fortress Press.

Fackenheim, Emil L. (1978). *The Jewish Return into History.* New York: Schocken Books.

—— (1993). *Encounters between Judaism and Modern Philosophy: A Preface to Future Jewish Thought.* New York: Basic Books.

Feuerbach, Ludwig (1957). *The Essence of Christianity.* New York: Harper & Row.

Glick, Leonard B. (1994). "Religion and Genocide," in Israel W. Chamy (ed.), *The Widening Circle of Genocide. Genocide: A Critical Bibliographic Review.* Vol. 3. New Brunswick, NJ: Transaction Publishers, 43–74.

Hegel, G. W. F. (1948). "The Spirit of Christianity and Its Fate," in *Early Theological Writings.* Chicago, Ill.: University of Chicago Press, 182–301.

Heidegger, Martin (1979). "Will to Power as Art," in *Nietzsche.* Translated from the German with notes and analysis by David Farrell Krell. San Francisco, Calif.: Harper & Row, 1–223.

Heschel, Abraham Joshua (1955). *God in Search of Man: A Philosophy of Judaism.* New York: Farrar, Straus and Giroux.

Huggler, Justin and Sa'id Ghazali (2003). "Palestinians Cheer Executions of 'Collaborators.'" *The Independent.* 23 October, 16.

Kant, Immanuel (1979). *The Conflict of the Faculties.* New York: Abaris.

—— (1985). *The Critique of Pure Reason*. New York: Macmillan.

Kisiel, Theodore (1992). "Heidegger's Anthropology: Biology and Philosophy and Ideology," in Rockmore, Tom, and Margolis, Joseph, eds., *The Heidegger Case: On Philosophy and Politics* (Philadelphia: Temple University Press), 11–54.

Kuper, Leo (1990). "Theological Warrants for Genocide: Judaism, Islam and Christianity." *Terrorism and Political Violence*, 2(3): 351–71.

Levinas, Emmanuel (1969). *Totality and Infinity: An Essay on Exteriority*. Pittsburgh, Pa.: Duquesne University Press.

Maimonides, Moses (1956). *The Guide for the Perplexed*. Translated from the original Arabic text by M. Friedlander. New York: Dover.

Maza, Bernard (1986). *With Fury Poured Out: A Torah Perspective on the Holocaust*. Hoboken, N.J.: Ktav.

Mazen, Dana (2002). "Palestinians in Hebron Kill Suspected Collaborators." Reuters News Service news report, 23 April 2002. Available through the Internet at: http://freerepublic.com/focus/news/671154/posts.

Mosse, George L. (1966). *Nazi Culture: Intellectual, Cultural, and Social Life in the Third Reich*. New York: Grosset & Dunlap.

Nietzsche, Frederick (1966). *Beyond Good and Evil: Prelude to a Philosophy of the Future*. New York: Vintage Books.

Radlaur, Dan (2002). *An Engineered Tragedy: Statistical Analysis of Casualties in the Israeli-Palestinian Conflict, September 2000–September 2002*. Herzilya, Israel: International Policy Institute for Counter-Terrorism Report released 24 June 2002 and updated 29 September 2002.

Rose, Paul Lawrence (1990). *German Question/Jewish Question: Revolutionary Anti-semitism from Kant to Wagner*. Princeton, N.J.: Princeton University Press.

Rosenzweig, Franz (1999a). *Franz Rosenzweig's "The New Thinking."* Edited and translated by Alan Udoff and Barbara E. Galli. Syracuse, N.Y.: Syracuse University Press.

—— (1999b). *Understanding the Sick and the Healthy: A View of World, Man, and God*. Cambridge, Mass.: Harvard University Press.

Rummel, R. J. (1994). *Death by Government*. New Brunswick, N.J.: Transaction Publishers.

Sacks, Jonathan (1992). *Crisis and Covenant: Jewish Thought after the Holocaust*. Manchester, England: Manchester University Press.

Wood, Allen W. (1992). "Rational Theology, Moral Faith, and Religion," in Paul Guyer (ed.), *The Cambridge Companion to Kant*. Cambridge: Cambridge University Press; 94–116.

12

The Ten Commandments, the Holocaust, and Reflections on Genocide

Paul R. Bartrop

THE DECALOGUE, THE NAZIS, AND THE HOLOCAUST

In the 1970 Columbia Pictures movie *Cromwell*, set during the English Civil War of the seventeenth century, the character of Oliver Cromwell (played by Richard Harris) is engaged in an argument with one of his generals, Henry Ireton (played by Michael Jayston). At the height of the argument, Ireton states that God is on the side of the parliamentary forces ranged against those of the king. Responding angrily, Cromwell replies, in a memorable line: "It is an odd thing, Mr. Ireton, that every man who wages war believes that God is on his side. I'll warrant God must often wonder who is on his!"

How often have we been witness to the acts of people who maintain, regardless of their behavior, that they are supported by divine assent? How often, indeed, do people claim more than just approval, but outright commission? In war, this has happened frequently, as soldiers have gone marching off to the strains of "*Gott mit Uns,*" "God Save the King," or variations on that theme. Such thoughts are no doubt inspired by a need on the part of those engaging in acts of combat to justify—to others, as well as to themselves—why they are putting themselves or their country's future on the line. People need to know that they are fighting for a higher cause, one from which the nation will derive benefit if it is successful, or in which it may nonetheless claim a final heavenly reward if they are not.

Those who commit genocide often endow their actions with some sort of religious meaning, frequently putting forth the assertion that, in destroying entire groups of people, they are doing God's work. History is replete with accounts of people being put to the sword, in their thousands and millions, as part of what is justified as some sort of divinely revealed plan of extirpation and annihilation. Religious wars of extermination are so ingrained in the popular consciousness that, even three and four centuries ago, it had become a given that religion is a root cause of violence, war, and mass murder.

Within the Jewish religious tradition, however, another set of givens prevails, these stemming from the revealed legal and ethical codes enunciated in the Torah and embracing 613 *mitzvot*, or divine commandments. These are scattered throughout the Torah and other sacred Jewish literature, which normative Judaism holds to be the literal word of God. Some are specific to men, others to women; many pertain to the ancient temple ritual, redundant since the destruction of the Second Temple in CE 70. Chronological, in both time and in the structure of the Torah, is the injunction to "be fruitful and multiply" (Genesis 1:28); this order to keep the species alive is, literally, the first commandment.

But of all the obligations ordained in the Torah, it is the Ten Commandments given by God to Moses in Exodus 20:1–14, and repeated in Deuteronomy 5:6–18 with variations, that most readily spring to mind for Jews and Christians whenever the notion of divinely mandated behavior is raised. In summary form, these read as follows:

1. I am the Lord your God, Who brought you out of the Land of Egypt, out of the house of bondage;
2. You shall have no other gods before me;
3. You shall not take the Lord's name in vain;
4. Remember the Sabbath day, to keep it holy;
5. Honor your father and your mother;
6. You shall not murder;
7. You shall not commit adultery;
8. You shall not steal;
9. You shall not bear false witness against your neighbor; and
10. You shall not covet.

As a legal code, these commandments represented, for the Jews standing at the foot of Mount Sinai, a revelation of the most profound—even revolutionary—power. Having emerged as a nation out of several hundred years of slavery in polytheistic, absolutist Egypt, they were now confronted with a number of radical new propositions: a single deity, whose existence is greater than anything else in the universe; a weekly day of rest; and adherence to a strict moral code whereby parents are respected, murder and theft are forbidden, and adultery, lying, and wanting beyond one's measure are all prohibited. These laws, moreover, were to apply to *everyone* within the House of Israel, from the meanest beggar to Moses himself—by extension, from the lowliest in society to its elites, even its princes. The Ten Commandments widened the scope of the earlier Noachide Code (implicit in Genesis 9, but expounded upon fully in the Babylonian Talmud, Sanhedrin 56a, according to which all of humanity is enjoined not to worship idols, or to blaspheme, murder, steal, engage in sexual immorality, or to consume the limb of a live animal, but to establish courts of law in order to live a godly and just life) and bound the Jews within a new covenantal relationship to God. Henceforth, their adherence to a system based on a divinely ordained code of ethics was to be rooted in the belief that God wanted them to act this way. And more than "wanted": the word of God being recognized as the ultimate authority, the Jews saw that they had to act morally because God had *instructed* them to do so, in a theophany so intense that, as Jewish tradition has it, all Jews then standing at Sinai, together with the souls of every Jew yet to be born and every convert yet to come to Judaism, were made aware of God's demands. Henceforth, the divine message would be revealed through the history and behavior of a specific people, the Jews—from which the belief in Jewish chosenness, or divine election, emerges.

The Decalogue became the linchpin holding together the Jewish ethical framework, but it did not stop there: with the emergence of Christianity and that tradition's absorption of the Hebrew Bible as the larger part of its own canon, the Ten Commandments also became a constituent aspect of church teaching. In the 2,000 years that followed the emergence of Christianity, there was no deviation from the idealization of the Decalogue for either religious code, not even during Christianity's most testing times or doctrinal upheavals. The Ten Commandments, in short, became—and have remained—one of the most crucial elements of religio-moral doctrine for both Jews and Christians down to the present day.

Which brings us to the period of the Third Reich, a time in which Europe was plunged into a new Dark Age by forces antithetical to everything the Jewish and Christian religious traditions had been working toward for millennia. This is not to suggest that European history until then had seen one long upward climb that was only interrupted by the arrival of the Nazis; on the contrary, it could be said that European development had been a succession of moral highs and lows that resemble a pattern of peaks and troughs rather than a J-curve leading skyward. But the social, political, economic, and cultural progress that began with the eighteenth-century Enlightenment had certainly led Europeans to hold that society could never again regress to a state devoid of civil and human rights, where life would

be so totally devalued and the principles enshrined in the Ten Commandments would become so utterly debased. How wrong they were. The inac-
curacy of such thinking would become all too apparent as the worst years
of the twentieth century unfolded.

Hugo Gryn (1928–1996), a Czech-born English Reform rabbi who as a
young man survived the Auschwitz extermination camp, reflected on this
later in a statement that has become acclaimed for its insight. During the
Holocaust, said Gryn, the ethical code of both Jews and Christians was
"denied and reversed":

> If you take the Ten Commandments, from the very first which starts: "I am
> the Lord your God who brought you out of the land of Egypt," here you had
> people who set *themselves* up to be gods, to be masters of life and death, and
> who took you *into* Egypt: into an Egypt of the most bizarre and most obnox-
> ious kind, and all the way to creating their own set of idols, to taking God's
> name in vain, to setting generations at each other so that children dishonoured
> parents.
>
> Certainly they murdered. Certainly they committed robbery. Certainly there
> was a great deal of coveting, of envy, involved in it. In other words, you had
> here an outbreak of the very opposite of everything that civilization was build-
> ing towards. (Gilbert, 1986: 826)

The Holocaust, in short, was for Rabbi Gryn "a denial of God, [and] a denial of man; it was the destruction of the world, in miniature form," as he
stated in the 1982 BBC documentary "Auschwitz and the Allies."

In an earlier work, this chapter's author wrote that Nazism contained
"all the elements of a repressive and anti-human ideology which rejected
the most fundamental ideals and freedoms fought for since Europe had
emerged from the Dark Ages" (Bartrop, 2000: 21). To this could be added,
in the current context, that Nazism's moral code was also the clearest and
most unequivocal statement the movement could make about itself—and
this is hardly a flattering observation. This might come as something of
a surprise to those who hold that the Christian churches remained intact
under Nazism, in an environment where church membership remained
at a high level throughout the duration of the Third Reich. The key to facing up to the dilemma posed by this is, of course, the notion of belief: we
need to consider the degree to which Germans during the period of the
Third Reich continued to *believe* in the fundamental tenets of Christianity, as enunciated in John 1:6–7 ("There was a man sent from God, whose
name was John, who came as a witness to bear witness of the Light, that all
men through him might believe"), rather than simply continue to attend
church or to affirm membership. It is a significant question, impossible to
answer, as no one may claim to know what intimate beliefs are held by
another—and even less, by an entire population. This is something that

cannot be quantified. We can, however, look into the actions of a people, and assess the extent to which they are aligned with the set of ideas or beliefs they claim to follow, in order to draw conclusions about the degree to which their behavior is or is not true to what they profess. While there are certainly exceptions, it must be concluded that the vast majority of Germans and Austrians, through their actions or their acquiescence between 1933 and 1945, did not put their proclaimed Christian adherence—what they claimed were their Christian beliefs—into practice. Membership in the religious community, in short, did not make them religious, at least insofar as the core doctrines of Christianity were concerned.

A number of historians have looked into this issue, in recent times most notably Robert P. Ericksen and Susannah Heschel (1999), Richard Steigmann-Gall (2004), and Doris L. Bergen (1996). While in certain respects there is no complete consensus between these authors about the relationship of Nazism to Christianity, there is one argument to which all would accede: Nazi ideology found much to admire in the structure of the Church (and in particular, the Roman Catholic Church) that was worthy of emulation. Just how far such admiration extended to doctrinal belief, however, is open to debate. Indeed, Steigmann-Gall considers the leaders of the Nazi movement, while on the whole opposed to Roman Catholicism, too have been more or less inconclusive when it came to the various forms of Protestantism in Germany. Many, regardless of confession, held themselves to be good Christians in accordance with their personal conception of what that entailed—though it may be surmised that the nature of the Nazi state saw much internal conflict raging within the hearts and souls of people who saw themselves this way. Put slightly differently, it can be said that church membership alone did not make the German people moral, a lesson they learned between 1933 and 1945, when both their sense of right and wrong and the effectiveness of church teachings were put to the ultimate test.

Quite simply, many of those who said they were Christians, and even *believed* they were Christian, did not for the most part *act* as Christians should. Germany was a society that viewed itself as being Christian, but the Nazi state gave the lie to the reality of that view. Max I. Dimont, in a telling paragraph, has shown how fragile Christian behavior was during the Third Reich:

New industries develop special skills, and the concentration camp industry was no exception. Adept *Sonderkommandos* learned how to apply grappling hooks with skill to separate the bodies. Trained technicians learned to pry dead lips apart and deftly knock out gold-filled teeth. Talented barbers dextrously shaved the heads of dead women. Six days a week, the new elite worked in the concentration camps. On Sunday they rested, went to church with their wives and children, and after church talked with horror about the eastern front where

Russians were killing German soldiers, and commented on the barbarity of the
Americans who were dropping bombs on civilians. (Dimont, 1962: 383)

As Franklin H. Littell, the doyen of Christian scholars who have addressed
this issue, has written, "the God of Abraham, Isaac and Jacob . . . is also
the Christians' God, *when they remember who they are*" (emphasis added)
(Littell, 1975: 57). It may well be argued that, with all too few exceptions,
those claiming Christian adherence in Germany between 1933 and 1945
did not so remember.

Nazism did not follow Christianity in its ideologies or its doctrines,
regardless of what its leaders professed. Adolf Hitler, for example,
considered the Ten Commandments to be "a code of living to which there's
no refutation. These precepts correspond to irrefragable needs of the human
soul; they're inspired by the best religious spirit" (Steigmann-Gall, 2004:
256). While this is certainly a glowing recommendation, it says nothing
about Hitler's degree of observance, his personal relationship to Jesus or
to God, or to religious dogma generally. When we examine the anatomy
of the Nazi state, we see that, for all the declarations of Christianity that
emanated from Germany between 1933 and 1945, it was a state that acted
in a distinctly *non*-Christian way.

To develop this argument further, one can juxtapose each of the
Commandments enunciated in the Decalogue against a feature characteristic
of the Nazi regime. The findings are highly illustrative of what might be
termed Nazism's true essence.

The first three Commandments focus on the nature of God and what
God expects of those professing belief. Where Nazi Germany is concerned,
the first Commandment was overturned completely. Here, instead of
recognizing God for what God is, we find a regime in which religious
beliefs have been denied and monotheism itself has been abandoned.
Again, it must be reiterated that here we are discussing the nature of the
regime, not of German society; and again it must be reiterated that while
there were many in the Nazi Party (and even its higher echelons) who
thought themselves to be good Christians, the reality of their actions—and
even more, of their party—did not bear this out.

Proceeding from this, the second Commandment is replaced in Nazism
by an ideology that elevates the nation-state to a position as the supreme
arbiter of right and wrong, introducing new idols to worship in the form of
Ein Volk, Ein Reich, Ein Führer, and the various ways they are lauded. And
while the third Commandment concerns itself with the swearing of oaths
in the name of God, the Nazis took the idea and corrupted it by requiring
that all members of the German armed forces swear a personal oath to Adolf
Hitler, in a parody of what all oath-swearing until that time had been. Prior
to this time, oath taking was a solemn appeal to God, who would serve as

a witness that a statement would be true, or that a promise about to made would be kept. The Nazi oath of loyalty, too, was an oath before God, but it enjoined one to swear unconditional obedience to the person of Adolf Hitler, unto death; it was not an oath to the state, or to the defense of the monarch through whom the state was governed, but to the Nazi dictator *himself*—the presumption being that Hitlerian policies and practices would be something God's law would have endorsed (which, given its commitment to moral behavior as outlined in the remaining Commandments, it could not).

The fourth Commandment, regarding the holiness of the Sabbath day, can be examined from the perspective of the slave labor force into which Europe's Jews were marched throughout the war years—a slavery that made a mockery of the Jews' liberation from Pharaoh in Egypt over 3,000 years earlier, at the very time of the theophany that led to the Decalogue in the first place. The Shabbat is an island in time, a day of holiness and spirituality—in short, a day of rest. This can be contrasted with the relentlessness of the Nazis' brutality, and their enslavement of the Jews. The Shabbat is to be considered an *"Oneg,"* a delight, on which humans are to be left free to worship God. Nazi slavery, on all days of the week, must be considered its diametric opposite.

In looking at the fifth Commandment, consideration could be made of the values the Nazis fostered in their children's organizations, specifically the Hitler Youth and the League of German Girls. Here, children were encouraged to participate actively in a culture of informing on their parents, dishonoring them through domestic betrayal for the greater good of the state (Grunberger, 1971). Little elaboration is necessary with regard to the sixth Commandment: the Nazis initiated a campaign of complete racial extermination against Jews, began and waged aggressive war throughout Europe, North Africa, and on the world's oceans, and murdered political opponents both before and after they came to power. To this must be added the millions of other Nazi-perpetrated murders that took place among all the nations of occupied Europe. German Nazism was an ideology, in short, that legitimized murder and broadened its scope to hitherto unparalleled proportions.

The seventh Commandment was overturned by the Nazis through the policy of selective breeding in Nazi "stud farms" established through the Lebensborn program, whereby young women who conformed physically to the "Aryan" ideal were encouraged to bear the children of young male Nazis equally endowed, regardless of marriage or even mutual attraction (Clay and Leapman, 1995; Neumann, 1958: 80–85). This promotion of sexual immorality runs counter to the spirit motivating the seventh Commandment, and is another example of a Nazi policy that is the direct opposite of the sanctified moral code that has underpinned Western morality for millennia.

Theft, the theme of the eighth Commandment, can be addressed by reference to the Nazis' plundering of European art galleries and industrial enterprises, as well as its expropriation of property (and in particular, Jewish property) on racial grounds in accordance with Nazi ideology (Nicholas, 1994; Kladstrup and Kladstrup, 2002; Feliciano, 1997; James, 2001). The ninth Commandment can refer to the operation of justice in the Third Reich: the swearing of false oaths, the legitimation of perjury in order to meet political or racial ends, and the entire sham legality behind the functioning of the *Volksgericht,* or "people's court" (Koch, 1989; Miller, 1995). Where the tenth Commandment is concerned, the theme of coveting looms large in the Nazi worldview: from the dream of regaining lands (such as Danzig, the Polish Corridor, and Alsace-Lorraine) that were lost as a result of the Treaty of Versailles, the Nazis cast avaricious eyes toward areas that were neither "lost" (the Sudetenland, for example, had never belonged to Germany) nor German (such as Czechoslovakia), and ultimately plotted the conquest of more and more territory in keeping with a long-held ideal of the acquisition of *Lebensraum* (as in the ambitions held for the German colonization of Poland, western Russia, and Ukraine) (Stoakes, 1986; Kallis, 2000; Cecil, 1975).

All these are but examples that illustrate some of the ways in which Germany's Nazi regime showed itself to be diametrically opposed to the ideals and ethics embodied within the Ten Commandments. Other examples could be cited but need not be pursued here; it is sufficient to show that each of the Ten Commandments has at least one opposite that can be derived from the behavior of the Nazi regime during the Third Reich. As Rabbi Gryn stated, the Holocaust represented *both* a denial of God *and* a denial of humanity. For this reason alone, it is deserving of study, but there is more to it than that: by looking at the Holocaust relative to the Decalogue, we can come closer to understanding why Judaism's ethical and moral values represent the opposite of such general forces as tyranny and dictatorship, and why, as a consequence, such forces must be combated. When all is said and done, the Ten Commandments provide a code that simultaneously requires humility before God and cooperation between human beings. Humility and cooperation are not ideals one can normally align with tyranny and dictatorship, much less mass murder and genocide.

Despite this, it should be noted that the Jewish religious tradition does not subscribe to a belief system that is totally passive, as scriptural references to the destruction of the Amalekites show (see, e.g., Exodus 17:8–16; Deuteronomy 25:17–19; or I Samuel 15:2–8); nor does the story of Joshua's revenge over the inhabitants of Jericho (Joshua 6:20–21) suggest that the ancient Hebrews were prepared to hold back from inflicting physical harm on their enemies if God commanded it. A most startling expression of violence within the Jews' belief system is to be found in Deuteronomy 7, as discussed elsewhere in this volume by Zev Garber. Yet even here, the Jewish concept of war—*milchamah*, in Hebrew—was surrounded by a number of restrictions governing how it was to be waged and the circumstances within which noncombatants should be treated humanely and spared wherever possible. After the theophany at Mount Sinai, all aspects of Jewish life, even the waging of war (as expatiated by the rabbis over the centuries with regard to the notion of *milchemet mitzvah*—a mandatory war, commanded by God—and *milchemet reshut*—an optional war, in which the king may fight with other nations in order to remove a potential threat, or expand the boundaries of Israel so as to strengthen the state), were to be conditioned by the values enunciated in the Ten Commandments. A literal reading of Jewish scripture without this understanding robs the Decalogue of its most essential meaning.

That said, it has unfortunately been the case throughout history that those professing to follow the Ten Commandments from within the Christian tradition have often lost sight of what is actually stipulated therein. Two post-Holocaust examples can help to explain.

RWANDA AND BOSNIA

In Rwanda, in a little more than three months in 1994, up to a million people, mostly Tutsi, were annihilated by their Hutu neighbors in a society where killing became a civic virtue and in which Hutu Christian clergy were often at the forefront of the killing (Mamdani, 2001: 226–27). As accounts collected by the World Council of Churches show, not only did the Roman Catholic Church that prevailed throughout Rwanda do little or nothing to stop the killing; in numerous cases it provided the churches, schools, and other locations by which the Tutsi population could be concentrated prior to their destruction (McCullum, 1996; Gourevitch, 1998). Here, those most directly responsible for upholding the Ten Commandments, and for bringing them to the people, were found wanting at the very time the Decalogue's message was needed the most.

While the tragedy of Rwanda was taking place, a longer-lasting series of conflicts had already entered its fourth year. In the wars accompanying the disintegration of Yugoslavia between 1991 and 1995, and again in 1998–1999, interreligious conflict plumbed depths unsurpassed since the sixteenth century, as first Catholic Croats and Orthodox Serbs slaughtered each other in a quest to obtain, retain, or regain territory, and then Orthodox Serbs launched a concerted campaign of "ethnic cleansing" to rid vast areas of Bosnia of its Muslim population—through killing, deportations, mass rape, massive cultural destruction, and other activities (Cigar, 1995; Gutman, 1993; Maass, 1996). A third round of bloodshed took place in Kosovo at the century's end, as Christian Orthodox Serbs practiced ethnic cleansing against Muslim Kosovars. Regardless of the message of the Ten Commandments, and in a fashion often comparable to the Nazis, the Serbs effectively tore up the Decalogue while at the same time assuring the faithful that, in performing these deeds, they were performing holy work. Such activities were frequently supported, and even carried out, by Serbian Orthodox clergy (Mojzes, 1998; Sells, 1996; Anzulovic, 1999).

Examples of genocide (and even of extensive human rights violations) committed by those purporting to follow the Ten Commandments abound throughout history and are confined neither to the Holocaust nor to the twentieth century. The vast number of occasions on which genocides have been perpetrated by people claiming adherence to the Ten Commandments indicates, however, that the message of the Decalogue has not penetrated as deeply as the leaders of the religious traditions themselves, particularly among some Christians, would have liked. And the Judeo-Christian concept of a moral-ethical Decalogue is not unique among the traditions of the world. Islam has a Decalogue similar to the Ten Commandments of the Hebrew Bible (see Qur'an XVII:22–39), as does Buddhism in the teachings known as the *dasa-sila*, or the Ten Precepts; so also do the Analects of Confucius have at their base an ethical foundation about how best to live a good life.

The Ten Commandments first related in the Hebrew Bible in Exodus 20, and reaffirmed later in Deuteronomy 5, have a definitive relationship with the moral and ethical values that genocide so diametrically opposes. Quite literally, the one is the antithesis of the other. When God states in Isaiah 45:7, "I am the Lord, and there is none else, I form the light, and create darkness: I make peace and create evil," we have a clear statement regarding the ultimate in opposites, through which God, as the Infinite, embraces both. The Ten Commandments, on the other hand, do not provide humanity with such options. In this list, we have God's expressed command of his intentions of how humans are to behave, with no room for the kind of activities that can lead to genocide or justify it.

It is this realization that makes the Holocaust, Rwanda, Bosnia, and all other manifestations of genocide so thoroughly untenable on religious grounds. Antihuman actions are, in the long term, ungodly, as stipulated in the very foundational documents of the religious traditions themselves. Regardless of the justifications offered by some clergy who support or authorize the actions of perpetrator regimes, there is no way that the Ten Commandments can be squared with any form of genocidal behavior, under any circumstances.

CONCLUDING THOUGHTS

At the time of the giving of the Ten Commandments, the Midrash tells us, Moses was taken to Heaven to receive the words directly from God. The angels protested the presence of a living mortal amidst the heavenly hosts, until Moses, authorized by God, made a statement that justified not only his presence there, but also the bestowal of the Commandments upon humanity. To the angels he replied:

> It says in the Torah, "I am the Lord your God, Who brought you out of the land of Egypt, out of the house of bondage." Were you in Egypt? Were you enslaved by Pharaoh? It says, "You shall have no other gods." Do you live among idolatrous nations? The Torah commands, "Remember the Sabbath day, to keep it holy." Do you work, that you should be in need of a Sabbath rest? The Torah says, "You should not take the Lord's name in vain." Do you conduct business deals that you should have to swear? "Honor your father and your mother." Do you have parents? The Torah prohibits murder. Is there bloodshed in Heaven? It says, "You shall not commit adultery." Are you married and in need of this warning? It states, "You shall not steal." Is there silver for you to steal in Heaven? The Torah commands not to covet another's property. Are there houses, fields, or vineyards among you that you should need this admonition? You do not possess a *yetser ha-ra* [evil inclination], as do human beings. How then do the Torah-prohibitions apply to you? (Weissman, 1980, 233–34)

The Jewish religious tradition holds that God's preference would be for all humanity to come voluntarily to an understanding that the Commandments are necessary for building an ideal life, and it would appear somewhat obvious that many terrible things would be avoided if everyone followed the Ten Commandments. That people do not do so, however, and instead develop systems that deny and negate the Decalogue, has roots deep in scripture: even as Moses was receiving the Ten Commandments directly from God, the Torah relates, the people of Israel were, of their own volition, making themselves an idol in the form of a golden calf, and had turned away from God (Exodus 32:1-6). It was only after a divinely decreed earthquake had caused substantial loss of life that the children of Israel again witnessed the reality of God's power, and finally recognized the need to follow his words to the letter.

The overall message is clear. Nazism, as developed in Germany between 1933 and 1945, was probably the most genocidal regime and ideology in history. It possessed a value system that was, quite simply, antithetical to that espoused in the Ten Commandments, and that led in a straight line to the Holocaust. Other expressions of genocide, even when perpetrated by nations and individuals professing to follow the Commandments, are equally opposed to the values of the Decalogue. In this sense, the phenomenon of genocide is not only morally degrading and physically destructive; it is also self-defeating, a social, political, economic, and cultural movement that is undertaken against the best interests of all humanity, not just those who are genocide's victims—for if a moral code that is a universal and absolute good can be reversed so dramatically (and with such devastating results), hope for the future must be diminished. It is against that prospect that those who would uphold the Ten Commandments must rededicate themselves, the better to confront the forces of genocidal destruction. If the twentieth century has taught us anything, it is that the twenty-first can be better. The values and ethics of the Decalogue, no less than the laws and conventions of democracy, must be among the key means to make it so.

BIBLIOGRAPHY

Anzulovic, Branimir (1999). *Heavenly Serbia: From Myth to Genocide*. New York: New York University Press.

Bartrop, Paul R. (2000). *Surviving the Camps: Unity in Adversity during the Holocaust*. Lanham, Md.: University Press of America.

Cecil, Robert (1975). *Hitler's Decision to Invade Russia, 1941*. London: David-Poynter.

Cigar, Norman L. (1995). *Genocide in Bosnia: The Policy of "Ethnic Cleansing."* College Station: Texas A&M University Press.

Clay, Catherine, and Michael Leapman (1995). *Master Race: The Lebensborn Experiment in Nazi Germany*. London: Hodder & Stoughton.

Dimont, Max I. (1962). *Jews, God, and History*. New York: New American Library.

Feliciano, Hector (1997). *The Lost Museum: The Nazi Conspiracy to Steal the World's Greatest Works of Art*. New York: Basic Books.

Gilbert, Martin (1986). *The Holocaust: The Jewish Tragedy*. London: Collins.

Gourevitch, Philip (1998). *We Wish to Inform You That Tomorrow We Will Be Killed with Our Families: Stories from Rwanda*. New York: Farrar, Straus and Giroux.

Grunberger, Richard (1971). *A Social History of the Third Reich*. London: Weidenfeld and Nicholson.

Gutman, Roy (1993). *A Witness to Genocide: The 1993 Pulitzer Prize-Winning Dispatches on the "Ethnic Cleansing" of Bosnia*. New York: Macmillan.

James, Harold (2001). *The Deutsche Bank and the Nazi Economic War against the Jews: The Expropriation of Jewish-Owned Property*. Oxford: Cambridge University Press.

Kallis, Aristotle A. (2000). *Fascist Ideology: Territory and Expansionism in Italy and Germany, 1922–1945*. London: Routledge.

Kladstrup, Don, and Petie Kladstrup (2002). *Wine and War: The French, the Nazis and the Battle for France's Greatest Treasure*. New York: Broadway Books.

Koch, H. W. (1989). *In the Name of the Volk: Political Justice in Hitler's Germany*. New York: St. Martin's Press.

McCullum, Hugh (1996). *The Angels Have Left Us: The Rwandan Tragedy and the Churches*. Geneva, Switzerland: WCC Publications.

Maas, Peter (1996). *Love Thy Neighbor: A Story of War*. New York: Alfred A. Knopf.

Mamdani, Mahmood (2001). *When Victims Become Killers: Colonialism, Nativism, and the Genocide in Rwanda*. Princeton, N.J.: Princeton University Press.

Miller, Richard Lawrence (1995). *Nazi Justiz: Law of the Holocaust*. Westport, Conn.: Praeger.

Mojzes, Paul (ed.) (1998). *Religion and the War in Bosnia*. Atlanta, Ga.: Scholars Press,

Neumann, Peter (1958). *Other Men's Graves*. London: Weidenfeld and Nicholson.

Nicholas, Lynn H. (1994). *The Rape of Europa: The Fate of Europe's Treasures in the Third Reich and the Second World War*. New York: Alfred A. Knopf.

Sells, Michael A. (1996). *The Bridge Betrayed: Religion and Genocide in Bosnia*. Berkeley: University of California Press.

Steigmann-Gall, Richard (2004). *The Holy Reich: Nazi Conceptions of Christianity, 1919–1945*. Cambridge: Cambridge University Press.

Stoakes, Geoffrey (1986). *Hitler and the Quest for World Domination*. Leamington Spa, U.K.: Berg.

Weissman, Moshe (ed.) (1980). *The Midrash Says: On the Weekly Haftaros. Vol. 2: Shemot, Exodus*. Book 2. Brooklyn, N.Y.: Benei Yakov Publications.

13

Coming to Terms with Amalek: Testing the Limits of Hospitality

Henry F. Knight

RELIGION AND VIOLENCE

Religion and violence build a terrifying alliance when they work in partnership with each other. Since September 11, 2001, the image of planes full of people flying into towers has haunted American thoughts about the connections between religion and violence. Some deny the linkage. Some see only the linkage. Since September 11, we have heard our own leaders declare that what happened in our nation on that day had nothing to do with Islam. What happened was a sheer act of terror, erroneously linked to a distorted view of Islam. At stake: to avoid labeling that religion in toto as a religion of violence. The motives have been understandable, whether they have been solely political or a mix of political wisdom and spiritual grace.

On the other hand, some wise souls have been warning us not to overlook the religious nature of what happened. While it would be wrong to cast a totalizing glance at the religion of Islam as violent, it would be equally wrong, as well as unwise, to fail to see that what happened was, indeed motivated in part, by religious sensibilities and understood to have divine sanction. As Andrew Sullivan reminded his readers in his 7 October essay for the *New York Times Sunday Magazine*, "this was a religious war" (Sullivan, 2001). But, as Sullivan also pointed out, the religious sensibilities at work are not found only in Islam. They are the sensibilities of revolutionary fundamentalism or, what Thomas Friedman, in a later editorial for the *New York Times*, called "religious totalitarianism" (Friedman, 2001). What

Sullivan and Friedman each have grasped is that there is a form of fundamentalism that is so single-mindedly fanatic that it denies the legitimacy
of any other faith claim except its own. Friedman explains, quoting Rabbi
David Hartman, "the opposite of religious totalitarianism is an ideology of
pluralism—an ideology that embraces religious diversity and the idea that
my faith can be nurtured without claiming exclusive truth. America is the
Mecca of that ideology, and that is what bin Laden hates and that is why
America had to be destroyed" (Friedman, 2001).

Whether or not this phenomenon is the explicit cause or one among
several contributing factors behind bin Laden's motivation to commit the
September 11 atrocity, the issues captured by Friedman's and Sullivan's
analyses are real and troubling. One could argue that the issues most
disturbing to bin Laden have to do with his perception that the United
States has succumbed to the decadence of modern life and is simply a
moral abomination. His disdain, therefore, would not be oriented toward
religious pluralism or modernity per se, but toward the failure of Western
culture, personified by the United States, to embody a cultural reality with
sufficiently moral limits and values at its core. Still, the pervasive expression
of violence toward another who does not fit within one's moral universe of
value and concern is prevalent.

Sullivan, in his article, called attention to the violence located not simply in Islamic tradition but in Jewish and Christian tradition as well. None
of the three great Abrahamic traditions are exempt from this problem.
Sullivan's point was to challenge public debate to recognize the religious
dimensions of violence without failing to see how embedded it has been
in Christianity and Judaism, even as he called attention to the violence undertaken in the name of Islam. Regina Schwartz, in her unsettling book *The
Curse of Cain*, has sought to do the same thing, but predating the September 11 tragedy and linking the problem to matters of identity when one's
identity is built on a logic of scarcity requiring that one's identity negate the
claims of others because they each contend for the same ground of divine
confirmation. In other words, the mythic constitution of one's identity can
define the world in such fashion that others are viewed as adversaries of the
most fundamental kind, in direct competition for what is good and holy.
More specifically, our sacred texts have clothed our adversaries in mythic
garb that, while disclosing important truths about ourselves, can shield or
cut us off from the humanity we share. Since 1993, I have participated in a
midrashic dialogue with three colleagues, two Jews (Zev Garber and Steven
Jacobs) and one other Christian (James Moore), in which we have wrestled
with this issue, probing the ways in which violence is embedded in our
texts and searching for ways to reconceive our relationship to those texts,
to each other, and to the identities they configure. In 2002, I joined them
in looking at one of the most troubling of biblical references, the figure of

Amalek and the related texts that call for Amalek's complete destruction, in reflecting on the aftermath of the attack of September 11, 2001.

A DISTURBING ENCOUNTER

Who is Amalek? In the biblical texts, scripture describes Amalek as a marauding, nomadic figure, a tribe of the Sinai Peninsula who attacks the people of Israel from the rear as they make their way through the wilderness following their liberation from Egypt. Furthermore, the testimony of Exodus 17 specifies that Israel was particularly vulnerable at the time they were attacked. Joshua, under the direction of Moses standing above him on a prominent hilltop, leads the battle against Amalek, winning when Moses's arms are raised holding his staff and losing when, in fatigue, Moses lowers his arms. Eventually, with the help of Aaron and Hur, Moses keeps the staff aloft and the Israelites are victorious, with God declaring, "Write this as a reminder in a book and recite it in the hearing of Joshua: I will utterly blot out the remembrance of Amalek from under heaven" (Ex. 17:14).

According to Genesis 36:12, Amalek is the grandson of Esau by way of a liaison between Esau's son Eliphaz and a concubine named Timna. In other words, while he is of Abraham's lineage, the connection is tainted. On the Sabbath before Purim, the Torah portion, *Zakhor*, Deuteronomy 25:17–19, is read, admonishing Jews to remember what happened when Amalek attacked them in the wilderness on their journey of liberation, and to blot out the name of Amalek while doing so. In that regard, I Samuel 15:1–34 is read as the *Haftarah*. Behind each of these readings, of course, is Exodus 17:8–16, which describes the ambush in the wilderness. The texts tell the story of egregious violence perpetrated by the Amalekites and command the Israelites to remember what happened in the wilderness, to forget the name of Amalek, and then to destroy Amalek's descendants completely when they are encountered later in the time of King Saul. Furthermore, these texts are read just before Purim because Haman, the oppressor of the Israelites who sought their destruction at the time of Esther, is seen to be a descendent of Agag, the king of the Amalekites about whom King Saul was confronted by the prophet/judge Samuel for having disobeyed the divine commandment to destroy all the Amalekites by sparing their king.

The violence in the passages is unsettling. In each of them, utter destruction is bearing down on the children of Israel, and in each case, God sides with them in their battle to survive and destroy their attackers. However, the utter viciousness of the violence is disclosed in the scene from I Samuel, where Samuel confronts Saul with the divine expectation that every Amalekite was to be slain: "Now go and attack Amalek, and utterly destroy all that they have; do not spare them, but kill both man and woman, child and infant, ox and sheep, camel and donkey'" (I Samuel 15:3). What else is this but genocide, divinely sanctioned genocide at that?

After Auschwitz, we cannot gloss over this. However, Jewish scholars before Auschwitz did not gloss over it without showing their discomfort with the violence in the text. My colleague Zev Garber recalled the resistance of Kabbalistic theology in his chapter on Amalek in his 1994 book, *Shoah: The Paradigmatic Genocide.* He writes: "The moral imperative of the *Zachor* commandment is for each individual to join together to eliminate evil, not by destroying the sinners, but by eliminating sins." Garber cites Psalm 104:35, *midrashically*: "May sinners disappear from the earth, and the wicked be no more," reading "not *hattaim* (sinners) [with the doubled/dageshed *tet*] but *hataim* [without the doubled *tet*] (sinful acts)" (Garber, 1994: 132). Wiesel makes a similar point in his essay "Myth and History," saying: "The law commands any living Jew who meets a living Amalekite to kill that Amalekite. The law is the law, but at the same time our sages adopt all measure to prevent us from identifying an Amalekite. So he has become myth" (Wiesel, 1985a: I, 362).

AMALEK RETURNS

To say Amalek is myth, however, is not to say that Amalek is not historical. Indeed, Amalek has returned in the guise of others displaying his hatred for Jews and what they represent. That is the ongoing significance of Purim. Amalek returned to confront Israel in the identity of Haman and once more Israel prevailed. So Israel remembers at the same time Israel blots out the name of Amalek of the line of Haman. Sadly, however, the cycle did not end with Haman. Haman has given way to Antiochus. Antiochus has given way to Titus, and he to Hadrian; then to Torquemada, Khmielnitzki, and eventually to Hitler. As Gunther Plaut points out in his commentary on the *Torah*, "Amalek has appeared and reappeared in many guises" (Plaut, 1981: 514).

Indeed, Amalek, the mythic enemy of Israel, has found a human face again and again in history. That is, Amalek, however mythic, is also very real. And with the pogroms of the second millennium, followed by the *Shoah*'s definitive exclamation point at the end of it, we find ourselves pondering an inexplicable dilemma. A figurative reading of the Amalek story is not strong enough. Over and over again, Jews find themselves ambushed by those who hate them for no other reason than they hold themselves to be a people set apart by God for covenant, which stirs up such animosity that they are attacked with genocidal ferocity. At the same time, as a people victimized by genocide and often devoted to humanistic principles, they cannot accept a (seemingly) divine mandate to do the same to others. Nevertheless, in coming to terms with the literal truth that Amalek returns, the literal command to destroy Amalek returns as a sober mandate for survival. Yet, how do Jews read their scriptural obligation to remember Amalek, knowing how very real Amalek is without becoming the figure that they themselves fear when that memory retains a mandate to destroy Amalek utterly? Self-defense and survival appear to be at odds, even an impasse, with sacred vocation. How can Jews make their way without sacrificing one or the other of these mutually binding obligations?

Perhaps there is a clue in pondering Amalek's return. In each biblical record of battling Amalek, there is a report involving the extensiveness of what is at stake. In Exodus 17, God declares to Moses that God will utterly blot out any memory of Amalek. In Deuteronomy 25, God declares that when the time comes that Israel is free from all its enemies God will blot out the memory of Amalek completely. Then, in I Samuel, the text reports that Saul had utterly destroyed all the Amalekites except for Agag, their king. Samuel confronts Saul over his failure to destroy their king, and then slays Agag himself. Complete destruction is accomplished. Then, in II Samuel, an Amalekite, one who had taken the life of King Saul after he had fallen on his spear, reports the king's demise to David and hands him the crown that this Amalekite took from Saul. Not surprisingly, David has the Amalekite killed for taking the life of the Lord's anointed. Then, centuries later, when Haman acts with genocidal intent toward the people of Israel, the text cites that he is descended from Agag. The point: the biblical record continues to report that the Amalekites have been defeated, destroyed—even declaring a complete destruction in I Samuel after the killing of King Agag by Samuel. But again and again, the Amalekites return. Is the biblical record oblivious to this flawed assertion, or is this recurrence after their presumed destruction significant? Of course, until the Samuel passage, there is only an implication of total defeat and a remnant of the Amalekites can be presumed. But after the Samuel passage, the incongruity is unavoidable.

Surely this incongruity would not have been missed by those compiling the scriptures, or overlooked by later scholars. Just as surely, we should not miss it. When we think that Amalek has been defeated and removed from the historical flow of events, he returns, unexpectedly, to claim his place in the story of Israel. The biblical authors, like the Rabbinic sages, we might argue, were more concerned about ideological lines, not bloodlines. That may be true, but I cannot help thinking they wanted the incongruity to show nonetheless. That is, whenever it appears that Amalek has been removed from history and banished to the realm of myth only, he reappears, ambushing Israel once again. When we read the command to remember, perhaps it is this we must remember more than anything else: when we least expect it, Amalek will return, and we must be prepared for that.

FACING AMALEK

Facing Amalek is dangerous work. On the one hand, Amalek is real and a threat. He is particularly a threat when the people are fatigued from their struggle to make their way from exile and slavery to freedom and the promised land. But that fatigue, no matter how prominent it might be, is never a final cause—even when the fatigue is spiritual, as Wiesel points out in his reading of the Exodus 17 text:

> Just before Amalek attacked Israel, you read a description of the moral atmosphere, of the moral climate among the wandering Jews. Suddenly they began doubting themselves, their spirit, their destiny, and the sentence which expresses this in the text is *Hayesh Adoshem b'kinbeynu?* They suddenly began wondering one to the other, "Is God really with me?" That was the moment of weakness. And because of that weakness Amalek attacked. (Wiesel, 1985a: I, 138)

Note well, the cause is instrumental, explaining why Amalek attacked when he did—not why he sought to attack the Israelites in the first place. Amalek simply strikes when Amalek has the greatest advantage. Amalek just happens.

But even though Amalek is real, recognizing Amalek is difficult. Amalek strikes from behind. Amalek strikes by ambush, when and where the people are vulnerable. Providing a face to the mythic name is therefore difficult—until Amalek strikes. However, providing a contemporary name for Amalek in disguise is dangerous for another reason. When that is done, one identifies another as the irreconcilable enemy of Israel and of God. That other, whether an individual or a people, is cast beyond the boundaries of mutual, moral regard. That other no longer counts within one's moral universe of concern. That is what happened to Jews as victims of anti-Semitism in Western Europe. They were cast outside Christendom's universe of moral concern. They became Christendom's Amalek. From the perspective of our time, we must not fail to see the demonization of the other that occurs when one is identified as Amalek. After identifying someone or some group as Amalek, the particular identity of that other is lost. Hereafter one relates to a cipher, not to a human being. After Auschwitz, that is an abomination that can no longer be tolerated.

We must be careful with this caution from a more idealistic standpoint as well. Just as the mythic dimension of Amalek demonizes the other, the mythologization of every human being as redeemable can participate in the same totalizing logic that voids the humanity of the other with whom we interact. In this case, the other is idealized and disappears as a real human being with faults and foibles. This, too, is an undoing of creation that must be resisted while we remember Amalek. Just as we cannot take God's place to determine who Amalek is, we cannot take God's place to determine who can never be or become Amalek. We must learn to face every human being in accord with the humanity that he or she embodies—however flawed, however gracious. Likewise, we must learn to face evil in its appropriate human proportions, even when those proportions may be extreme. In other words, we cannot fall into the easy trap of declaring that remembering Amalek is a *Jewish* mandate for which Christians offer a contrasting caution in their unswerving commitment to the possible redemption of *every* human being. That is a misleading dichotomization that must be resisted. Instead, the danger of mythologizing the other must be recognized regardless of perspective.

As strong as these cautions are, the story of Amalek reminds us that, while there may be good, strong moral and spiritual reasons to resist identifying anyone with Amalek, Amalek exists nonetheless. He returns no matter how we might try to get rid of him. He has not been eradicated from history. God's people, representing the way of generous hospitality to others, remain vulnerable to attack by those who live without covenantal regard for others. Amalek exists in every generation.

The message is strong and disturbing. Amalek cannot be eradicated completely even when he is pursued relentlessly. It is in the structure of creation that Amalek can and will return. Indeed, Amalek is aligned with the primal chaos present from the beginning of creation, for Amalek opposes the movement of liberation and the abundant unfolding of life. Amalek, in relation to others, is the undoer of creation. That is, the very hospitality that makes room for our freedom makes room for that other who cannot accept hospitality's welcome. Of course, Amalek will bring destruction upon himself, but he will destroy every other as well if he is allowed. Therefore Amalek must be resisted. Israel and any who would join in Israel's cause must stay on guard. Amalek works by ambush. Amalek obstructs God's people and their journey toward freedom and indeed, any people's movement to fulfill life, to flourish. Amalek is like a cancer in this regard. Amalek returns, again and again. Remember that. Be on guard. But do not let Amalek win by allowing Amalek to be in control. Do not honor Amalek nor allow Amalek to define the terms of resistance. Blot out Amalek's name and significance thoroughly each time Amalek returns. But do not become Amalek in the process, lest Amalek win.

Perhaps this is a variation of Emil Fackenheims's well-known and oft-cited 614th commandment: "Do not give Hitler [read Amalek] a posthumous victory." Remember, but remember in a way that retains the identity of being God's people; do not become Amalek when remembering Amalek. Perhaps we can draw the implication further. Amalek is real and must be remembered, because Amalek will return and ambush his victims from the rear when they are weak and where they are vulnerable. At the same time, one must beware of identifying anyone with Amalek, lest in doing so they become the *other-denying one* they fear. Instead, we must all learn to ask if someone or some group *could* be Amalek but without drawing the final conclusion. If we are not careful in this regard, we may discover, to our regret, that Amalek has taken on the image of our own reflection. This must be the limit beyond which we dare not go.

FACING AMALEK IN OUR TIME

Who then is Amalek? Amalek is the other who opposes Israel (and any of us who identify with Israel) so viciously, so completely, so utterly that he/she opposes not just Israel (or those who identify with Israel) but God and God's intentions for life and all creation. Amalek is that other whom my hospitality will never be able to make welcome in the world because Amalek's identity and place in the world requires that certain others be eliminated. Amalek is that other whom hospitality cannot welcome because Amalek's identity denies the validity of hospitality even when it welcomes Amalek.

When we face the other in our post-*Shoah*, violence-riddled world, we are called to move beyond tribal, cultural, and religious parochialisms. Indeed, we are led there in a shared Exodus from the confining regions of oppression and bigotry. We follow Israel as Israel bears witness to the liberating intention for every people. As we make our way, we will be ambushed from behind when we are most vulnerable. However, our vulnerability, like Israel's, is not the cause of the ambush. The ambush happens because Amalek exists. Indeed, Amalek is the embodiment of that chaotic force that resists the generous and hospitable ordering of the universe as creation.

In a post-*Shoah* world, we cannot escape Amalek's presence. We are mandated to remember that for the sake of our Jewish friends as well as for our own. But how? How should we remember? Furthermore, we are still called forward with all of God's people, in the movement of redemption and liberation toward the promised land. Likewise, we must ask, How? How shall we move forward, especially as we ponder the stalking presence of Amalek in the shadows behind us? We will, most probably, be ambushed, yet we must wage a struggle for survival, not only for ourselves but for every other engaged in the movement of liberation toward the promise of a full and free life. How shall we engage Amalek when the ambush occurs? How shall we defeat him, now, millennia later? While we may be able to postpone the ambush, we cannot prevent Amalek from being Amalek; but we can control how we respond to the ambush and to him when it happens.

In other words, in facing Amalek, we must also come to terms with another telling fact of life. Every attempt to eradicate this *other-destroying other* has failed. Even though in each telling of Israel's story, it appears that

Amalek has been destroyed, another generation finds itself ambushed by this returning figure. Why? Amalek returns, even when Israel has done everything within its human power to eradicate him. How does anyone defeat such an enemy?

We may state the other side of this insight as a limit. We cannot finally identify Amalek until he has perished. The story of Amalek is a story of memory, Jewish memory, for the sake of the future and the present. We can fear someone is Amalek, we can beware of Amalek in any circumstance, but we cannot know until afterward, for Amalek is the one who is irreconcilable. As long as that person or group is alive, he or she or they may surprise us yet again by showing us that they are *not* Amalek but one who seeks to return in penitence from exile—*not* in chaos against life. In other words, Amalek is named as an act of memory in order to be alert in the present. To do otherwise risks becoming the one who is named.

While we may fear that another can or may be Amalek in our time, we must learn to differentiate types and levels of evil, remembering that, when we identify someone as Amalek, we mythologize the one we so identify. The mythic dimensions of that act demonize the other, removing the particularities of his or her identity from our view. We begin to relate to Amalek, not to the one who stands before us, or who may literally stalk us. When we do that, we reduce another human being to a cipher and participate in the undoing of creation.

Not all tragic actions are full embodiments of the evil Amalek represents. Not every evil can be identified as an expression of the nihilism we associate with Amalek. But refraining from the mythic language of Amalek does not mean we embrace, endorse, or even understand why someone has acted as they have. Nor does it mean we cannot recognize the act they perpetrate as evil. But we also know that, when Amalek is identified as a living other, that other ceases to retain his or her humanity as a child of God before whom we share our moral accountability. More importantly, we know what can happen when others are identified with Amalek. Religious fanatics can burst into sanctuaries of prayer and slaughter persons in them without remorse if they believe they are attacking such a figure. This is true regardless of whether the figure is named Amalek or Satan. We may cite Baruch Goldstein's murderous deed in Hebron as well as the actions aimed at the World Trade Center. As heinous as they are, each event is still understandable as a fanatical action undertaken by perpetrators who believe themselves to be acting under divine sanction. We may call the attack on the World Trade Center an atrocity, as Michael Berenbaum claims we should, to distinguish it from Goldstein's angry deed. But neither one is a nihilistic act. Rather, they are understandable if those who perpetrated them thought they were attacking a figure like Amalek who had to be utterly destroyed. Nevertheless, we must be careful of slipping into a mythic identification that can dehumanize all parties and perpetuate the survival of Amalek in new disguise.

Christians need look no further than their own historic misuse of this kind of mythic identification preserved in scripture. Whenever we deal with the presence of violence in our own identity and our relationship to our Jewish siblings, we come face to face with scriptural contempt in the accusatory treatment of Jews in the Gospels. In the case of Matthew 27:25, following the crowd's request to release Barabbas, Matthew states, "Then the people as a whole answered, 'His blood be on us and on our children!'" Matthew appears to have turned *midrashically* to II Samuel 1:16 and adopted David's statement condemning the Amalekite who killed King Saul for taking the life of God's anointed: "Your blood be on your head for you have taken the life of the Lord's anointed." In other words, with his *midrashic* use of this passage, accusing other Jews of being Amalek, he has set up the demonizing logic that flows from this passage in subsequent generations. In the hands of later Christians, this language led to actions that drew forth telling fears from Jewish quarters that the Church had become Amalek in their time. Only penitential action and changed attitudes lie between that fear and its confirmation in actuality.

While the issues remain troubling and complex, I hope that this analysis not only underscores the problem of demonization, but also shows how mythologizing a very difficult conflict only makes the conflict worse, more intractable, setting two groups at odds with each other, each one accusing the other of being opposed to their mutual existence. When this happens, each group is driven by these mythic dynamics into accusing the other of being their ultimate fear personified.

TERRORISM, GENOCIDE, AND POWER

We cannot complete our analysis of Amalek without attending to some unsettling dynamics about the nature of mythologizing the other and using that mythic view of the other to justify violence against him or her. Helen Fein, in her sustained analyses of genocide, has identified at least four preconditions to genocidal action that bear mention in this context:

- Mythic Othering (my own term): The victims of genocide are typically "defined outside the universe of obligation of the dominant group."
- Crisis: A political or cultural crisis of national identity threatens the dominant group's future and generates a climate of either-or conflict.
- Power: An elite group that adapts a political formula or myth to justify the nation's domination or expansion rises to power, idealizing the singular rights of the dominant group.

- Changing Calculus of Costs: The calculus of political and moral costs changes as perpetrators successfully engage the resistance of protesting voices and actions of those within and beyond the ruling parties move forward with their plans for genocidal action. (Fein, 1979: 9)

In the case of terrorist activity, one need only substitute Fein's description of an elite group exercising legitimate political power with an elite group adapting a mythic or political formula to legitimize their resistance to a dominating and unjust power to characterize the dynamics of such action. The point does not turn on whether or not one agrees or disagrees with the mythic legitimation or that group's characterization of injustice. Rather, the key issue linking terrorist activity with genocidal activity is the mythic dimension of defining the other as having no moral claim of obligation on the legitimating party in a situation of extensive political and cultural crisis. The difference between terrorism and genocidal activity rests on access to power.

What Fein points out is that, without serious checks on the use and abuse of power or on the mythologization of the other, the preconditions for genocide and/or terrorism are in place. In this regard, internal protest and democratic institutions that check and challenge any ruling elite are essential. The political conflict they generate serves the larger entity of the state by removing one of the conditions that allows for unmitigated violence to the problematic other in one's midst. In addition, the recognition of the mythic dimension signals the importance of other strategies hinted at above. First, mythic identification of any living other is problematic. Even if the mythologization were all positive, the dynamics of myth-making sever the human connections with the other, rendering him or her beyond the pale of shared moral obligations. When the other is identified with Amalek, he or she is defined as beyond even the reach of divine forgiveness: as evil. Once that happens, anyone so identified loses his or her claims of shared humanity with anyone else, becoming superfluous to the moral calculus employed to work out appropriate strategies of survival in critical times.

Furthermore, victims of such demonization can be blamed for their own victimization by identifying them with the ultimate adversary who must be resisted at all costs. That is, what happens to them is a consequence of their adversarial opposition to how life is blessed and served in the encompassing narrative that grounds the dominant group. However, the irony of such identification is that those who demonize the other in such ways can only do so by usurping the role of judge in that mythic universe. In other words, such action can only be justified by idolatrous action on the part of those who mythologize the other in this fashion.

Still, the actions of Amalek are real. Suicide bombers who destroy schools and terrorize public transportation enact the role of Amalek. When they strike, we see Amalek at work in their actions. Nonetheless, their identification with a group of disenfranchised people cannot lead to identifying the people with whom the terrorists share ethnic, cultural, or religious identity with Amalek. Amalek acts in and through particular individuals. Yet Amalek can be known only after the violence is done, and even then we must be cautious in presuming to judge as only God can judge.

THE LIMITS OF HOSPITALITY

In both Christian and Jewish traditions, there is a strong mandate to see in the face of every other the image of God. In that spirit, we are called to embody hospitality to the other. As Emmanuel Levinas has reminded us, the face of the other is our summons to ethical action, our *ayecha* (Where are you?) to which we are summoned to reply *hineni* (Here I am!). But in the face of modern violence, particularly understanding its religious expressions in revolutionary forms of fundamentalism, we must not forget that Amalek ambushes all of us from behind, even, perhaps especially, doing so in the guise of religious fundamentalism. When that happens, Amalek grows in strength, feeding off religious passion that Amalek uses for the destruction of life, as a cancer feeds off its otherwise life-giving host. Hospitality is vulnerable to this as well.

When we are truly practicing hospitality we are welcoming others into our households and other domains. As we do, we expand our worlds, our life space, and take responsibility for those who have entered into our domain. We serve them as our guests, and as their hosts we take responsibility for their safety and welfare. Consequently, we cannot place them in harm's way, exposing them to the wrath and violence of Amalek, even if we might wish to risk being open to one we might suspect is Amalek. This is Samuel's strong word for Saul, which we must hear even as we resist Samuel's support of genocide. Saul was king, and therefore responsible for the welfare of an entire people, not just himself. When we are hosts, we are responsible for others, not just ourselves.

Many of us who face Amalek from the Christian side will wonder what we do with Jesus' language about turning the other cheek and loving our enemies as we do ourselves. Is not Amalek the personification of the enemy? Are we not called to embrace Amalek according to the dynamic of agapeic love? That is what we have been taught as the way of Christ. But we can only offer ourselves in sacrificial relationship to others. We cannot offer others on our behalf. Here, Jesus' words about hospitality are especially instructive. As he admonishes his disciples at the beginning of Matthew 10 to go out in search of hospitality in the surrounding cities and to announce its healing and life-giving significance where it is encountered and embodied, he also warns his disciples about the dangers of hostility that does not welcome them. Move on; do not tarry in those places. Be wise as serpents, gentle as doves. Know the difference and act accordingly. Then, as he concludes his comments, he warns his followers that hospitality will generate its own conflict, though it most probably will surface in the familiar domains of household and family, between parents and children, and between siblings. His additional caution is focused interpersonally. In other words, Jesus recognizes the limits of hospitality as well as its promise and its risk. When we practice hospitality and welcome others into our domain, we promise to provide them protection and care, serving them responsibly as they dwell with us as our guests. We cannot offer them to Amalek when he attacks our households, when more life is at stake than just our own. Especially there, we must be honest about the face of Amalek. For Amalek does not want our shelter; rather, Amalek seeks to destroy it.

This caution about Amalek is focused within a broader range of social interactions. Its scope is social and cultural as well as tribal, and in our time, religious. There are limits to hospitality at the micro and macro levels. Beware. Be alert. Be wise as serpents; gentle as doves. Remember. But remember as well, that Jews and Christians have undertaken a larger journey, moving from exile to the promised land: from bondage to liberation; from survival to covenantal wholeness. As long as we have not arrived, Amalek is a threat. As long as Amalek is a threat, we have not arrived.

SUMMARY AND CONCLUSION

What then does it mean for us to remember Amalek? Is it enough to know the story? Clearly not. The plain meaning of the text, whether we encounter it in Exodus 17, Deuteronomy 25, I Samuel 15, or in other allusions to the Amalekites elsewhere in scripture, is unsettling. It tells of an utterly destructive enemy as well as a summons to destroy that enemy. However, when we allow the plain meaning of the text to include all the encounters with Amalek, the text, as often happens, provides doorways for increased understanding and opportunities for important critical leverage. Such is the case with these texts as we encounter the mythic dimensions of Amalek along with the historical reality of Amalek's returning presence in the story of Israel.

The biblical, along with the mythic identifications the scriptures open up, invite the probing analyses of *derash*, explaining implications hidden in what the text says and does not say. As well, we draw from the wrestlings of others who, over the years, have encountered these texts, preserving, as it were, their *remez*—those meanings external to the text, most notably those provided by their contexts. But the secret of how to live with even this inclusivity does not come without the uneasy sense that we are not to live with these texts comfortably. Consequently, we find ourselves wrestling with the same question we posed at the beginning: How do we live with the returning presence of Amalek and honor, as well, the summons to live hospitably with every other? Our response must be: carefully, indeed, cautiously, ever alert.

No one lives outside the possibility of reconciliation except those who keep themselves there. And that can be known only after they have succeeded, not before. What they succeed in doing is destroying their own place in the domain of life, not the domain of life itself, which they seek to reduce to something less than what it is. Still, in doing this, they destroy the lives of others, without remorse. In our gratitude that no one dwells beyond the possibility of reconciliation, we cannot forget that some, in the freedom they have to return, have the same freedom to oppose the hospitality and generosity that makes that return possible. Creation is always exposed to this risk. For many, it is costly beyond measure.

Those of us who live out this perilous promise cannot forget the dangers represented by Amalek. Neither can we overlook the conflict we may introduce in our most intimate or our most treasured groups when we insist on living within a commitment to hospitality toward the other that refrains from closing the circle of hospitality prematurely by relating to the other as a cipher, not a person—even if, later, that same individual may prove to be Amalek himself or herself. But we cannot know that until memory gives us that perspective. We can, however, place ourselves in the dilemma and choose to live with it, holding fast to the memory of Amalek even as we resist both his obvious and more insidious attempts to redefine our world.

BIBLIOGRAPHY

Abrahamson, Irving (ed.) (1985). *Against Silence: The Voice and Vision of Elie Wiesel.* New York: Holocaust Library.
Berenbaum, Michael (2002). "Filling the Void, in Space and in Our Hearts." Available through the Internet at: www.newsday.com.
Fein, Helen (1979). *Accounting for Genocide: National Responses and Jewish Victimization during the Holocaust.* New York: Free Press.
Friedman, Thomas (2001). "The Real War." *New York Times,* 19.
Garber, Zev (1994). *Shoah: The Paradigmatic Genocide.* Lanham, Md.: University Press of America.
Juergensmeyer, Mark (2000). *Terror in the Mind of God: The Global Rise of Religious Violence.* Berkeley: University of California Press.
Kimball, Charles (2002). *When Religion Becomes Evil.* San Francisco, Calif.: HarperCollins.

Plaut, W. Gunther (1981). *The Torah: A Modern Commentary.* New York: Union of American Hebrew Congregations.

Schwartz, Regina (1997). *The Curse of Cain: The Violent Legacy of Monotheism.* Chicago, Ill.: University of Chicago Press.

Sullivan, Andrew (2001). "This Really Is a Religious War." *New York Times Sunday Magazine,* 44–53.

Wiesel, Elie (1985a). "Myth and History," in Irving Abrahamson (ed.), *Against Silence: The Voice and Vision of Elie Wiesel* (New York: Holocaust Library), I, 361–66.

—— (1985b). "The Burden on Jewish Youth," in Irving Abrahamson (ed.), *Against Silence: The Voice and Vision of Elie Wiesel.* New York: Holocaust Library, II, 131–38.

IV

THEOLOGIES AND PRACTICES
OF RECONCILIATION

14

Post-Shoah Restitution of a Different Kind

John K. Roth

The Holocaust remains a highly combustible issue.

—Stuart Eizenstat

As the twentieth century drew to a close and the twenty-first got under way, the *Shoah* remained both combustible and newsworthy. Many reports covered the struggle over financial reparations for Jewish survivors of the Shoah and their heirs as well as for non-Jewish slave laborers who suffered under Nazi tyranny. Other accounts emphasized the restitution of Jewish property, including art looted from the Shoah's victims. Tension-filled negotiations—national and international—with governments, corporations, insurance firms, art museums, law offices, and numerous other agencies and agents eventually produced a modicum of what Stuart Eizenstat has aptly called "rough justice" (Eizenstat, 2003: 130, 137–38, 353; Bazyler, 2003). While these post-Shoah bargains and settlements about bank accounts, insurance policies, financial settlements, and property claims took place with widespread public attention focused upon them, a less publicized but immensely important and still unresolved issue about restitution remained a key part of the Shoah's legacy: the debt that Christianity owes to Jews and Judaism for centuries of anti-Jewish hostility that foreshadowed, and in some quarters still exists after, the Shoah.

In a post-Shoah world, which unfortunately remains one where human beings fall prey to terror, mass murder, and genocide, how far can and should restitution try to go? With that question in mind, I will use this essay to reflect on restitution in the context of Christian-Jewish relations. As my

241

analysis will show, many of the post-Shoah issues surrounding what I call restitution of a different kind form minefields that, arguably, are even more difficult to traverse and disarm than those that have made the recent material claims settlements so volatile. Restitution issues within Christian-Jewish relations must be handled with care lest hasty inquiry, insensitive judgment, or premature closure set off explosions that broaden harm's way.

CONSCIOUSNESS AND CONSCIENCE AFTER THE SHOAH

Adolf Hitler and his Nazi regime intended the annihilation of Jewish life to signify the destruction of the very idea of a common humanity that all people share. Jean Améry, who noted that the Nazis "hated the word 'humanity,'" amplified such points when he stated: "Torture was no invention of National Socialism. But it was its apotheosis" (Améry, 1986: 30-31; Roth, 2004: 85-99). Améry meant that the Third Reich aimed to produce men, women, and children whose hardness would transcend humanity in favor of a racially pure and culturally superior form of life that could still appropriately be called Aryan or German but not merely "human." Insofar as *humanity* referred to universal equality, suggested a shared and even divine source of life, or implied any of the other trappings of weakness and sentimentality that Hitler and his most dedicated followers attributed to such concepts, National Socialism intentionally went beyond humanity. Such steps entailed more than killing so-called inferior forms of life that were thought to threaten German superiority. Moving beyond humanity made it essential to inflict torture—not only to show that "humanity" or "sub-humanity" deserved no respect in and of itself, but also to ensure that those who had moved beyond humanity, and thus were recognizing the respect deserved only by Germans or Aryans, had really done so.

Jonathan Glover echoed these strains of Nazi "logic" in his important (1999) study, *Humanity: A Moral History of the Twentieth Century.* Convinced that "the Nazi genocide has a terrible darkness all its own," he locates it in the Nazis' "views about cruelty and hardness, and the appalling new Nazi moral identity." Reflected in pedagogy that would train the Nazi young to show cruelty to racial and cultural "inferiors" without dismay, that new moral identity, Glover makes clear, took its goals to include demolishing the idea that Germans, Slavs, and Jews shared the same humanity. Joseph Stalin and Mao Zedong took more lives than Hitler, but Glover thinks that Stalin and Mao defended "hardness and inhumanity," however implausibly, "as the supposed means to a more humane world." By contrast, the Nazis' "twisted deontology" made those qualities desirable in themselves, for they were key characteristics of a National Socialist identity that had moved beyond humanity (Glover, 1999: 327 and 396).

If Améry and Glover are right, and I think they are, then National Socialism entailed that not only Jews but also Judaism and every aspect of Jewish life must disappear. Eventually, Nazi "logic" would have put Christianity at risk too, but unquestionably, the racially anti-Semitic core of National Socialism made the elimination of every trace of Jewish life a "logical," if not political, priority that no other exceeded. Hitler and his Nazi followers did not succeed completely in implementing their anti-Semitism, but they went far enough in establishing as a principle what Améry aptly called "the rule of the antiman," that none of our fondest hopes about humanity can be taken for granted (Améry, 1986: 31). Jews inhabit the post-Shoah world in a distinctive way. To the extent that they confront the Shoah, their consciousness includes memory that is qualitatively different from any other. Here I want to choose my words carefully, because debates continue about whether the Nazis clearly and distinctly intended that other nationalities or ethnic groups (Sinti and Roma, for example) should also disappear root and branch. So I will make my point as follows: Jewish post-Shoah consciousness is different from every other form of consciousness because it involves the recognition, beyond doubt or question, that one is part of a people who have been targeted for utter elimination—every trace, root and branch—from existence anywhere and everywhere.

(This recognition grips me as a Christian who has taught and written about the Shoah for more than thirty years. Non-Jews can and should do such work, but our consciousness in doing this is fundamentally different from that of the Jews because we are not part of the Jewish people, the ones who were targeted for destruction and death. Especially in post-Shoah circumstances, this crucial difference between Jew and non-Jew remains, no matter how much we non-Jews may express solidarity with the Jewish people, and that difference deserves respect. We non-Jews carry our own Shoah legacies—which are usually related to bystanders or perpetrators, including the fact that most of the former and many of the latter would have identified themselves as Christians of one kind or another. Those responsibilities are awesome enough, but they are not the same as the trauma that stalks Jews whose families were decimated and who themselves would not be alive today if National Socialism's "logic" had prevailed.)

The anger and rage to which I have alluded spring from particularities that general references to the Shoah cannot encompass. What must be faced is not only that Jews were left in harm's way, but, also, how *in detail* they were put and left in that condition. Crucial to that perspective is awareness that the Shoah's details—like the specific torture that Améry experienced at the hands of Gestapo agents in a prison at Fort Breendonk, Belgium, in July 1943—show that Jews were abandoned to *useless experience*, whose particularities are as diverse as its wreckage is vast.

In *The Drowned and the Saved*, the Auschwitz survivor Primo Levi explores useless experience concentrated on the Shoah's "useless violence," which was characterized by the infliction of pain that was "always redundant, always disproportionate." Levi probes deeply precisely because he does not dwell on the obvious—beatings or hangings, for example. Instead his catalog of useless violence recalls the cattle cars that shipped Jews to Auschwitz. Their "total bareness" revealed a "gratuitous viciousness" that left people neither privacy nor dignity when they had to relieve themselves. Or, he observed, the loot collected from the arrivals at Auschwitz meant that there were tens of thousands of spoons in that place. None were given to prisoners; they had to fend as best they could, which might mean spending precious food from the camp's starvation diet to buy a spoon on the camp's black market. There were plenty of ways to identify prisoners, but at Auschwitz the Nazis implemented "the violence of the tattoo," which Levi describes as "an end in itself, pure offense" (Levi, 1988: 106, 109, 111, and 119).

Levi's list continues. Its detail corroborates both Améry's judgment that "torture was not an accidental quality of this Third Reich, but its essence" (Levi, 1988: 24), and Glover's claim that "hardness over compassion was central to the Nazi outlook" (Glover, 1999: 326). In turn, Levi's account resonates with these claims when he concludes by acknowledging that National Socialism's useless violence did have one unredeeming element of utility: "Before dying," Levi observed, "the victim must be degraded, so that the murderer will be less burdened by guilt. This is an explanation not devoid of logic but it shouts to heaven: it is the sole usefulness of useless violence" (Levi, 1988: 126). Levi forbore to add, but might have gone on to say that the Nazi goal was not simply to lessen guilt's burden, but to create practitioners of useless violence who would feel no guilt at all.

Useless violence entails useless suffering, a topic that the Jewish philosopher Emmanuel Levinas explored in an influential post-Shoah essay that he published on the latter theme in 1982. As a French prisoner of war, Levinas did forced labor under the Nazis, and almost all of his Lithuanian family perished in the Shoah. This had a profound impact upon him. Calling the twentieth century one of "unutterable suffering," he wrote that "the Shoah of the Jewish people under the reign of Hitler seems to me the paradigm of gratuitous human suffering, in which evil appears in its diabolical form." Suffering of the kind that the Nazis and their collaborators wreaked on European Jewry is "for nothing." To try to justify it religiously, ethically, politically—as the Nazis did when they made the practice of useless violence essential to the German "superiority" that they envisioned—was what Levinas called "the source of all immorality" (Levinas, 1998: 94, 97, and 99).

When Levinas said that the useless suffering administered during the Shoah was "for nothing," he did not overlook Nazi "logic" and what it meant. To the contrary, he saw that National Socialism was ultimately about destruction, its grandiose rhetoric about the creation of a thousand-year Reich notwithstanding. The chief element in National Socialism's destructive arrogance was that regime's resolve to deface the human face—not in some abstract way but by useless suffering visited upon Jewish women, children, and men—with remorseless determination that made its anti-Semitic prerogatives dominant until overwhelming force stopped them from doing more of their worst.

For those who survive such disasters or contemplate them secondhand, useless violence and useless suffering entail useless knowledge. Hence, it is worth noting that whereas Charlotte Delbo was not Jewish, her arrest for resisting the Nazi occupation of her native France made her experience the Shoah when she was deported to Auschwitz in January 1943. Delbo survived the Nazi onslaught to bear witness to what happened to European Jewry. In 1946, she began to write the trilogy that came to be called *Auschwitz and After*. Her work's anguished visual descriptions, profound reflections on memory, and diverse writing styles make it an unrivaled Shoah testimony.

Delbo called the second part of her trilogy *Useless Knowledge*. Normally we think that knowledge is useful, and it certainly can be, but Delbo showed how the Shoah produced knowledge about hunger and disease, brutality and suffering, degradation and death that did nothing to unify, edify, or dignify life. "The sound of fifty blows on a man's back is interminable," she recounted. "Fifty strokes of a club on a man's back is an endless number" (Delbo, 1995: 58–59). This was only one example of what Delbo called useless knowledge. Its vast accumulation drove home her point: for the most part, what happened in the Shoah divided, besieged, and diminished life forever.

Illustrated by Levi, Levinas, and Delbo, useless experience particularizes the Shoah's ongoing devastation. It remains to be seen how far-reaching that devastation will be, which is where restitution-in-spite-of-the-Shoah comes back into play. Primo Levi concluded *The Drowned and the Saved* by contending that "there are no problems that cannot be solved around a table, provided there is good will and reciprocal trust" (Levi, 1988: 200). Emmanuel Levinas thought that awareness of the other's useless suffering could evoke responses, intensely meaningful ones, to try to relieve that suffering. If there is to be post-Shoah reconciliation between Christians and Jews, it will require a courage that refuses to let skepticism dismiss the hopes of Levi and Levinas too easily. At the hands of non-Jews, including Christians who stood by or aided and abetted the perpetrators of the Shoah—if only by uncritical participation in a tradition whose millennia-long hostility toward Jews helped to set them up for the Nazi kill—Jewish life was abandoned to, and nearly destroyed by, useless experience that did not have to be. Furthermore, it must be said that in many cases, the torturers, the teachers of "useless knowledge," and the practitioners of "useless violence" were, at least in part, the products of a predominantly Christian society that accepted them without repentance—during the genocide and after it ended as well. No honesty can or should remove entirely the raw edges of memory that remain, but Charlotte Delbo joins Levi and Levinas to urge that the post-Shoah situation should not be left there alone. "Do something," she wrote, "something to justify your existence / . . . because it would be too senseless / after all / for so many to have died / while you live /doing nothing with your life" (Delbo, 1995: 230). No false conciliatoriness could fulfill Delbo's sensibly impassioned imperative, but the courage to keep trying for reconciliation in spite of the Shoah, which includes doing as much as Christians and Jews can to relieve the useless suffering of others, would help.

THE LONG JOURNEY OF RESTITUTION

Daniel Jonah Goldhagen would argue, however, that the steps noted above are only the beginning of a long journey of restitution that is required for reconciliation between Christians and Jews. For reconciliation to go deep down, restitution is required, because restitution entails more than words that express repentance. Restitution requires concrete actions to make amends, to compensate people who have been unjustly harmed. It is an understatement to say that Shoah-related restitution can only be partial at best, but restitution remains important because without it, reconciliation between Christians and Jews may never escape the false conciliatoriness that Jean Améry despised. I turn to Goldhagen because his book *A Moral Reckoning: The Role of the Catholic Church in the Shoah and Its Unfulfilled Duty of Repair* (2002) not only emphasizes restitution more than do most discussions about post-Shoah Christian-Jewish relations, but also contains a restitution agenda that arguably surpasses any other in its ambition and long-term significance.

Thus far, there have been two chief reactions to Goldhagen's book, neither of them very encouraging. First, in contrast to the noisy reception of his first book, *Hitler's Willing Executioners* (1996), relative silence has surrounded *A Moral Reckoning.* I suspect that Goldhagen's call for concrete actions and responses was sufficiently hard-hitting and convincing to embarrass and daunt many Christians to such an extent that they preferred to ignore the book rather than to deal forthrightly with it. Second, the silence was only relative, and by no means complete, because critics have often defensively dismissed *A Moral Reckoning* as historically inaccurate, excessively critical of Christianity, and extreme in its recommendations. To some extent those latter judgments are valid, but the question is whether those flaws are sufficient to doom the credibility of his analysis. In my view, they are not. In particular, the restitution challenges that Goldhagen poses for Christians still deserve consideration and definitely have their place in the broad context of post-Shoah restitution studies.

Goldhagen argues that Roman Catholics and Christians generally should provide what I am calling post-Shoah restitution of a different kind. As we shall see, the restitution he has in mind is not of the financial type that grabbed so many headlines in recent years. Goldhagen's call for restitution is more fundamental than that. Whether it will help or hinder Christian-Jewish reconciliation is a good question. According to Goldhagen, Pope Pius XII was an anti-Semite, the Roman Catholic Church was "more a collaborator than a victim of Nazism," and the New Testament's "libelous and hate-inducing passages about Jews" must go (Goldhagen, 2002: 241 and 261). In short, he calls for a radical reformation to remove from Christianity the anti-Semitism that implicated it in the Shoah and still leaves that tradition immorally mired in deception and hypocrisy.

Unpretentious, indecisive, moderate, and patient are not words that come to mind when reading Goldhagen. Insisting that it is high time to "call a spade a spade," his post-Shoah moral reckoning with Christianity and the Roman Catholic Church in particular pulls few punches and guarantees a hard-hitting bout over history, ethics, and theology. Goldhagen's book is unlikely to leave its readers indifferent (Goldhagen, 2002: 193). Its significance, however, depends less on immediate reactions and more on what happens ten, twenty, or even a hundred years after its appearance. Goldhagen may be helping to create a new Christianity. It will take time to tell. *Hitler's Willing Executioners* was widely criticized on the grounds that its views were oversimplified, empirically questionable, and arrogantly argued, the latter complaint incited by his petulant tendency to think that no scholar before him got much of anything right about the Shoah. As time passed, and especially owing to the book's favorable reception in Germany, Goldhagen's work withstood much of the criticism. *A Moral Reckoning* has not fared as well, perhaps because it chides scholars of all persuasions. The defenders of Pope Pius XII, for example, have created a "moral blackout" regarding the Vatican's anti-Semitism. With exceptions such as James Carroll, the author of *Constantine's Sword* (2001), Goldhagen thinks that even most of the post-Shoah critics of the Roman Catholic Church fail to go far enough; they have barely begun to press the issues of repentance and restitution. If Goldhagen is to be believed, his scholarship and, considerably important here, his moral judgments trump the field. This single-mindedness may not be good public relations, but it would be foolish to dismiss him on those grounds. His case is carefully argued.

Goldhagen's reckoning begins in two places. First, he believes that the Roman Catholic Church, the Vatican, and the wartime popes Pius XI and especially Pius XII should be judged no differently from any other institutions or persons—with one qualification: the Church, its members, and particularly its leaders should also be held accountable to the highest ethical standards of justice and love that they profess as Christians. Second, Goldhagen identifies the anti-Semitism that lies at the heart of his indictment. Deeply rooted in falsehoods about Jews—none worse than the New Testament's allegation that the Jews are Christ-killers or even the offspring of Satan—anti-Semitism's many varieties reflect and inflame hostility against Jews "simply because they are Jews" (Goldhagen, 2002: 21). It follows, Goldhagen contends, that an anti-Semite is one who falsely accuses Jews of "noxious qualities or malfeasance," regarding those qualities or behaviors as the result of Jewishness and focusing "criticism disproportionately or exclusively on Jews" (Goldhagen, 2002: 23).

In Goldhagen's judgment, any Christian who believes or advances that tradition's falsehoods about Jews should be identified as an anti-Semite. Goldhagen finds that such falsehoods abound in Christianity. Correctly referring to what he calls "the Christian Bible's assault on Jews," Goldhagen sums it up as follows: "The Jews killed the son of God who is God. All Jews are guilty for this crime. Because Jews do not hear Jesus, they do not hear God. For their rejection of Jesus, they are to be punished. Jews, the willful spurners of Jesus, cannot gain salvation, cannot go to heaven. And their religion, which cannot bring them to salvation, has been made invalid, superseded, replaced by Christianity" (2002: 267).

Goldhagen acknowledges that the post-Shoah Church has gradually repudiated the allegations of Jewish responsibility for the killing of Jesus. It has also rejected collective Jewish guilt and punishment for that crime. Before and during the Shoah, however, such repudiations by Christians—Protestants as well as Catholics—were few and far between. To the contrary, Goldhagen documents that the Church's anti-Semitism was institutional. As the Church's anti-Jewish teachings were transmitted from one generation to another, Western civilization became increasingly drenched in anti-Semitism's poison.

The anti-Semitism that Christianity embodied, inspired, and inflamed was "eliminationist." Clarifying a point central to controversy that swirled when *Hitler's Willing Executioners* appeared, Goldhagen underscores that eliminationist anti-Semitism "does not necessarily mean killing," and that "the Catholic Church was doctrinally opposed to, and itself did not advocate, killing Jews" (2002: 167). That said, Goldhagen adds that the lack of persistent and public Church protest against the Third Reich's slaughter of European Jewry scarcely inspires confidence that the Church was completely opposed to the mass annihilation.

Goldhagen rejects the apologetics that excuse the lack of public protest against the persecution and murder of Jews. He finds it morally incredible to hold that Nazi threats were too severe for stands to be taken in defense of Jews. He utterly rejects any reasoning that tries to excuse Pope Pius XII, in particular, on the grounds that if he had spoken out more forthrightly in their favor, then the Jews would have suffered even more under Hitler. Cutting in the opposite direction, his analysis of the evidence points to a devastating conclusion: the Church found that "letting Jews die was preferable to intervening on their behalf" (2002: 15). Goldhagen does not go so far as to state this outright, but his analysis leaves a nagging suspicion. Despite deplorably bloody tactics in which the Church would not involve itself directly, did its leaders feel, without ever saying so, that it would be beneficial to be rid of the Jews one way or another?

Regarding Jews as dire threats, Christian anti-Semitism had long harbored eliminationist attitudes about them. Christianity's tendencies were to restrict and isolate Jews or to insist on their assimilation or conversion. Even they did not advocate physical elimination, many Christians sought the social or religious elimination of Jews for reasons that were rooted in anti-Semitic stereotypes or allegations. In a fundamental disagreement with "We Remember," the Roman Catholic Church's official statement on the Shoah in 1998, Goldhagen finds the Church speaking nonsense when it asserts that the Nazis' racial anti-Semitism "had its roots outside of Christianity" ("We Remember," in Rittner, et al., 2000: 260). He argues persuasively that "the Church's accusations against Jews were often virtually indistinguishable from those of the racist antisemites" (Goldhagen, 2002: 80). At the time of the Shoah, for example, Nazi and Catholic anti-Semitism agreed that the Jews were increasingly linked to communism, an ideology loathed by Pope Pius XII and many other Catholic leaders. In sum, Goldhagen shows that "examples of the Church's incitement to radical anti-Jewish action are legion" (2002: 165). Absent the seedbed and support provided by Christian anti-Semitism, the Nazis' racist anti-Semitism could not have been so powerfully credible to the Germans and their allies, who eventually attempted the total elimination of the Jews in the Shoah.

Other critics made similar points long before Goldhagen reiterated them, but he goes farther than most in holding the Church accountable. Accountability requires truth telling and restitution. The Church, Goldhagen appropriately contends, has not told the whole truth and nothing but the truth about its anti-Semitism and its failure during the Shoah. A moral reckoning requires it to do so, but that step would not be sufficient. The Church, Goldhagen adds, must make amends to Jews and reform itself.

Goldhagen uses the word "must" frequently and unabashedly. His list of "musts" for the Church is as challenging as it is long. Especially after the Shoah, three types of restitution are crucial: material, political, and moral.

Wherever the Church was implicated in exploiting Jews or in expropriating their property, it must work to set every account straight. Goldhagen notes that the German Catholic Church has taken steps in that direction, and he gives credit where it is due, as he does throughout his book. Political restitution is more complicated because Goldhagen links it to the state of Israel. At the very least, he insists, the Church will fail in its moral responsibility toward Jews if it acts to "weaken the foundation of Israel" or takes measures that "might imperil its existence or the lives of many of its citizens" (Goldhagen, 2002: 219).

If those arguably vague criteria create a minefield, moral restitution does so even more. The most basic task of moral restitution sounds simple—eradicate anti-Semitism from Christianity—but it is not. By Goldhagen's reckoning, conciliatory language, goodwill, apologies, and even the most heartfelt expressions of sorrow, regret, and contrition are not enough. Nothing less than fundamental reform will do. The changes must go deep down because anti-Semitism lies at the very roots of Christianity. What, then, should the Church do, and how must it change?

For starters, Goldhagen prods the Church to name names. It should identify the individual leaders who came up short during the Shoah and repudiate them, including "all relevant Popes, bishops, and priests" (Goldhagen, 2002: 246). It should halt immediately the canonization of any person—read, Pius XII specifically—who aided and abetted the persecution of Jews. The Church should develop memorials that bear witness to the Shoah-related suffering and death in which it is implicated. A lengthy papal encyclical should be forthcoming; it should detail the history of the Church's anti-Semitism, denouncing that history, and any perpetuation of it, as sinful. These steps, however, only begin to deal with Goldhagen's list.

Anti-Semitism, Goldhagen believes, is inseparable from the Church's authoritarian and imperialistic pretensions. Therefore, the Church must abandon papal infallibility, dissolve the Vatican as a political state, embrace religious pluralism to make clear that salvation does not come through the Church alone, and revise its official Catechism to make unmistakable that any teaching smacking of anti-Semitism is "wrong, null, and void" (Goldhagen, 2002: 259). The biggest issue, however, is the Church's "Bible problem" (2002: 207).

THE "BIBLE PROBLEM"

Goldhagen's reading of the New Testament leaves him with two striking impressions: First, Christianity is "a religion of love that teaches its members the highest moral principles for acting well. Love your neighbor. Seek peace. Help those in need. Sympathize with and raise up the oppressed.

Do to others as you would have them do to you" (Goldhagen, 2002: 3). Second, the New Testament's "relentless and withering assault on Jews and Judaism" is not incidental because it portrays the Jews as "the ontological enemy" of Jesus, goodness, and God (2002: 262 and 266).

The "Bible problem," moreover, is not just that two apparently contradictory perspectives collide, but that the collision takes place in texts that are regarded as sacred and divinely inspired. The need, Goldhagen contends, is for Christians to rewrite the New Testament, to expunge anti-Semitism from it. He recognizes how difficult, perhaps insurmountable, that task may be; nevertheless, Goldhagen does not despair. He thinks that the Christian tradition can be self-corrective, resilient, and revitalized if Christians find the will to be true to their tradition's best teachings about love and justice.

Wisely, Goldhagen does *not* presume to rewrite the New Testament. Nor does he venture to define everything that a truly post-Shoah Church should be. His book contains touches of modesty after all. Meanwhile, if the Roman Catholic Church, and by implication all churches, moved in his direction, it would not be the first time that a Jewish teacher has shown Christians the way. Goldhagen seems to be betting that Christianity can gain new life by letting its old one die. How many Christians will welcome such prospects remains unknown, but hope of that kind should be familiar to them. It would be good for post-Shoah followers of Jesus to embrace it. Doing so would advance restitution and reconciliation, two of the afterwords on which good relations between post-Shoah Christians and Jews so much depend.

RAISING VOICES

Even if Christianity does not change in ways that satisfy Goldhagen, perhaps the raising of his critical voice along with those of many others can make us Christians and our churches—Catholic, Protestant, Orthodox— more attuned to avoiding complicity in genocide, and more determined to intervene as best we can to thwart genocidal impulses. By using his voice to challenge Christianity, Goldhagen may not achieve the aims that he stated explicitly, but he might find that the senses of shame and responsibility that he has helped to produce can assist Christians in preventing the repetition of past errors and in making their tradition anti-genocidal. This hope is one that we Christians can ill afford to squander.

Every form of power includes, even depends upon, raising voices. Leaders have to raise their voices to state their principles, express their visions, and rally their supporters. Governments have to raise their voices to define policies, defend interests, and justify decisions. Religious communities and institutions, including churches and many others as well, are no different.

Supporters of leaders, governments, and religious communities have to raise their voices to back visions and policies; otherwise the power of principles, interests, and traditions declines and even disappears.

Genocide also depends on raising voices. It cannot exist unless divisions between people are constructed by speech, fears are expressed in ideology and propaganda, and killing is unleashed by voices that proclaim it to be necessary. No religion is automatically immune to sins of this kind. Genocide also depends on "unraising" voices; it counts on the muting of criticism, the silencing of dissent, and the acquiescence of bystanders. No religion is automatically immune from involvement in sins of this kind either. Every voice unraised against genocide gives aid and comfort to those who call for and support that crime of crimes. Genocide can be prevented before it happens, and it can be stopped after it is underway. Neither prevention nor successful intervention, however, can happen without power. Religion's power is not the same as political or economic power, and it is definitely not the same as military might. But religion has its power nonetheless, and there is scarcely a genocide in human history that could not have been checked or prevented if religiously-inspired voices had been raised in support of that cause.

Daniel Goldhagen challenged Christianity to make restitution not only of a different kind but also of very specific kinds. Where the latter are concerned, he may not get much of what he wants. The Roman Catholic Church is unlikely to give up the Vatican. Christians are unlikely to rewrite the New Testament. But thanks to evaluations and judgments that he and other critics have offered, Christians and churches might indeed make restitution of a different kind by speaking out now and in the future in voices that are raised clearly and persistently against genocidal threats. All religious traditions and their followers can do the same. If they did, one could be more confident that *yes* can answer the question "Will genocide ever end?"

BIBLIOGRAPHY

Améry, Jean (1986). *At the Mind's Limits: Contemplations by a Survivor on Auschwitz and Its Realities.* New York: Schocken Books.

Bazyler, Michael (2003). *Holocaust Justice: The Battle for Restitution in America's Courts.* New York: New York University Press.

Carroll, James (2001). *Constantine's Sword: The Church and the Jews—A History.* Boston, Mass.: Houghton Mifflin Company.

Delbo, Charlotte (1995). *Auschwitz and After.* Translated by Rosette C. Lamont. New Haven, Conn.: Yale University Press.

Eizenstat, Stuart (2003). *Imperfect Justice: Looted Assets, Slave Labor, and the Unfinished Business of World War II.* New York: Public Affairs.

Glover, Jonathan (1999). *Humanity: A Moral History of the Twentieth Century.* New Haven, Conn.: Yale University Press.

Goldhagen, Daniel Jonah (1996). *Hitler's Willing Executioners: Ordinary Germans and the Holocaust.* New York: Alfred A. Knopf.

——— (2002). *A Moral Reckoning: The Role of the Catholic Church in the Holocaust and Its Unfulfilled Duty of Repair.* New York: Alfred A. Knopf.

Levi, Primo (1988). *The Drowned and the Saved.* Translated from the Italian by Raymond Rosentahl. New York: Summit Books.

Levinas, Emmanuel (1998). *Entre-Nous: On Thinking-of-the-Other.* Translated from the French by Michael B. Smith and Barbara Harshav. New York: Columbia University Press.

Roth, John K. (2004). "Useless Experience: Its Significance for Reconciliation after Auschwitz" in David Patterson, and John K. Roth (eds.). *After-Words: Post-Holocaust Struggles with Forgiveness, Reconciliation, Justice.* Seattle: University of Washington Press, 85–99.

"We Remember: A Reflection on the Shoah," in Carol Rittner, Stephen D. Smith, and Irena Steinfeldt (eds.) (2000). *The Holocaust and the Christian World: Reflections on the Past, Challenges for the Future.* New York: Continuum, 257–62.

15

The Holocaust, Genocide, and the Catholic Church

Donald J. Dietrich

1.

The Holocaust and the genocide in Rwanda have challenged the Catholic Church to critique its own theology and to address the issue of empathetic reconciliation (Appleby, 2000; Dietrich 1995; Tschuy, 1997). Because of its historical roots in European society, the Catholic Church has had to reexamine those of its doctrines that have supported anti-Semitism, ethnocentrism, and the resultant marginalizing tactics. Scholars, for example, have spent about four decades trying to clarify the Church's role in the "Final Solution" and are now faced with understanding its participation in the genocide in Rwanda (Phayer, 2000; Zuccotti, 2001; Carroll, 2001; Kertzer, 2001; Dietrich, 1988).

With respect to the Nazi Holocaust, the Church's historical attachment to religious and political anti-Semitism led to a marginalization of the Jewish people that was confronted only after World War II. Nationalism, eugenics, and ethnocentrism played their role in making the German people and their churches susceptible to anti-Semitism and to Hitler, their charismatic leader, who sought to unify the *Volk* in order to eliminate the "fragmented" political structure that plagued the Weimar Republic as well as to impose a radical anti-Jewish policy in accordance with Nazi ideology (Gellately, 2001; Kershaw, 2000). A great deal is now known about the political, social, economic, and intellectual structures that influenced Germans as well as Europeans in general and facilitated their murderous policies (Roth and Maxwell, 2001) toward the Jews and others.

The Catholic Church played a crucial role in this drama and has had to deal with its responsibility for the Shoah since 1945. Vatican II launched a reexamination of the church in the modern world and, through *Nostra Aetate*, reversed the church's historic anti-Semitic policies. Such theologians as Johanne Baptist Metz have provided theological tools that have helped the Church to respond critically to its own contributions in support of political brutality. Beginning with Vatican II, the Church condemned anti-Semitism, and for several decades since then it has attempted to forge authentic links between Jews and Christians. Yet even as Catholics take pride in the Church's post-*Nostra Aetate* efforts, another dark event in Rwanda has reminded the faithful that much has still to be done.

Similar to Catholic attitudes and behavioral patterns during the *Hitlerzeit*, the Church has manifested a surprising moral inconsistency in Rwanda— indeed, has shown a grave lack of moral responsibility. Aside from its own divisive role in evangelization and its participatory role in fomenting ethnocentrism, not only has the Church remained silent before genocidal atrocities, but in many cases its members—from lay Christians to church leaders—have been involved in this genocide (Tschuy, 1997: 24; Rutayisire et al., 2000: 15). This essay will reflect on the initiatives of the Church in Vatican II, the development of the theology of Metz, and the Church's role in Rwanda, which has stimulated such theologians as Robert Schreiter to develop a much needed theology of reconciliation.

2.

The Church transformed its ecclesial and theological milieu radically during Vatican II; with its fifteen carefully modulated sentences, *Nostra Aetate* was finally passed by an overwhelming majority (for the text of *Nostra Aetate*, see Wigoder, 1988: 143–44). The stress on the spiritual bond between the Church and the Jewish people, as well as the statement that the Church "received the Old Testament through the Jewish people, with whom God concluded the Ancient Covenant," were unprecedented and crucially needed for the Catholic Church to engage the world of marching soldiers. The acknowledgement of the obviously Judaic roots of Christianity, including, of course, the Jewish background of Jesus, unlocked new vistas in public ecclesial discussions. Stating that God did not reject the Jews reversed the church's traditional position. Stressing that "what happened in the passion of Christ cannot be charged against all Jews without distinction living at that time and certainly not against the Jews living today" was the keystone of the Catholic Church's response to its Jewish heritage. This repudiation of historical anti-Semitism alongside an insistence on mutual understanding through fraternal dialogue, opened an exciting era in

Catholic-Jewish relations. Even the document's ambivalence helped open the way for discussion in future decades.

In 1974 the Vatican issued a second document on Jewish-Christian relations (for the text see Wigoder, 1988: 144–49) entitled "Guidelines for the Implementation of *Nostra Aetate*." These "Guidelines" provided explicit and formal expressions by which to accommodate the new attitudes emerging as Jews and Christians examined their past and present relationships and designed the parameters for future interchanges. Christians, the document asserted, should begin learning how Jews have historically defined themselves through their own integral religious experiences. Judaism was no longer to be labeled as a religion of fear and legalism that ignored the love of God and neighbor. The document also repudiated the Christian accusation that Judaism had become fossilized after the destruction of the Temple (CE 70). Jews, it insisted, had continued to develop a rich religious tradition that can now help educate Christians as they continue to work out their own salvific history. Anti-Semitism was now not merely deplored but condemned. Supersessionist implications were to be excised, and Christians were told that they had to understand the difficulties that arise as Jews reflect on God in the face of the Christian Incarnation. The bishops (Fisher et al., 1986: 218ff.) of the United States and other national groups have subsequently insisted that the Church has to reflect on its own self-understanding of the Jews as a covenanted people. The Christian Testament itself cannot be understood without reflecting on the Jewish awareness of God. Virtually all of the documents from the national conferences of bishops and Catholic scholars have reminded the faithful that the Church has not displaced the Jewish people in God's plan.

John Paul II (Fisher et al., 1986: 215ff.) also continuously reminded Catholics that the two religious communities were linked in God's revelation. In 1985, under his leadership, the Vatican published "Notes on the Correct Way to Present the Jews and Judaism in the Preaching and Catechesis of the Catholic Church" (for the text of the document, see Wigoder, 1988: 149–59). On the positive side, the "Notes" incorporated the Pope's 1980 statement in Mainz, Germany (Dietrich, 1995: 78–80) and focused on the notion that the Jewish covenant had never been revoked. A further statement warned that the traditional Christian scriptural texts had to be read carefully because so many of the hostile references toward the Jews occurred in the context of Christians forging their own identity.

Unfortunately, the "Notes" also restate that the Church and Judaism cannot be perceived as two parallel and equal roads to salvation and that the Church *must* witness Christ as the redeemer for *all* (Hvalvik, 1990: 87–107). Although this statement was subsequently qualified by an expression pledging respect for religious liberty, it appears, even in *Dominus Jesus* (6 August 2000), to imply that all non-Christian faiths seem to have existential, but not theological, legitimization (Pope and Hefling, 2002). In essence, the "Notes" strongly suggest that "divergence" in the two covenants should be seen only as temporary, and that ultimately convergence is still to be considered normative for salvation. Since the final synthesis has not been achieved, the dialogue is to continue.

The "Notes" (D'Costa, 1985: 259–68) also do not directly confront the Christian responsibility for the creation of anti-Semitism; they only deplore it. Particularly unfortunate is the restriction of the significance of the Holocaust to its "meaning for the Jews," which seems to ignore its meaning for the church as well as for its universal implications for all men and women. The universal implications of the Holocaust, many scholars insist, have an impact on society as a whole (Horowitz, 2002; Barnett, 1999) as well as on Christianity, the nominal religion of the perpetrators. Subsequently, other contributions toward creating a positive milieu emerged. John Paul II's visit to and comments in the synagogue in Rome in 1986 reinforced the dialogue, as did his later insertion of a prayer into the Western Wall in Jerusalem.

In 1998 the Vatican issued the document "We Remember: A Reflection on the Shoah" (http://www.bc.edu/research/cjl/resources/documents/catholic), which summarized thirty years of Jewish-Catholic dialogue and explicated the persistent issues that still had to be addressed. One issue caught the attention of all. "We Remember" sorrowfully reminded its readers that individual Catholics had been guilty of horrific crimes, but that the Church "as such" was innocent. The institutional church, within which Jesus has continued his mission, it was thought, could not be guilty of the malevolent acts that culminated in the Holocaust. People were guilty, not the institution (Carroll, 2001; Tessis and Fried, 2001). The institutional church as a formative source in our culture, many scholars have insisted, has transmitted nefarious values. In short, individual sinners have helped create structural sin, and the church as an institution, some think (Hinze, 2000: 207–38), must bear that sin and admit that it has been and still is a sinful church, since it is composed of sinners. In *Lumen Gentium* and *Gaudium et Spes* Vatican II articulated the notion of a "sinful church," but such a viewpoint continues to be a source of anxiety for some Church leaders.

During the last four decades, the collective reflection of the Catholic Church has helped clarify both the continuities and discontinuities existing between the two faith communities (Boys, 2000). Since the conversation among scholars has included such topics as covenant, Christology, and scapegoating, this historical issue of anti-Semitism and its ramifications has become part of a broader theological rethinking of the meaning of moral development and of the human condition itself. Along with the institutional church, such theologians as Johannes Metz have tried to reappropriate the meaning of revelation and to expose the past theological corruption that helped support policies of sanctioned murder.

3.

Metz (Pinnock, 2002; Ashley, 1998: 191–204) critiques all abstract theologies that do not recognize the socially critical character of faith. For Metz, faith is to respond with a critical consciousness to what Marx and the Frankfurt School have termed "material" historical conditions, i.e., the economic, political, and social phenomena that are the causes of suffering. In the process, Metz rejects any type of theodicy, for example, that attributes suffering to the logical or ultimately benevolent progress of history. The kind of faith that is plausible in the face of brutality, he feels, is the prophetic model of faith found in the Bible, which directly responds to individual and collective suffering. When faced with the Holocaust, he accuses theodicy in all its theological forms of being bankrupt, since theodicy tends to suppress protests against suffering (Pinnock, 2002: 82).

The Holocaust was a crucial formative crisis for Metz as a German theologian (Pinnock, 2002: 164; Schuster, 1999). Drawing on his own experience as a teenager in Germany during World War II, Metz identified with those scholars and Holocaust survivors who have focused their attention on God's seeming indifference to suffering. He has asserted that a Christian response to suffering ought to give Holocaust victims the ultimate authority to remember and to speak about the religious interpretation of this catastrophe. Metz's systematic critique of any theological apathy toward suffering contains an insistence that men and women have a duty to change history (Metz, 1980: 127).

The horror of the *Shoah* cannot be given a patina of "good" in terms of moral development, economic progress, or divine self-revelation. The testimony of each victim demands, Metz has insisted, that any authentic post-Holocaust theology must articulate a protest against systemic evil and a commitment to change political, social, and economic configurations. In taking this position (Metz, 1980: 130; 1998: 70) Metz has rejected the views of Karl Rahner, his teacher, and Hans Urs von Balthasar, who see in the incarnation and crucifixion of Jesus ways to reconcile suffering and love. God, they say, has himself participated in suffering, so it has to be expected as part of the human condition. Metz disagrees with such a theological avoidance of the tangible brutality imposed on the Jews. He has instead promoted a narrative theology focusing on critical memory and on the story of Jesus as a source of hope. Theology must articulate, he insists, the memory of past salvations connected to historical events. Opposing Jürgen Moltmann, Metz maintains that the anguish of Jesus is not comparable to the anguish and suffering of anyone in Auschwitz, because whereas Jesus made conscious choices that led to his crucifixion, those who suffered during the Holocaust were unwilling victims (Metz, 1998: 69–70). In essence (Pinnock, 2002: 90), Metz refuses to rely on theoretical responses to history. Theology should fundamentally center on the narrative memory of concrete suffering and on the biblical hope for redemption.

Metz sees in the Hebrew Bible the original embodiment of faith language and hence the source and model for a faith response to suffering. For him, the narratives of this Bible are rooted in dangerous memories, because in response to the oppression of the poor, we are reminded of those persons who protested suffering and anticipated the possibility of political change in history with hope, solidarity, and resistance. For Christians, the resurrection can also be a dangerous memory that signifies (Metz, 1969: 88; 1980: 111) the overcoming of injustice, the release from oppression, and the promise of human freedom for all in the course of moving toward God's kingdom.

Narratives that highlight suffering uncover the truth that history is brimming with oppression. Examples of such suffering are embedded in the Jewish and Christian faith traditions and must not be ignored. Narratives must also be explicated to analyze the causes of suffering, a preliminary step necessary for developing political strategies of resistance (Dietrich, 2003). Remembering the past for the sake of the future in the context of our distorted and brutally imperfect world can involve danger because the Jewish and Christian hopes for redemption can and should spark a protest against suffering. Memory, therefore, is designed to play a liberating function for religious narratives (Metz, 1980: 66, 68, 195), which can help assist contemporaries in becoming conscious of freedom as well as of the potential for human agency and self-determination in history. Such narratives can also spur hope, which can help us transform history. Narratives of suffering can catalyze a sense of moral shock that can lead to solidarity with victims and to protests against the brutalization of others (Pinnock, 2002: 93–96; Lamb, 1982).

To make faith stimulate men and women into confronting the past and responding concretely to alleviate current suffering, Metz seems to consider protest and resistance integral to an authentic theological discourse. Christian faith, focused on universal redemption, should help increase our awareness of the horror of suffering. Christians, he feels, have to carve out a political approach to faith, in which the historical event becomes seminal to "doing" theology within a specific historical context.

4.

In light of the Church's initiatives after *Nostra Aetate* and Metz's theological reflections, the Catholic response to discrimination and genocide in Rwanda has to be seen as astounding. When European Catholic missionaries first came to Rwanda after the country was placed under Belgian control by the League of Nations, they were strongly influenced by the nineteenth-century anthropological and racial studies that served as the pillars of the colonial enterprise (Semujanga, 2003). Making no attempt to know the people or understand their culture, these missionaries simply rejected anything related to Rwandan religious and cultural traditions and espoused marginalizing tactics that continued to subordinate the Hutus to the Tutsis, since this tactic seemed useful for evangelization and for purposes of consistency in colonial policies. Catholic missionaries after 1918 endorsed the ethnic division already fostered by German colonial rule among the Hutus and Tutsis, and conceptualized it by maintaining the Hutus and Tutsis as exclusive groups. They totally disregarded what the two groups have in common: the same culture, religion, and habitat. In traditional Rwandan culture, for example, pastoralism was associated with wealth and prestige and was originally dominated by the Tutsis. Hutus engaged in agriculture and had less status. Due to economic mobility, however, a rich Hutu could become classified as a member of the leadership elite. What came to exacerbate divisions, then, was not the simple fact of belonging to either of these two groups, but the ethnic interpretation given by the missionaries and colonialists to an issue that was basically socioeconomic.

By the 1950s, the Tutsi elite aspired to independence and clearly rejected the colonizers and their policies. In response, the Belgian colonial administration, together with Church leaders, felt betrayed and reversed the Tutsi elitist policy. The Belgians and the Church hierarchy shifted their support to the Hutus, blaming the politically divisive colonial policies on the Tutsis. These Tutsis, once hailed for their "inborn" leadership qualities, now were marginalized as outsiders who had actually been exploiting their socioeconomic inferiors. The colonizers ignored their own role in that exploitation (Rutayisire et al., 1995: 428; Longman, 1997). Murder, torture, and ultimately by the 1990s, genocide, became part of Rwandan history. Even after the genocide, the Church's attitude remained the same. The Church in Rwanda refused to recognize its historical and ethnocentric role in dividing the Rwandan people and in the subsequent genocide. Following its past habit of supporting the existing political order, the Church insisted that Rwandans were engaged in a civil war, not a genocide.

When the genocide began, Church leaders in the Vatican and in Rwanda did not protest. While human rights were being flagrantly violated, with murders taking place in churches and Catholic schools and even carried out by Christians on other Christians, Church officials remained silent. In fact, some Catholic clergy were busy gathering the Tutsis into churches to be killed, telling them they were looking out for safe hiding places. Priests and nuns not only served as accomplices, but were even involved in direct acts of murder (*Golias Magazine*, 1996).

The Rwandan Catholic Church has been reluctant to recognize its historic role in the division of the Rwandan people as well as its participation, implicitly and explicitly, in the policy of genocide. When the survivors of the genocide and the new government urged that some churches where people had been slaughtered be used as memorials to their beloved dead, the Rwandan bishops refused. Even more scandalous was the Church's attitude of justifying genocide as civil war, so that it could avoid its own responsibility for supporting sanctioned murder (Roth and Maxwell, 2004).

5.

Given the Church's role in the Holocaust and Rwanda as well as its shameful support of dictatorships in the twentieth century, such theologians as Robert Schreiter (1992) have focused on reconciliation issues. Several conditions, he has emphasized, seem necessary to promote genuine reconciliation. First, the Church must forbear to advance "cheap reconciliation" by calling on victims to merely forgive and forget. Secondly, the Church must accept a mandate to concentrate on restoring the truth and revealing the root causes and psychopolitical dynamics that led to such events as the Rwandan tragedy. Thirdly, the Church is not to forget its origins by considering reconciliation simply as a managed human process.

Schreiter (1992: 19-21; see also Volf, 1996) sees "cheap reconciliation" as dealing only nominally with a history of violence by suppressing its memory and "moving on." Suppressing memory does not reduce or eliminate the violence, but only postpones its expurgation. Reconciliation is not merely a cessation of violence and is more than an insistence on Christian forgiveness. The process of reconciliation involves memory, justice to the victims, and a theology rooted in Jesus' message itself. Since memory is linked to identity, to ignore remembering has moral implications that need to be taken seriously. In fact, to deny memory is ultimately to side with the perpetrator. To forget about the dead, Schreiter has asserted, is to kill them again.

The Church, Schreiter asserts, should promote "truth telling" and establish the responsibilities for its own heinous acts and for the brutal events perpetrated in society at large. To bring about an authentic reconciliation, the Church has to expose the real causes of violence and try to eradicate them. According to Schreiter, political conflict cannot be considered peripheral during the reconciliation process, but must be met at its very heart. If the sources of the conflict are not candidly examined, reconciliation can never be realized.

Authentic reconciliation cannot be a managed process. Reconciliation itself (Schreiter, 1992: 25) is not merely conflict mediation, an instrumental mechanism that tries to attain a tolerant consensus between two or more conflicting parties. Such a process initially sounds attractive, since it recognizes each side's agenda of legitimate interests. Reconciliation is needed, however, in situations where social relations have almost completely deteriorated and social bonds have been radically fractured (Schreiter, 1992: 26, 60). According to Scott Appleby, reconciliation becomes more of an attitude than an acquired skill. Real and not just superficial reconciliation is a stance assumed before a broken world rather than just simply an instrumentalized tool to repair that world (Appleby, 2000: 167) and is oriented toward the larger goal of healing relationships, rebuilding communities, and transforming society into a harmonious and peaceful community.

Some Church leaders have now recognized that if faith is to help shape a nurturing culture, doctrine and theology must be rooted in historical events. The Holocaust and the genocide in Rwanda are historical events that have inspired Metz, Schreiter, and others to insist that the real world is the context in which any authentic theology that can help heal our culture must be grounded.

BIBLIOGRAPHY

Appleby, R. Scott (2000). *The Ambivalence of the Sacred: Religion, Violence, and Reconciliation*. Lanham, Md.: Rowman and Littlefield Publications.

Ashley, James Matthew (1998). *Interruptions: Mysticism, Politics and Theology in the Work of Johann Baptist Metz*. Notre Dame: University of Notre Dame Press.

Barnett, Victoria (1999). *Bystanders: Conscience and Complicity during the Holocaust*. Westport, Conn.: Greenwood Press.

Boys, Mary (2000). *Has God Only One Blessing? Judaism as a Source of Christian Self-Understanding*. New York: Paulist Press.

Carroll, James (2001). *Constantine's Sword: The Church and the Jews*. Boston: Houghton Mifflin.

D'Costa, Gavin (1985). "Elephants, Ropes, and a Christian Theology of Religions." *Theology*, 88: 259–69.

Dietrich, Donald J. (1988). *Catholic Citizens in the Third Reich: Psycho-Social Principles and Moral Reasoning*. New Brunswick, N.J.: Transaction Books.

—— (1995). *God and Humanity in Auschwitz: Jewish-Christian Relations and Sanctioned Murder*. New Brunswick, N.J.: Transaction Publishers.

—— (ed.) (2003). *Christian Responses to the Holocaust: Moral and Ethical Issues*. Syracuse, N.Y.: Syracuse University Press.

Fisher, Eugene, A. James Rudin, and Marc H. Tenenbaum (eds.) (1986). *Twenty Years of Jewish-Christian Relations*. New York: Paulist Press.

Gellately, Robert (2001). *Backing Hitler: Consent and Coercion in Nazi Germany*. Oxford: Oxford University Press.

Golias Magazine (1996). N48/49.

Hinze, Bradford (2000). "Ecclesial Repentance and the Demands of Dialogue." *Theological Studies,* 61: 207–38.
Horowitz, Irving Louis (2002). *Taking Lives: Genocide and State Power.* 5th ed. rev. New Brunswick, N.J.: Transaction Publishers.
Hvalvik, Reidar (1990). "A 'Sonderweg' for Israel: A Critical Examination of a Current Interpretation of Romans 11:25–27." *Journal for the Study of the New Testament,* 38: 87–107.
Kershaw, Ian (2000). *Hitler, 1936–1945: Nemesis.* New York: W. W. Norton.
Kertzer, David I. (2001). *The Popes against the Jews: The Vatican's Role in the Rise of Modern Anti-Semitism.* New York: Alfred A. Knopf.
Lamb, Matthew (1982). *Solidarity with Victims: Toward a Theology of Social Transformation.* New York: Crossroad.
Longman, T. (1997). "Empowering the Weak and Protecting the Powerful: The Contemporary Nature of Christian Churches in Rwanda, Burundi, and the Democratic Republic of the Congo." Lecture. New Haven, Conn.: Yale University, 26 September.
Metz, Johannes (1980). *Faith in History and Society.* Trans. by David Smith. New York: Seabury Press.
——— (1998). "Theology as Theodicy?" in J. Matthew Ashley (ed.), *A Passion for God: The Mystical-Political Dimension of Christianity.* New York: Paulist Press, 54–71.
——— (1969). *Theology of the World.* New York: Herder and Herder.
Phayer, Michael (2000). *The Catholic Church and the Holocaust, 1930–1965.* Bloomington: Indiana University Press.
Pinnock, Sarah (2002). *Beyond Theodicy: Jewish and Christian Continental Thinkers Respond to the Holocaust.* Albany: State University of New York Press.
Pope, Stephen and Charles Hefling (eds.) (2002). *Sic et non: Encountering Dominus Iesus.* Maryknoll, N.Y.: Orbis Books.
Roth, John K., and Elisabeth Maxwell (eds.) (2001). *Remembering for the Future: the Holocaust in an Age of Genocide.* 3 Volumes. New York: Palgrave.
Rutagambwa, Elisee (1999). *The Rwandan Genocide: Moral Indictment and Ethical Challenge for the International Community and the Church.* Thesis for the Licentiate in Sacred Theology. Cambridge, Mass.: Weston Jesuit School of Theology.
Rutayisire, Paul, J.-P. Karegeye, and F. Rutembesa (2000). *Rwanda: L 'Eglise Catholique a l'epreuve du genocide.* Greenfield Park, Quebec: Les Editions Africana.
Schreiter, Robert (1992). *Mission and Ministry in a Changing Social Order.* Maryknoll, N.Y.: Orbis Books.
Schuster, Ekkehard (1999). *Hope against Hope: Johann Baptist Metz and Elie Wiesel Speak Out on the Holocaust.* Trans. by J. Matthew Ashley. New York: Paulist Press.
Semujanga, Josias (2003). *Origins of Rwandan Genocide.* Amherst, N.Y.: Humanity Books.
Tessis, Daniel, and Sylvia Fuks Fried (eds.) (2001). *Catholics, Jews, and the Prism of Conscience.* Waltham, Mass.: Brandeis University.
Tschuy, Theo (1997). *Ethnic Conflict and Religion: Challenge to the Churches.* Geneva: WCC Publications.
Verschave, Francois-Xavier (1994). *Complicite de genocide? La politique de la France au Rwanda.* Paris: La Decouverte.

Volf, Miroslav (1996). *Exclusion and Embrace: A Theological Exploration of Identity, Otherness, and Reconciliation.* Nashville, Tenn.: Abingdon Press.

Wigoder, Geoffrey (1988). *Jewish-Christian Relations since the Second World War.* Manchester, England: Manchester University Press.

Zuccotti, Susan (2001). *Under His Very Windows: The Vatican and the Holocaust in Italy.* New Haven, Conn.: Yale University Press.

16

Catholic Views on the Holocaust and Genocide: A Critical Appraisal

John T. Pawlikowski

For a century or so, the institutional Catholic Church in Europe battled the forces of liberalism and what was termed "freemasonry." This "hundred years' war" was rooted in the belief on the part of popes and Vatican officials that fundamental liberal notions of human rights and religious freedom would undermine Catholic moral hegemony in countries where Catholics constituted a majority, such as Italy, Austria, and Poland. Even in countries where Catholics did not dominate the political scene, as in Germany and France, they frequently fought strongly against such notions, which were labeled as "Satanic" in origin (Modras, 1994; 2001; Pawlikowski, 1998). While such opposition on the part of the papacy, the Vatican, and local church leaders did not automatically generate support for genocide and eventually the Holocaust, it certainly weakened any sustained protests against genocidal or near-genocidal actions by governments, and eventually against the Holocaust. Moral opposition to genocide and Holocaust is ultimately based in notions of individual human equality. By devaluing notions of human equality in the nineteenth and twentieth centuries, Catholicism contributed, even if only indirectly, to prevailing notions of religious and racial superiority that would provide an indispensable seedbed for genocides and the Holocaust. The failure of Vatican Council I to see growing anti-Semitism as a major social force that needed direct attention is a case in point.

This hundred years' war against liberal notions of human dignity came to an end only at Vatican Council II. After a fierce battle within the council, the bishops endorsed the importance of notions of human rights and religious liberty *for the first time*. Pope John XXIII made a major contribution through his social encyclical *Pacem in Terris*, in which he laid out, for the first time in Catholic history, a Charter of Human Rights (O'Brien and Shannon, 2002). It is documents such as Vatican II's *Declaration on Religious Liberty* and *Nostra Aetate*, as well as *Pacem in Terris*, which provide a basis within contemporary Catholic social ethics for a response to genocide. If they had been available at the time of the Holocaust, they may well have made some difference in the quality of the Catholic institutional response to Hitler's attack on the Jews as well as Poles, Roma, disabled people, and homosexuals.

While the issue of genocide has never been addressed in a formal, comprehensive way within official Catholic social teaching, that of the Holocaust has. For that reason, I will turn to that subject first, and then go on to explore Catholic responses to genocide.

After many years of delay, the Vatican released "We Remember," a comprehensive statement on the Holocaust on 16 March 1998 (NCCB, 1998). Its principal architect was Cardinal Edward ldris Cassidy, then the president of the Pontifical Council for Christian Unity and of the Holy See's Commission for Religious Relations with the Jews. But Cardinal Cassidy had to submit the text to the Vatican's doctrinal office—headed by Cardinal Joseph Ratzinger, now Pope Benedict XVI—and to the Vatican secretariat of state, directed by Cardinal Angelo Sodano. The latter in particular mandated certain changes in the document that would be responsible for future controversy.

In some quarters, mostly Catholic, the document was greeted with considerable enthusiasm. A number of Jewish leaders also saw very positive elements in the document (Banki, 2001). It clearly acknowledged the Holocaust as a historical fact—so that Holocaust denial was not an acceptable Catholic option—it expressed genuine regret for Catholic complicity in the Holocaust, and it mandated education in the Holocaust for Catholic students at all levels of schooling throughout the world. But it also had some serious drawbacks that were noted both by Catholic and Jewish scholars. Important Catholic publications such as *Commonweal* and *The Tablet* weighed in with significant critiques. In March 1999 most of these criticisms were discussed at a major symposium on the document, with Cardinal Cassidy as an active participant, held at the Catholic Theological Union (CTU) in Chicago, Illinois, under the auspices of CTU's Bernardin Center and the Tanenbaum Center for Interreligious Understanding (Banki and Pawlikowski, 2001).

My own assessment of "We Remember" is rather mixed. I do see it as a document that establishes the Holocaust as a permanent and vital issue of Christian self-reflection. But at the same time I believe it falls short, from a scholarly point of view, in several critical areas. On the whole, though, it brings the issues raised by the Holocaust to the heart of Catholic theological reflection far more directly than any previous document—and with papal endorsement—helps provide a mandate for Holocaust education within the Christian community.

"We Remember" also clearly implicates Catholics at all levels of the Church—even at the very highest levels, as Cardinal Edward Cassidy has reiterated—in the sin of anti-Semitism. The document distinguishes between the "pure" mystical or sacramental Church, the Body of Christ, and the wayward "sons and daughters" of the Church, a division rooted in a theological perspective no longer acceptable to leading theologians, who regard such a perspective as not fully congruent with the vision laid out in Vatican II's document on the Church. "We Remember" does at least argue that important Catholics were guilty of serious moral failure in their attitudes toward the Jewish people during the Nazi era.

While "We Remember" is certainly the most important document on Catholic-Jewish relations released by the Vatican since *Nostra Aetate* itself, some perspectives that are incomplete and sometimes even misleading mark it. I would like to focus on three such areas. The first has to do with the distinction between the sinful actions of the "sons and daughters" of the Church and the fundamental holiness of the Church itself. As I suggested above, and as Cardinal Cassidy has emphasized in several of his own commentaries on the document, this distinction is based on a long-standing perception that views the Church as a sacramental reality that remains fundamentally unaffected by the sinful realities of history. In a public discussion of "We Remember" in Chicago soon after the release of the document, Cardinal Francis George spoke of a conversation he had with Pope John Paul II on this matter in which the Pope strongly insisted that the Church itself, as a theological reality, couldn't be blamed for anti-Semitism or for the Holocaust. Without question, Catholics must take this classical theological position seriously, even if one feels that it can lead to serious misinterpretation or that it is overly ahistorical. But it is likewise important to recognize that other, more historically based theologies of the Church emerged in the discussions at the Vatican II, as Robert Schreiter shows in his contribution to the scholarly symposium on "We Remember" (Schreiter, 2001).

Surely the authors of "We Remember" were in no position to resolve this basic theological issue. Nonetheless, "We Remember" could have, and should have, made it clearer that the "sons and daughters" of the Church who fell into the sin of anti-Semitism did so because of what they had learned from teachers, theologians (the Church Fathers in particular), and preachers sanctioned by the institutional Church, as well the artwork in churches that depicted the Jewish community after Christ as blind and decrepit. Yet we know from many studies of anti-Semitism, such as the late Father Edward Flannery's classic volume *The Anguish of the Jews* (Flannery,

1965), as well as more recent studies such as *The Jewish-Christian Controversy: From the Earliest Times to 1789* by Samuel Krauss (Krauss, 1995), Heinz Schreckenberg's *The Jews in Christian Art* (Schreckenberg, 1996), and the volume by Marvin Perry and Frederick Schweitzer *Antisemitism: Myth and Hate: From Antiquity to the Present* (Perry and Schweitzer, 2002), that for centuries, anti-Semitism permeated Catholic catechesis and preaching, as well as the popular culture they generated. The famous facade of the medieval cathedral in Strasbourg, France, with its depiction of the vibrant Church represented as a young woman and the bedraggled and blindfolded synagogue presented in the guise of a bent-over old woman, is an apt illustration of how deeply anti-Semitism was embedded in the Church's attitudes.

"We Remember" is remiss in not connecting its members' sinful actions relative to Jews much more directly to the anti-Semitic perspectives presented within the tradition of Catholic worship and education. Pope John Paul II's recognition of anti-Semitism in Christian history, in his plea for forgiveness for anti-Semitism and failures on the part of Catholics with respect to other peoples and cultures, represents a bit of an advance on "We Remember." The significance of this papal statement regarding anti-Semitism was enhanced through the Pope's gesture of inserting a copy of it into the Western Wall during his historic visit to Jerusalem.

The second problematic area of "We Remember" is its contention that there were *no* substantive links between Christian anti-Judaism (a hostility toward the Jewish religion) or Christian anti-Semitism (the attempt to marginalize Jews and make them miserable as a people, a process that sometimes led to the death of the Jews) on the one hand, and the anti-Semitism propagated by Nazi ideology, which encouraged the complete annihilation of the Jewish people, on the other. There is some basis to the distinction, but "We Remember" has overdrawn it. Certainly there is a body of scholarly opinion that would posit too direct a line between classical Christian anti-Judaism and anti-Semitism and the fundamental theories of the Third Reich. Nazi ideology, however, is in the final analysis something quite beyond the most gruesome forms of traditional anti-Judaism and anti-Semitism. Important Jewish and Christian scholars have acknowledged this, and it is a view to which I have subscribed in my own writings on the Holocaust (Pawlikowski, 2000; 2001).

"We Remember" does the Church the service of reminding Christians that classical Christian anti-Judaism and anti-Semitism differ significantly from Nazi ideology. Christian anti-Judaism and anti-Semitism by themselves would not have generated the Holocaust. But "We Remember" leaves the distinct impression that there was no inherent connection between Nazi ideology relative to the Jews and classical Christian anti-Judaism and anti-Semitism. This is basically false. Among Europe's Christian population, Christian anti-Judaism and anti-Semitism had everything to do with widespread acquiescence and even collaboration with the Nazi policy devoted to the destruction of the Jews. I like to speak of classical Christian anti-Judaism and anti-Semitism as providing a *seedbed* for Nazism. Nazi ideologues drew upon classical anti-Jewish Catholic Church legislation while developing the laws they would use to dispossess Europe's Jews, and they exploited Catholic-based cultural entities (such as the Oberammergau passion play) to promote Nazi ideology among the masses.

In a May 1998 address to the national meeting of the American Jewish Committee in Washington, D.C., Cardinal Cassidy addressed the criticism that "We Remember" does a disservice by leaving the impression that Christian anti-Semitism played no significant role in the spread of Nazism. He argued that the document does imply that actions of members of the Catholic Church aided the cause of Nazism. As principal author of the text, Cardinal Cassidy's interpretation must be taken seriously. The U.S. Bishops' Conference publication of "We Remember" contains Cardinal Cassidy's interpretive commentary for this very reason. Nonetheless, there remain some troubling points in the Cardinal's address. First, he couples his assertion of Catholic complicity during the Holocaust with an oblique phrase asserting that one should be careful in assessing the motives of Catholic collaborators who assisted the Nazis. I have never believed that there was only one motive impelling the Nazis and their allies to terrorize and murder Jews. But documentary evidence has sufficiently established that the teachings of the Church on Jews and Judaism surely were a key factor enabling the behavior of those who planned and carried out the anti-Semitic policies of the Third Reich.

Cardinal Cassidy's insistence that Catholics played a role in the Holocaust is definitely a step forward, and should help persuade those reading "We Remember" that it is linked to the perspective of Pope John Paul II, who has described anti-Semitism as a sin on more than one occasion, including in his book *Crossing the Threshold* (John Paul II, 1991: 204; 1994), and his introductory letter to "We Remember" (published as an integral part of the document). But Cardinal Cassidy's Washington address does not go far enough in linking the sinful actions of Christians in the Third Reich with the Catholic tradition as such.

The second problematic statement in Cardinal Cassidy's address in Washington involves the witness of Catholics who opposed Nazism. Cardinal Cassidy is perfectly correct in emphasizing that these Catholics—in Holland, France, Poland, Italy, and elsewhere—must be honored for their outstanding moral courage. But, in making this point right after discussing the collaboration of Catholics, he unfortunately leaves the impression, intended or not, that those who rescued or otherwise helped Jews somehow "balanced" the collaborators and bystanders within the Church. No such balance existed within Nazi-era Catholicism or Christianity as a whole.

The final point I would raise about "We Remember" concerns its depiction of Pope Pius XII. Most of this material was added to the text at the insistence of Cardinal Angelo Sodano and came from Fr. Peter Gumpel, S.J., the promoter of the cause of Pius XII for canonization as a saint. I do believe there is definite value in We Remember's insistence that a number of important Jewish leaders during the Nazi era regarded Pius XII in favorable terms. Popular journalism and the legacy of Rolf Hochhuth's play The Deputy (Hochhuth, 1964) have generated a serious misrepresentation of his record. However, we need to take a much more comprehensive look at how Pius XII's contemporaries regarded him. And we need to ask: Did he make saving Jews a high enough priority item? Did he use all available means at his disposal (such as interventions by papal nuncios)? And did he act soon enough? Moreover, there are also some indications that, as Pius XII was rethinking his general outlook on the social order (something evident in his Christmas addresses in the early 1940s), his efforts on behalf of Jewish rescue intensified. This connection has been insufficiently probed to date.

"We Remember" seems to imply that Pius XII's response to the Jews' coming under attack by the Nazis was unquestionably positive. This is simply not the case, but we need to know a lot more before a final assessment of the man can be made. In sum, new scholarly investigations of Pius XII's record should be pursued in earnest. The Church's moral integrity will not permit anything but sound scholarship in this regard (Pawlikowski, 2002).

One general conclusion has emerged so far from scholarly studies on Pius XII. Pius appears to have been profoundly committed to what we can term a diplomatic, rather than a prophetic, vision of the Church. In such a vision diplomatic channels, rather than public pronouncements, assume primary importance in achieving results. Part of Pius's profound commitment to the diplomatic church model was the result of his desire to preserve Catholicism as an institutional force against the onslaught, as he saw it, of Bolshevism and liberalism. His concern about liberalism is not as well known as his antipathy toward Bolshevism. But Pius, until the 1940s, was a fervent believer and participant in the century-long struggle of the Catholic Church against the growing power of the liberal political order in Western Europe. Pius, as well as many of his allies in the Church (as well as many in the Protestant churches), saw the so-called Berlin culture as a fundamental threat to the continuation of a European civilization in which Christianity would set the moral, cultural, and even political tone for societies. In some ways, Pius took this liberal "threat" more seriously than even Bolshevism because it was subtler and because it was stronger in Western Europe.

Pius XII's and the Vatican's conduct during the Nazi era provides Catholics with extremely valuable reference points as today's Church confronts difficult new social situations, especially those in which genocide looms as a possibility. It seems that the Catholic Church, consciously or not, is beginning to learn from the failings of its policy of reserve during the 1930s and 1940s. Challenges in the last decade to unjust regimes in South Africa, Malawi, the Philippines, and elsewhere, plus the forthright manner in which the February 1989 Pontifical Commission for Justice and Peace statement condemned apartheid, anti-Semitism, and anti-Zionism by name, attest to a decided movement away from the public caution so evident during the papacy of Pius XII. Certainly the framers of "We Remember" were in a position to examine that caution in great detail. But when they did not do so, a great opportunity was lost to provide Catholics—and other Christians as well— with the means to ponder how religious institutions should respond when human dignity is under attack in massive fashion. While the diplomatic model of the Church has not totally disappeared in Catholic circles, there now appear clear signs that the Church is increasingly beginning to forsake this model to speak out publicly when human life is threatened. Speaking out on such matters unquestionably carries some measure of risk for the Church's institutional well-being. In some cases, such as those of Argentina and Rwanda (as we shall see shortly), it has failed to take this risk. But in the situations cited above, it has shown willingness to make defense of human life an absolute priority whatever the risk to its institutional well-being.

There are other issues that "We Remember" could have highlighted with respect to the Holocaust that would contribute to an overarching theology against genocide. The first is the realization that violent religious language greatly contributes to "softening" a society for genocide. The turnabout in Christian language relative to Jews after Vatican II represents a remarkable transformation of social imagery that could be a model for other social situations. Religion remains a powerful force in most current societies. If religious language in a given society continues to demean people who do not share the dominant faith system, and even denies them full rights of citizenship, it certainly opens the door for physical assaults on such groups in times of social tension. Contrariwise, positive language about the "religious other" can serve as a barrier to such assaults.

Religion also has a role to play in insuring that groups in society are not "neutralized" in terms of their fundamental humanity. Some years ago the Holocaust scholar Henry Friedlander showed some parallels between the neutral language in reporting daily death counts in the Nazi extermination camps and the language used by the U.S. military in reporting Vietnamese casualties during the Vietnam War (Friedlander, 1980). Religion must always fight against such neutralization, even of an enemy, for if neutralization of particular groups in society is allowed a foothold, it exposes these groups to the possibility of more violent attacks that again, in times of social crises, can turn into genocide or near-genocidal actions against them.

Finally, "We Remember" might have also taken up the issue of the basic definition of the Church in light of the Holocaust. Within an ecclesiastical framework dominated by self-preservation, as I would argue was the case during the pontificate of Pius XII, Jews, Poles, Sinti and Roma, and other victim groups became, to use the term coined by Nora Levin, "unfortunate expendables" (Levin, 1973: 693). Polish-American historian Richard Lukas (1986: 16) and Catholic historian John Morley (1980) have both noted, for example, strong Polish criticism of Pius XII within Poland itself and from the Polish government-in-exile in London. The fact that human rights were seen as a centerpiece of the discredited liberal tradition associated with the alleged Masonic conspiracy against Christianity only enhanced the Catholic Church's capacity to push concern for individual victims to the periphery, or even beyond the edge, of moral concern.

In light of the experience of the Holocaust, any authentic notion of ecclesiology must make human rights a central component. The vision of the Church that must direct post-Holocaust Christian thinking is one in which the survival of all persons is integral to the authentic survival of the Church itself. "Unfortunate expendables" must disappear from authentic ecclesial self-definition. Jews, Poles, the Roma, homosexuals, and the disabled should not have been viewed as "unfortunate expendables" during the Nazi period—and there is no place for any similar classification today. There is no way for Christianity, or any other religious tradition, to survive meaningfully if it allows the death or suffering of other people to become a by-product of its efforts for self-preservation. For Catholics the *Document on Religious Liberty* from Vatican II can serve as a foundational resource, for it argued for the basic dignity of every human being expressed in the freedom of conscience, even to the point of protecting the right not to believe. Human dignity, not right belief, becomes the fundamental cornerstone of any just society. All other identities, though important, become secondary. They can never be used as the basis for a massive assault on human life.

As for the wider issue of genocide, there is no official Catholic document that parallels "We Remember." The 1989 Pontifical Justice and Peace Commission's document touches upon the issue of genocide, especially in its condemnation of apartheid in South Africa, and there have been occasional statements from the Vatican legations at the United Nations in New York and Geneva at the time of important United Nations discussions relative to mass human killings. But the Catholic Church *as an institution* has thus far not undertaken a comprehensive examination of the genocide questions, nor of its possible involvement in the fostering of a genocidal mentality in certain countries.

Certainly the most challenging situation for the Catholic Church in terms of genocide has to be Rwanda, which in terms of percentage was home to the largest Catholic population in Africa. Several years ago, the Synod for Africa convened by Pope John Paul II in Rome brought together hundreds of bishops from throughout the continent to discuss fundamental questions facing the Church. Yet only a few voices were heard regarding the role of the Catholic Church in the genocide, and this issue was not raised in the final report from the synod. Catholic leaders, whether at the Vatican or in Rwanda, have said little publicly regarding the brutality that consumed the country since the end of the genocide. When they have spoken, it has usually been in defense of a particular priest or nun charged with crimes against humanity by the post-genocide international tribunal.

Without question, any discussion of Catholic responsibility during the genocide in Rwanda must be done carefully. No one wants a repeat of the exaggerated statements made by some authors, such as John Cornwell (Cornwell, 1999) or Daniel Goldhagen (Goldhagen, 2002), regarding the role of Pius XII and the Vatican during the Holocaust. But an honest accounting based on solid scholarship is a moral requirement. The Church cannot serve as moral leader in other areas of injustice if it fails to undertake a thorough investigation of its actions, or lack thereof, during the Nazi period and during the Rwandan genocide. Individual Catholic leaders deserve support if charged by the international tribunal. But this cannot be official Catholicism's only response to mass murder in a country where the Church had apparently established deep roots.

Scholarly studies on the Rwandan genocide are still at a relatively early stage (Adelman and Suhrke, 1999; Melson, 2003). This is especially the case with regard to the role of the Church. But they are beginning to appear, and even if one grants some exaggeration, the accounts are far from pretty. There is growing evidence that the Church in Rwanda, though its leaders sometimes condemned the genocide, did so in a manner that had racist tones, i.e., in ways that give an impression of Hutu superiority in terms of the annihilation of roughly 80 percent of the minority Tutsi population. Some priests directly cooperated with the genocidal effort by turning over Tutsi who, on occasion, had sought refuge in the cities. And the Church leadership largely remained silent. This was no doubt due to the fact that, as Timothy Longman has pointed out, "the churches were integrated into wider structures of power that allowed wealth and privilege to become concentrated in the hands of a select few" (Longman, 2003). Though Catholic and Protestant leaders did sign a joint statement calling for an end to the massacres, this letter contained no strong condemnation of what was taking place and never referred to the situation as genocide. An indication of how deeply intertwined the Catholic leadership was with the government responsible for the genocide is to be seen in the flight of many of these church leaders out of Rwanda in advance of the collapse of the government responsible for the massacres.

On a day-to-day basis, the Church leadership provided little or no moral guidance for the Catholic community, particularly the Hutus, who carried out most of the genocidal activities. This lack of moral guidance enabled many Catholics to participate in the genocide with little or no compunction. At times, it appears people stopped to pray at churches on their way to slaughter Tutsi. In one parish in the town of Nagoma, a Tutsi priest hidden by a Hutu colleague told of Catholic Hutu coming to their parish and demanding the celebration of Mass. "People came to mass each day to pray," he reported, "then they went out to kill" (Longman, 2003: 157).

In my judgment, the Catholic Church in Rwanda, with the assistance of the Vatican, would contribute to the overall moral integrity of the Catholic Church by undertaking a comprehensive and honest accounting of the genocide in that nation, just as the diocese of Lyon, France, did a full accounting some years ago of its activities during the Nazi era. Trying to bury the issue only weakens the Church's moral credibility. Such an investigation could become the basis for a statement on genocide by the Vatican that would also lay out guidelines for the conduct of church leaders and ordinary members during a time of massive human brutality.

Pope John Paul II, in his first papal encyclical on the redemption of humanity, described human rights as integral to any full understanding of Christology. One cannot know Christ and go out and engage in massive human brutality. It is clear that the Church of Rwanda did not know Christ during the period of genocide. And the Vatican did little to challenge Rwandan Catholics during this period of moral darkness. Only an honest accounting of what went wrong—and why—can provide some healing in the face of this moral failure.

BIBLIOGRAPHY

Adelman, Howard, and Astri Suhrke (eds.) (1999). *The Path of Genocide: The Rwanda Crisis from Uganda to Zaire.* New Brunswick, N.J.: Transaction Publishers.

Banki, Judith H. (2001). "Vatican II Revisited" in Judith H. Banki, and John T. Pawlikowski (eds.), *Ethics in the Shadow of the Holocaust: Christian and Jewish Perspectives.* Franklin, Wisc.: Sheed & Ward, 211–13.

Banki, Judith H., and John T. Pawlikowski (eds.) (2001). *Ethics in the Shadow of the Holocaust: Christian and Jewish Perspectives.* Franklin, Wisc.: Sheed & Ward.

Bartov, Omer, and Phyllis Mack (eds.) (2003). *In God's Name: Genocide and Religion in the Twentieth Century.* New York: Berghahn Books.

Bemporad, Jack, John T. Pawlikowski, and Joseph Sievers (eds.) (2000). *Good and Evil after Auschwitz: Ethical Implications for Today.* Hoboken, N.J.: Ktav.

Cornwell, John (1999). *Hitler's Pope: The Secret History of Pius XII.* New York: Viking.

Flannery, Edward H. (1965). *The Anguish of the Jews: Twenty-three Centuries of Anti-Semitism.* New York: Macmillan.

Friedlander, Henry (1980). "The Manipulation of Language" in Henry Friedlander, and Sybil Milton (eds.), *The Holocaust: Ideology, Bureaucracy, and Genocide. The San Jose Papers.* Millwood, N.Y.: Kraus International, 103–13.

Gellately, Robert, and Ben Kiernan (eds.) (2003). *The Specter of Genocide: Mass Murder in Historical Perspective.* Cambridge, Mass.: Cambridge University Press.

Goldhagen, Daniel (2002). *A Moral Reckoning: The Role of the Catholic Church in the Holocaust and Its Unfulfilled Duty of Repair.* New York: Alfred A. Knopf.

Hochhuth, Rolf (1964). *The Deputy.* New York: Grove Press.

John Paul II (1991). *Crossing the Threshold of Hope.* New York: Alfred A. Knopf.

—— (1994). *The Way to Christ: Spiritual Exercises.* New York: HarperOne.

Krauss, Samuel (1995). *The Jewish-Christian Controversy: From the Earliest Times to 1789.* Edited and revised by William Horbury. Tubingen, Germany: J. C. B. Mohr.

Lespinay, Charles de (2003). "The Churches and the Genocide in the East African Great Lakes Region" in Omer Bartov, and Phyllis Mack (eds.), *In God's Name: Genocide and Religion in the Twentieth Century.* New York: Berghahn Books, 161–79.

Levin, Nora (1973). *The Holocaust: The Destruction of European Jewry, 1933–1945.* New York: Schocken Books.

Longman, Timothy (2003). "Christian Churches and Genocide in Rwanda," in Omer Bartov, and Phyllis Mack (eds.), *In God's Name: Genocide and Religion in the Twentieth Century.* New York: Berghahn Books, 139–60.

Lukas, Richard (1986). *Forgotten Holocaust: The Poles under German Occupation, 1939–1944.* Lexington: University of Kentucky Press.

Melson, Robert (2003). "Modern Genocide in Rwanda: Ideology, Revolution, War, and Mass Murder in an African State," in Robert Gellately, and Ben Kiernan (eds.), *The Specter of Genocide: Mass Murder in Historical Perspective.* Cambridge, Mass.: Cambridge University Press, 325–38.

Modras, Ronald E. (1994). *The Catholic Church and Antisemitism: Poland, 1933–1939.* Chur, Switzerland: Harwood Academic Publishers.

—— (2001). "Jewish Citizenship in Emerging Nation States: Christian Anti-Semitism, Nationalism, and Nazi ideology," in Judith H. Banki, and John T. Pawlikowski (eds.), *Ethics in the Shadow of the Holocaust: Christian and Jewish Perspectives.* Franklin, Wisc.: Sheed & Ward, 81–101.

Morley, John (1980). *Vatican Diplomacy and the Jews during the Holocaust, 1939–1943.* New York: Ktav.

NCCB [National Conference of Catholic Bishops] (1998). *Catholics Remember the Holocaust.* Washington, D.C.: United States Catholic Conference.

O'Brien, Daniel J., and Thomas A. Shannon (eds.) (2002). *Catholic Social Thought: The Documentary Heritage.* Maryknoll, N.Y.: Orbis Books.

Pawlikowski, John T. (1998). "Liberal Democracy, Human Rights and the Holocaust." *Catholic International,* 9(10): 454–58.

—— (2000). "God: The Foundational Ethical Questions after the Holocaust," in Jack Bemporad, John T. Pawlikowski, and Joseph Sievers (eds.), *Good and Evil after Auschwitz: Ethical Implications for Today.* Hoboken, N.J.: Ktav, 53–66.

—— (2001). "The Holocaust: Its Challenges for Understanding Human Responsibility," in Judith H. Banki, and John T. Pawlikowski (eds.), *Ethics in the Shadow of the Holocaust: Christian and Jewish Perspectives.* Franklin, Wisc.: Sheed & Ward, 261–89.

———. (2002). "The Papacy of Pius XII: The Known and the Unknown," in Carol Rittner, and John Roth (eds.), *Pope Pius XII and the Holocaust* London: Leicester University Press, 56–69.

Perry, Marvin, and Frederick M. Schweitzer (2002). *Antisemitism: Myth and Hate from Antiquity to the Present.* New York: Palgrave/Macmillan.

Rittner, Carol, and John K. Roth (eds.) (2002). *Pope Pius XII and the Holocaust.* London: Leicester University Press.

Schreckenberg, Heinz (1996). *The Jews in Christian Art: An Illustrated History.* New York: Continuum.

Schreiter, Robert J. (2001). "The Church as Sacrament and as Institution: Responsibility and Apology in Ecclesial Documents," in Judith H. Banki, and John T. Pawlikowski (eds.), *Ethics in the Shadow of the Holocaust: Christian and JewishPerspectives.* Franklin, Wisc.: Sheed & Ward, 51–59.

17

Terror Out of Zion: Making Sense of Scriptural Teaching

Zev Garber

BY WAY OF INTRODUCTION

Let me begin by acknowledging that I have a problem with scholars who assume, adjudicate, and adjure that divine will not human propensity is the influential force that wreaks terror in the Holy Land of Israel. I was born in the Bronx, New York City, in the early 1940s to European-born, Yiddish-speaking parents, who early on exposed me to the Jewish traditional way of life, exemplified by yeshiva learning and Orthodox Jewish observance. My moral banner was hoisted at Yeshiva Rabbi Israel Salanter in the Bronx by refugee rabbis, survivors of the *Shoah* (Holocaust), who taught me in the spirit of *musar* (moral deliberation) that God's covenant with the Jewish people is absolute and eternal—and that the mission of the Jews is to apply ethical monotheism to everyone everywhere at all times and under all circumstances. The Covenant at Sinai, enshrined in truth and justice, forged a "covenant-people," whose ideals will lead to a unity of peace among the peoples of the world. "I am the Lord, I have called you in righteousness, I have taken you by the hand and kept you; I have given you as a covenant to the people, a light unto the nations" (Isaiah 42:6). Then followed several years of high school at Manhattan Talmudic Academy (affiliated with Yeshiva University), where I was immersed in Jewish sacred texts, traditionally divided into Scriptures and Talmud (Garber, 1994c; 1994d). In a classroom in Washington Heights, I was initiated into a virtual Jewish textual experience stretching back 2,000 years through modern and medieval Europe to ancient Babylonia and Palestine.

In the course of my intensive Jewish day school education, I sang the
triumphant song of Moses and the Israelites at the crossing of the Sea of
Reeds (Exodus 15) and the victorious hymn of Deborah and Barak (Judges
5); with Joshua and the Judges I conquered the land of Canaan; I relished
the empire and temple building of David and Solomon; I swam in the sea
of the Talmud; I traversed the Code of Maimonides (1135–1204), the Code
of Joseph Karo (the *Shulhan Arukh*) (1488–1575), the biblical commentaries of Rashi (1040–1105) and Ibn Ezra (1092/3–1167), and the philosophy
and poetry of Judah Halevy (1075–1141). I was dazzled by the tomes of
responsa (replies to inquiries seeking the wisdom of Jewish law) and *hid-
dushim* (critically innovative interpretations to Jewish law); I was mystified
by the hidden wisdom of Kabbalah; I relished the novellas of the *musarists*
and Hasidic masters; I felt the throes of the *Shoah*; and I rejoiced in Zion
reborn and redeemed. Succinctly speaking, my formative years engendered
and nourished in me collective self-respect, pride of heritage, social justice,
and the meaning of life, sacrifice, and death as a proud Jew for the sake of
Heaven and humankind.

My parochial education was religious and spiritual, but at the university
(Hunter College, N.Y., 1958–1962) and graduate school in California
(UCLA, 1962–1965; USC, 1965–1968), I learned to be academic and critical. For example, I read rabbinic passages not against broad history, but as
self-contained literary constructions within a literary genre. By this method,
I not only read about rabbinics but also confronted the process itself. This
enabled me to discover the wisdom of the rabbinic dictum, *'ein muqtam
u-memuchar ba-torah* ("there is neither before nor after in the word of the
Lord"), meaning that for the Sages, all of the Torah (written and oral), in
all periods, is of one piece. So my lectures, teaching, and writing on Jewish
matters are more historiosophy than historiography—paradigmatic history
rather than pragmatic history, though the former is tied to the latter. In
short, for me, the continuity of the Jews lies more in actual ethnic memory
than factual historical details. Faith knowledge and its corollary, "mythiciz-
ing history," was and is the way of Torah, whose teachings observant Jews
believe and live by (Garber, 1994b).

My approach to scholarship is therefore grounded in the language,
text, and culture of the Jewish canon yet grafted onto the tree of Western
knowledge. Such an alliance requires a learning and wisdom that is beyond
the pale of Western categories of thought. It is distressing to read seasoned
scholars' commentary on Jewish atrocities based on the Holy Writ, when
these authors have no knowledge of Jewish textual tradition and interpretation (Glick, 1994). It is painful to see how bias, resentment, competitive-
ness, and blameful ignorance of Jewish law and lore fester among Israelis
vis-à-vis Palestinians on the land. All this suggests that we urgently need
some fresh thinking on terror in the name of the Lord that goes beyond the

politicians, professors, and pundits who comment on the Israeli-Palestinian crisis at this moment in time.

BLOOD IN ZION'S NAME

In Zionist lore, the religio-mystical philosophy of Rav Abraham Isaac Kook (1865–1935), grounded in kabbalistic particularity ("The People of Israel, the Torah, and the Land of Israel are One") though soaring to heights of universality ("the whole earth, and all therein, is His creation"), is widely admired. Kook's Zionism is expressed in transnatural metaphors: love of God is fully demonstrated in the love for all God's creation; the impurity of the Exile, a cosmic distortion, is corrected by the return to Zion, a cosmic restoration; and the efforts of religious and secular Jews on the land to make Zion a fit place in which to live, is an outpouring of divine "Light unto the Nations," perfecting the world (*tikkun 'olam*) through reconciliation, harmony, and peace. Rav Kook's intellectual sincerity and piety remains a giant step in bridging the chasm between secular Zionism and the religious tradition.

On the night of 4 November 1995, Yigal Amir, a religious Jew, fired three bullets into the body of Israel's prime minister, Yitzhak Rabin, shattering a utopian facade and exposing an Israeli society where conflicting political, cultural, and religious ideologies split over fundamental issues of consciousness, identity, and peace. Friends and foes of the slain prime minister united to condemn this horrendous crime as completely unacceptable to Israel and the nations. Few voices were heard in support of Amir's actions, and what faint support he garnered from the "right-wing religious fanatics" was correctly denounced by the religious ideologues of the Religious Zionists and Settlement Movement. Representative of the majority reaction were the remarks of Professor Moshe Kaveh, president and rector of Bar-Ilan University, at the memorial assembly on the campus of Bar-Ilan University (October 24, 1996): "The assassination of the Prime Minister (one year ago) was a base attempt to destroy a people, a history, a cultural heritage, a faith. Our Declaration of Independence outlines a vision of common destiny and common fate; the horrifying gunfire stamped out a life, and sought to extinguish a dream."

The murder of Prime Minister Rabin generated a plethora of articles, essays, and public comments. Biographers such as Robert Slater (1993) and Dan Kurzman (1998) write reverently about Rabin and accept the official version of his death. Staff writers of *Haaretz*, *Jerusalem Post*, and the *Jerusalem Report* treat only an aspect of the assassination or deal with the making of a murderer. Israeli journalists Michael Karpin and Ina Friedman's (1998) *Murder in the Name of God: The Plot to Kill Yitzhak Rabin* surveys the full range of the nationalist expression and activity, concluding that the assassin was influenced by a wide incitement campaign from the religio-nationalist camp.

However, Barry Charmish's (2000) *Who Killed Yitzhak Rabin?* moves the argument away from why the prime minister was eliminated to how he was murdered. His questions about the three shots fired, the composition of the bullets, the angle of trajectory, and the points of entry into Rabin's body are noted and discussed by David Morrison (2000) in his book *Lies: Israel's Secret Service and the Rabin Murder.* Morrison raises a number of points that he feels the Shamgar Commission, convened to investigate the security lapses that permitted the murder of Rabin, failed to investigate properly. Why the insufficient security around Rabin? Why were shouts of "blanks" and "exercise" heard? Why the discrepancy in reporting Rabin's real wounds and the seeming fault and negligence in medical preparedness? Why the conflicting conclusions in the autopsy report? Who altered the testimony on the finding of Amir's gun? How to explain conflicting eyewitness accounts? Why the obtuse answers to the role played by agent-provocateur Avishai Raviv?

The tendency to omit evidence, alter facts, and sanitize Shabak (Israel's Secret Service) actions points to a serious obstruction of justice. For Morrison, this rush to justice so soon after an "Amir-alone" conviction, followed by governmental and journalistic silence, should be unsettling to all who believe in a democratic Israel.

The murder of a sitting prime minister of Israel is horrible, and the unwillingness of responsible government leaders to investigate all leads and uncover all involved individuals, in and out of office, is dastardly. In addition, a shocking statistic has surfaced: at the time of the assassination and in Israel today, 10 percent of the Israeli public is willing to engage in illegal nonviolent means and another 10 percent is willing to engage in illegal violent measures to protest unacceptable government policies. Why is this so? And is Israel's administrative structure safe for democracy in light of the events leading to and from the first-ever assassination of a prime minister? These are among the questions posed by *The Assassination of Yitzhak Rabin*, edited by Yoram Peri (2000).

Editor Yoram Peri and fourteen contributors from a range of disciplinary viewpoints—historical, psychological, anthropological, political, and cultural—survey the causes, countdown to, meaning of, and fallout from the assassination; analyze media, rhetoric, and public reaction, from Israel's radical right to the voices of Israeli youth to the reaction of the Arab population; construct and deconstruct the grief and mourning; and ask what lessons can be learned from this cowardly and ghastly act. The answers given can neither definitively satisfy all questions nor calm the hurt nor comfort the loss nor silence the political protest of a nation distraught by an unprecedented act of homegrown violence.

Nonetheless, the volume's central theme is disturbing: the assassination showed how militant nationalist-clerical groups can usurp the will of the people, hit an enlightened Western democratic state broadside, and cause it to languish as an ethnocentric, xenophobic backwater. Referring to Rabin as "traitor, "informer," and "collaborator" advanced a process of defamation and vilification that created the dangerous atmosphere of permissive assassination. Ironically, the book claims, the killing of Rabin, portrayed in the biblical terms of scapegoat and sacrifice, halted the descent to political violence and possibly civil war. The *Realpolitik* is explosive: Israel is surrounded by enemies poised to obliterate her, and there is seemingly no dialogue of compromise on the home front between the Israeli left, which sees the West Bank as occupied territory, and the Israeli right, which views Judea and Samaria (i.e., West Bank) as liberated territories.

Volatile language that excuses unconscionable acts of violence is found in the literature and rhetoric of extreme right-wing radicals and should be condemned in the strongest terms. But neither are liberal intellectuals strangers to intolerant talk or behavior—for example, making light of the revelation that extreme right-wing leader Avishai Raviv was an agent-provocatur of the General Security Services. Further, labeling the right wing as fascist or suggesting that the "ultra-Orthodox" settlers are messianic and not pragmatic is not entirely fair. Many religious Zionists are ethical and commanded to be so by the Halakhah (Jewish law) that molds their lives. Alas, both groups have misused the moment of opportunity, converting necessary dialogue into endless disputation and creating an endless cycle of charges and countercharges.

How can peacemakers penetrate Israel's perpetual dilemma—the collision between the classic Zionist vision of a democratic, humane Jewish state as a refuge for the oppressed de facto, and religious-nationalist Zionism, which demands theocracy and Jewish occupation of the entire biblical Land of Israel de jure? A possible solution lies in vigilant civil discourse that preempts *sin'at chinam* (hatred without reason) by all means necessary and not necessary managing and creating so-called spin after the crisis.

The clarion call from Zion teaches that the communal experience be expressed in righteousness, justice, and moral action. A presently divided Israel requires it as does a united one. There is no alternative.

THE COMMANDMENT OF *HEREM*

The Torah of Moses, in whose image Jewish ethnicity and religion are formed, is a system derived from contact between the human and the divine that instructs by means of narrative, aphorisms, laws, commandments, and statutes, providing rules of life for individuals, nature, and society; the goal provided by the Torah is to achieve spiritual and temporal happiness in the full realization of the divine will. Yet the Giver of the Ten Commandments and the *Shema* (Deuteronomy 6:4; see, also, Leviticus 19:8; Matthew 22:36–40; Mark 12:28–38; and Luke 10:25–28) is the grantor of genocide against the Seven Nations of Canaan: "(W)hen the Lord your God gives them over to you and you defeat them; then you must utterly destroy them. Make no covenant with them and show them no mercy" (Deuteronomy 7:2 and 20:17). How to explain this warrant for genocide, which scholars across the disciplines and denominational spectrum see as the underbelly of Israelite religion and a feeder to contemporary Israelis to kill from within and without in the name of God?

The commandment to annihilate the Seven Nations (Hittites, Girgashites, Amorites, Canaanites, Peruzites, Hivites, and Jebusites) is intrinsically connected to the biblical doctrine of *herem*, a legal injunction forbidding contact with a human, animal, or thing either because it is proscribed as an abomination to God (*to'evah*), or because it is irrevocably consecrated to Him in a private or communal vow as *qadosh* ("holy"). The latter are normally seen as priestly offerings; the former, including defeated enemies and enemy towns sworn as *herem* are utterly destroyed (Leviticus 27:28; Numbers 18:14; Ezekiel 44:29; Numbers 21:1–3). It appears that *herem* was administered differently to entities outside and inside the pre-exilic Israelite community, for example, the destruction of Jericho, Ai, Hazor, and Zephat versus the punishment of the people of Jabesh-Gilead and the Benjaminites (Joshua 6:17ff., 8:26, 10:39, 11:13; Judges 1:17, 20–21). Exceptionally severe is the divine admonition against Amalek, whom the Lord swore to "utterly blot out"; Moses vowed "war with Amalek from generation to generation" (Exodus 17:14; Garber 1994a). There are situations of devastation and dedication where *herem* is clear-cut but the terminology is lacking; e.g., Moses' instruction to the Levites to kill the worshippers of the golden calf, and the war against Midian described as the "Lord's vengeance on Midian" (Exodus 32:27; Numbers 31:3).

The negativity of *herem* goes back to the hoary origins of Israelite ethnic religion: "You shall have no other gods beside me" and "he that sacrifices unto the gods, save unto the Lord only, shall be utterly destroyed" (Exodus 20:3; Deuteronomy 5:7; Exodus 22:19). In addition to passages proscribing for idolatry and apostasy, there are religious ground rules for wars of settlement: invoke the favor of God to guarantee victory on the battlefield. Thus, in desperate times, the land-hungry Israelites enlisted the God of Israel as their standard bearer in the conquest of the Canaanite lands, called the Promised Land, which, together with male circumcision, represented the virtual Abrahamic covenantal promise of possession (Genesis 17:7–8). This is reflected in the narratives of Deuteronomy and Joshua, which speak of the indigenous populations as enemy *herem*, and thus fair game in wars of aggression and attrition. Deuteronomy speaks of utter conquests in Transjordan where man, woman, and child are put to death but the livestock and other assets are left intact (Numbers 21:24; Deuteronomy 2:34, 3:6, 10:28–40, 11:10ff.). Yet, in the severest type of *herem*, livestock are killed and burnt as an offering to the Lord and no spoils are taken (Joshua 6–7; Judges 21:5–11; I Samuel 15:1–9).

Meanwhile, the decree against the Seven Nations reflects a bilateral legislation. Exodus law speaks of their dispossession and expulsion lest they cause the Israelites to depart from the way of the God of Israel (Exodus 23:27–33, 32:2–3, 34:11ff.; Numbers 33:50–56). Deuteronomy adds extermination and regulates it as a religious duty, no doubt because these major populations of the Promised Land threatened the purity of the Israelite faith and nation (Thomas, 1958: 197).

BEYOND BIBLICAL VIOLENCE

At the third international conference "Remembering for the Future 2000" (Oxford and London, 16–23 July 2000), Bruce Zuckerman (University of Southern California) and I presented a paper that explored the nature of an extreme, political act—the Rabin assassination—from a biblical perspective (Garber and Zuckerman, 2003). When Yigal Amir assassinated Yitzhak Rabin, he conceived of himself as God's agent, acting with divine sanction to save God's chosen people from the disastrously wrong path down which Israel's leaders—and especially Rabin—would have led them. The Torah holds ample precedent, and potential sanction, for such extremism. In particular, the prophetic literature depicts a small, extremist minority—sometimes even a minority of one—opposing the political establishment with extreme words intended to bring about extreme action.

We tend to forget how extreme and distasteful the words of the prophets were to their contemporary audiences—indeed, how basically unreasonable they were. That the prophets of the Bible spoke in the name of God, that the views they expressed have been vindicated by history, are now the "givens" of Judaism. What, in biblical times, was extremist, marginal, prophetic rhetoric has become, in our time, the sacred mainstream. One may well suspect that Yigal Amir saw himself in a prophetic perspective: misunderstood, even vilified, by his contemporaries, but certain of his divine mission, which the longer perspective of history will, through God's will, eventually vindicate.

But how are we to judge? How do we know if someone's radical views and deeds have divine authority? What distinguishes a prophet from a crazed extremist? This is precisely the dilemma that the priest Amaziah faced when he was confronted by his own extremist, the prophet Amos—a

radical who declared that God sanctioned the overthrow of the government and its leader by violent means. Amos claimed that he was a prophet,
speaking in the name of God; but Amaziah was not sure. Utilizing this
biblical model as a basis of comparison, and in accordance with talmudic
and halakhic parameters, we examined Yigal Amir and his contemporary,
extreme act "in the name of God." What clues do the Bible and Jewish law
leave us by which to judge whether his were the tragically misguided actions of one man on behalf of himself or the inspired actions of a prophetic
agent on behalf of God? Simply put but deeply perplexing: Is divinely sanctioned violence (conceived or perceived) a product of chance, or is it fated
by historical inevitability? If the former, does the effect follow a necessary
cause? If the latter, what will prevent a morally repugnant act, by choice or
by obligation, from being repeated in the Land of Israel? How to answer the
national-religious fervor among many of the settlers in Judea and Samaria,
who view the Palestinian population as the embodiment of the evil Amalek
and the Seven Nations?

The answer lies in the conduct of warfare spelled out in Deuteronomy 20.
This chapter calls for trust in the Lord during war and delineates protocols
of holy war in three sections: (1) verses 1–9, stipulating exemption from
battle for individuals who have not completed significant life-orienting
acts that ensure continuity of life (e.g., the newly married) and prohibiting
exemptions for the cowards, the powerful, and aspiring martyr; (2) verses
10–18, laying out rules of engagement in the capture of heathen cities; and
(3) verses 19–20, prohibiting the felling of fruit-bearing trees, for "are trees
in the field human beings that they should come under siege from you?"
(Deuteronomy 20:19).

Verses 16–18 are of particular interest for they speak of a total ban against
the nations of Canaan and the total destruction (*hakharem takharimem*) of
"the Hittitites and the Amorites, the Cannaanites and the Peruzites, the
Hivites and the Jebusites—just as the Lord your God has commanded"
(Deuteronomy 20:17). Verses 10–15 mandate a call for peace before attacking any city that lies outside the land promised, Israel. This reduces the
incentive to go to war and inhibits wanton killing in nonobligatory war
(*milchemet reshut*), for example, war to increase the boundary of Israel or
improve its strategic position. If war ensues and the enemy is defeated, only
combatants may be killed, and women and children are deemed vassalage.
Even in the obligatory war (*milchemet mitzvah*) against the Seven Nations,
decimation was limited to the leadership in the "towns of the kings" who
were seen as a threat to Israel's religion, and was not applicable to the population living in common cities or in the rural area; "this was according to
instruction of Moses" (Joshua 11:10–15).

The end of the ban against the Seven Nations and other indigenous
groups of pre-Israelite Canaan is signaled when Solomon (tenth century

BCE) employed them as slave labor in his building activities (I Kings 5:13–18, 9:20–21). This policy of enforced segregated living continued down to the period of the Babylonian exile of the Judeans (Jews) from the land (586 BCE).

Halakhah follows the lead of Maimonides in determining Torah laws of warfare:

> You cannot wage war against people on earth until you first approach them with an offer of peace; this is true concerning all wars; optional wars as well as wars we are commanded to fight (the war against the Seven Nations and the war against Amalek) if they agree to make peace and accept upon themselves the obligation of the Seven Noachide Laws it is forbidden to kill a single soul; they can be taxed, and they have to accept the jurisdiction of the courts of Israel (Law of Kings 6:1).

War is treated in Jewish tradition as the clash between diverse ideas on basic humanity. The minimum Torah requirement for defining a population as humane is the commitment to live by the Seven Noachide Laws (based on Genesis 9). These laws include the establishment of courts of justice and prohibitions against blasphemy, idolatry, incest, bloodshed, robbery, and eating flesh taken from a living animal. Less than minimal is viewed as uncivilized; still, such peoples are not to be annihilated. Thus, Judaism the religion neither condones nor sanctions assassination, killing, murder, or genocide as glory to God Most High. Acts so done are the way of man not the will of God, merciful creator and judge of all.

A FINAL-BEGINNING WORD

Elsewhere I have written on anti-Semitism as a factor in the current Israeli-Palestinian crisis (Garber, 2002). Here I want to say that the Palestinians are neither the descendants of the Seven Nations of Canaan nor the embodiment of Amalek, and that the settlers in Judea and Samaria are dead wrong in seeing them as such. Likewise pitiful is the position of many Christian Zionists who see the current conflict between Israelis and Palestinians and the Christian West against Islam as a prelude to a final Armageddon (Rev. 16:16). Such a stance gives credence to a divine curse to obliterate the accursed enemy, including the innocents among them. After Auschwitz, this is an unbearable and morally repugnant notion.

If the crimes of militant Palestinian militias Hamas, Islamic Jihad, al-Aqsa Brigade, and splinter groups are judged as unconscionable, it is in this respect: these groups are purveyors of terror. It is a sick society that calls acts of willful murder deeds for the glory of Heaven, and proclaims killers of innocent people heroic freedom fighters. Morally wrong is the logic that equates protection against attack with the brutality of the act; e.g., regarding the assassination of Hamas military chief Salah Shehadeh, who planned the indiscriminate murder of many Israelis, as comparable to the attack at the Hebrew University on 31 July 2002. Worse yet is a rationale that proudly parades children in suicide bomber's clothing and exhibits mothers openly praying that their children be blown up when Jews are killed. Most damaging is to educate the young and the innocent with propaganda advocating hated and killing rather than hope and life. To live free, Palestinians need to break free from the snare of fanatical Palestinianism (Grossman, 1998; Ozick, 2003).

"Genocide in the name of God" reads religion as the cause and genocide as the effect in the seemingly never-ending game of humanity that some call the "cycle of violence." This need not be. At creation, God said, "Let there be light," and at Sinai, he declared, "Choose life:" These are the formulae for cosmos banishing chaos (Genesis 1:3; Deuteronomy 30:19). The alternative is unacceptable and unthinkable.

BIBLIOGRAPHY

Charmish, Barry (2000). *Who Killed Yitzhak Rabin?* Cambridge, Mass.: Brookline Books.

Garber, Zev (2002). "America Attacked and Zion Blamed—Old-New Anti-Semitism: *Fatwa* against Israel." *Shofar*, 20(2): 1–4.

—— (1994a). "Deconstructing Theodicy and Amalekut: A Personal Apologia," in Zev Garber, *Shoah: The Paradigmatic Genocide-Essays in Exegesis and Eisigesis.* Lanham, Md.: University Press of America, 119–36.

—— (1994b). "The Ninety-Three Beit Ya'akov Martyrs: Towards the Making of a Historiosophy," in Zev Garber, *Shoah: The Paradigmatic Genocide—Essays in Exegesis and Eisigesis.* Lanham, Md.: University Press of America, 97–118.

—— (1994c). "Talmud," in John K. Roth (ed.), *Ethics, Vol. 3: Pessimism and Optimism—Zoroastrian Ethics.* Pasadena, Calif.: Salem Press, 872–75.

—— (1994d). "Torah," in John K. Roth (ed.), *Ethics, Vol. 3: Pessimism and Optimism—Zoroastrian Ethics.* Pasadena, Calif.: Salem Press, 852–54.

Garber, Zev, and Bruce Zuckerman (2003). "The Rabin Assassination in the Long View and the Short View: Biblical Radicalism in a Modern Context. *Hakirah*, 1, 69–88.

Glick, Leonard B. (1994). "Religion and Genocide," in Israel W. Charny (ed.), *The Widening Circle of Genocide. Genocide: A Critical Bibliographic Review. Vol. 3.* New Brunswick, N.J.: Transaction Publishers, 43–73.

Grossman, David (1998). "Fifty Is a Dangerous Age: After Half a Century, the Nation Changes in Unexpected Ways." *The New Yorker*, 74(9), 20 April, 55.

Karpin, Michael I., and Ina Friedman (1998). *Murder in the Name of God: The Plot to Kill Yitzhak Rabin.* New York: Metropolitan Books.

Kurzman, Dan (1998). *Soldier of Peace: The Life of Yitzhak Rabin, 1922–1995.* New York: HarperCollins.

Morrison, David (2000). *Lies, Israel's Secret Service and the Rabin Murder.* New York, N.Y., and Jerusalem: Gefen Books.

Ozick, Cynthia (2003). "Where Hatred Trumps Bread: What Does the Palestinian Nation Offer the World? *Wall Street Journal*, 30 June 2003. Available through the Internet at: http://www.opinionjournal.com/editorial/feature.html?id-110003690.

Peri, Yoram (ed.) (2000). *The Assassination of Yitzhak Rabin.* Stanford, Calif.: Stanford University Press.

Roth, John K. (ed.) (1994). *Ethics, Vol. 3: Pessimism and Optimism Zoroastrian Ethics.* Pasadena, Calif.: Salem Press.

Slater, Robert (1993). *Rabin of Israel: Warrior for Peace.* New York: St. Martin's Press.

Thomas, D. Winton. (1958). *Documents from Old Testament Times.* New York: Harper.

18

Rape, Religion, and Genocide: An Unholy Silence

Carol Rittner

Rape is . . . always an intrinsically evil act.

—Catechism of the Catholic Church, #2356

the entire community should . . . help [women] transform
the act of violence into an act of love and acceptance.

—From the text of a letter sent by Pope John Paul II to
Archbishop Vinko Puljic of Sarajevo, 2 February 1993

INTRODUCTION

In 1948, the French philosopher and author Albert Camus addressed a group of Roman Catholic monks at the Dominican Monastery of Latour-Maubourg in Paris. Asked to speak about what "unbelievers" expect of Christians when they confront evil in the world, Camus said that

> What the world expects of Christians is that Christians should speak out, loud and clear, and that they should voice their condemnation in such a way that never a doubt, never the slightest doubt, could rise in the heart of the simplest man. [T]hey should get away from abstraction and confront the blood-stained face history has taken on today. (Camus, 1960: 71)

Camus's words remain disturbingly relevant. The purpose of this chapter is very specific: to ascertain what, if anything, the leadership[1] of the Roman

291

Catholic Church has had to say about the use of rape as a weapon of war and genocide (Saltzman, 2001: 63–64). Has the Church[2] had anything to say about this issue? Has the "great voice . . . in Rome" spoken (Camus, 1960: 71)? Have the bishops, archbishops, or cardinals spoken? What guidance have they given "the faithful" on this matter? What words of compassion have they offered to the victims of rape used as a weapon of war and genocide? What has the male leadership of the Church had to say to male *genocidaires* who use their penises as weapons of war and genocide?

WAR AND GENOCIDE IN THE 1990S

Many commentators (e.g., Elliot, 1972; Horowitz, 1997; Rummel, 1994; Staub, 1989; Totten et al., 2004; Weitz, 2003) would agree that the last years of the twentieth century were difficult ones for humankind generally but particularly savage for women and children. Consider, for example, these statistics: "in World War I, the ratio of military personnel killed to civilians killed was 8:1; in World War II it was 1:1; in the many smaller wars since 1945, the ratio has been 1:8," with the vast majority being women, children, and the elderly (Barstow, 2000: 3). What happened? Why such a dramatic change?

Some[3] think the dramatic change is linked to the concept of "total war," which made its entrance onto the world stage during World War I. Now there is no such thing as a "non-combatant."[4] Everyone from the factory worker to the farmer is a "fair" target of weapons more sophisticated than knives, guns, and conventional bombs. Others (e.g., Tschuy, 1997; Naimark, 2001) think the increase in civilian deaths is linked to an upsurge in deadly ethnic conflicts in various parts of the world where wholesale, deliberate violence is inflicted on entire populations, and the combatants sanction any method or means of warfare, legal or illegal, no matter how horrific. Still others (Barstow, 2000: 3) think it is because of the escalation of "guerrilla conflicts," in which "the main objective is to destroy villages and crops in order to starve out the enemy or force them to flee." Whatever the reasons, what we know is that, since the end of World War II and the Holocaust, more than 250 violent conflicts, wars, and genocides have resulted in 23 million casualties, with women, children, and the elderly suffering disproportionately vis-à-vis combatant and noncombatant casualties. Nowhere has this been more evident than in the former Yugoslavia (1992–1995) and Rwanda (1994), two areas of the world where genocide occurred during the last decade of the twentieth century.

Rwanda, the smallest country in Africa, is one of that continent's most densely populated.[5] At the beginning of the twentieth century, Rwanda was under German colonial control, but, after Germany's defeat in World War

I (1914–1918), the League of Nations handed Belgium colonial control of Rwanda, inhabited by three main ethnic groups: Hutu, comprising about 85 percent of the population, Tutsi, about 12 percent, and Twa (a pygmoid people), about 3 percent of the population. Belgian authorities systematized indirect rule over Rwanda through the Tutsis, who were educated in Catholic missionary-run schools and whom the Belgians considered "ethnically superior" to the other two ethnic groups. The Belgians placed Tutsis in positions of civil and ecclesiastical authority. It was an unjust social system supported by secular and ecclesiastical colonial authorities until well into the 1950s (Rittner et al., 2004: 49–63, 229–49). But a reversal occurred when "the Belgian administration became fearful of the ascendance of the educated Tutsi elite" (Green, n.d.), although Timothy Longman (echoing the British scholar Ian Linden) thinks the reversal happened because, "in the post-war period, a number of missionaries who came to Rwanda were influenced by social-democratic philosophies and became concerned by the plight of the Hutu people who despite constituting more than 80 percent of the population, were entirely excluded from political office and other opportunities for advancement . . . the new progressive priests and their Hutu protégés helped raise the consciousness among the Hutu masses of their exploitation, and in the late 1950s, ethnic tensions increased sharply" (Longman, 2001). What followed was an endless series of bloody conflicts between the displaced Tutsi ethnic minority and the newly privileged Hutu ethnic majority.

By the late 1980s, a generation of Tutsis had grown up in forced exile in countries neighboring Rwanda. They formed a rebel army, the Rwanda Patriotic Front (RPF), and in 1990 the RPF launched a military invasion of Rwanda.[6] Whether in response to this invasion, or simply as a continuation of what had become hateful and often deadly discrimination against the Tutsi population, the increasingly politically extremist Hutu-controlled Rwandese government launched a series of mini-pogroms against Tutsis across Rwanda, with the result that between 1990 and 1993, some 2,000 Tutsis were murdered (Jones, 2006: 237). This proved to be a prelude to the 1994 genocide, which claimed approximately a million lives, overwhelmingly from the Tutsi minority (Farrington, 2004: 93).

Even as Rwanda was awash in ethnic violence, further to the north on the European continent, Yugoslavia, a multiethnic, multinational state composed of Serbs, Croats, Slovenes, Bosnian Muslims, Macedonians, and Albanians, was experiencing its own ethnic tensions. Cobbled together after World War I from the remnants of the disintegrated Ottoman Empire, Yugoslavia had been held together for thirty-five years by Marshal Josep Broz Tito (1892–1980), a Communist strongman of Croat and Slovene background. After Tito's death in 1980, Yugoslavia fractured along ethnic and religious lines. Nationalist leaders like Franjo Tudjman (1922–1999) and Slobodan Milošević (1941–2006), among others, exploited these ethnic and religious rivalries[7] as they jockeyed for positions of power. After Croatia and Slovenia declared their independence from Yugoslavia (June 1991), a bloody war broke out involving the major ethnic-religious groups (Croat Catholics, Bosnian Muslims, and Serb Orthodox Christians). By the time former Yugoslavia had achieved some measure of stability, thousands were dead, hundreds of thousands were displaced, and horrors the world thought it would never again see in Europe were all too evident.

For the first time since the end of World War II and the Holocaust, newspapers and magazines around the world carried photographs of sealed railroad cars carrying desperate people to unknown destinations. Publications such as *Time*, *Newsweek*, and the *Economist* carried photos of skeletal men gazing out from behind barbed wire fences. TV news programs broadcast reports of civilians forced from cities and villages. And Bosnia, the most ethnically heterogeneous of Yugoslavia's republics (43 percent Muslim, 35 percent Orthodox Serb, and 18 percent Roman Catholic Croat) (Power, 2002: 247), was on the verge of being destroyed as a multicultural, multiethnic society: "The Bosnian Serb army—with the active assistance of the Yugoslav Army and paramilitary groups from Serbia proper—began a drive to 'ethnically cleanse' all non-Serbian inhabitants from much of Bosnia. As part of its 'ethnic cleansing' campaign, Bosnian forces used tactics such as siege warfare, systematic persecution involving widespread torture, murder, rape, beatings, harassment, de jure discrimination, intimidation, forced displacement of people, confiscation and destruction of property, and the destruction of cultural objects such as mosques and Catholic churches" (Smith, 2002: 179). Other countries in Europe, unwilling to involve themselves in these bloody and vicious ethnic conflicts, stood by and watched as the dissolution of Yugoslavia "brought genocide back to Europe after nearly half a century" (Jones, 2006: 237). For three long years (1992–1995), people in Europe and beyond could tune into their evening news programs and watch genocide as it happened in parts of Yugoslavia where only a few years before they had watched athletes from around the world compete in the 1984 Winter Olympics.

GENOCIDE

Genocide is as old as history, but it was only in 1944 that humanity had a word for it. That word, "genocide"—from the Greek *genos* (race, tribe) and the Latin *cide* (killing)—was coined by Raphael Lemkin (1900–1959), a Polish Jewish jurist who wanted to describe what he had witnessed, and his family had suffered, in Nazi-dominated Europe. In November 1944 he published his book, *Axis Rule in Occupied Europe*. In that volume he described genocide as a coordinated plan of different actions aimed at the annihilation of a national or ethnic group. After World War II and the Holocaust ended, Lemkin went on to lobby the fledgling United Nations (UN), urging member states to pass the 1948 UN Convention on the Prevention and Punishment of the Crime of Genocide (Rittner, et al., 2002: 209–210). According to Article II of that convention, genocide comprises a range of organized actions,

> . . . committed with intent to destroy, in whole or in part, a national, ethnical, racial or religious group, as such:
>
> (a) Killing members of the group;
> (b) Causing serious bodily or mental harm to members of the group;
> (c) Deliberately inflicting on the group conditions of life calculated to bring about its physical destruction in whole or in part;
> (d) Imposing measures intended to prevent births within the group; and
> (e) Forcibly transferring children of the group to another group.

As is all too obvious, according to Article II of the UN Convention, people can be destroyed by killing, but also by acts short of killing.

SEXUAL VIOLENCE AGAINST WOMEN

For centuries, in times of conflict and violence, women have been raped as an act of violence and a demonstration of power. In the former Yugoslavia, particularly in Croatia and Bosnia, between 1992 and 1995, sexual violence against women was rampant. (Men and boys also were sexually violated, but never as extensively or systematically as were women and girls.) While all sides raped, Serb soldiers and paramilitary groups raped women and girls on a massive scale (Allen, 1996; Gutman, 1993; MacKinnon, 2006; Stiglmayer, 1999). They did so because they wanted to destroy non-Serbs (mostly Bosnian Muslims, but also Croat Catholics). The Serbs raped and sodomized women and girls in an effort aimed at ejecting non-Serbs from territory Serbs claimed or had "conquered" during the ensuing conflict. In Rwanda during the 1994 genocide, sexual violence was ubiquitous. Members of the Hutu extremist militia known as the *interahamwe* committed widespread rape. Their victims were Tutsi women as well as some politically moderate Hutu women (Neuffer, 2002: 271–92; Hatzfield, 2005; Human Rights Watch, 2006; Whitworth, 2006).

In neither Rwanda nor Yugoslavia was the massive rape of women an incidental adjunct to armed conflict. In both countries, rape was a deliberate strategy, and it was organized and systematic (Saltzman, 2000: 63–64, 70–71). In both countries, the *genocidaires* "chose" to rape. There were no mistakes.[8] Men used rape as a weapon to maim, mutilate, and destroy women, and through them the ethnic groups of the women they raped, just as these same men used their machetes and tire chains, their M-16s and grenade launchers, as weapons to maim, mutilate, and murder. In both Rwanda and the former Yugoslavia, men raped and sodomized, spreading HIV-AIDS and other sexually transmitted diseases, and they did so with purpose.

In Rwanda, thousands of Tutsi women were sexually violated in the most sadistic and brutal manner imaginable. Genocidaires not only raped, they sodomized women, raping them with objects such as sharpened sticks or gun barrels, holding them in sexual slavery for days and weeks, sexually mutilating them (Human Rights Watch, 1996: 39). René Degni-Segui, the UN Special *Rappateur* on Rwanda after the genocide, said that "Calculating backward from the number of pregnancies caused by rape . . . at least 250,000 women—and as many as 500,000—[were] raped in Rwanda in 1994" (Neuffer, 2002: 276). The exact number of women raped by *genocidaires* during the 1994 genocide will never be fully known, but human rights observers and medical workers think that during the 100 days of genocide in Rwanda, rape was the rule and its absence the exception.

A fact-finding team sent to the former Yugoslavia by the European Community (EC) estimated that, during the conflict in Bosnia alone, Serb forces, military and paramilitary, raped more than 20,000 Muslim women.[9] The Bosnian Ministry of the Interior estimated the number of rape victims, including both Serbian and Croatian women, to be significantly higher—50,000 (Stiglmayer, 1994: 85). Again, as in Rwanda, the *genocidaires* not only raped, they sodomized women, held them in sexual slavery for weeks and even months, and they did so with purpose. According to Todd Salzman,

> While rape and sexual assault have frequently accompanied wars, the Bosnia-Herzegovina conflict . . . utilized this atrocity to attain the objective of the conflict itself, ethnic cleansing. In and through rape, and in particular rape for the purpose of impregnation, Serbs utilized the female gender violating her body and its reproductive capabilities as a "weapon of war." This policy was systematically planned by Serbian political and military leaders and strategically executed with the support of the Serbian and Bosnian Serb armies and paramilitary groups as a policy of ethnic cleansing or genocide in order to create a "greater Serbia," that is, a religiously, culturally, linguistically homogenous Serbian nation. (Saltzman, 2000: 79)

RAPE AS A WEAPON OF GENOCIDE

Rape is so widespread in war and genocide because it is so effective in ethnic wars. "It has . . . devastating effects on communities, particularly in traditional societies or very religious communities where the virginity and fidelity of women can be central to the makeup of that society" (Cohen, 1998: 1). In cultures that see a woman as the property of a man, as was the case in Rwanda and Yugoslavia, both solidly traditional, patriarchal societies, violating women was an indirect yet potent way of attacking and violating male enemies (Saltzman, 2000: 79). As Elizabeth Neuffer writes, "Rape as a part of warfare is not just about having sex, it is also about having someone else's property. Booty and beauty, historically, have simply been expected spoils of victory" (2002: 272).

Men raped women because women were part of the unwanted "ethnic other." They raped women because raping women enabled men to interrupt the ethno-continuity of their enemy's ethnic group (Huttenbach, 1996: 5). They raped women because they wanted to destroy their enemy. The widespread use of rape in the genocides of the 1990s reflects the unique terror it held for women, the unique power it gave rapists over their victims, and the unique contempt it displayed for its victims.

Who were the rapists? In former Yugoslavia, all sides raped—Bosnians, Croats, and Serbs (Fitzpatrick, 2001: 78), but the Serbs set the pattern. They were determined to create a "Greater" Serbia, and to do so they needed to drive out Bosnian Muslims and Croat Catholics, thus making sure Serbs were the ethnic majority population in Serb-controlled areas. They set up concentration camps where Bosnian and Croat men were beaten, tortured, starved, sexually abused, and frequently executed by firing squads. They set up "rape camps," where Bosnian and Croat women were raped, sodomized, forcibly impregnated, and denied medical attention or access to abortions. The Serbs did this "to humiliate and demoralize [their enemies], as part of a program to terrorize, to drive away the unwanted ethnic 'other,' to boost the military's morale. It was a broad, systematic—even strategic—campaign . . . one encouraged by authorities" (Stiglmayer, 1999: 327). The Serbs did this because they wanted Bosnian Muslim and Croat Catholic women to give birth to Chetnick (Serb) babies who "would kill Muslims" when they grew up (Saltzman, 2000: 73).

In Rwanda, Hutu extremists targeted Tutsi women as early as December 1990, in their so-called Hutu Ten Commandments. The first three commandments dealt with Tutsi women, and, by innuendo, their sexual attractiveness. The hatred mobilized against Tutsi women by the extremist Hutu elements before and during the 1994 genocide "allowed the most inhumane acts of sexual violence to take place" (quote in Melvern, 2000: 73, fn. 9; see also Gourevitch, 1998: 87–88). The Hutu-controlled Rwandan government urged, even ordered, Hutu men to rape, sodomize, and impregnate Tutsi women during the genocide. Here too, sexual violence was not incidental to the "genocidal intent" of the Hutu extremist government in Rwanda, not incidental but central. "The pattern of sexual violence in Rwanda shows that acts of rape and sexual mutilation were not accessory to the killings, or for the most part, opportunistic assaults. Rather, according to the actions and statements of the perpetrators, as recalled by survivors, these acts were carried out with the aim of eradicating the Tuts" (quote in Fitzpatrick, 2001: 79).

THE CHURCH AND RAPE

During the days, weeks, months, even years that these genocides raged in the former Yugoslavia and Rwanda, what was the reaction of Roman Catholic Church leadership to what was happening in these two countries, both of which have significant Roman Catholic populations? In Rwanda, for example, according to the 1991 census, "89.8 percent of the population claimed membership in a Christian Church—62.6 percent claimed to be Catholic, 18.8 percent Protestant, and 8.4 percent Seventh Day Aventists" (Government of Rwanda, 1994: 126–28). On the surface, Rwanda appeared to be a model of national piety, with high levels of church attendance among both Catholics and Protestants. In addition, the churches were "important centers of power" (Longman, 2001: 149), exercising significant influence at all levels of government and among the general population. Yugoslavia, not as overwhelmingly Roman Catholic as Rwanda, still had a fairly large Roman Catholic population (about 20 percent of the overall population of Bosnia-Herzegovina, Croatia, and Serbia, or approximately 4.4 million people, were Roman Catholic) (*World Fact Encyclopedia*, 2003: 154). In addition, there were large numbers of Serbian Orthodox Christians living in the former Yugoslavia, as well as a significant number of Muslims (*World Fact Encyclopedia*, 2003: 154).

I do not think that, just because there are large numbers of Roman Catholics in a country, the leadership of the Roman Catholic Church will concern itself with issues I or others may think are important, such as the use of rape as a weapon of war and genocide. But, given that the leadership of the Catholic Church often speaks out on issues involving sex and sexual morality, I think it is reasonable to ask if the Vatican, that is, the pope, his cardinals, archbishops, and bishops, took notice of the widespread sexual violence during the genocides in former Yugoslavia and Rwanda during the 1990s.

WHAT WAS SAID

During both conflicts, the Pope and other leaders of the Roman Catholic Church, at the Vatican and elsewhere, were "out front" and vocal in their general condemnations of violence, war, and "ethnic cleansing." For example, Cardinal Bernard Law in Boston (1992: 366), Cardinal Franjo Kuharic in Zagreb,[10] Archbishop Renato R. Martino at the United Nations in New

York (Martino, 1992: 367–68), and Pope John Paul II himself at the Vatican[11] all spoke out against the violence and human misery in Yugoslavia. The Pope called the conflict there "'an absurd and cruel war,' driven by the 'glaring anachronism' of intolerant nationalism." The warring parties, he said, must find a way to stop the violence and to live once again together in fraternity and peace (quoted in Martino, 1992: 366). And their concern did not end with the cessation of conflict. Even as late as July 2002, Cardinal Law wrote a letter to then American Secretary of State Colin Powell about the 1992–1995 conflict in former Yugoslavia, calling it "the worst outbreak of ethnic and fratricidal war in Europe since World War II" and urging the U.S. government to support the continuation of the United Nation's peace-keeping mission in that part of the world (Law, 2002).

The leadership of the Church also spoke out about the genocide in Rwanda. On 10 April 1994, four days after the killings began, Pope John Paul II publicly pleaded with the *genocidaires* in Rwanda, to "stop these acts of violence! Stop these tragedies! Stop these fratricidal massacres!"[12] Four days later, on 14 April 1994 Cardinals Francis Arinze, Christian Wiyghan Tumi, and Paulos Tzadua, presidents of the African Synod of Bishops meeting at the Vatican with Pope John Paul II, appealed for peace in Rwanda, "We make a heartfelt plea to all concerned in the conflict to lay down their arms and stop the atrocities and killings" (Rittner, et al., 2004: 13). Two weeks later, on 27 April 1994, Pope John Paul II spoke out once again (2004: 77), and two months after that, from 24–29 June 1994 the Pope sent Cardinal Roger Etchegaray, president of the Pontifical Council for Justice and Peace, as his personal envoy to Rwanda. Cardinal Etchegaray celebrated Requiem Mass in the Cathedral of Kabgayi and delivered, in Pope John Paul II's name, messages to the interim president of Rwanda and to the president of the Rwandan Patriotic Front. Speaking as the pope's emissary, Etchegaray said: "this senseless war must be stopped. . . . I implore all the political and military authorities to meet once again and declare a ceasefire and to maintain it at all costs . . . ceasefire means laying down your arms—machetes and spears" (2004: 128).

Relative to the conflict in the former Yugoslavia, in February 1993 the Vatican released the text of a letter signed by Pope John Paul II and sent to Archbishop Vinko Puljic of Sarajevo. In it, the Pope addressed the situation in Bosnia—Herzegovina, appealing for peace and encouraging efforts to achieve reconciliation between and among the various ethnic groups, beginning with families. His hope was that "the violence and tribulations in progress will soon cease and yield to reconciliation and peace." He continued:

> It is particularly necessary that Pastors and all the faithful responsible for the family apostolate sense an urgency in looking after the situation of the mothers, wives and young women who have been subjected to violence because of an

outburst of racial hatred or brutal lust. These women, who have been the object of such a serious offense, must find the support of understanding and solidarity in the community. Even in such a tragic situation they must be helped to distinguish between the act of deplorable violence which they have suffered from men who have lost all reason and conscience, and the reality of these new beings who have been given life. . . . In every case it should be emphasized most clearly that since the unborn child is in no way responsible for the disgraceful acts accomplished, he or she is *innocent* and therefore cannot be treated as the *aggressor*. Therefore, the entire community should be close to these women who have been so tragically offended and to their families, in order to help them transform the act of violence into an act of love and acceptance.[13]

This letter, written by the Pope in good faith and no doubt with every good intention tells the violated and forcibly impregnated women of Bosnia-Herzegovina that they should accept what has happened to them: accept the children growing in their wombs, and "transform the act of violence into love and solidarity." The "barbarous acts of hatred and and racism," writes the Pope, "must be answered with the strength of love and solidarity."[14] The Pope's emphasis in his letter of 2 February 1993 is on the life of the unborn child, not on the life of the woman who has been violated and forcibly impregnated, and not on the actions of the men who perpetrated these deeds "of hatred and racism."

WHAT WAS NOT SAID

Whatever may be one's opinion of the advice given to the violated women of the Balkans, Pope John Paul II's letter of 2 February 1993 to Archbishop Vinko Puljic of Sarajevo should have contained the strongest possible condemnation of the men who perpetrated these vicious acts against women and the clearest possible statement condemning the use of rape as a weapon of war and genocide, declaring that those who pervert the act of love by turning it into a weapon of evil show themselves to be minions of the darkness beyond the pale of our common humanity. But it did not. There were no words of condemnation of the *genocidaires*, no words of empathy or sympathy for the women who faced agonizing decisions about whether or not to bring their pregnancies to term. There were no words of understanding, empathy, or sympathy for the women who may have attempted suicide because they were desperate, no words of care or concern for the women who somehow would have to make their way back into a patriarchal society that devalued women generally, and, especially those who had been sexually violated. There were only words asking the Church community as well these violated women "to distinguish between the act of deplorable violence they have suffered from men who have lost all reason, and the reality of these new human beings who have been given life." Only words pleading for women "to transform the act of violence into an act of love and acceptance."

The only statement I have found that comes close to condemning the sexual violence during the conflict in former Yugoslavia is a 1992 statement jointly issued by Cardinal Franjo Kuharic, Roman Catholic Archbishop of Zagreb, and Pavle I, Serbian Orthodox Patriarch of Belgrade. In it, they said: "We especially express our horror at the perpetration of extremely immoral misdeeds, at the mistreatment of older and younger women and girls, which only monsters can perpetrate, no matter what name they give themselves" (RCC, 1992: 367). They do call the perpetrators "of extremely immoral misdeeds . . . monsters," yet, even in this statement, these church-men were unable to use the words "rape," "sexual violence," or "penis" used as weapons of war and genocide, although those do seem to be the issues they are addressing, even if obliquely.

What about in Rwanda? What did the leadership of the Church have to say to the people of Rwanda about the widespread rape and sexual violence that occurred there during the 1994 genocide? What words of compassion and understanding did the men of the Church offer to the women of Rwanda who were the victims of sexual violence, who were impregnated by *genocidaires*, many of them also infected with HIV/AIDS? What did the Pope, his cardinals, archbishops, and bishops have to say to the Rwandan men who used rape as a weapon of war and genocide?

Unfortunately, nowhere have I found a statement alluding to, much less condemning, these gender-based crimes or the use of rape as a weapon of war and genocide. Nowhere have I found statements expressing care, empathy, or understanding for the violated and impregnated women. Such statements may exist deep in the files of the Vatican or in some diocesan archive in Rwanda, or elsewhere, but I have not found them. I have found statements issued by the Pope and members of the Roman Catholic hierarchy deploring sterilization and sex outside of marriage, statements condemning the so-called "morning after pill," statements condemning abortion and euthanasia, but not a single letter or statement in clear, concrete, understandable language addressing, much less condemning, rape as a weapon of war and genocide in the former Yugoslavia or Rwanda—or in Kosovo, Chechnya, Congo, Sierra Leone, East Timor, Darfur, or any place in the world for that matter.

CONCLUSION: AN UNHOLY SILENCE

What is one to make of this silence? What is one to make of these men of the Church who are so vocal about abortion, sterilization, birth control, and euthanasia, but so silent about rape and the men who use their penises as weapons of war and genocide? What should one make of such an unholy silence?

One could argue that these days, neither Roman Catholics nor anyone else pays much attention to letters or statements from the Pope, his cardinals, archbishops, and bishops about sex and sexual morality, much less about war and peace in various parts of the world. One could even argue that ecclesiastical statements in today's secular world no longer have any impact on either the faithful or the faithless. Still, I think even the most cynical among us expects the "great voice . . . in Rome" to speak out, to utter a word of condemnation when necessary, or to utter words of care, concern, and compassion when needed by the human family. Words, weak though they may be, are all we human beings have to express our deepest beliefs and our highest aspirations. Words are what separate us from the rest of life on this planet, which, as far as we can tell, is incapable of self-reflection and self-evaluation, of sorrow and repentance, of compassion and love.

I can only conclude that the leadership of the Roman Catholic Church, the Pope, and his cardinals, archbishops, and bishops, unlike the God of Abraham, Isaac, and Jacob in Exodus 3:7–10, failed to *witness* the affliction of God's people (women) in Yugoslavia and Rwanda, failed to *hear the cry of complaint* God's people (women) uttered against the men who used rape as a weapon of war and genocide in Rwanda and Yugoslavia, and failed, failed utterly to *know well* what God's people (women) were suffering in the 1990s, and still suffer today.

I, for one, still wait for the "great voice . . . in Rome" to speak out and condemn the evil of rape as a weapon of war and genocide. I wait for the leadership of the Roman Catholic Church to condemn the men who use their penises as weapons of war and genocide to achieve political and strategic objectives. I wait for the Pope and his hierarchy, men steeped in a respect for life and horror for abortion, to find "new" words that will enable them to move beyond the "old" category of excessive violence in times of conflict to the "new" category of the sacrilege of the human person in times of genocide. I wait for the "great voice . . . in Rome" to speak words of compassion to the thousands and thousands of violated women in Rwanda, the former Yugoslavia, and elsewhere in the world who have been raped, impregnated, infected with HIV/AIDS, and left to care for the children of *genocidaires*. Thus far, however, the only words I hear are Albert Camus's words, spoken in 1948 to those monks at the Dominican Monastery of Latour-Maubourg in Paris, and I find that very troubling indeed.

NOTES

1. By "the leadership" of the Church, I am speaking about the Pope and the members of the hierarchy (cardinals, archbishops, and bishops).

2. When I use the term, "the Church" in this essay, I am referring specifically to the Roman Catholic Church.

3. See further, Program 2, "Total War" in the BBC/PBS series, *The Great War and the Shaping of the Twentieth Century* (1996). Also see Hardach (1980), Keegan (1976), and Winter (2000).

4. See "Total War."

5. See further, http://www.prb.org/TemplateTop.cfm?Section=PRB_Country_ Profiles&template=/customsource/countryprofile/countryprofiledisplay .cfm&Country=331 (Accessed: 28 July 2006).

6. For a much more complete explanation of the situation in Rwanda before, during, and after the Belgians colonial period, see further, Ian Linden, *Church and Revolution in Rwanda* (Manchester, U.K.: Manchester University Press, 1977), and L. R. Melvern, *A People Betrayed: The Role of the West in Rwanda's Genocide* (New York: Zed Books, 2000).

7. For a more complete explanation of the breakup of Yugoslavia, see Cohen (1998).

8. I base my comments here on Llezlie L. Green's analysis of the situation that prevailed in Rwanda in her essay, "Sexual Violence and Genocide against Tutsi Women" (n.d.), on the Human Rights Watch report *Shattered Lives* (1996), and on various essays in Stiglmayer (1994).

9. European Council Investigative Mission into the Treatment of Muslim Women in the former Yugoslavia, *Report to the European Council Foreign Ministers*, 8 January 1993, paragraph 14.

10. Cardinal Kuharic of Zagreb and Serbian Orthodox Patriarch Pavle I of Belgrade, in a joint statement called for an immediate ceasefire in Bosnia-Herzegovina and the unconditional release of all prisoners after they met in Geneva, Switzerland, in September 1992.

11. See further, "Crisis in Yugoslavia—Position and Action of the Holy See (1991–1992)," published by the Holy See.

12. See further, Homily of Pope John Paul II at the Mass of the Inauguration of the African Synod at St. Peter's Basilica, Rome, 10 April 1994: 4.

13. Pope John Paul II, 2 February 1993: http://priestsforlife.org/magisterium/ 93-02-02poperapeandab.htm (Accessed 20 August 2006).

BIBLIOGRAPHY

Allen, Beverly (1996). *Rape Warfare: The Hidden Genocide in Bosnia-Herzegovina*. Minneapolis: University of Minnesota Press.

Barstow, Ann Llewellyn (ed.) (2000). *War's Dirty Secret: Rape, Prostitution and Other Crimes Against Women*. Cleveland, Ohio: Pilgrim Press.

Bartov, Omer, and Phyllis Mack (eds.) (2001). *In God's Name: Genocide in the Twentieth Century*. New York: Berghahn Books.

Brandt, Don (ed.) (2003). *Violence against Women: From Silence to Empowerment*. Monrovia: World Vision.

Camus, Albert (1960). *Resistance, Rebellion, and Death*. New York: Vintage Books.

Cohen, Roger (1998). *Hearts Grown Brutal: Sagas of Sarajevo*. New York: Random House.

des Forges, Alison (1999). *Leave None to Tell the Story: Genocide in Rwanda*. New York: Human Rights.

Eliot, Gil (1972). *The Twentieth Century Book of the Dead*. New York: Charles Scribner.

Farrington, Marie Julianne (2004). "Rwanda—100 Days," in Carol Rittner, John K. Roth, and Wendy Whitworth (eds.), *Genocide in Rwanda: Complicity of the Churches?* St. Paul, Minn.: Paragon House.

Fitzpatrick, Brenda (2001). "Rape as Genocide: Lessons from the Balkans and Rwanda in the 1990s," in Don Brandt (ed.), *Violence against Women: From Silence to Empowerment*. Monrovia: World Vision.

Gourevitch, Philip (1998). *We Wish to Inform You That Tomorrow We Will Be Killed with Our Families*. New York: Farrar, Straus, Giroux.

Government of Rwanda (1994). *Recensement General de la Population et de l'Habitat au 15 Août 1991*. Kigali.

Green, Llezlie (n.d.). "Sexual Violence and Genocide against Tutsi Women." Available on the Internet at http://academic.udayton.edu/race/06hrights/GeoRegions/Africa/Rwanda01.htm. Accessed 9 September 2005.

Gutman, Roy (1993). *A Witness to Genocide: The First Inside Account of the Horrors of 'Ethnic Cleansing.'* Rockport, N.Y.: Element.

Gutman, Roy, and David Rieff (eds.) (1999). *Crimes of War: What the Public Should Know*. New York: W. W. Norton & Company.

Hardach, Gerd (1980). *The First World War*. London: Penguin.

Hatzfield, Jean (2005). *Machete Season: The Killers in Rwanda Speak*. New York: Farrar, Straus, Giroux.

Horowitz, Irving Louis (1997). *Taking Lives: Genocide and State Power*. 4th Edition. New Brunswick, N.J.: Transaction Publishers.

Human Rights Watch (1996). *Shattered Lives: Sexual Violence during the Rwandan Genocide*. New York: Human Rights Watch.

Huttenbach, Henry R. (1996). "Mass Rape and Gendercide: Gender Victimization as Aspects of Genocide in Bosnia." *The Genocide Forum*. No. 9: 3–4.

Jones, Adam (2006). *Genocide: A Comprehensive Introduction*. New York: Routledge.

Keegan, John (1976). *The Face of Battle*. London: Penguin.

Law, Bernard Cardinal (2002). "Letter of July 2, 2002 to U.S. Secretary of State Colin Powell." Available on the Internet at http://www.usccb.org/sdwp/international.bosnia.html. Accessed 10 October 2006.

Linden, Ian (1977). *Church and Revolution in Rwanda*. Manchester, N.Y.: Manchester University Press.

Longman, Timothy (2001). "Christian Churches and Genocide in Rwanda," in Omer Bartov and Phyllis Mack (eds.). *In God's Name: Genocide in the Twentieth Century*. New York: Berghahn Books.

MacKinnon, Catherine A. (2006). *Are Women Human?* Cambridge, Mass.: Harvard University Press.

Martino, Renato P. (1992), "The Plague of Ethnic Cleansing," *Origins*: 367-368.

Melvern, Linda R. (2000). *A People Betrayed: The Role of the West in Rwanda's Genocide*. New York: Zed Books.

Naimark, Norman M. (2001). *Fires of Hatred: Ethnic Cleansing in the Twentieth Century*. Cambridge, Mass.: Harvard University Press.

Neuffer, Elizabeth (2002) *The Key to My Neighbor's House: Seeking Justice in Bosnia and Rwanda*. New York: Picador.

Power, Samantha (2002). *"A Problem from Hell": America in the Age of Genocide*. New York: Basic Books.

Rittner, Carol, John K. Roth, and James M. Smith (eds.) (2002). *Will Genocide Ever End?* St. Paul, Minn.: Paragon House.

Rittner, Carol, John K. Roth, and Wendy Whitworth (eds.) (2004). *Genocide in Rwanda: Complicity in the Churches?* St. Paul, Minn.: Paragon House.

Roman Catholic Church (RCC). "Message of Patriarch Pavle and Cardinal Kuharic following their meeting in Geneva on 23 September 1992," www.georgefox.edu/academics/undergrad/...ree/Pavle_Message?misc_art.pdf.

Rummel, R. J. (1994). *Death by Government*. New Brunswick, N.J.: Transaction Publishers.

Saltzman, Todd (2000). "'Rape Camps,' Forced Impregnation and Ethnic Cleansing: Religious, Cultural and Ethical Responses to Rape Victims in the Former Yugoslavia," in Ann Llewellyn Barstow (ed.), *War's Dirty Secret: Rape, Prostitution, and Other Crimes against Women*. Cleveland, Ohio: Pilgrim Press.

Smith, Helmut Walzer (ed.) (2002). *The Holocaust and Other Genocides: History, Representation, Ethics*. Nashville, Tenn.: Vanderbilt University Press.

Staub, Erwin (1989). *The Roots of Evil: The Origins of Genocide and Other Group Violence*. New York: Cambridge University Press.

Stiglmayer, Alexandra (ed.) (1994). *Mass Rape: The War against Women in Bosnia Herzegovina*. Lincoln: University of Nebraska Press.

Stiglmayer, Alexandra (1999). "Sexual Violence: Systematic Rape," in Roy Gutman and David Rieff (eds.), *Rimes of War: What the Public Should Know*. New York: W. W. Norton and Company.

Totten, Samuel, William S. Parsons, and Israel W. Charny (eds.) (2004). *A Century of Genocide: Critical Essays and Eyewitness Accounts*. 2nd Edition. New York: Routledge.

Tshuy, Théo (1997). *Ethnic Conflict and Religion: Challenges to the Churches*. Geneva: World Council of Churches Publication.

Weitz, Eric E. (2003). *A Century of Genocide: Utopias of Race and Nation*. Princeton, N.J.: Princeton University Press.

Whitworth, Wendy (ed.) (2006). *We Survived Genocide in Rwanda*. Newark: Quill Press.

Winter, J. M. (2000). *The Great War and the Twentieth Century*. New Haven, Conn.: Yale University Press.

World Fact Encyclopedia. Washington, D.C.: Brassey's Inc.

Convention on the Prevention and Punishment of the Crime of Genocide

Adopted by Resolution 260 (III) A of the United Nations General Assembly on 9 December 1948.

ARTICLE 1

The Contracting Parties confirm that genocide, whether committed in time of peace or in time of war, is a crime under international law which they undertake to prevent and to punish.

ARTICLE 2

In the present Convention, genocide means any of the following acts committed with intent to destroy, in whole or in part, a national, ethnical, racial or religious group, as such:

(a) Killing members of the group;
(b) Causing serious bodily or mental harm to members of the group;
(c) Deliberately inflicting on the group conditions of life calculated to bring about its physical destruction in whole or in part;
(d) Imposing measures intended to prevent births within the group; and
(e) Forcibly transferring children of the group to another group.

ARTICLE 3

The following acts shall be punishable:

(a) Genocide;
(b) Conspiracy to commit genocide;
(c) Direct and public incitement to commit genocide;
(d) Attempt to commit genocide; and
(e) Complicity in genocide.

ARTICLE 4

Persons committing genocide or any of the other acts enumerated in Article 3 shall be punished, whether they are constitutionally responsible rulers, public officials or private individuals.

ARTICLE 5

The Contracting Parties undertake to enact, in accordance with their respective Constitutions, the necessary legislation to give effect to the provisions of the present Convention and, in particular, to provide effective penalties for persons guilty of genocide or any of the other acts enumerated in Article 3.

ARTICLE 6

Persons charged with genocide or any of the other acts enumerated in Article 3 shall be tried by a competent tribunal of the State in the territory of which the act was committed, or by such international penal tribunal as may have jurisdiction with respect to those Contracting Parties which shall have accepted its jurisdiction.

ARTICLE 7

Genocide and the other acts enumerated in Article 3 shall not be considered as political crimes for the purpose of extradition.

The Contracting Parties pledge themselves in such cases to grant extradition in accordance with their laws and treaties in force.

ARTICLE 8

Any Contracting Party may call upon the competent organs of the United Nations to take such action under the Charter of the United Nations as they consider appropriate for the prevention and suppression of acts of genocide or any of the other acts enumerated in Article 3.

ARTICLE 9

Disputes between the Contracting Parties relating to the interpretation, application or fulfillment of the present Convention, including those relating to the responsibility of a State for genocide or any of the other acts enumerated in Article 3, shall be submitted to the International Court of Justice at the request of any of the parties to the dispute.

ARTICLE 10

The present Convention, of which the Chinese, English, French, Russian and Spanish texts are equally authentic, shall bear the date of 9 December 1948.

ARTICLE 11

The present Convention shall be open until 31 December 1949 for signature on behalf of any Member of the United Nations and of any non-member State to which an invitation to sign has been addressed by the General Assembly.

The present Convention shall be ratified, and the instruments of ratification shall be deposited with the Secretary-General of the United Nations.

After 1 January 1950, the present Convention may be acceded to on behalf of any Member of the United Nations and of any non-member State which has received an invitation as aforesaid.

Instruments of accession shall be deposited with the Secretary-General of the United Nations.

ARTICLE 12

Any Contracting Party may at any time, by notification addressed to the Secretary-General of the United Nations, extend the application of the present Convention to all or any of the territories for the conduct of whose foreign relations that Contracting Party is responsible.

ARTICLE 13

On the day when the first twenty instruments of ratification or accession have been deposited, the Secretary-General shall draw up a proces-verbal and transmit a copy of it to each Member of the United Nations and to each of the non-member States contemplated in Article 11.

The present Convention shall come into force on the ninetieth day following the date of deposit of the twentieth instrument of ratification or accession.

Any ratification or accession effected subsequent to the latter date shall become effective on the ninetieth day following the deposit of the instrument of ratification or accession.

ARTICLE 14

The present Convention shall remain in effect for a period of ten years as from the date of its coming into force.

It shall thereafter remain in force for successive periods of five years for such Contracting Parties as have not denounced it at least six months before the expiration of the current period.

Denunciation shall be effected by a written notification addressed to the Secretary-General of the United Nations.

ARTICLE 15

If, as a result of denunciations, the number of Parties to the present Convention should become less than sixteen, the Convention shall cease to be in force as from the date on which the last of these denunciations shall become effective.

ARTICLE 16

A request for the revision of the present Convention may be made at any time by any Contracting Party by means of a notification in writing addressed to the Secretary-General.

The General Assembly shall decide upon the steps, if any, to be taken in respect of such request.

ARTICLE 17

The Secretary-General of the United Nations shall notify all Members of the United Nations and the non-member States contemplated in Article 11 of the following:

(a) Signatures, ratifications and accessions received in accordance with Article 11;
(b) Notifications received in accordance with Article 12;
(c) The date upon which the present Convention comes into force in accordance with Article 13;
(d) Denunciations received in accordance with Article 14;
(e) The abrogation of the Convention in accordance with Article 15; and
(f) Notifications received in accordance with Article 16.

ARTICLE 18

The original of the present Convention shall be deposited in the archives of the United Nations.

A certified copy of the Convention shall be transmitted to all Members of the United Nations and to the non-member States contemplated in Article 11.

ARTICLE 19

The present Convention shall be registered by the Secretary-General of the United Nations on the date of its coming into force.

Universal Declaration of Human Rights

Preamble

Whereas recognition of the inherent dignity and of the equal and inalienable rights of all members of the human family is the foundation of freedom, justice and peace in the world,

Whereas disregard and contempt for human rights have resulted in barbarous acts which have outraged the conscience of mankind, and the advent of a world in which human beings shall enjoy freedom of speech and belief and freedom from fear and want has been proclaimed as the highest aspiration of the common people,

Whereas it is essential, if man is not to be compelled to have recourse, as a last resort, to rebellion against tyranny and oppression, that human rights should be protected by the rule of law,

Whereas it is essential to promote the development of friendly relations between nations,

Whereas the peoples of the United Nations have in the Charter reaffirmed their faith in fundamental human rights, in the dignity and worth of the human person and in the equal rights of men and women and have determined to promote social progress and better standards of life in larger freedom,

Whereas Member States have pledged themselves to achieve, in co-operation with the United Nations, the promotion of universal respect for and observance of human rights and fundamental freedoms,

Whereas a common understanding of these rights and freedoms is of the greatest importance for the full realization of this pledge,

Now, therefore,

THE GENERAL ASSEMBLY

Proclaims this Universal Declaration of Human Rights as a common standard of achievement for all peoples and all nations, to the end that every individual and every organ of society, keeping this Declaration constantly in mind, shall strive by teaching and education to promote respect for these rights and freedoms and by progressive measures, national and international, to secure their universal and effective recognition and observance, both among the peoples of Member States themselves and among the peoples of territories under their jurisdiction.

Article 1

All human beings are born free and equal in dignity and rights. They are endowed with reason and conscience and should act towards one another in a spirit of brotherhood.

Article 2

Everyone is entitled to all the rights and freedoms set forth in this Declaration, without distinction of any kind, such as race, colour, sex, language, religion, political or other opinion, national or social origin, property, birth or other status.

Furthermore, no distinction shall be made on the basis of the political, jurisdictional or international status of the country or territory to which a person belongs, whether it be independent, trust, non-self-governing or under any other limitation of sovereignty.

Article 3

Everyone has the right to life, liberty and the security of person.

Article 4

No one shall be held in slavery or servitude; slavery and the slave trade shall be prohibited in all their forms.

Article 5

No one shall be subjected to torture or to cruel, inhuman or degrading treatment or punishment.

Article 6

Everyone has the right to recognition everywhere as a person before the law.

Article 7

All are equal before the law and are entitled without any discrimination to equal protection against any discrimination in violation of this Declaration and against any incitement to such discrimination.

Article 8

Everyone has the right to an effective remedy by the competent national tribunals for acts violating the fundamental rights granted him by the constitution or by law.

Article 9

No one shall be subjected to arbitrary arrest, detention or exile.

Article 10

Everyone is entitled in full equality to a fair, and public hearing by an independent and impartial tribunal, in the determination of his rights and obligations and of any criminal charge against him.

Article 11

1. Everyone charged with a penal offence has the right to be presumed innocent until proven guilty according to law in a public trial at which he has had all the guarantees necessary for his defence.
2. No one shall be held guilty of any penal offence on account of any act or omission which did not constitute a penal offence, under national or international law, at the time when it was committed. Nor shall a heavier penalty be imposed than the one that was applicable at the time the penal offence was committed.

Article 12

No one shall be subjected to arbitrary interference with his privacy, family, home or correspondence, nor to attacks upon his honour and reputation. Everyone has the right to the protection of the law against such interference or attacks.

Article 13

1. Everyone has the right to freedom of movement and residence within the borders of each State.
2. Everyone has the right to leave any country, including his own, and to return to his country.

Article 14

1. Everyone has the right to seek and to enjoy in other countries asylum from persecution.
2. This right may not be invoked in the case of prosecutions genuinely arising from non-political crimes or from acts contrary to the purposes and principles of the United Nations.

Article 15

1. Everyone has the right to a nationality.
2. No one shall be arbitrarily deprived of his nationality nor denied the right to change his nationality.

Article 16

1. Men and women of full age, without any limitation due to race, nationality or religion, have the right to marry and to found a family. They are entitled to equal rights as to marriage, during marriage and at its dissolution.
2. Marriage shall be entered into only with the free and full consent of the intending spouses.
3. The family is the natural and fundamental group unit of society and is entitled to protection by society and the State.

Article 17

1. Everyone has the right to own property alone as well as in association with others.
2. No one shall be arbitrarily deprived of his property.

Article 18

Everyone has the right to freedom of thought, conscience and religion; this right includes freedom to change his religion or belief, and freedom, either alone or in community with others and in public or private, to manifest his religion or belief in teaching, practice, worship and observance.

Article 19

Everyone has the right to freedom of opinion and expression; this right includes freedom to hold opinions without interference and to seek, receive and impart information and ideas through any media and regardless of frontiers.

Article 20

1. Everyone has the right to freedom of peaceful assembly and association.
2. No one may be compelled to belong to an association.

Article 21

1. Everyone has the right to take part in the government of his country, directly or through freely chosen representatives.
2. Everyone has the right of equal access to public service in his country.
3. The will of the people shall be the basis of the authority of government; this shall be expressed in periodic and genuine elections which shall be by universal and equal suffrage and shall be held by secret vote or by equivalent free voting procedures.

Article 22

Everyone, as a member of society, has the right to social security and is entitled to realization, through national effort and international co-operation and in accordance with the organization and resources of each State, of the economic, social and cultural rights indispensable for his dignity and the free development of his personality.

Article 23

1. Everyone has the right to work, to free choice of employment, to just and favourable conditions of work and to protection against unemployment.

2. Everyone, without any discrimination, has the right to equal pay for equal work.
3. Everyone who works has the right to just and favourable remuneration ensuring for himself and his family an existence worthy of human dignity, and supplemented, if necessary, by other means of social protection.
4. Everyone has the right to form and to join trade unions for the protection of his interests.

Article 24

Everyone has the right to rest and leisure, including reasonable limitation of working hours and periodic holidays with pay.

Article 25

1. Everyone has the right to a standard of living adequate for the health and well-being of himself and of his family, including food, clothing, housing and medical care and necessary social services, and the right to security in the event of unemployment, sickness, disability, widowhood, old age or other lack of livelihood in circumstances beyond his control.
2. Motherhood and childhood are entitled to special care and assistance. All children, whether born in or out of wedlock, shall enjoy the same social protection.

Article 26

1. Everyone has the right to education. Education shall be free, at least in the elementary and fundamental stages. Elementary education shall be compulsory. Technical and professional education shall be made generally available and higher education shall be equally accessible to all on the basis of merit.
2. Education shall be directed to the full development of the human personality and to the strengthening of respect for human rights and fundamental freedoms. It shall promote understanding, tolerance and friendship among all nations, racial or religious groups, and shall further the activities of the United Nations for the maintenance of peace.
3. Parents have a prior right to choose the kind of education that shall be given to their children.

Article 27

1. Everyone has the right freely to participate in the cultural life of the community, to enjoy the arts and to share in scientific advancement and its benefits.

2. Everyone has the right to the protection of the moral and material interests resulting from any scientific, literary or artistic production of which he is the author.

Article 28

Everyone is entitled to a social and international order in which the rights and freedoms set forth in this Declaration can be fully realized.

Article 29

1. Everyone has duties to the community in which alone the free and full development of his personality is possible.
2. In the exercise of his rights and freedoms, everyone shall be subject only to such limitations as are determined by law solely for the purpose of securing due recognition and respect for the rights and freedoms of others and of meeting the just requirements of morality, public order and the general welfare in a democratic society.
3. These rights and freedoms may in no case be exercised contrary to the purposes and principles of the United Nations.

Article 30

Nothing in this Declaration may be interpreted as implying for any State, group or person any right to engage in any activity or to perform any act aimed at the destruction of any of the rights and freedoms set forth herein.

The United Nations Convention on the Non-Applicability of Statutory Limitations to War Crimes and Crimes Against Humanity (1968)

Adopted and opened for signature, ratification and accession by General Assembly resolution 2391 (XXIII) of 26 November 1968
Entry into force 11 November 1970, in accordance with article VIII

PREAMBLE

The States Parties to the present Convention,

Recalling resolutions of the General Assembly of the United Nations 3 (I) of 13 February 1946 and 170 (II) of 31 October 1947 on the extradition and punishment of war criminals, resolution 95 (I) of 11 December 1946 affirming the principles of international law recognized by the Charter of the International Military Tribunal, Nurnberg, and the judgment of the Tribunal, and resolutions 2184 (XXI) of 12 December 1966 and 2202 (XXI) of 16 December 1966 which expressly condemned as crimes against humanity the violation of the economic and political rights of the indigenous population on the one hand and the policies of apartheid on the other,

Recalling resolutions of the Economic and Social Council of the United Nations 1074 D (XXXIX) of 28 July 1965 and 1158 (XLI) of 5 August 1966 on the punishment of war criminals and of persons who have committed crimes against humanity,

Noting that none of the solemn declarations, instruments or conventions relating to the prosecution and punishment of war crimes and crimes against humanity made provision for a period of limitation,

Considering that war crimes and crimes against humanity are among the gravest crimes in international law,

Convinced that the effective punishment of war crimes and crimes against humanity is an important element in the prevention of such crimes, the protection of human rights and fundamental freedoms, the encouragement of confidence, the furtherance of co-operation among peoples and the promotion of international peace and security,

Noting that the application to war crimes and crimes against humanity of the rules of municipal law relating to the period of limitation for ordinary crimes is a matter of serious concern to world public opinion, since it prevents the prosecution and punishment of persons responsible for those crimes,

Recognizing that it is necessary and timely to affirm in international law, through this Convention, the principle that there is no period of limitation for war crimes and crimes against humanity, and to secure its universal application,

Have agreed as follows:

Article 1

No statutory limitation shall apply to the following crimes, irrespective of the date of their commission:

(a) War crimes as they are defined in the Charter of the International Military Tribunal, Nurnberg, of 8 August 1945 and confirmed by resolutions 3 (1) of 13 February 1946 and 95 (I) of 11 December 1946 of the General Assembly of the United Nations, particularly the "grave breaches" enumerated in the Geneva Conventions of 12 August 1949 for the protection of war victims;

(b) Crimes against humanity whether committed in time of war or in time of peace as they are defined in the Charter of the International Military Tribunal, Nurnberg, of 8 August 1945 and confirmed by resolutions 3 (I) of 13 February 1946 and 95 (I) of 11 December 1946 of the General Assembly of the United Nations, eviction by armed attack or occupation and inhuman acts resulting from the policy of apartheid, and the crime of genocide as defined in the 1948 Convention on the Prevention and Punishment of the Crime of Genocide, even if such acts do not constitute a violation of the domestic law of the country in which they were committed.

Article 2

If any of the crimes mentioned in Article 1 is committed, the provisions of this Convention shall apply to representatives of the State authority and private individuals who, as principals or accomplices, participate in or who directly incite others to the commission of any of those crimes, or who conspire to commit them, irrespective of the degree of completion, and to representatives of the State authority who tolerate their commission.

Article 3

The States Parties to the present Convention undertake to adopt all necessary domestic measures, legislative or otherwise, with a view to making possible the extradition, in accordance with international law, of the persons referred to in Article 2 of this Convention.

Article 4

The States Parties to the present Convention undertake to adopt, in accordance with their respective constitutional processes, any legislative or other measures necessary to ensure that statutory or other limitations shall not apply to the prosecution and punishment of the crimes referred to in Articles 1 and 2 of this Convention and that, where they exist, such limitations shall be abolished.

Article 5

This Convention shall, until 31 December 1969, be open for signature by any State Member of the United Nations or member of any of its specialized agencies or of the International Atomic Energy Agency, by any State Party to the Statute of the International Court of Justice, and by any other State which has been invited by the General Assembly of the United Nations to become a Party to this Convention.

Article 6

This Convention is subject to ratification. Instruments of ratification shall be deposited with the Secretary-General of the United Nations.

Article 7

This Convention shall be open to accession by any State referred to in Article 5.

Instruments of accession shall be deposited with the Secretary-General of the United Nations.

Article 8

1. This Convention shall enter into force on the ninetieth day after the date of the deposit with the Secretary-General of the United Nations of the tenth instrument of ratification or accession.

2. For each State ratifying this Convention or acceding to it after the deposit of the tenth instrument of ratification or accession, the Convention

shall enter into force on the ninetieth day after the date of the deposit of its own instrument of ratification or accession.

Article 9

1. After the expiry of a period of ten years from the date on which this Convention enters into force, a request for the revision of the Convention may be made at any time by any Contracting Party by means of a notification in writing addressed to the Secretary-General of the United Nations.
2. The General Assembly of the United Nations shall decide upon the steps, if any, to be taken in respect of such a request.

Article 10

1. This Convention shall be deposited with the Secretary-General of the United Nations.

2. The Secretary-General of the United Nations shall transmit certified copies of this Convention to all States referred to in Article 5.

3. The Secretary-General of the United Nations shall inform all States referred to in Article 5 of the following particulars:

(a) Signatures of this Convention, and instruments of ratification and accession deposited under Articles 5, 6 and 7;

(b) The date of entry into force of this Convention in accordance with Article 8; and

(c) Communications received under Article 9.

Article 11

This Convention, of which the Chinese, English, French, Russian and Spanish texts are equally authentic, shall bear the date of 26 November 1968.

IN WITNESS WHEREOF the undersigned, being duly authorized for that purpose, have signed this Convention.

Index

Contributors

Paul R. Bartrop is a graduate of La Trobe and Monash Universities in Melbourne, Australia. As an Honorary Research Fellow in the Faculty of Arts at Deakin University, Melbourne, and a faculty member at Bialik College, Melbourne, where he teaches courses in comparative genocide studies, Jewish religion, modern history, and international studies. He has published six books, among them *Australia and the Holocaust, 1933–1945* (1994); *False Havens: The British Empire and the Holocaust* (editor, 1995); *Surviving the Camps: Unity in Adversity during the Holocaust* (2000); and *Bolt from the Blue: Australia, Britain, and the Chanak Crisis* (2003). A former president of the Australian Association of Jewish Studies, he serves on the executive boards of a number of Holocaust and genocide-related journals. He lives in Melbourne.

Donald J. Dietrich is Professor of Theology at Boston College, Boston, Massachusetts. He is on the Committee on Christian Relations and the Holocaust at the United States Holocaust Memorial Museum in Washington, D.C. He has written several books including *God and Humanity in Auschwitz: Jewish-Christian Relations and Sanctioned Murder* (1984), and *Christian Responses to the Holocaust: Moral and Ethical Issues* (2003).

Mohammad Omar Farooq is Associate Professor of Economics and Finance and Director of the Institute of Entrepreneurial Studies at Upper Iowa University. He received his PhD from the University of Tennessee, Knoxville, Tennessee. He has written more than fifty essays on a broad range of Islamic topics and maintains a website devoted to the genocide in Bangladesh, which he personally experienced in 1971.

Zev Garber was Professor and Chair of Jewish Studies at Los Angeles Valley College, Van Nuys, California, and taught as Visiting Professor in religious studies at the University of California at Riverside. He has written extensively in the fields of Judaica and Shoah. Among his publications are *Methodology in the Academic Teaching of Judaism* (1988); *Teaching Hebrew Language and Literature at the College Level* (1991); *Shoah: The Paradigmatic Genocide* (1994); *Perspectives on Zionism* (1994); *What Kind of God? Essays in Honor of Richard L. Rubenstein* (1995, consultant editor); *Peace in Deed: Essays in Honor of Harry James Cargas* (1998); *Academic Approaches to Teaching Jewish Studies* (2000); *Double Takes: Thinking and Rethinking Issues of Modern Judaism in Ancient Contexts* (with Bruce Zuckerman, 2004). He is editorial advisor to *Western States Jewish History* and has served as president of the National Association of Professors of Hebrew (United States).

Leonard B. Glick was, until his retirement, Professor of Anthropology at Hampshire College, Amherst, Massachusettes, where he taught cultural anthropology and European Jewish history. Author of numerous articles on anthropological approaches to religion and ethnicity, he is also the author of *Abraham's Heirs: Jews and Christians in Medieval Europe* (1999).

Stephen R. Haynes is Associate Professor of religious studies at Rhodes College, Memphis, Tennessee, where he has taught since 1989. He holds degrees from Emory University, Columbia Theological Seminary, Florida State University, and Vanderbilt University. His publications include *Reluctant Witnesses: Jews and the Christian Imagination* (1995) and *Noah's Curse: The Biblical Justification for Slavery in America* (2001). He offers courses on the Holocaust, religion and racism, and religion and literature. His research interests include Jewish-Christian relations, Dietrich Bonhoeffer, and religion and higher education.

Steven Leonard Jacobs holds the Aaron Aronov Endowed Chair of Judaic Studies in the Department of Religious Studies at the University of Alabama, Tuscaloosa, Alabama, where he is also Associate Professor of Religious Studies. His publications include *Shirot Bialik: A New and Annotated Translation of Chaim Nachman Bialik's Epic Poems* (1987); *Raphael Lemkin's Thoughts on Nazi Genocide: Not Guilty?* (1992); *Contemporary Christian and Contemporary Jewish Religious Responses to the Shoah* (1993; 2 volumes); *Rethinking Jewish Faith: The Child of a Survivor Responds* (1994); *The Holocaust Now: Contemporary Christian and Jewish Thought* (1996), *Encyclopedia of Genocide* (associate editor, 1999); *Pioneers of Genocide Studies* (co-editor, 2002); *Dismantling the*

Big Lie: The Protocols of the Elders of Zion (2003). He currently serves as First Vice President of the International Association of Genocide Scholars, as well as in a number of Holocaust- and genocide-related organizations.

Henry F. Knight is the director of the Cohen Center for Holocaust Studies, Keene State College, Keene, New Hampshire. For sixteen years he served the Jewish Federation of Tulsa, Oklahoma, as director of the Council for Holocaust Education, taught "The Christian Problem of the Holocaust" at Phillips Theological Seminary, and was University Chaplain and the Applied Associate Professor of Hermeneutic and Holocaust Studies at the University of Tulsa. He received his BA from the University of Alabama and his M.Div. and DM degrees from Emory University, Atlanta, Georgia. An ordained Methodist minister, he specializes in post-Holocaust Christian theology. His publications include *Confessing Christ in a Post-Holocaust World: A Midrashic Experiment* (2000) and *Celebrating Holy Week in a Post-Holocaust World* (2005)

Leo Kuper (1908–1994). One of the foremost scholars of genocide until his death, Kuper originally practiced law in his native South Africa. After the Second World War, he moved to England, where he taught sociology at the University of Birmingham. In 1961, he joined the faculty of the University of California, Los Angeles, as Professor of Sociology and Director of its African Studies Center. Among his pioneering works were *Genocide: Its Political Use in the Twentieth Century* (1981) and *The Prevention of Genocide* (1985). He was also a founder of International Alert, based in London, addressing both genocide early warnings and interventions.

Paul Mojzes is Professor of Religious Studies at Rosemont College, Rosemont, Pennsylvania, and until recently was the Provost and Academic Dean. He is a native of Yugoslavia who came to the United States in 1957. He studied at Belgrade University Law School, then received the AB *summa cum laude* from Florida Southern College and his PhD from Boston University. He is the co-editor of the *Journal of Ecumenical Studies*, and founder and editor of *Religion in Eastern Europe*. He was the author of five and editor of several more books, and has written close to 100 articles. He is president of Christians Associated for Relationships with Eastern Europe and a member of the European Forum of the National Council of Churches. At the time of the writing of this essay, he was the Ida E. King Chair of the Distinguished Visiting Professor of Holocaust and Genocide at the Richard Stockton College of New Jersey in Pomona, New Jersey.

James F. Moore is Professor of Theology at Valparaiso University, Valparaiso, Indiana, and the director of the Inter-faith AIDS Project at the Zygon

Center for Religion and Science in Chicago, Illinois. He is the author of *Christian Theology after the Shoah* (1993) and many other essays related to Christian theology and the Holocaust. He serves on the Advisory Committee for the Annual Scholars Conference on the Holocaust and the Churches, the editorial board of *Studies in the Shoah* series at the University Press of America, and the academic advisory board of the David S. Wyman Institute for Holocaust Studies.

Chris Mato Nunpa was Associate Professor of Indigenous Nations and Dakota Studies at Southwest Minnesota State University, Marshall, Minnesota, and is a Wahpeton Dakota from the Upper Sioux Community New Granite Falls, Minnesota. He received his BA from St. Cloud University, and his MA and PhD from the University of Minnesota. For the past sixteen years he has served as Coordinator for the Dakota-English Dictionary Project.

David Patterson holds the Bomblum Chair in Judaic Studies at the University of Memphis, Tennessee, and is director of the University's Bomblum Judaic Studies Program. A winner of several book awards, including the Koret Jewish Book Award, he has published more than 100 articles and book chapters on philosophy, literature, Judaism, and Holocaust Studies. His works include *Along the Edge of Annihilation* (1999); *Sun Turned into Darkness* (1998); *The Greatest Jewish Stories Ever Told* (1997); *When Learned Men Murder* (1996); *Exile* (1995); *Pilgrimage of a Proselyte* (1993); *The Shriek of Silence* (1992); *In Dialogue and Dilemma with Elie Wiesel* (1991); *Literature and Spirit* (1988); *The Affirming Flame* (1988); and *Faith and Philosophy* (1982). He is the editor and translator of the English edition of *The Complete Black Book of Russian Jewry* (2002), and co-editor of the *Encyclopedia of Holocaust Literature* (2002), and *After-Words: Post-Holocaust Struggles with Forgiveness, Reconciliation, Justice* (2003).

John T. Pawlikowski, a Servite priest, is Professor of Social Ethics at Catholic Theological Union, Chicago, Illinois, where he also directs the Catholic-Jewish Studies Program in the school's Cardinal Bernardin Center. He is the author or editor of fifteen books on social ethics, Holocaust studies, and Jewish-Christian relations. He has been a member by presidential appointment of the United States Holocaust Memorial Council since 1980, and currently serves as president of the International Council of Christians and Jews.

Gary A. Phillips is the Dean of the College, Wabash College, Crawfordsville, Indiana. Before that he was Professor of Religion and Chair of the Religion Department at the University of the South, Sewanee, Tennessee. Prior to arriving at Sewanee in 1998, he taught at the College of the Holy

Cross, in Worcester, Massachusetts. He has authored, co-authored, and co-edited eight books, including *Bible and Ethics of Reading, The Postmodern Bible, Reading Community Reading Scripture, The Holocaust and Other Genocides,* and *Levinas and the Bible.* In addition, he has contributed more than thirty-five articles and translations to journals, edited volumes, dictionaries, and encyclopedias.

Carol Rittner is Distinguished Professor of Holocaust and Genocide Studies at the Richard Stockton College of New Jersey. A graduate of College Misericordia, the University of Maryland, the Pennsylvania State University, and St. John's Seminary, she, also, holds three Honorary Doctorates (College Misericordia, King's College, and Monmouth University). Her many publications include *The Courage to Care: Rescuers of Jews during the Holocaust* (1986); *Elie Wiesel: Between Memory and Hope* (1991); *Different Voices: Women and the Holocaust* (1993); *The Holocaust and the Christian World* (2000); *Will Genocide Ever End?* (2002); and *The Church & Genocide: Rwanda, 1994* (2004). She is, also, the associate editor of *The Genocide Forum* and editor of the *Aegis Review of Genocide.*

John K. Roth was the Edward J. Sexton Professor of Philosophy, Director of the Center for the Study of the Holocaust, Genocide, and Human Rights, and chair, Department of Philosophy and Religious Studies at Claremont McKenna College, Claremont, California, where he taught since 1966. In addition to service on the United States Holocaust Memorial Council, and on the editorial board for *Holocaust and Genocide Studies,* he has published hundreds of articles and reviews and more than thirty-five books, including, most recently, *Holocaust Politics, Pope Pius XII and the Holocaust, Will Genocide Ever End?,* and a revised edition of *After Auschwitz: The Holocaust and Its Legacy* (with Richard Rubenstein). He has been Visiting Professor of Holocaust Studies at the University of Haifa, Israel, and his Holocaust-related research appointments include a 2001 Koerner Visiting Fellowship at the Oxford Centre for Hebrew and Jewish Studies in England, as well as a 2004–2005 appointment as the Ina Levine Senior Scholar in the Center for Advanced Holocaust Studies at the United States Holocaust Memorial Museum, Washington, D.C. In 1988, he was named U.S. National Professor of the Year by the Council for Advancement and Support of Education and the Carnegie Foundation for the Advancement of Teaching.

Richard L. Rubenstein is President Emeritus and Distinguished Professor of Religion at the University of Bridgeport, Connecticut. He is the author of numerous books and articles on theology, history, Jewish-Christian relations and the Holocaust, including *After Auschwitz: Religion and Contemporary Judaism; The Cunning of History; Approaches to Auschwits* (2003; 2nd

Edition; with John Roth); *The Age of Triage; My Brother Paul; The Religious Imagination*. His works have been translated into French, German, Hutch, Swedish, Korean, Japanese, and Italian. He is, also, a member of the Executive Committee of The Aegis Trust (UK).

Marc I. Sherman edited and unified the bibliographic entries in this volume. He is Cataloging Librarian at the Weismann Institute of Science, Rechovot, Israel. He is also Assistant Director of the Institute on the Holocaust and Genocide in Jerusalem, and Director of Holocaust and Genocide Review in the forthcoming Genocide Prevention Now (GPN) wordwide website. He has served as bibliographic editor of the Encyclopedia of Genocide(1999). He co-edited *Medical and Psychological Effects of Concentration Camps on Holocaust Survivors* (1997; with Robert Krell), served as Associate Editor of the series *Genocide: A Critical Bibliographic Review*, and co-edited *Human Rights: An International and Comparative Law Bibliography* (1995). He received his MLS from Syracuse University, and lives in Modi'in, Israel.

Made in the USA
San Bernardino, CA
16 January 2016